Introduction to Leadership

Concepts and Practice

Sixth Edition

Peter G. Northouse

Western Michigan University

 Sage

FOR INFORMATION:

2455 Teller Road
Thousand Oaks, California 91320
E-mail: order@sagepub.com

1 Oliver's Yard
55 City Road
London, EC1Y 1SP
United Kingdom

Unit No 323-333, Third Floor, F-Block
International Trade Tower Nehru Place
New Delhi 110 019
India

18 Cross Street #10-10/11/12
China Square Central
Singapore 048423

Printed in the United States of America

Library of Congress Cataloging-in-Publication Data

Names: Northouse, Peter G., author.

Title: Introduction to leadership: concepts and practice / Peter G. Northouse, Western Michigan University.

Description: Sixth edition. | Thousand Oaks, California: SAGE, [2025] | Includes bibliographical references and index.

Identifiers: LCCN 2023038761 | ISBN 9781071942253 (paperback) | ISBN 9781071928059 (looseleaf) | ISBN 9781071884942 (epub) | ISBN 9781071884959 (epub) | ISBN 9781071884966 (pdf)

Subjects: LCSH: Leadership.

Classification: LCC HM1261.N667 2025 | DDC 303.3/4--dc23/eng/20230816

LC record available at https://lccn.loc.gov/2023038761

Acquisitions Editor: Lily Norton

Content Development Editor: Megan O'Heffernan

Production Editor: Tracy Buyan

Copy Editor: Melinda Masson

Typesetter: diacriTech

Cover Designer: Gail Buschman

Marketing Manager: Jennifer Haldeman

BRIEF CONTENTS

DETAILED CONTENTS

PREFACE

Leadership is a highly valued commodity. Recent world affairs such as the global COVID-19 pandemic, climate change, war in Ukraine and the Middle East, and even the U.S. national political climate have only fueled the public's desire for constructive leadership to new, higher levels. People continue to be fascinated by who leaders are and what leaders do. They want to know what accounts for good leadership and how to become good leaders. Despite this strong interest in leadership, very few books clearly describe the complexities of practicing leadership. I have written *Introduction to Leadership: Concepts and Practice* to fill this void.

Each chapter describes a fundamental principle of leadership and how it relates in practice to becoming an effective leader. These fundamentals are illustrated through examples, profiles of effective leaders, and case studies. The text comprises 12 chapters: **Chapter 1, "Understanding Leadership,"** analyzes how different definitions of leadership have an impact on the practice of leadership. **Chapter 2, "Recognizing Your Traits,"** examines leadership traits found to be important in social science research and explores the leadership traits of a select group of historical and contemporary leaders. **Chapter 3, "Understanding Leadership Styles,"** explores how a person's view of people, work, and human nature forms a personal philosophy of leadership and how this relates to three commonly observed styles of leadership: authoritarian, democratic, and laissez-faire. **Chapter 4, "Attending to Tasks and Relationships,"** describes how leaders can integrate and optimize task and relationship behaviors in their leadership role. **Chapter 5, "Developing Leadership Skills,"** considers three types of leadership skills: administrative, interpersonal, and conceptual. **Chapter 6, "Engaging Strengths,"** discusses the emerging field of strengths-based leadership, looking at how several assessment tools can help one to recognize their own strengths and those of others and then put those strengths to work as an effective leader. **Chapter 7, "Creating a Vision,"** explores the characteristics of a vision and how a vision is expressed and implemented. **Chapter 8, "Working With Groups,"** explores the development of groups, the roles individuals play in groups, and how to lead groups through creating a constructive climate, providing structure, clarifying norms, building cohesiveness, promoting standards of excellence, and addressing out-group members. **Chapter 9, "Embracing Diversity and Inclusion,"** discusses the importance of inclusive leadership and best practices for creating inclusive environments. **Chapter 10, "Managing Conflict,"** addresses the question of how we can manage conflict and produce positive change. **Chapter 11, "Addressing Ethics in Leadership,"** explores six factors that are related directly to ethical leadership: character, actions, goals, honesty, power, and values. Finally, **Chapter 12, "Exploring Destructive Leadership,"** analyzes the causes of toxic leadership and discusses practical ways to confront and nullify it.

NEW TO THIS EDITION

This edition retains the essence of the previous edition but has been expanded and enhanced in several ways:

- First, this edition includes a **new chapter**, "Working with Groups." This chapter examines the nature of groups including the stages of development, the roles individuals play in groups, and how to lead groups through creating a constructive climate, providing structure, clarifying norms, building cohesiveness, promoting standards of excellence, and addressing out-group members.

- Second, this edition includes **new and updated case studies** that illustrate the chapter content and challenge the reader to use this information to solve "real world" leadership challenges.

- Third, it includes **six new leadership snapshots** on leaders, including Damien Hooper-Campbell, Ridley Scott, U.S. Supreme Court justice Ruth Bader Ginsburg, and Google's Project Aristotle, which use stories of the successes and failures of leaders in a variety of fields to illustrate chapter concepts.

- Fourth, this edition includes a **new questionnaire on group leadership** that helps students understand the dimensions of group leadership as well as their own styles when it comes to leading groups.

SPECIAL FEATURES

Introduction to Leadership: Concepts and Practice is designed to help the reader understand how to become a better leader. While the book is grounded in leadership theory, it describes the basics of leadership in an understandable and user-friendly way. Each chapter focuses on a fundamental aspect of leadership, discusses how it can be applied in real leadership situations, and provides a relevant profile of a leader.

Perhaps the most notable features of this book are the four applied activities included in every chapter, which allow the reader to explore leadership concepts and real-world applications:

- **Case studies** illustrate the leadership concepts discussed in the chapter. At the end of each case, thought-provoking questions help the reader analyze the case using ideas presented in the chapter.

- **Self-assessment questionnaires** help the reader determine their own leadership style and preferences. Students may want to complete this questionnaire before reading the chapter's content. By completing the questionnaire first, the reader will be more aware of how the chapter's content specifically applies to their leadership tendencies.

- **Observational exercises** guide the reader in examining behaviors of leaders from their own life experiences.

- **Reflection and action worksheets** stimulate the reader to reflect on their leadership style and identify actions to take to become more effective.

AUDIENCE

A practice-oriented book, *Introduction to Leadership: Concepts and Practice* is written in a user-friendly style appropriate for leadership courses across disciplines. Specifically, it is well suited for programs in leadership studies and leadership courses in schools of agriculture, allied health, business, communication, education, engineering, management, military science, nursing, political science, public administration, religion, and social work. In addition, this book is appropriate for programs in continuing education, corporate training, executive development, in-service training, and government training. It is also useful for student extracurricular activities.

TEACHING RESOURCES

This text includes an array of instructor teaching materials designed to save you time and to help you keep students engaged. To learn more, visit sagepub.com or contact your Sage representative at sagepub.com/findmyrep.

ACKNOWLEDGMENTS

I would like to express my appreciation to many individuals who directly or indirectly played a role in the development of this book. First, I would like to thank the many people at SAGE Publishing, especially editors Maggie Stanley and Lily Norton, who guided this revision from the beginning review phase through the production phase. In addition, I would like to thank content development editor Megan O'Heffernan, copy editor Melinda Masson, and production editor Tracy Buyan. In their own unique ways, each of these people made valuable contributions that enhanced the overall quality of the book. Collectively, they are an extraordinary team that demonstrates the very highest standards of excellence.

In addition, I would like to thank Terry Hammink and Isolde Anderson, who reviewed and made comments on drafts of the new chapter, and in particular Paul Yelsma for his insights and suggestions regarding small groups as well as his contributions to the development of the group leadership questionnaire.

Above all, I am grateful to Marie Lee for her editing and competence and Laurel Northouse for her insights and steadfast support. It takes a lot of dedicated people to write a book, and I feel fortunate to have those people in my life.

For their thoughtful and constructive feedback on this latest edition, I would like to thank the following reviewers:

Hilda Cecilia Contreras Aguirre, *New Mexico State University*

Katya Armistead, *University of California, Santa Barbara*

Jessica Hirshorn, *Arizona State University*

Kim C. Roberts, *Athens State University*

Scott A. Cook, *Longwood University*

Suha R. Tamim, *University of South Carolina*

Haley M. Woznyj, *Longwood University*

Barbara H. Zwadyk, *High Point University*

Yuying Tsong, *California State University, Fullerton*

For comprehensive reviews of past editions, I would like to thank the following reviewers:

Cecily J. Ball, *Bethune-Cookman University*

Jamie L. H. Brown, *Central Michigan University*

Kimberly A. Carlson, *Virginia Tech*

Kelly L. Coke, *Texas A&M University–Texarkana*

Randy Danielsen, *Nova Southeastern University*

Sally Elizabeth Deck, *University of Washington Tacoma*

David DeMatthews, *University of Texas at Austin*

Susan Bramlett Epps, *East Tennessee State University*

Lorraine Godden, *Queen's University at Kingston*

Michelle Hammond, *Oakland University*

Stephen J. Linenberger, *Bellevue University*

Andrew W. Mayer, *University of New Haven*

Joseph W. T. Pugh, *Immaculata University*

Wayne R. Sass, *University of Southern California*

Tracey Honeycutt Sigler, *The Citadel, Military College of South Carolina*

Maureen Baldwin, *Saint Ambrose University*

Jens Beyer, *Hochschule Anhalt Standort Bernburg*

Carl Blencke, *University of Central Florida*

Barry L. Boyd, *Texas A&M University*

Linda L. Brennan, *Mercer University*

Shannon Brown, *Benedictine University*

Lisa Burgoon, *University of Illinois at Urbana-Champaign*

Tom Butkiewicz, *University of Redlands*

Patricia Cane, *Klamath Community College*

Stephen C. Carlson, *Piedmont College*

Melissa K. Carsten, *Winthrop University*

Roger Clark, *NWN Corporation*

James R. "Chip" Coldren Jr., *Governors State University*

Barbara Collins, *Cabrini College*

Stacey A. Cook, *College of Marin*

Ronald J. Cugno, *Nova Southeastern University*

Dan Cunningham, *McDaniel College*

Greg Czyszczon, *James Madison University*

Douglas Davenport, *Truman State University*

Edward Desmarais, *Salem State University*

Marco Dowell, *California State University, Dominguez Hills*

Susan Bramlett Epps, *East Tennessee State University*

Tiffany Erk, *Ivy Tech Community College of Indiana*

Leon Fraser, *Rutgers Business School*

Jim Fullerton, *Idaho State University*

Jennifer Garcia, *Saint Leo University*

Don Green, *Lincoln Christian University*

Francesca Grippa, *Northeastern University*

D. Keith Gurley, *University of Alabama at Birmingham*

Sat Ananda Hayden, *University of Southern Mississippi*

Yael Hellman, *Woodbury University*

Vanessa Hill, *University of Louisiana at Lafayette*

Martha A. Hunt, *NHTI—Concord's Community College*

Jean Gabriel Jolivet, *Southwestern College*

Sharon Kabes, *Southwest Minnesota State University*

Ruth Klein, *Le Moyne College*

Renee Kosiarek, *North Central College*

Robert Larison, *Eastern Oregon University*

Lorin Leone, *Independence University*

Karen A. Longman, *Azusa Pacific University*

Maureen Majury, *Bellevue College*

Douglas Micklich, *Illinois State University*

James L. Morrison, *University of Delaware*

Terry W. Mullins, *University of North Carolina Greensboro*

Jane Murtaugh, *College of DuPage*

Joanne E. Nottingham, *University of North Carolina Wilmington*

Ramona Ortega-Liston, *University of Akron*

Ron Parlett, *Nova Southeastern University*

Bryan Patterson, *Johnson C. Smith University, Northeastern University*

Bruce Peterson, *Sonoma State University*

Deana Raffo, *Middle Tennessee State University*

Melody Rawlings, *Northern Kentucky University*

Bronte H. Reynolds, *California State University, Northridge*

Robert W. Robertson, *Independence University*

Louis Rubino, *California State University, Northridge*

Lou L. Sabina, *Stetson University*

Stephanie Schnurr, *University of Warwick*

Laurie A. Schreiner, *Azusa Pacific University*

Thomas Shields, *University of Richmond*

Pearl Sims, *Peabody College of Vanderbilt University*

Douglas Threet, *Foothill College*

Bruce Tucker, *Santa Fe Community College*

Mary Tucker, *Ohio University*

John Tummons, *University of Missouri*

Sameer Vaidya, *Texas Wesleyan University*

Natalie N. Walker, *Seminole State College*

Simone Wesner, *Birkbeck, University of London*

Paula White, *Independence University*

Cecilia Williams, *Independence University*

Amy Wilson, *University at Buffalo*

Laurie Woodard, *University of South Florida*

Critiques by these reviewers were invaluable in helping to focus my thinking and writing during the revision process.

ABOUT THE AUTHOR

Peter G. Northouse, PhD, is Professor Emeritus of Communication in the School of Communication at Western Michigan University. In addition to publications in professional journals, he is the author of *Leadership: Theory and Practice* (9th ed.) and coauthor of *Health Communication: Strategies for Health Professionals* (3rd ed.) and *Leadership Case Studies in Education* (3rd ed.). His scholarly and curricular interests include models of leadership, leadership assessment, ethical leadership, and leadership and group dynamics. Currently, he is a consultant and lecturer on trends in leadership research, leadership development, and leadership education. He holds a doctorate in speech communication from the University of Denver, and master's and bachelor's degrees in communication education from Michigan State University.

1 UNDERSTANDING LEADERSHIP

INTRODUCTION

This book is about *what it takes to lead*. Everyone, at some time in life, is asked to be a leader, whether to lead a classroom discussion, coach a children's soccer team, or direct a fundraising campaign. Many situations require leadership. Leadership, according to Rost (1991), is a mutual influence *process*, involving both leaders and followers. But, in every leadership situation, expectations and demands are placed upon one or more individuals to initiate and take responsibility for a decision, an event, or another need. A leader may have a high profile (e.g., an elected public official) or a low profile (e.g., a volunteer leader), but in every situation, leadership demands are placed on the individual who is the leader. Being a leader is challenging, exciting, and rewarding, and carries with it many responsibilities. This chapter discusses different ways of looking at leadership and their impacts on what it means to be a leader.

At the outset, it is important to address a basic question: *What is leadership?* Scholars who study leadership have struggled with this question for many decades and have written a great deal about the nature of leadership (Antonakis et al., 2004; Bass, 1990; Conger & Riggio, 2007). With the development of the social sciences during the 20th century, inquiry into leadership became prolific. Studies on leadership have emerged from a wide range of disciplines such as anthropology, business administration, educational administration, history, military science, nursing administration, organizational behavior, philosophy, political science, public administration, psychology, sociology, and theology (Rost, 1991). It's important to note that most of the scholarship on leadership has been generated from research conducted in Western, industrialized countries (such as the United States and Europe) and tends to reflect biases particular to those cultures.

WAYS OF VIEWING LEADERSHIP

As scholars have studied leadership over the years, they have developed a number of different approaches and theories. While the words are often used interchangeably, approaches and theories are different conceptually. An **approach** is a general way of thinking about a phenomenon, not necessarily based on empirical research. A **theory** usually includes a set of hypotheses, principles, or laws that explain a given phenomenon. Theories are more refined and can provide a predictive framework in analyzing the phenomenon.

Not unlike fashion, approaches to and theories of leadership have evolved, changed focus and direction, and built upon one another during the past century. For example, Rost (1991) identified more than 100 different definitions of leadership in the literature, and Curtin (2022), more recently, identified 700 definitions of leadership and ways to lead. Despite the scope and vastness of these definitions, it is important and useful to differentiate between the various common ways of viewing leadership. In the following section, six distinct ways of conceptualizing leadership are discussed, including leadership as a *trait*, an *ability*, a *skill*, a *behavior*, a *relationship*, and an *influence process*.

Leadership Is a *Trait*

First, for many people, leadership is thought of as a trait. A **trait** is a distinguishing quality of an individual, and defining leadership as a trait means that each individual brings to the table certain qualities that influence the way they lead. Some leaders are confident, some are decisive, and still others are outgoing and sociable.

Early on, the **trait approach** focused on identifying the innate qualities and characteristics possessed by widely revered social, political, and military leaders. Also called **"Great Man" theories**, these studies of leadership traits were especially strong from 1900 to the early 1940s, enjoying a renewed emphasis in the 1970s as researchers began to examine charismatic leadership. In the 1980s, researchers linked leadership to the **"Big Five" personality factors** while interest in **emotional intelligence** as a trait gained favor in the 1990s. (For a discussion of *emotional intelligence* and leadership, see Chapter 5.)

Saying that leadership is a trait places a great deal of emphasis on the leader and on the leader's special gifts. It follows the often-expressed belief that "leaders are born, not made"—that leadership is innate rather than learned. Some argue that focusing on traits makes leadership an elitist enterprise because it implies that only a few people with special talents will lead. Although there may be some truth to this argument, it can also be argued that all of us are born with a wide array of unique traits, many of which can have a positive impact on our leadership. Because traits are relatively fixed and not easily changed, this perspective focuses more on people's attributes, giving less emphasis to how people learn and develop leadership.

Through the years, researchers have identified a multitude of traits that are associated with leadership. In Chapter 2, we will discuss some key leadership traits, and in Chapter 6, we will explain how strengths-based leadership is a variation of trait leadership. Although there are many important leadership traits, what is most important for leaders is having the required traits that a particular situation demands. For example, a chaotic emergency room at a hospital requires a leader who is insightful and decisive and can bring calm to the situation. Conversely, a high school classroom in which students are bored demands a teacher who is inspiring and creative. Successful leadership is more likely when the leader has the right traits and exhibits these traits in the right place at the right time.

Leadership Is an *Ability*

In addition to being thought of as a trait, people often conceptualize leadership as an ability. A person who has leadership **ability** is *able* to be a leader—that is, has the capacity to lead. While the term *ability* frequently refers to a natural capacity, ability can be acquired. For example, some people are naturally good at public speaking, while others rehearse to become comfortable speaking in public. Similarly, some people have the natural physical ability to excel in a sport, while others develop their athletic capacity through exercise and practice. In the same vein, some people find that math and mathematical concepts come easy to them, while others must study and practice math concepts in order to learn and be able to use them. In leadership, some people have the natural ability to lead, while others develop their leadership abilities through hard work and practice.

An example of leadership as an ability is the legendary University of California at Los Angeles basketball coach John Wooden, whose teams won seven consecutive National Collegiate Athletic Association titles. Described first as a teacher and then as a coach, Wooden implemented four laws of learning into his coaching: explanation, demonstration, imitation, and repetition. His goal was to teach players how to do the right thing instinctively under great pressure. Less visible or well known, but also an example of leadership as an ability, is the unheralded but highly effective restaurant manager who, through years of experience and learning, is able to create a successful, award-winning restaurant. In both of these examples, it is the individuals' abilities that create outstanding leadership.

Leadership Is a *Skill*

Third, people think of leadership as a skill. Conceptualized as a **skill**, leadership is a *competency* developed to accomplish a task effectively. Skilled leaders are competent people who know the means and methods for carrying out their responsibilities. For example, a skilled leader in a fundraising campaign knows every step and procedure in the fundraising process and is able to use this knowledge to run an effective campaign. Similarly, a skilled editor of a magazine knows how to edit, how to select articles that fit the magazine's established content style, and how to adapt that content to the publication's audience. In short, skilled leaders are competent—they know what they need to do, and they know how to do it.

Describing leadership as a skill makes leadership available to everyone because skills are competencies that people can learn or develop. Even without natural leadership ability, people can improve their leadership with practice, instruction, and feedback from others. Viewed as a skill, leadership can be studied and learned. If you are capable of learning from experience, you can acquire leadership.

Leadership Is a *Behavior*

Another way of thinking about leadership is as a behavior. It is *what leaders do* when they are in a leadership role. In the late 1930s, leadership research began to focus on leader behavior—what leaders say and the way they act. Unlike traits, abilities, and skills, leadership behaviors are observable. When someone leads, we see that person's leadership behavior.

Research on leadership has shown that leaders engage primarily in two kinds of general behaviors: task behaviors and relationship behaviors, which are discussed in depth in Chapter 4. **Task behaviors** are used by leaders to get the job done (e.g., a leader prepares an agenda for a meeting). **Relationship (process) behaviors** are used by leaders to help people feel comfortable with other group members and at ease in the situations in which they find themselves (e.g., a leader helps individuals in a group to feel included). Since leadership requires both task and relationship behaviors, the challenge for leaders is to know the best way to combine them in their efforts to reach a goal.

An aspect of viewing leadership as a behavior also arose in the development of situational theories. The premise of these theories is that different situations demand different kinds of leadership behavior. Examination of the **situational approach** to leadership began in the late 1960s by Hersey and Blanchard (1969) and Reddin (1967) and continued to be refined and revised from the 1970s through the 1990s (Vecchio, 1987). One of these approaches, **path–goal theory**, examines how leaders use employee motivation to enhance performance and satisfaction. Another situational approach, **contingency theory**, focuses on the match between the leader's style and specific situational variables.

All these theories underpin the approach that leadership is about how leaders perform and act rather than the unique qualities of the leader. Interestingly, it also provides a unique window into leaders' ethics and whether they do the right thing. For example, elected school boards have had to grapple with many thorny issues over the past few years, from COVID-19 protocols to their stance on books with LGBTQ+ themes in school libraries to how negative aspects of U.S. history are taught. The way a board's president and members respond (or behave) toward the public when dealing with these issues says a great deal about their leadership. Do they bend to the will of the loudest constituents, or do they make decisions with the education of all students firmly in mind? Similarly, the leadership of a junior high basketball coach can be described by how the coach treats their team's players in practice and in games. The coach's leadership is about what they do and how they affect the players in their coaching role.

Leadership Is a *Relationship*

Another, and a somewhat unusual, way to think about leadership is as a relationship, centering on the communication between leaders and followers.

In traditional leadership, authority is often a top-down, linear one-way event, but when thought of as a relationship, leadership becomes an interactive activity, a process of collaboration that occurs between leaders and followers (Rost, 1991). A leader affects and is affected by followers, and both leader and followers are affected in turn by the situation that surrounds them. This premise is expressed in recognized **relational approaches** such as **leader–member exchange (LMX) theory** (Graen & Uhl-Bien, 1995), which focuses on the quality of leader–follower relationships, and Lipman-Blumen's (2000) **connective leadership**, which focuses on how leaders can work with followers in ways that affirm followers' distinct identity and embrace their diversity.

When leadership is defined as a relationship, it becomes available to everyone. Authority and influence are shared, and leadership is not restricted to the formally designated leader in a group. For example, a team marketing project may involve a designated team leader, but all the idea generation, planning, problem solving, and decision making might be made with active input from all members. When the final proposal is presented to the client, everyone's contribution is reflected.

In addition, the relationship approach has an ethical overtone because it stresses the need for leaders to work with followers to achieve their mutual purposes. Stressing mutuality lessens the possibility that leaders might act toward followers in ways that are forced or unethical. It also increases the possibility that leaders and followers will work together toward a common good (Rost, 1991).

The premise of working toward a common good is embodied in the work of Susan R. Komives and her colleagues (Komives et al., 2013; Komives et al., 2016), particularly in the area of civic engagement. She and her coauthors envision leadership as a relationship among multiple partners, but with the additional goal of attempting to accomplish positive change in an ethical manner.

According to Komives and colleagues (2013), civic engagement entails "the sense of personal responsibility individuals should feel to uphold their obligations, as part of any community" (p. 24). This can include watching out for older or vulnerable neighbors, creating a positive climate in the workplace, cleaning up roadsides with a group of friends, confronting unjust treatment of others when you observe it, and just generally contributing to the public good.

Leadership Is an *Influence Process*

Another way of thinking about leadership is as an influence process. This is the perspective that will be emphasized in this book.

> **Leadership** *is a process whereby an individual influences a group of individuals to achieve a common goal.*

Defining leadership as an influence process means that it is not a trait or an ability that resides in the leader, but rather an interactive event that occurs between the leader and the followers. Influence is central to the process of leadership because leaders *affect* followers. Leaders direct their energies toward influencing individuals to achieve something together. Stressing common goals gives leadership an ethical dimension because it lessens the possibility that leaders might act toward followers in ways that use coercion or are unethical.

The Urban Farming Guys (2023) in Kansas City took this approach when moving into and revitalizing a run-down neighborhood in their city. They began with urban gardening, converting overgrown yards to food production; started aquaponics in their limited space; invited neighbors into the process; taught gardening and construction skills to people; and created community. No single individual is responsible; it is a collective effort and is making a difference.

New and Evolving Approaches to Leadership

Since the 1980s, a number of new leadership approaches have emerged that comprise many of the different views of leadership identified earlier. Beginning with the work of Bass (1985, 1990), leadership studies generated **charismatic leadership** theories. From these approaches developed **transformational leadership theory**, which describes leadership as a process that changes people and organizations. In that same vein, **adaptive leadership** examines how leaders help people address problems, face challenges, and adapt to change. Adaptive leadership stresses that the leaders don't solve the problems but, rather, encourage others to do the problem solving and adapt to change.

Other emerging approaches include the following:

- **Authentic leadership** looks at the authenticity of leaders and their leadership.

- **Spiritual leadership** considers how leaders use values, a sense of "calling," and membership to motivate followers.

- **Servant leadership** emphasizes the "caring principle" with leaders as "servants" who focus on their followers' needs in order to help these followers become more autonomous, knowledgeable, and like servants themselves.

- **Gender-based studies**, which view how one's gender affects and differentiates one's leadership, have gained momentum as women continue to become more dominant in the workforce, especially on a global level.

- **Ethical leadership**, examining a leader's character, duties, decision making, and decision outcomes, has recently come to center stage out of concern about dishonest or unethical behavior occurring within organizations and professions.

The historical timeline in Figure 1.1 is not intended to represent the development of leadership theories and approaches as separate and distinct eras only to disappear from the picture when a new theory appears. Instead, many of these theories and approaches occur concurrently, building upon one another. Even when a certain approach's period of popularity has waned, the theory continues to influence further study and the development of new leadership approaches.

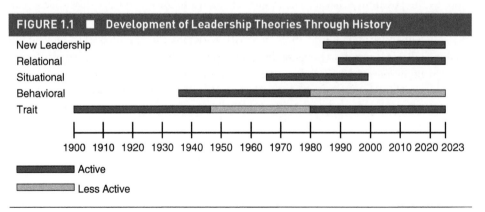

FIGURE 1.1 ■ Development of Leadership Theories Through History

Source: Adapted from Antonakis, J., Cianciolo, A. T., & Sternberg, R. J. (Eds.). (2004). *The nature of leadership.* Sage, p. 7.

LEADERSHIP AND MANAGEMENT

In any explanation of what leadership is, it is important to make a distinction between leadership and management. Leadership and management are not the same. Management emerged out of the industrialization of work in the early 20th century, and its purpose is to structure and coordinate various functions within organizations (Northouse, 2019). In contrast, leadership has been studied for thousands of years, across multiple contexts—politics, the military, religion, and more.

Frederick Taylor was a key figure in the development of management theory. At the turn of the 20th century, Taylor pioneered the concept of the scientific management of labor. This involved measuring every detail of a worker's tasks to make work more efficient, consistent, and predictable. According to Taylor, the responsibility of workers was to provide the labor, and the responsibilities of managers were to design the "one best way" for each task to be done and then train, monitor, and evaluate each worker. This approach was applied to many U.S. industries in the first half of the 20th century and is still in use today in assembly lines, fast-food restaurants, and other industries (Modaff et al., 2017).

Management theory was further developed by Chester Barnard, whose work in the areas of cooperation and authority helps us understand how management and leadership can sometimes overlap. Barnard (1938) conceptualized two types of authority: authority of position and authority of leadership. Authority of position is the power to direct the work of an individual, by someone in a higher position in an organization's structure. Authority of leadership is not based on position, but ascribed to those in the organization who have the knowledge and ability needed for a task. Barnard argued that both types were necessary for organizations to function well (Modaff et al., 2017).

Both leadership and management involve influence, but leadership is about seeking constructive change, and management is about establishing order. For example, it is often said that "managers are people who do things right, and leaders are people who do the right thing." Since both leaders and managers are engaged in influencing people toward goal accomplishment, our discussion in this book will treat the roles of managers and leaders similarly and not emphasize the differences between them.

LEADERSHIP AND CULTURE

While there are many different approaches to leadership throughout the world, the definition and concepts of leadership outlined in this chapter are from an American perspective. If you were to travel to nations across the world, you would no doubt encounter different views of leadership specific to those ethnic and political cultures.

In 2004, Robert J. House led a group of 160 researchers in an ambitious study to increase our understanding of the impact culture has on leadership effectiveness. The GLOBE (Global Leadership and Organizational Behavior Effectiveness) studies drew on the input of 17,000 people in 62 countries in determining how leadership varies across the world. Among the many findings generated by the GLOBE studies was the identification of positive and negative leadership characteristics that are universally accepted worldwide (see Table 1.1).

TABLE 1.1 ■ Universal Leadership Attributes		
Positive Leader Attributes		
Trustworthy	Just	Honest
Foresighted	Plans ahead	Encouraging
Positive	Dynamic	Motivator
Builds confidence	Motivational	Dependable
Intelligent	Decisive	Effective bargainer
Win-win problem solver	Communicative	Informed
Administratively skilled	Coordinator	Team builder
Excellence oriented		
Negative Leader Attributes		
Loner	Asocial	Noncooperative
Irritable	Nonexplicit	Egocentric
Ruthless	Dictatorial	

Source: Adapted from House, R. J., Hanges, P. J., Javidan, M., Dorfman, P. W., & Gupta, V. (Eds.). (2004). *Culture, leadership, and organizations: The GLOBE study of 62 societies.* Sage, pp. 677–678. Reprinted with permission.

LEADERSHIP'S "DARK SIDE"

Finally, it is important to note that the same characteristics and behaviors that distinguish leadership can also be used by leaders in nonpositive ways (Conger, 1990). The **dark side of leadership** is the destructive side of leadership where a leader uses their influence or power for personal ends. Lipman-Blumen (2005) suggests that such leaders are "toxic," where their leadership leaves their followers worse off than they found them, often violating the basic human rights of others and playing to their followers' basest fears. While many cite Adolf Hitler as the prime example of the dark side of leadership, there are many current examples in the world today, from religious extremist groups such as the Taliban, which has banned education for women in Afghanistan, to corporate leaders who engage in unethical behavior such as sexual misconduct, fraud, bribery, and insider trading. In fact, Bobby Allyn (2019) found that scandals caused by bad behavior rather than a company's poor financial performance were the leading cause of leadership dismissals among the world's 2,500 largest public companies.

In Chapter 12, "Exploring Destructive Leadership," we discuss more fully the complexities that allow the dark side of leadership to exist, including examining how and why it occurs, the characteristics of destructive leadership, and how to deal with it.

UNDERSTANDING EFFECTIVE LEADERSHIP

The meaning of leadership is complex and includes many dimensions. For some people, leadership is a *trait* or an *ability*, for others it is a *skill* or a *behavior*, and for still others it is a *relationship* or an *influence process*. In reality, leadership probably includes components of all of these dimensions. Each dimension explains only a facet of leadership.

LEADERSHIP SNAPSHOT

Michelle Obama, Former U.S. First Lady

When Michelle Obama became the U.S. First Lady after her husband, Barack Obama, was elected U.S. president in 2008, she began to embody the words she spoke earlier that year at the Democratic National Convention: "We have an obligation to fight for the world as it should be" (White House Historical Association, 2018).

Photo by Fotonoticias/WireImage

Before she was Barack Obama's wife, Michelle Robinson grew up on the South Side of Chicago, the daughter of a pump operator for a Chicago water treatment plant and a stay-at-home mother. In her neighborhood, the "feeling of failure" predominated (Obama, 2018, p. 44), but her parents refused to buy in and continually emphasized hard work and education to her and her brother, Craig. As a result, Robinson was driven in her studies, ultimately testing into one of Chicago's top public high schools. Even though she excelled at school, she was continuously plagued by thoughts of "Am I good enough?" But when a high school counselor told Robinson she "wasn't Princeton material," Robinson refused to believe her, applying and being accepted to the Ivy League school.

Robinson ultimately earned a bachelor's degree from Princeton University and went on to earn a Juris Doctor degree from Harvard Law School. She returned to Chicago to work as a lawyer for a large firm, but found her energies becoming more and more devoted to wanting to make a difference for the people of Chicago and those in her neighborhood, especially youth. Even though she took a 50% pay cut, she accepted a job working as an assistant to Chicago's mayor, Richard Daley, and as a liaison to several departments including Health and Human Services. She left City Hall to become the founding executive director of the Chicago chapter of Public Allies, an AmeriCorps program that prepares young people to work in nonprofits and public service, a job where she "felt I was doing something immediately meaningful, directly impacting the lives of others while also staying connected to both my city and my culture" (Obama, 2018, p. 180).

Three years later, Michelle Obama took a job working at the University of Chicago to develop its first community service program. Despite the fact that the university was located in Obama's former neighborhood, most South Side residents felt that it had its back turned to the neighborhood. Obama was hired to lower those walls and get students more involved in the neighborhood and residents with the university. During this time, Obama also became a mother of two daughters, Malia and Sasha, having to balance the competing responsibilities of motherhood and career. She worked part-time in her position for several years, but shortly after Sasha was born, she began a new job at the University of Chicago Medical Center, as the executive director of community affairs working to improve the university's community outreach. She brought along her three-month-old daughter to her interview for the job, which sent the message that she was going to be both: a mother and a professional.

She was promoted to vice president of community and external affairs at the university, where among her accomplishments was establishing a program connecting South Side residents with regular health care providers, regardless of the residents' ability to pay.

During this time, Obama's husband, who had been involved in politics on the local and state level, was elected to the U.S. Senate. Because she was invested in her career and her children were settled, Obama opted not to uproot the family to move to Washington, DC, continuing to be a full-time working mother with a spouse who was often away from home.

Just three years later, Barack Obama threw his hat into the ring to run for president of the United States, and Michelle Obama was thrust into an additional new role—that of the wife of a presidential candidate. She found herself on the campaign trail, speaking to crowds of people in support of her husband's candidacy. The public scrutiny on her was intense, but Obama was determined "to be myself, to speak as myself" (Obama, 2018, p. 236). When Barack Obama won the 2008 presidential election, Michelle Obama would assume yet another role: First Lady of the United States.

While Obama made it clear from the start that her first priority was as "mom-in-chief" to her daughters, her position as First Lady thrust her into the national spotlight and offered her an opportunity to make an impact on a larger scale. As First Lady, Obama exhibited charisma, compassion, and passion.

"A First Lady's power is a curious thing—as soft and undefined as the role itself. . . . Tradition called for me to provide a kind of gentle light, flattering the president with my devotion, flattering the nation primarily by not challenging it. I was beginning to see though, that wielded carefully, the light was more powerful than that," she wrote. "I had influence in the form of being something of a curiosity—a black First Lady, a professional woman, a mother of young kids. . . . With my soft power I was finding I could be strong" (Obama, 2018, p. 372).

Initially, Obama used that "soft power" to promote efforts to support military families, help women balance career and family, and end childhood obesity. She initiated the Let's Move! program, which brought together elected officials, business leaders, educators, parents, and faith leaders to work to provide more nutritious food in schools, bring healthy and affordable food into underserved communities, plant vegetable gardens across the United States, and provide new opportunities for kids to be more active.

When her husband was elected to his second term as president, Obama directed her energies toward education, on both a national and international level. She spearheaded the Reach Higher Initiative to help U.S. students understand job opportunities and the education and skills they need for those jobs. Telling them to "Never view your challenges as obstacles," she encouraged youth to continue their educations beyond high school at technical schools, colleges, and universities (White House Historical Association, 2018). Worldwide, she championed the education of girls and women, launching the Let Girls Learn initiative that funded education projects tackling everything from leadership to poverty to combating the challenges girls encounter in their communities.

Through all this, Obama was authentic, talking openly about her personal life, including her experiences as a Black woman at an elite school and her fight against stereotypes to help spread a message of encouragement to youth. On January 6, 2017, in her final speech as First Lady, she took the opportunity to tell American youth to continue to fight for their futures:

> I want our young people to know that they matter, that they belong. So don't be afraid. You hear me, young people? Don't be afraid. Be focused. Be determined. Be hopeful. Be empowered. Empower yourself with a good education. Then get out there and use that education to build a country worthy of your boundless promise. Lead by example with hope; never fear. (Obama, 2017)

Since leaving the White House, Michelle Obama has continued to be an enormously popular public figure. Her autobiographical memoir, *Becoming*, was the best-selling book of 2018, and was published in 33 languages. She published a second book, *The Light We Carry*, in 2022 in which she details some of her leadership practices like "starting kind," "going high," and assembling a "kitchen table" of trusted friends and mentors. She has also continued her promotion of education for girls, launching the Girls Opportunity Alliance to support more than 1,500 grassroots organizations that help empower girls worldwide through education.

"I'm an ordinary person who found herself on an extraordinary journey," she wrote in *Becoming*. "For every door that's been opened to me, I've tried to open my door to others . . . There's power in allowing yourself to be known and heard, in owning your unique story, in using your authentic voice. And there's grace in being willing to know and hear others" (Obama, 2018, pp. 420–421).

In considering these various definitions of leadership and based on the results of your Conceptualizing Leadership Questionnaire, which dimension seems closest to how you think of leadership? How would you define leadership? Answers to these questions are important because *how you think* about leadership will strongly influence *how you practice* leadership.

There is a strong demand for effective leadership in society today. This demand exists at the local and community levels, as well as at the national level, in this country and abroad. People feel the need for leadership in all aspects of their lives. They want leaders in their personal lives, at school, in the work setting, and even in their spiritual lives. Everywhere you turn, people are expressing a need for strong leadership.

When people ask for leadership in a particular situation, it is not always clear exactly what they want. For the most part, however, they want effective leadership. Effective leadership is intended influence that creates change for the greater good. Leadership uses positive means to achieve positive outcomes. Furthermore, people want leaders who listen to and understand their needs and who can relate to their circumstances. The challenge for each of us is to be prepared to lead when we are asked to do so.

SUMMARY

All of us at some time in our lives will be asked to show leadership. When you are asked to be the leader, it will be both demanding and rewarding. How you approach leadership is strongly influenced by your definitions of and beliefs about leadership. Through the years, writers have defined leadership in a multitude of ways. It is a complex, multidimensional process that is often conceptualized in a variety of ways by different people. Some of the most common ways of looking at leadership are as a trait, as an ability, as a skill, as a behavior, as a relationship, and as an influence process. The way you think about leadership will influence the way you practice leadership.

Despite being studied for nearly a century, new ways of theorizing about leadership are constantly being developed. Technology has allowed society to become more globally connected and aware, and while early studies by House et al. (2004) explored the leadership attributes recognized in other cultures, how ethnic and political cultures impact one's views on leadership is gaining more attention. At the same time, technology has amplified the visibility of instances of destructive leadership, and researchers are giving more attention to why it occurs and how to deal with it.

KEY TERMS

ability

adaptive leadership

approach

authentic leadership

"Big Five" personality factors

charismatic leadership

connective leadership

contingency theory

dark side of leadership

emotional intelligence

ethical leadership

gender-based studies

"Great Man" theories

leader–member exchange (LMX) theory

leadership

path–goal theory

relational approach

relationship (process) behaviors

servant leadership

situational approach

skill

spiritual leadership

task behaviors

theory

trait

trait approach

transformational leadership theory

Application

1.1 Case Study—King of the Hill

Denny Hill's career as a high school swimming coach didn't start out well. The seniors on his team quit in the first season because he required them to come to all the workouts. The team only won three meets the whole season. That was 40 years ago. Since that time, the high school chemistry teacher's success as a swimming coach has been extraordinary; his winnings include more than 900 boys' and girls' dual meets and a phenomenal 31 state titles.

Denny is noted for creating a team effort out of what is usually considered an individual sport. He begins every season with a team sleepover, followed by "Hell Week," a two-week grueling regimen in which team members swim at least 5 miles a workout and 10 miles a day. He acknowledges this is a bonding experience for the swimmers, regardless of their skill, because they are "all in the same boat."

Denny passes the mantle of leadership onto his team members. Seniors are expected to be mature leaders who inform the freshmen of the team goals and expectations. Juniors are to be role models, while sophomores serve as quiet leaders who are still learning but have a foundation in the team culture. Even the freshman members have a job: They are required to pay attention to the coaches and other team members as they learn the team's culture and what's expected.

Denny holds a 20-minute team meeting each Monday where every member has the opportunity to present a rose or a complaint to anyone on the team including the coaches. He is tough on swimmers and makes them work, but when they need support, he is always there to put an arm around them. Denny also uses humor, often making jokes that help take the edge off long, hard workouts.

And despite his teams' successes, Denny isn't about winning; he's more about preparing to win—telling his swimmers that by preparing to win, everything takes care of itself. When you do win, he says, you've done it the right way.

Questions

1. What leadership *traits* account for Denny Hill's success?

2. How would you describe Denny's leadership *abilities*?

3. Leadership includes administrative skills, interpersonal skills, and conceptual skills. How does Denny stack up on these *skills*?

4. How does Denny integrate task and relationship *behaviors* in his leadership?

5. From a *relational* perspective, how would you describe Denny's leadership?

6. In what way does Denny's coaching exemplify leadership as an *influence process*?

1.2 Case Study—Charity: Water

When Scott Harrison created Charity: Water in 2006, he wanted not only to bring clean drinking water to millions around the world but also to redefine philanthropy by converting thousands of formerly skeptical "non-givers" to join and fund his cause.

When Scott was young, his devoutly religious family relocated to New Jersey for his father's job—a move that proved extremely detrimental to Scott's mother's health. Their new home had a carbon monoxide leak that permanently damaged her immune system. At a young age, Scott became a caregiver for her as she essentially lived in isolation, spending her time in a "clean room" and wearing a charcoal mask on her face to protect her from ingesting toxins from the air.

As a teen, however, Scott rebelled, joining a rock band and, after barely graduating from high school, leaving for New York to pursue music and attend New York University. He became a nightclub promoter, working for 40 different clubs over 10 years to attract the "beautiful people"—the wealthy and powerful who would easily pay $10,000 for a night of partying and the opportunity to be seen in the hippest, most trendy places.

Scott became an influencer; a few phone calls made by him to the right people could put a nightclub on the map. In return, Scott received a percentage of a club's sales, making $3,000 to $5,000 on a good night (Clifford, 2018), as well as endorsement deals, being paid well just to be seen drinking a particular brand of alcohol.

By outside appearances, Scott had an enviable life, but he had become disillusioned with his lifestyle, believing he was "polluting" himself with drugs, alcohol, and pornography, and feeling disconnected from the spirituality and morality of his childhood (Fields, 2018). He began seeking the opposite of what he was doing, applying to work with humanitarian efforts. With only his experience as a club promoter to offer, he received numerous rejections until Mercy Ships, a nonprofit hospital ship that delivers medical care to places where such care is not available, responded. The organization was looking for a photojournalist to document its efforts in Liberia. For this opportunity, Scott would pay Mercy Ships $500 per month. For him, it was perfect: the opposite of his current life, working in an impoverished country ravaged by civil war and paying for the pleasure to do so.

Scott's first Mercy Ships tour was on a 525-foot hospital ship, equipped with 42 beds, a few operating rooms, and an MRI machine. The ship traveled to Liberia, which had no operating hospitals and only two surgeons in the entire country. He documented the work on the ship and photographed every patient both before and after medical intervention, and his images and stories were used to raise awareness and inspire donors to contribute to the organization's work.

Scott realized that the wealthy and powerful people who had followed him when he was a club promoter could prove helpful in assisting Mercy Ships with its mission and that the skills he had developed to lure people to nightclubs could also be effective at rallying people in support of a good cause. He compiled a list of 15,000 potential donors who could make significant financial contributions and began blasting them with emails filled with images and stories of Mercy Ships patients. While he received dismissal from some, he found many more were moved by the stories and wanted to help.

On Scott's second Mercy Ships tour, he ventured into the Liberian countryside and the villages that were home to the organization's patients. He was struck by the morbid conditions of these villages' water sources—learning that 50% of the country was drinking unsafe, dirty contaminated water, which contributed directly to many of the illnesses and suffering of Mercy Ships patients. Scott had gone from witnessing wealthy club patrons buying $10 bottles of designer water, which they didn't open, to seeing people die from a lack of clean drinking water. The contrast was not lost on him, and he had found a cause that deeply resonated with him.

He had no money, was $30,000 in debt, and had no experience in building an organization, but when he returned to New York, he jumped in, making 8–10 presentations a day to interest others in his mission of providing clean drinking water for the 1 billion people in the world without it. His presentations met with little success in the way of donations; instead, he learned that there was a profound distrust of and cynicism toward charities. To be successful, he would have to "reimagine" the giving process.

Scott created Charity: Water and a four-pronged plan to reinvent the charity model. The first element is to guarantee that 100% of donations directly finance clean water projects. Following the model of multibillionaire Paul Tudor Jones of the Robin Hood Foundation, he established two separate accounts. Every public donation goes into the first account to be used exclusively to fund the water projects. A second account, called The Well, funded by a small group of private donors dedicated specifically to financing operating expenses, pays the salaries and overhead of the organization.

The second prong is "proof," visibly showing donors the impact of their contributions using technology. The organization's partners in foreign countries use GPS devices, take photos, and upload and post the GPS coordinates and pictures for each project on Google Earth and Google Maps.

Third, Scott replaced the "poverty mentality" most charities use in their marketing with the idea that giving should be an opportunity and a blessing, not an obligation or a debt. Through stories focused on hope, opportunity, and fun, Charity: Water offers a "grand invitation" to join the effort in creating a world where every person has clean drinking water.

The last prong is to use local partners in the countries where Charity: Water has its projects. For the work to be sustainable and culturally appropriate, it has to be led by local people. Charity: Water raises awareness of the issue and the money to solve it, while the locals are "the heroes," who use that money to bring clean water to their communities.

Charity: Water began at the start of a major world financial crisis, but still managed to raise $1.7 million in its first year. Donations grew 490% in the first three years of operations, while net giving in the United States dropped by 8% during the same period. Charity: Water now has raised more than $689 million and provided more than 15 million people around the world with access to clean water through more than 111,000 projects in 29 different countries (Charity: Water, 2023).

At the same time, Scott has stuck to his vision to radically change the charitable giving landscape by tapping into people's desire to make a difference, and provide complete transparency, thus raising the standards for an entire industry.

Questions

1. What leadership *traits* account for Scott Harrison's success?

2. How would you describe Scott's leadership *abilities*?

3. Leadership includes administrative skills, interpersonal skills, and conceptual skills. In what ways does Scott exhibit these *skills*?

4. Based on the definition of leadership as an *influence process*, how would you describe Scott's leadership?

5. Though Scott was a well-paid, successful club promoter with a long list of "followers," would you characterize that element of his career path as "leadership"? Why or why not?

Application

1.3 Conceptualizing Leadership Questionnaire

Purpose

1. To identify how you view leadership
2. To explore your perceptions of different aspects of leadership

Directions

1. Consider for a moment your own impressions of the word *leadership*. Based on your experiences with leaders in your lifetime, what is leadership?
2. Using the scale provided, indicate the extent to which you agree or disagree with the following statements about leadership.

Statement	Strongly disagree	Disagree	Neutral	Agree	Strongly agree
1. When I think of leadership, I think of a person with special personality traits.	1	2	3	4	5
2. Much like playing the piano or tennis, leadership is a learned ability.	1	2	3	4	5
3. Leadership requires knowledge and know-how.	1	2	3	4	5
4. Leadership is about what people do rather than who they are.	1	2	3	4	5
5. Followers can influence the leadership process as much as leaders.	1	2	3	4	5
6. Leadership is about the process of influencing others.	1	2	3	4	5
7. Some people are born to be leaders.	1	2	3	4	5
8. Some people have the natural ability to be leaders.	1	2	3	4	5

Statement	Strongly disagree	Disagree	Neutral	Agree	Strongly agree
9. The key to successful leadership is having the right skills.	1	2	3	4	5
10. Leadership is best described by what leaders do.	1	2	3	4	5
11. Leaders and followers share in the leadership process.	1	2	3	4	5
12. Leadership is a series of actions directed toward positive ends.	1	2	3	4	5
13. A person needs to have certain traits to be an effective leader.	1	2	3	4	5
14. Everyone has the capacity to be a leader.	1	2	3	4	5
15. Effective leaders are competent in their roles.	1	2	3	4	5
16. The essence of leadership is performing tasks and dealing with people.	1	2	3	4	5
17. Leadership is about the common purposes of leaders and followers.	1	2	3	4	5
18. Leadership does not rely on the leader alone but is a process involving the leader, followers, and the situation.	1	2	3	4	5
19. People become great leaders because of their traits.	1	2	3	4	5
20. People can develop the ability to lead.	1	2	3	4	5
21. Effective leaders have competence and knowledge.	1	2	3	4	5

Statement	Strongly disagree	Disagree	Neutral	Agree	Strongly agree
22. Leadership is about how leaders work with people to accomplish goals.	1	2	3	4	5
23. Effective leadership is best explained by the leader–follower relationship.	1	2	3	4	5
24. Leaders influence and are influenced by followers.	1	2	3	4	5

Scoring

1. Sum scores on items 1, 7, 13, and 19 (trait emphasis)
2. Sum scores on items 2, 8, 14, and 20 (ability emphasis)
3. Sum scores on items 3, 9, 15, and 21 (skill emphasis)
4. Sum scores on items 4, 10, 16, and 22 (behavior emphasis)
5. Sum scores on items 5, 11, 17, and 23 (relationship emphasis)
6. Sum scores on items 6, 12, 18, and 24 (influence process emphasis)

Total Scores

1. Trait emphasis: _____
2. Ability emphasis: _____
3. Skill emphasis: _____
4. Behavior emphasis: _____
5. Relationship emphasis: _____
6. Influence process emphasis: _____

Scoring Interpretation

The scores you receive on this questionnaire provide information about how you define and view leadership. The emphasis you give to the various dimensions of leadership has implications for how you approach the leadership process. For example, if your highest score is for *trait emphasis*, it suggests that you emphasize the role of the leader and the leader's special gifts in the leadership process. However, if your highest score is for *relationship emphasis*, it indicates that you think leadership is centered on the communication between leaders and followers, rather than on the unique qualities of the leader. By comparing your scores, you can gain an understanding of the aspects of leadership that you find most important and least important. The way you think about leadership will influence how you practice leadership.

Application

1.4 Observational Exercise—Defining Leadership

Purpose

1. To develop an understanding of the complexity of leadership
2. To become aware of the different ways people think about leadership

Directions

1. In this exercise, select five people you know and interview them about leadership.
2. Ask each person to give you their definition of leadership, and to describe how they conceptualize it. Have them elaborate on the question: What is leadership?
3. Record each person's response on a separate sheet of paper.
   Person #1 (name) _____
   Person #2 (name) _____
   Person #3 (name) _____
   Person #4 (name) _____
   Person #5 (name) _____

Questions

1. What differences did you observe in how these people define leadership?

2. What seems to be the most common view of leadership?

   a. In the beginning of this chapter, we discussed six ways of viewing leadership. Which of these ways was highlighted most frequently by your interviewees? And which was highlighted least?

   b. Of the people interviewed, whose descriptions come closest to your own? Why?

1.5 Reflection and Action Worksheet—Understanding Leadership

Reflection

1. Each of us has our own unique way of thinking about leadership. What leaders or people have influenced you in your thinking about leadership? Discuss what leadership means to you and give your definition of leadership.

2. What do the scores you received on the Conceptualizing Leadership Questionnaire suggest about your perspective on leadership? Of the six dimensions on the questionnaire (trait, ability, skill, behavior, relationship, and influence process), which one is the most similar to your own perspective? Which one is least like your own perspective?

3. Do you think leadership is something everyone can learn to do, or do you think it is a natural ability reserved for a few? Explain your answer.

Action

1. Based on the interviews you conducted with others about leadership, how could you incorporate others' ideas about leadership into your own leadership?

2. Treating leadership as a relationship has ethical implications. How could adding the *relationship* approach to your leadership make you a better leader? Discuss.

3. Think about your own leadership. Identify one trait, ability, skill, or behavior that you could develop more fully to become a better leader.

2 RECOGNIZING YOUR TRAITS

INTRODUCTION

Why are some people leaders while others are not? What makes people become leaders? Do leaders have certain traits? These questions have been of interest for many years. It seems that all of us want to know what characteristics account for effective leadership. This chapter will address the traits that are important to leadership.

Since the early 20th century, hundreds of research studies have been conducted on the traits of leaders. These studies have produced an extensive list of ideal leadership traits (see Antonakis et al., 2004; Bass, 1990). The list of important leadership traits is long and includes such traits as diligence, trustworthiness, dependability, articulateness, sociability, open-mindedness, intelligence, confidence, self-assurance, and conscientiousness. Because the list is so extensive, it is difficult to identify specifically which traits are essential for leaders. In fact, nearly all of the traits are probably related to effective leadership.

What traits are important when you are asked to be a leader? To answer this question, two areas will be addressed in this chapter. First, a set of selected traits that appear by all accounts to be strongly related to effective leadership in everyday life will be discussed. Second, the lives of several historical and contemporary leaders will be examined with a discussion of the traits that play a role in their leadership. Throughout this discussion, the unique ways that certain traits affect the leadership process in one way or another will be addressed.

LEADERSHIP TRAITS EXPLAINED

From the beginning of the 20th century to the present day, researchers have focused a great deal of attention on the unique characteristics of successful leaders. Thousands of studies have been conducted to identify the traits of effective leaders. The results of these studies have produced an extensive list of important leadership traits; each of these traits contributes to the leadership process.

For example, research studies by several investigators found the following traits to be important: achievement, persistence, insight, initiative, self-confidence, responsibility, cooperativeness, tolerance, influence, sociability, drive, motivation, integrity, confidence, cognitive ability, task knowledge, extroversion, conscientiousness, and openness (Judge et al., 2002; Kirkpatrick & Locke, 1991; Stogdill, 1974). On the international level, Robert J. House and colleagues (2004), in a study of 17,000 managers in 62 different cultures, identified a list of 22 valued traits that were universally endorsed as characteristics of outstanding leadership in these countries. The list, which was outlined in Table 1.1 in Chapter 1, "Understanding Leadership," includes such attributes as being trustworthy, just, honest, encouraging, positive, dynamic, dependable, intelligent, decisive, communicative, informed, and a team builder. As these findings indicate, research studies on leadership traits have identified a wide array of important characteristics of leaders.

However, these research findings raise an important question: If there are so many important leadership traits, which *specific traits* do people need to be successful leaders? While the answer to this question is not crystal clear, the research points to *six key traits: intelligence, confidence, charisma, determination, sociability*, and *integrity*. In the following section, we will discuss each of these traits in turn.

Intelligence

Intelligence is an important trait related to effective leadership. Intelligence includes having good language skills, perceptual skills, and reasoning ability. This combination of assets makes people good thinkers, and makes them better leaders.

While it is hard for a person to alter their IQ, there are certain ways for a person to improve intelligence in general. Intelligent leaders are well informed. They are aware of what is going on around them and understand the job that needs to be done. It is important for leaders to obtain information about what their leadership role entails and learn as much as possible about their work environment. This information will help leaders be more knowledgeable and insightful.

For example, a few years ago, a friend, Chris, was asked to be the coach of his daughter's middle school soccer team even though he had never played soccer and knew next to nothing about how the game is played. Chris took the job and eventually was a great success, but not without a lot of effort. He spent many hours learning about soccer. He read how-to books, instructor's manuals, and coaching books. In addition, Chris subscribed to several soccer magazines. He talked to other coaches and learned everything he could about playing the game. By the time he had finished the first season, others considered Chris to be a very competent coach. He was smart and learned how to be a successful coach.

Regarding intelligence, few if any of us can expect to be another Albert Einstein. Most of us have average intelligence and know that there are limits to what we can do. Nevertheless, becoming more knowledgeable about our leadership positions gives us the information we need to become better leaders.

Confidence

Being confident is another important trait of an effective leader. Confident people feel self-assured and believe they can accomplish their goals. Rather than feeling uncertain, they feel strong and secure about their positions. They do not second-guess themselves but, rather, move forward on projects with a clear vision. Confident leaders feel a sense of certainty and believe that they are doing the right thing. Clearly, **confidence** is a trait that has to do with feeling positive about oneself and one's ability to succeed.

If confidence is a central trait of successful leaders, how can you build your own confidence? First, confidence comes from *understanding* what is required of you. For example, when first learning to drive a car, a student is low in confidence because they do not know *what* to do. If an instructor explains the driving process and demonstrates how to drive, the student can gain confidence because they now have an understanding of how to drive. Awareness and understanding build confidence. Confidence can also come from having a mentor to show the way and provide constructive feedback. This mentor may be a boss, an experienced coworker, or a significant other from outside the organization. Because mentors act as role models and sounding boards, they provide essential help to learn the dynamics of leadership.

Confidence also comes from *practice.* This is important to point out, because practice is something everyone can do. Consider Michael Phelps, one of the most well-known athletes in the world today. Phelps is a very gifted swimmer, with 23 Olympic gold medals and the record for winning the most medals, 28, of any Olympic athlete in history. But Phelps also spent an enormous amount of time practicing. His workout regimen included swimming six hours a day, six days a week. His excellent performance and confidence were a result of his practice, as well as his gifts.

In leadership, practice builds confidence because it provides assurance that an aspiring leader can do what needs to be done. Taking on leadership roles, even minor ones on committees or through volunteer activities, provides practice for being a leader. Building one leadership activity on another can increase confidence for more demanding leadership roles. Those who accept opportunities to practice their leadership will experience increased confidence in their leadership abilities.

Charisma

Of all the traits related to effective leadership, charisma gets the most attention. **Charisma** refers to a leader's special magnetic charm and appeal, and it can have a huge effect on the leadership process. Charisma is a special personality characteristic that gives a leader the capacity to do extraordinary things. In particular, it gives the leader exceptional powers of influence. A good example of a charismatic leader is former president John F. Kennedy, who motivated the American people with his eloquent oratorical style. President Kennedy was a gifted, charismatic leader who had an enormous impact on others.

At the same time, charisma can also be used by leaders in less positive ways. As we discuss in Chapter 12, "Exploring Destructive Leadership," charisma enhances a leader's ability to gain people's devotion. Incorporated with charisma are leaders' strong rhetorical skills, vision, and energy, which destructive leaders use to win others over and to exploit followers for their own ends. World history abounds with examples of leaders, from Adolf Hitler to InfoWars host Alex Jones, who use their charisma in a harmful way.

It is not unusual for many of us to feel challenged with regard to charisma because it is not a common personality trait. A few select people are very charismatic, but most of us are not. Since charisma appears in short supply, a question arises: What do leaders do if they are not naturally charismatic?

Based on the writings of leadership scholars, several behaviors characterize charismatic leadership (Conger, 1999; House, 1976; Shamir et al., 1993). First, charismatic leaders serve as *strong role models* for the values that they desire others to adopt. Mohandas Gandhi advocated nonviolence and was an exemplary role model of civil disobedience; his charisma enabled him to influence others. Second, charismatic leaders *show competence* in every aspect of leadership, so others trust their decisions. Third, charismatic leaders *articulate clear goals* and *strong values*. Martin Luther King Jr.'s "I Have a Dream" speech is an example of this type of charismatic leadership. Fourth, charismatic leaders communicate *high expectations* for followers and *show confidence* in their abilities to meet these expectations. Finally, charismatic leaders are an *inspiration* to others. They can excite and motivate others to become involved in real change, as demonstrated by Kennedy and King.

Determination

Determination is another trait that characterizes effective leaders. Determined leaders are very focused and attentive to tasks. They know *where* they are going and *how* they intend to get there. Determination is the decision to get the job done; it includes characteristics such as initiative, persistence, and drive. People with determination are willing to assert themselves, they are proactive, and they have the capacity to persevere in the face of obstacles. Being determined includes showing dominance at times, especially in situations where others need direction.

We have all heard of determined people who have accomplished spectacular things—the person with cancer who runs a standard 26.2-mile marathon, the blind person who climbs Mount Everest, or the single mom of four kids who graduates from college. A good example of determined leadership is Nelson Mandela, who is featured in the Leadership Snapshot in this chapter. Mandela's goal was to end apartheid in South Africa. Even though he was imprisoned for many years, he steadfastly held to his principles. He was committed to reaching his goal, and he never wavered from his vision. Mandela was focused and disciplined—a determined leader (Asmal et al., 2003).

What distinguishes all of these leaders from other people is their determination to get the job done. Of all the traits discussed in this chapter, determination is probably the one trait that can be acquired by those who lead. All it demands is perseverance. Staying focused on the task, clarifying the goals, articulating the vision, and encouraging others to stay the course are characteristics of determined leaders. Being determined takes discipline and the ability to endure, but having this trait will almost certainly enhance a person's leadership.

Sociability

Another important trait for leaders is **sociability**. Sociability refers to a leader's capacity to establish pleasant social relationships. People want sociable leaders—leaders with whom they can get along. Leaders who show sociability are friendly, outgoing, courteous, tactful, and diplomatic.

They are sensitive to others' needs and show concern for others' well-being. Sociable leaders have good interpersonal skills and help to create cooperative relationships within their work environments.

Being sociable comes easier for some than for others. For example, it is easy for extroverted leaders to talk to others and be outgoing, but it is harder for introverted leaders to do so. Similarly, some individuals are naturally "people persons," while others prefer to be alone. Although people vary in the degree to which they are outgoing, it is possible to increase sociability. A sociable leader gets along with coworkers and other people in the work setting. Being friendly, kind, and thoughtful, as well as talking freely with others and giving them support, goes a long way to establish a leader's sociability. Sociable leaders bring positive energy to a group and make the work environment a more enjoyable place.

To illustrate, consider the following example. This scenario occurred in one of the best leadership classes I have had in 40 years of teaching. In this class, there was a student named Anne Fox who was a very sociable leader. Anne was very caring and was liked by everyone in the class. After the first week of the semester, Anne could name everyone in class; when attendance was taken, she knew instantly who was there and who was not. In class discussions, Anne always contributed good ideas, and her remarks were sensitive of others' points of view. Anne was positive about life, and her attitude was contagious. By her presence, Anne created an atmosphere in which everyone felt unique but also included. She was the glue that held us all together. Anne was not assigned to be the leader in the class, but by the semester's end she emerged as a leader. Her sociable nature enabled her to develop strong relationships and become a leader in the class. By the end of the class, all of us were the beneficiaries of her leadership.

Integrity

Finally, and perhaps most important, effective leaders have **integrity**. Integrity characterizes leaders who possess the qualities of honesty and trustworthiness. People who adhere to a strong set of principles and take responsibility for their actions are exhibiting integrity. Leaders with integrity inspire confidence in others because they can be trusted to do what they say they are going to do. They are loyal, dependable, and transparent. Basically, integrity makes a leader believable and worthy of our trust.

Dishonesty creates mistrust in others, and dishonest leaders are seen as undependable and unreliable. Honesty helps people to have trust and faith in what leaders have to say and what they stand for. Honesty also enhances a leader's ability to influence others because they have confidence in and believe in their leader.

Integrity demands being open with others and representing reality as fully and completely as possible. However, this is not an easy task: There are times when telling the complete truth can be destructive or counterproductive. The challenge for leaders is to strike a balance between being open and candid and monitoring what is appropriate to disclose in a particular situation. While it is important for leaders to be authentic, it is also essential for them to have integrity in their relationships with others.

LEADERSHIP SNAPSHOT

Nelson Mandela, First Black President of South Africa

South Africa The Good News / www.sagoodnews.co.za CC BY 2.0 https://creativecommons.org/licenses/by /2.0/deed.en

In 1990, when Nelson Mandela was released from prison after serving 27 long years, he was determined not to be angry or vindictive, but instead to work to unite his country of South Africa, which had been fractured by generations of apartheid.

The descendant of a tribal king, Mandela was born in 1918 in a small African village and grew up in a country where whites ruled through subjugation and tyranny over Blacks and other racial groups. Mandela attended Methodist missionary schools and put himself through law school, eventually opening the first Black law partnership in 1942. His firm represented the African National Congress, which was engaged in resisting South Africa's apartheid policies, and during the 1950s, he became a leader of the ANC. Influenced by Mohandas Gandhi, Mandela was initially committed to nonviolent resistance but shifted to supporting violent tactics when the government refused to change its apartheid policies. In 1964, Mandela received a life sentence for plotting to overthrow the government by violence.

During the nearly three decades Mandela spent in prison, he became a symbolic figure for the anti-apartheid movement. But during those years, Mandela spent time examining himself, coming to see himself as others did: as an aggressive and militant revolutionary. He learned to control his temper and strong will and used persuasion instead to convince others. He listened to others' life stories, including those of the white guards, seeking to understand their perspectives. He was steadfast in maintaining his dignity, carefully refusing to be subservient while being respectful to the guards and others. As a result, he became a natural leader inside the prison, while outside, his fame framed him as a symbolic martyr not only to Black Africans but also to people across the globe. Free Mandela campaigns were building around the world, with other countries and international corporations being pressured by stockholders and citizens to "divest" in South Africa.

In 1990, South African president F. W. de Klerk, fearing civil war and economic collapse, released Mandela, at the time 71, from prison. Mandela emerged as a moral leader who stood by the principles of liberty and equal rights for all. He began speaking around the world, raising financial support for the ANC while seeking to bring peace to his fractured country. In 1992, the South African government instituted a new constitution and held a popular election with all parties represented, including the ANC. The result? In 1994, Mandela was elected as the first Black president of South Africa, effectively ending apartheid. For his role in negotiations to abolish apartheid, Mandela received the Nobel Peace Prize, sharing it with de Klerk.

As president of South Africa from 1994 to 1999, Mandela's mission was to transform a nation from minority rule and apartheid to a multiracial democracy. On the first day of his presidency, he set the tone with the predominantly white staff of the former president, telling them that those who wanted to keep their jobs were welcome to stay, stating "Reconciliation starts here." He developed a multiracial staff and cabinet, using his friendly smiling style and tactic of listening carefully to all viewpoints before making decisions to keep the staff focused on problems and issues rather than on partisanship.

Mandela served his five-year term as president but, at 76 years old, chose not to seek another term. In retirement, he continued to advocate for social causes, serving as a mediator in disputes outside of South Africa and bringing a message of peace and justice throughout the world. Mandela died in 2013. While it is difficult to summarize all that he accomplished, Mandela's legacy is best described by former U.S. president Bill Clinton, who in 2003 wrote, "Under a burden of oppression he saw through difference, discrimination and destruction to embrace our common humanity."

Integrity undergirds all aspects of leadership. It is at the core of being a leader. Integrity is a central aspect of a leader's ability to influence. If people do not trust a leader, the leader's influence potential is weakened. In essence, integrity is the bedrock of who a leader is. When a leader's integrity comes into question, their potential to lead is lost.

Former president Bill Clinton (1993–2001) is a good example of how integrity is related to leadership. In the late 1990s, he was brought before the U.S. Congress for misrepresenting under oath an affair he had engaged in with a White House intern. For his actions, he was impeached by the U.S. House of Representatives, but then was acquitted by the U.S. Senate. At one point during the long ordeal, the president appeared on national television and, in what is now a famous speech, declared his innocence. Because subsequent hearings provided information suggesting he might have lied during his television speech, many Americans felt Clinton had violated his duty and responsibility as a person, leader, and president. As a result, Clinton's integrity was clearly challenged and the impact of his leadership substantially weakened.

In conclusion, many traits are related to effective leadership. The six traits discussed here appear to be particularly important in the leadership process. As will be revealed in subsequent chapters, leadership is a very complex process. The traits discussed in this chapter are important but are only one dimension of a multidimensional process.

LEADERSHIP TRAITS IN PRACTICE

Throughout history, there have been many great leaders. Each of them has led with unique talents and in different circumstances. The following section analyzes the accomplishments and the traits of six famous leaders. Although there are hundreds of equally distinguished leaders, these six are highlighted because they represent different kinds of leadership at different points in history. All of these leaders are recognized as being notable leaders: Each has had an impact on many people's lives and accomplished great things.

It's important to know that singling out leaders for their admirable traits can be problematic. Leaders are, after all, human, and humans are not perfect. Given time and the hindsight of history, people who have been identified as having strong leadership traits may be found to have negative qualities as well. For example, George Washington, the first president of the United States, is widely regarded as the founding father of this country. He has been described by historians as having the traits of modesty, evenness, trustworthiness, balance, and integrity. His leadership was instrumental in leading the colonies to victory over Great Britain in the Revolutionary War and in the creation of the U.S. Constitution and establishment of the U.S. democratic government. However, despite his traits and leadership in the founding of the country, there is a dark side to Washington. During his presidency, he and his wife Martha held 317 enslaved people on their Virginia plantation, and it is said that he was a firm disciplinarian who ordered whippings of those enslaved people who were rebellious.

It is important to keep the imperfect nature of people in mind as you read about the leaders discussed here—Harriet Tubman, Winston Churchill, Mother Teresa, Dr. Anthony Fauci, Oprah Winfrey, and LeBron James. While each of these individuals has accomplished much and impacted many, they may also have made missteps along the way or will in the future. As you read about each of them, focus on the *traits* that make their leadership effective and think about how those traits contribute to their success as leaders.

Harriet Tubman (c. 1820–1913)

Harriet Tubman was an American activist who played a major role in the abolitionist movement in the years leading up to the Civil War (1861–1865). She was born enslaved in Dorchester County, Maryland. At the age of 12, she suffered a severe blow to the head while trying to assist a fellow

UniversalImagesGroup/Contributor via Getty Images

enslaved person who was being attacked. The wound she received caused intermittent black-outs for the rest of her life. In 1849, Tubman escaped by way of the Underground Railroad from Maryland to Philadelphia in the free state of Pennsylvania by traveling at night, using the North Star as her guide. After she gained her own freedom, Tubman became a "conductor" for the Underground Railroad. She subsequently made 13 return trips to the South and rescued as many as 300 other enslaved people. Tubman was known as "Moses" because she helped her people escape to freedom. During the Civil War, she became a spy and soldier for the North (for the Union Army) and was the first woman in the armed services to carry out a military operation: In 1863, she led the successful Combahee River Raid that freed more than 750 enslaved people. In her later years, she settled in Auburn, New York, where she established a home dedicated to the care of older African Americans. When she died in 1913, Tubman was 93 years old.

Traits and Characteristics

Harriet Tubman was a tenacious leader (C. Clinton, 2004; Wills, 1994). She had a far-reaching impact despite horrific treatment, a lack of formal education, and the seizures she experienced as a result of her head injury. She fought courageously to end slavery with persistent resolve. Devoted to her cause, she repeatedly risked her own life to bring freedom to others. She was determined, focused, strong, and unpretentious. Her leadership combined the spiritual and the practical; she believed in divine guidance but was pragmatic and methodical in her approach to tasks. Tubman was a remarkable leader and her accomplishments extraordinary.

Winston Churchill (1874–1965)

Winston Churchill was one of the greatest statesmen and orators of the 20th century. In addition, he was a talented painter and prolific writer; he received the Nobel Prize in Literature in 1953. Churchill served in the military during World War I, became prime minister of Great Britain in May 1940, and remained in that office through World War II, until 1945. It was at this time that his masterful leadership was most visible. When the Germans threatened to invade Britain, Churchill stood strong. He made many famous speeches that had far-reaching effects on the morale of the people of Great Britain and the Allied forces. On the home front, he was a social reformer. He served a second term as prime minister from 1951 to 1955. He died at the age of 90 in 1965.

Walter Stoneman/Stringer/Hulton Archive/Getty Images

Traits and Characteristics

Winston Churchill's leadership was remarkable because it emerged from a man who was average in many respects and who faced challenges in his personal life. In his education, he did not stand out as superior to others. On a societal level, he was a loner who had few friends. On a personal level, he suffered from bouts of depression throughout his life. Despite these characteristics, Churchill emerged as a leader because of his other unique gifts and how he used them (Hayward, 1997; Keegan, 2002; Sandys & Littman, 2003). A voracious reader, Churchill was plain speaking, decisive, detail oriented, and informed (Hayward, 1997). Furthermore, he was very ambitious, for himself, but also for his nation. He evoked strong reactions among his followers. His political opponents characterized him as pugnacious, egotistical, and dangerous while his supporters thought him charismatic, courageous, and a genius (Addison, 2005). His most significant talent was his masterful use of language. In his oratory, the normally plainspoken Churchill used words and imagery in powerful ways that touched the hearts of many and set the moral climate of the war (Keegan, 2002). He had the ability to build hope and inspire others to rise to the challenge. His stoicism and optimism were an inspiration to his people and all of the Allied forces (Sandys & Littman, 2003).

Mother Teresa (1910–1997)

A Roman Catholic nun considered a saint by many, Mother Teresa received the Nobel Peace Prize in 1979 for her work with people living in poverty in Kolkata, India, and throughout the world. Born in Macedonia, Mother Teresa came from a comfortable background. At the age of 18, she joined the Catholic Sisters of Loreto order and worked for 17 years as a high school teacher in Kolkata. Her awareness of poverty in Kolkata caused her to leave the convent in 1948 to devote herself to working full-time with people experiencing poverty in the city. In 1950, Mother Teresa founded a new religious order, the Missionaries of Charity, to care for people who did not have adequate access to housing, health care, and other basic necessities.

Today, more than 1 million workers are affiliated with the Missionaries of Charity in more than 40 countries. The charity provides help to people who have been hurt by floods, epidemics, famines, and war. The Missionaries of Charity also operate hospitals, schools, orphanages, youth centers, shelters, and hospices. For her humanitarian work and efforts for peace, Mother Teresa has been recognized with many awards, including the Pope John XXIII Peace Prize (1971), the Nehru Award (1972), the U.S. Presidential Medal of Freedom (1985), and the Congressional Gold Medal (1994). Although she struggled with deteriorating health in her later years, Mother Teresa remained actively involved in her work to the very end. She died at the age of 87 in 1997. In September 2016, Pope Francis declared Mother Teresa a saint, with the official name of Saint Teresa of Kolkata. In a statement announcing the canonization, the Vatican called her a "metaphor for selfless devotion and holiness" (Lyman, 2016).

Bettmann/Contributor/Bettmann/Getty Images

Traits and Characteristics

Mother Teresa was a simple woman of small stature who dressed in a plain blue and white sari, and who never owned more than the people she served. Mirroring her appearance, her mission was simple—to care for the poor. From her first year on the streets of Kolkata where she tended to one dying person to her last years when thousands of people were cared for by the Missionaries of Charity, Mother Teresa stayed focused on her goal. She was a true civil servant who was simultaneously determined and fearless, and humble and spiritual. She often listened to the will of God. When criticized for her stand on abortion and women's role in the family, or her approaches to eliminating poverty, Mother Teresa responded with a strong will; she never wavered in her deep-seated human values. Teaching by example with few words, she was a role model for others. Clearly, Mother Teresa was a leader who practiced what she preached (Gonzalez-Balado, 1997; Sebba, 1997; Spink, 1997; Vardey, 1995).

Dr. Anthony Fauci (1940–)

Dr. Anthony Fauci was the director of the U.S. National Institute of Allergy and Infectious Diseases from 1984 to 2022, a time during which he advised seven U.S. presidents but most Americans had never heard his name. During his 38 years as director, he oversaw efforts to prevent, diagnose, and treat established infectious diseases such as HIV/AIDS, respiratory infections, diarrheal diseases, tuberculosis, and malaria as well as emerging diseases such as Ebola, Zika, West Nile virus, and SARS. He became known for his groundbreaking work in HIV/AIDS research, persuading the presidential administration to take the crisis seriously, getting increased funding for AIDS research, and forging alliances with activists by allowing access to experimental drugs even as they were being tested in clinical trials. Most crucially, he developed an understanding of how HIV attacks the human defense system, sparking the creation of effective medications that cut down the mortality rate of the disease. But it was Fauci's leadership during the COVID-19 pandemic from 2020 to 2022 that led to him becoming a household name.

In January 2020, as reports of the novel coronavirus emerged from China, Fauci quickly assembled a research team to work on a vaccine. Within weeks, as deaths and illness from COVID-19 began to mount in other countries across the globe, he worked with colleagues at the Centers for Disease Control and Prevention to prepare the American public for what was to become a major global pandemic. Fauci became a fixture at news briefings alongside President Donald Trump, where sometimes he felt the need to rebut false or misleading statements that the president made about the virus or treatments for it. Fauci's calm demeanor and commitment to communicating only the hard facts about the virus propelled him to celebrity as the country, and the globe, endured an unprecedented shutdown. But as the public health crisis became politicized and divisive, some people began to challenge his decision making, scientific competence, and ethics. In fact, Fauci and his family members became subjects of harassment and death threats. Nevertheless, through governmental support and funding, several COVID-19 vaccines were developed during the pandemic, which were able to dramatically decrease the virus's transmission and effects. Ultimately, COVID-19 was responsible for more than 6.7 million deaths worldwide, including over 1.1 million in the United States. Mutations of the virus continue to affect people worldwide today, but the mortality rate of the virus has

AC NewsPhoto / Alamy Stock Photo

been greatly lessened through the use of the vaccines and treatments developed through and facilitated by Fauci's leadership. Fauci stepped down from his NIAID post and as chief medical advisor to the U.S. president in December 2022.

Traits and Characteristics

Dr. Anthony Fauci's remarkable and long career fighting infectious diseases and steering the United States' response to the COVID-19 pandemic is evidence of his strengths as a leader. Fauci's trait of determination was evident in his work to combat HIV/AIDS through his success in getting the U.S. government to fund research for the disease, which ultimately resulted in effective drug treatments. His sociability was a key factor in his ability to develop alliances with AIDS activists, who were angry about the government's slow reaction to the deadly disease, and gain their trust and support.

Fauci's intelligence was a significant factor in his distinguished and accomplished career and made him credible when discussing the complexities of HIV/AIDS and COVID-19. During the COVID-19 pandemic, he approached the public with confidence and integrity, providing information that was factually proven about the virus and treatments, and openly rebutting and disagreeing with false claims and information by the president and other elected officials. Despite distractions, which included threats to his family's well-being and heated exchanges during congressional hearings, he stayed on message, explaining the logic behind recommendations for COVID-19 restrictions. Fauci was focused and determined in his efforts to minimize the number of COVID-19 cases and deaths in the United States and facilitating the quick development of a vaccine and treatments for the disease. He held on to his resolve and commitment to deliver and communicate public health guidance based on the available data. While knowing the economic pain that resulted from business closures and shutdowns, he believed saving lives mattered more in the long term than saving jobs (National Institute of Allergy and Infectious Diseases, 2023; Ott, 2020; Segal, 2022).

Oprah Winfrey (1954–)

An award-winning television talk show host, Oprah Winfrey is one of the most powerful and influential people in the world. Born in rural Mississippi into a dysfunctional family, she was raised by her grandmother until she was 6. Winfrey learned to read at a very early age and skipped two grades in school. Her adolescent years were difficult: While living in Milwaukee with her mother, who worked two jobs, Winfrey was molested by a family member. Despite these experiences, she was an honors student in high school and received national accolades for her oratory ability. She received a full scholarship to Tennessee State University, where she studied communication and worked at a local radio station. Winfrey's work in the media eventually led her to Chicago where she became host of the highly acclaimed *Oprah Winfrey Show.* In 2007,

Frederick M. Brown/Stringer/Getty Images Entertainment/Getty Images

Winfrey was the highest-paid entertainer in television, earning an annual salary estimated at $260 million. She also is an actor, a producer, a book critic, and a magazine publisher and, in 2011, left her successful television show to concentrate on her television network, OWN. In 2013, Winfrey received the nation's highest civilian honor, the Presidential Medal of Freedom. In 2018, Winfrey won the Golden Globe Cecil B. DeMille Award for her contributions to the entertainment industry. Winfrey was the first Black woman to win this award.

Her total wealth is estimated at more than $3.1 billion. Winfrey is also a highly regarded philanthropist: Her giving has focused on making a difference in the lives of people experiencing poverty, natural disasters, and other hardships. Winfrey has paid special attention to the needs of people in Africa, raising millions of dollars to help AIDS-affected children there and creating a leadership academy for girls in a small town near Johannesburg, South Africa.

Traits and Characteristics

Oprah Winfrey's remarkable journey from rural poverty to influential world leader can be explained by several of her strengths (Harris & Watson, 2007; Illouz, 2003; McDonald, 2007). Foremost, Winfrey is an excellent communicator. Since she was a little girl reciting Bible passages in church, she has been comfortable in front of an audience. On television, she is able to talk to millions of people and have each person feel as if she is talking directly to them. Winfrey is also intelligent and well read, with a strong business sense. She is sincere, determined, and inspirational. Winfrey has a charismatic style of leadership that enables her to connect with people. She is spontaneous and expressive, and has a fearless ability to self-disclose. Because she has "been in the struggle" and survived, she is seen as a role model. Winfrey has overcome many obstacles in her life and encourages others to overcome their struggles as well. Her message is a message of hope.

LeBron James (1984–)

LeBron James is a professional basketball player for the Los Angeles Lakers, whose extraordinary athletic skills and accomplishments are recognized worldwide (Coombs & Cassilo, 2017; ESPN, 2019; Green, 2017). When James was in high school, his exceptional talent had already been recognized by National Basketball Association scouts, and he was selected as the Cleveland Cavaliers' first overall draft pick in 2003. James has been with three different teams during his professional career (Cleveland Cavaliers, Miami Heat, and L.A. Lakers), setting numerous scoring records and winning several Most Valuable Player awards. He has won two Olympic gold medals and four NBA championships—two with Miami, one with Cleveland, and one with Los Angeles.

Because of his skill and subsequent fame, James has considerable influence among his fans, his teammates, other professional athletes, and the wider public. In 2017, *Time* magazine identified him as one of the 100 Most Influential People in the World. James has used his stature to speak out about NBA rules he thinks should be changed, mistakes made by the Cavaliers' front office, and racist comments by NBA owners.

James has used his platform to champion racial equality and social justice. In 2020, James helped establish More Than A Vote, a nonprofit organization led by prominent Black athletes that is devoted to combating systemic, racist voter suppression through voter outreach and education.

Despite his superstar status, James is still true to his humble roots. He grew up in Akron, Ohio, under challenging circumstances that motivated him to give back to underresourced communities. He has supported numerous causes and community outreach programs, including Boys & Girls Clubs of America, the Children's Defense Fund, and a whole-house renovation for a needy family, where he contributed his own labor, fitting it in around his training schedule with the Cavaliers (Curtis, 2016). In 2004, in just his second year as a pro basketball player, James established the LeBron James Family Foundation to improve the lives of children and teens in Akron

Everett Collection Inc/Alamy Stock Photo

through educational and cocurricular programs. In 2018, the LJFF opened the *I PROMISE School*, of which James said, "This school is so important to me because our vision is to create a place for the kids in Akron who need it most—those that could fall through the cracks if we don't do something. We've learned over the years what works and what motivates them, and now we can bring all of that together in one place, along with the right resources and experts" (Evans, 2017).

Traits and Characteristics

LeBron James has many qualities that contribute to his effectiveness as a leader. He has physical power and the ability to dominate other players on the basketball court. He has great confidence in his basketball skills, which inspires teammates to perform at high levels as well. He is a consistent performer, being selected to play in 16 NBA All-Star Games. He is ambitious and determined to win championships. He has the endurance to play for many years to come, but even now is thinking about the next phase of his life, and the legacy he will leave behind. He operates out of a strong set of principles, such as giving back to his community. He has the emotional maturity and resilience to handle criticism and learn from it. His charisma has earned him spots on many magazine covers, and numerous invitations to host or be a guest on TV talk shows.

All of these individuals have exhibited exceptional leadership. While each of these leaders is unique, together they share many common characteristics. All are visionary, strong willed, diligent, and inspirational. As purpose-driven leaders, they are role models and symbols of hope. Reflecting on the characteristics of these extraordinary leaders will provide you with a better understanding of the traits that are important for effective leadership. Although you may not aspire to be another Dr. Fauci or Mother Teresa, you can learn a great deal from these leaders in understanding how your own traits affect your leadership.

SUMMARY

This chapter describes the traits required of a leader. Social science research has provided insight into leadership traits. Thousands of leadership studies have been performed to identify the traits of effective leaders; the results of these studies point to a very long list of important leadership traits. From this list, the traits that appear to be especially important for effective leadership are *intelligence, confidence, charisma, determination, sociability*, and *integrity*.

From an examination of a select group of well-known historical and contemporary leaders including Harriet Tubman, Winston Churchill, Mother Teresa, Dr. Anthony Fauci, Oprah Winfrey, and LeBron James, it is clear that exemplary leaders exhibit many similar traits. In the main, these leaders were or are visionary, strong willed, diligent, inspirational, purpose driven, and hopeful. These leadership figures provide useful models for understanding the traits that are important and desirable for achieving effective leadership.

Because leadership is a complex process, there are no simple paths or guarantees to becoming a successful leader. Each individual is unique, and each of us has our own distinct talents for leadership. Those who are naturally strong in the six traits discussed in this chapter will be well equipped for leadership. If you are not strong on all of these traits but are willing to work on them, you can still become an effective leader.

Remember that many traits are related to effective leadership. By becoming aware of your own traits and how to nourish them, you will be well on your way to becoming a successful leader.

KEY TERMS

charisma

confidence

determination

integrity

intelligence

sociability

Application

2.1 Case Study—NorthTown Doulas

Kamiah N. didn't like what she was seeing. The infant mortality rate of African American babies in her community was nearly four times that of babies who were white and of other racial groups. She had experienced this personally: When she was 19, her first child died four days after birth from conditions that, had she known, could have been prevented during pregnancy.

Kamiah grew up in an impoverished, mostly African American neighborhood in a mid-sized city, known as NorthTown. When she became pregnant, she relied on friends or others in her neighborhood to tell her what she needed to know. She didn't consider going to a doctor; regular health care was not readily accessible or affordable for the families in her neighborhood, most of whom were uninsured. In addition, Kamiah had heard rumors that the pregnant women from their neighborhood who did visit doctors were at risk of having their child taken away by Child Protective Services after birth because "they always run a drug screen on you to see if you used drugs during pregnancy" or because you neglected your and the baby's health during pregnancy.

But when Kamiah became pregnant again, she was determined to find out what could be done to make sure her second baby survived. She began researching infant mortality and discovered the leading causes of infant mortality in her community were low birth weight and shortened gestation periods. Most low-weight babies were born prematurely, and many that were full term were small because of the youngness of the mother or because the mother did not gain enough weight during pregnancy. She also discovered that many African American mothers are wary of hospitals and doctors. A 2018 National Vital Statistics Report by the Centers for Disease Control and Prevention showed that African American mothers are 2.3 times more likely than white mothers to wait to begin prenatal care until their third trimester of pregnancy or to not receive prenatal care at all (Osterman & Martin, 2018).

Despite her apprehensions, Kamiah went to a free clinic during her pregnancy and learned firsthand why young women like her would not want to visit a doctor. She felt judged by the clinic's white medical professionals, and when she said she wanted to have her baby at home because she couldn't afford a hospital, the doctors said that wasn't possible and that CPS could become involved if she did.

When Kamiah attended a Young Women's Christian Association (YWCA) conference on prenatal care, she learned about something she had never heard about before—*doulas*. Doulas are trained professionals who offer physical, emotional, and informational support to moms-to-be before, during, and after birth. But the price tag for doula care was anywhere from $250 to $2,000, which meant a doula was not an option for Kamiah or any of the low-income women in her neighborhood.

When she gave birth to her second child in the hospital, she says she remembers feeling "completely alone" and wished she'd had someone there to advocate for her while she was doing the hard work of giving birth. It was then that Kamiah decided not only to become a doula, but to become certified to train others in her community to be doulas as well.

Kamiah applied for and was awarded an educational grant offered by her neighborhood's community association to pay for her training as a doula. When she completed the training, she immediately began the certification process to become a doula trainer. At the same time, she met with the executive director of the local YWCA for advice on how to pursue her dream of providing doula services for the women in her neighborhood. The executive listened to Kamiah's plan and, without hesitation, offered to mentor her on how to set up a nonprofit organization and apply for grant funding, and how to identify and talk with potential donors, elected officials, and others who could support her efforts.

A year later, Kamiah established NorthTown Doulas, a nonprofit that funds and supports doula training for doulas of color. NorthTown Doulas trains doulas not only in the birth experience, but also to serve as advocates for women. Because so many of their clients were likely to be young Black mothers, the doulas were taught to "meet young Black mothers exactly where they are and not to dismiss them."

"When you go into a hospital and you don't feel supported because of your race, but you have an advocate there who is culturally the same as you and can speak for you so you can do the work of having a baby, it just makes all the difference," Kamiah says.

After forming NorthTown Doulas, Kamiah faced two challenges. The first was getting the word out to pregnant women that doula services were available. This required the women in her neighborhood first to understand what a doula was and then to trust one to help them with their pregnancies and births. From her own experience, Kamiah knew that the informal leaders in the neighborhood were the grandmothers, and she reached out to these women, many of whom she'd known since she was young. She knew if the older women in the neighborhood trusted her, it would help smooth the way with younger generations who needed her services.

Kamiah's second challenge was funding. Kamiah began talking to large groups, such as service clubs, women's organizations, and church groups, where the audiences were mostly white. Kamiah found that public speaking came naturally to her. She was able to talk openly about her own pregnancy and birth experiences and those of other low-income women of color, explaining their perceptions and their reality. Kamiah found that audiences responded to her transparency with empathy and appreciation, perhaps because many of them were mothers.

Within two years of its founding, NorthTown Doulas was on solid financial footing, and Kamiah had trained 14 doulas who provide their free services to clients who are low-income and of color. The doulas meet weekly with their pregnant clients, teaching them about nutrition and prenatal care and listening to their concerns and fears. The doulas are well informed on the social services available in the community and how to access these services for their clients, especially when it comes to securing adequate nutrition. In cases where the mothers-to-be need medical treatment, the doulas help the clients find doctors and midwives they will trust, often transporting their clients to appointments and staying with them through their visits. After the women have given birth, the doulas continue to provide them with assistance, teaching them how to care for their infants and manage being a new parent, and monitoring them and the babies for any health concerns.

Since she became a doula, Kamiah has helped more than 50 young women give birth to healthy babies. As the organization's leader, she has less time now to be a doula, which she admits she misses, but knows that through her organization and the doulas she's trained, she still has a hand in the healthy births of many children.

Questions

1. How would you describe Kamiah's leadership traits?

2. Of the six major traits described in the chapter (i.e., intelligence, confidence, charisma, determination, sociability, and integrity), which traits are Kamiah's strongest?

3. Of these traits, which do you think is naturally strong for Kamiah, and which did she learn?

4. What different traits did Kamiah exhibit in her ability to get others to support her, such as the executive director of the YWCA? The grandmothers in the neighborhood? The groups where the audiences were mostly white?

2.2 Case Study—The Three *B*s

The three *B*s are three recent college graduates at the precipice of their careers. Having each completed their education from prestigious American universities, all three are destined to become important and influential leaders. Following is a snapshot of the lives of each of these future leaders at the time of their college graduation. As you read through each person's biography, pay particular attention to the traits and characteristics of these graduates, noticing which will serve them as they mature into the leaders they become.

B1

B1 grew up in a rural, southern state and, at a young age, knew his path lay in politics. Influenced by John F. Kennedy and Martin Luther King Jr., B1 would later admit, "Sometime in my sixteenth year, I decided I wanted to be in public life as an elected official. I loved music and thought I could be very good, but I knew I would never be John Coltrane or Stan Getz. I was interested in medicine and thought I could be a fine doctor, but I knew I would never be Michael DeBakey. But I knew I could be great in public service. I thought I could make it without family wealth, or connections, or establishment southern positions on race and other issues."[1]

B1 was born to a widowed mother and never knew his father. His early years were influenced greatly by the two strong women in his life: his mother and his grandmother. His mother was fun loving and vivacious, leaving her young son in his grandparents' care while she studied nursing in a neighboring state. His grandmother, by contrast, was a strong-willed disciplinarian, instilling in B1 a lifelong love of reading. When B1 was 4, his mother married the man who would become his stepfather, a local car dealer and an abusive alcoholic. B1 often intervened in the violent arguments that broke out in his home and protected the secrets of his home life as the children of alcoholics often do. He was 15 when his mother ended the marriage.

B1 attended Catholic schools and, later, a local public high school. The high school was segregated, a dogma B1 had difficulty accepting. Charming, handsome, and intelligent, he was an active student leader and musician, playing the saxophone and winning first chair in the state band. Highly interested in politics, he participated in both Boys State and Boys Nation, which provided him the opportunity to meet his idol, President Kennedy.

B1 was mentored by his high school principal, a woman known for her commitment to "produce leaders who thought of personal success in terms of public service"[2] and who recognized B1 as a "young man of rare talent and ambition."[3] It was in the halls of his high school that B1 found his passion for law, informing his Latin teacher of his intent to study law after a mock trial exercise for her class.

Following high school, B1 attended Georgetown University, which he financed through scholarships and part-time jobs. He was a member of Phi Beta Kappa (the prestigious academic honor society), an honorary band fraternity, and a service fraternity. B1 was elected class president twice and interned and clerked for the senator from his home state.

Following his graduation with a degree in foreign service, B1 won a prestigious Rhodes Scholarship to University College, Oxford, England, but left Oxford after a year to study law at Yale University.

B2

B2 was the eldest child of a prestigious and wealthy family. His father and grandfather were prominent U.S. political leaders, and his mother the daughter of a successful publisher. B2's ancestry traced directly to the American colonists.

The death of his 3-year-old sister when B2 was 7 devastated his family. Left an only child for a time, he brought consolation to his mother through his humor, playfulness, and good cheer, a role he often relied upon as he matured into adulthood.[4]

After attending a prestigious prep school from seventh through ninth grade, B2 was accepted to Phillips Academy, a highly selective boarding school in Andover, Massachusetts. It was the same school both his father and grandfather had attended, but unlike his father, B2 was not an academic or athletic standout. He was very active and social, however, playing baseball and serving as head cheerleader, standing out among his classmates for his humor and antics.

B2 went on to Yale University, where he was admitted under the university's "legacy" policies that gave preferential treatment to children of alumni. Both B2's father and grandfather were Yale graduates.

While at Yale, B2 was an active fraternity member (serving as president his senior year), cheerleader, and member of the rugby team. He was also a member of Skull and Bones, an undergraduate secret society of which his father had also been a member. The secretive Skull and Bones is known for its prominent alumni and has often been the subject of conspiracy theories.

A self-proclaimed "average" student, B2 received a bachelor's degree in history with a C grade point average. Nevertheless, he was accepted by Harvard University's prestigious MBA program after serving a two-year commission in the Air National Guard. In the Air Guard, B2 was selected to serve as a pilot, despite low pilot aptitude tests and irregular attendance to air training. He was honorably discharged prior to attending Harvard.

Harvard classmates and professors remember B2 as having "a relaxed attitude and an unusual confidence that stood out even in a class of some of America's most confident."[5] Though an average student, B2 was described as a "quick study—not a very deep thinker, but an efficient one . . . more of a listener than a participant."[6] With a ready sense of humor, B2 stood out in team-based activities and was often chosen to lead. B2 completed his MBA, calling it "a turning point" that taught him "the principles of capital, how it is accumulated, risked, spent, managed."[7]

B3

B3's parents met and married while attending college. B3 was born six months later to his Kenyan father and white American mother. When B3 was 2 years old, his father (after receiving his graduate degree at Harvard University) abandoned the family and returned to his home. B3 would see his father only once more before his father's sudden death when B3 was 21.[8]

His mother subsequently remarried and moved B3 to Indonesia when he was 6. Though not religious, his family sent B3 to a Catholic school as well as a public school in a predominantly Muslim country, contributing to what the young biracial boy would later recall as "the multiplicity of cultures which fed me."[9] B3 became fluent in Indonesian and was known as a schoolyard peacemaker, acting as a mediator for his classmates' conflicts. His third-grade teacher remembered him as a boy who liked to be in charge and who wanted to be the best, though she admitted he would cede his place willingly if asked to do so.

When he was 10, his mother, concerned for his education, sent him back to the United States to live with his grandparents and attend Hawaii's elite, private Punahou School.[10] B3 was a good but not outstanding student. Popular and athletic, he was a member of the varsity basketball team.

Despite the racial diversity of Hawaii, B3 struggled with his racial identity. Though he had loving role models in his grandfather and stepfather and a multicultural upbringing, the young man had to resolve his own identity as a biracial man in America. In the absence of a father who could have provided much-needed guidance, B3 was left mostly on his own to figure things out for himself. "At some level I had to raise myself . . . if I think about how I have been able to navigate some pretty tricky situations in my life, it has to do with the fact that I had to learn to trust my own judgment; I had to learn to fight for what I wanted."[11]

Perhaps sensing his teenage grandson's struggle, B3's grandfather connected him with Frank Marshall Davis, a leading Black activist and writer. Davis introduced the young man, who was already an avid reader, to the world of Black literature and activism.

After graduating from high school, B3 moved to Los Angeles to attend Occidental College, transferring in his junior year to Columbia University in New York City. His college classmates described him as endearing and likable with a proclivity toward multiracial social circles and an ability to move easily between different groups. Deeply interested in political and international affairs, he graduated from Columbia with a bachelor's degree in political science.

Desiring to work as a community organizer, he applied unsuccessfully to several organizations. Frustrated and laden with student debt, he accepted a position with a global business consulting company. Appreciated for his intelligence and self-assurance, B3 was well liked by his supervisors and colleagues. He was described as a bit reserved, as if he was simply biding his time until he could pursue his true passions. The opportunity came when he was offered a job as an organizer for the New York Public Interest Research Group, where he worked to mobilize college students on a variety of city issues from rebuilding public transportation to increasing recycling efforts.

After two years, B3 was ready to leave New York and pursue causes that were important to him, and he accepted a job as a community organizer in Chicago's largely poor and Black South Side. His first assignment was to organize the community's low-income residents and pressure the city government to improve conditions in the crumbling housing projects. His efforts met with some success, but he soon came to the conclusion that to be truly effective he would need a law degree.

B3 attended Harvard Law School, excelling as a student and graduating magna cum laude. Reflecting on his choice to go to Harvard, B3 explained, "One of the luxuries of going to

Harvard Law School is it means you can take risks in your life. You can try to do things to improve society and still land on your feet. That's what a Harvard education should buy—enough confidence and security to pursue your dreams and give something back."[12]

He was elected president of the prestigious *Harvard Law Review*, the first African American ever to do so. A liberal, B3 won the election by persuading the journal's primarily conservative staffers that he would treat their views fairly, a promise he kept. Shortly after, when one of his professors approached B3 with an opportunity to clerk for a Supreme Court justice, B3 politely declined, explaining his desire to go back to Chicago to complete the work he had been doing and run for elected office.

His election to the *Law Review* garnered widespread media attention and resulted in a contract from a major publisher to write a book on race relations for which he was able to use the proceeds to help pay off his student loans.

Questions

Before the identities of these future leaders are revealed, complete Question 1.

1. Rank the strength of each person (on a scale of 1 to 10, with 10 as high) for each leadership trait listed. Use the "explanation" column to support your ranking.

	B1	
	RANK	**EXPLANATION**
INTELLIGENCE		
CONFIDENCE		
CHARISMA		
DETERMINATION		
SOCIABILITY		
INTEGRITY		

	B2	
	RANK	**EXPLANATION**
INTELLIGENCE		
CONFIDENCE		
CHARISMA		
DETERMINATION		
SOCIABILITY		
INTEGRITY		

	B3	
	RANK	EXPLANATION
INTELLIGENCE		
CONFIDENCE		
CHARISMA		
DETERMINATION		
SOCIABILITY		
INTEGRITY		

B1, B2, and B3 all became influential world leaders, serving as consecutive U.S. presidents. You may recognize them as President **B**ill Clinton (B1), President George W. **B**ush (B2), and President **B**arack Obama (B3).

2. The chapter strongly implies that leadership is about traits—people become leaders because of their traits. In light of what you know about these men and their presidencies, do you feel the trait approach adequately captures the essence of their leadership? Does nurturance play an equal or more important role? Why or why not?

3. Of all the traits exhibited by these three leaders, what one trait would you like to have for yourself? Explain why.

Notes

1. W. Clinton (2004).

2. Riley (n.d.).

3. Ibid.

4. Bruni (2002).

5. Solomon (2000).

6. Ibid.

7. Ibid.

8. Life Books (2008).

9. Nelson (n.d.).

10. Remnick (2010).

11. Meacham (2008).

12. Editors of *Life* magazine (2008).

Application

2.3 Leadership Traits Questionnaire

Purpose

1. To gain an understanding of how traits are used in leadership assessment
2. To obtain an assessment of your own leadership traits

Directions

1. Make five copies of this questionnaire. It should be completed by you and five people you know (e.g., roommates, coworkers, relatives, friends).
2. Using the following scale, have each individual indicate the degree to which they agree or disagree with each of the 14 statements regarding your leadership traits. Do not forget to complete this exercise for yourself.

_____ (your name) is

Statements	Strongly disagree	Disagree	Neutral	Agree	Strongly agree
1. Articulate: Communicates effectively with others	1	2	3	4	5
2. Perceptive: Is discerning and insightful	1	2	3	4	5
3. Self-confident: Believes in oneself and one's ability	1	2	3	4	5
4. Self-assured: Is secure with self, free of doubts	1	2	3	4	5
5. Persistent: Stays fixed on the goals, despite interference	1	2	3	4	5
6. Determined: Takes a firm stand, acts with certainty	1	2	3	4	5
7. Trustworthy: Is authentic, inspires confidence	1	2	3	4	5
8. Dependable: Is consistent and reliable	1	2	3	4	5

Statements	Strongly disagree	Disagree	Neutral	Agree	Strongly agree
9. Friendly: Shows kindness and warmth	1	2	3	4	5
10. Outgoing: Talks freely, gets along well with others	1	2	3	4	5
11. Conscientious: Is thorough, organized, and careful	1	2	3	4	5
12. Diligent: Is industrious, hardworking	1	2	3	4	5
13. Sensitive: Shows tolerance, is tactful and sympathetic	1	2	3	4	5
14. Empathic: Understands others, identifies with others	1	2	3	4	5

Scoring

1. Enter the responses for Raters 1, 2, 3, 4, and 5 in the appropriate columns on the scoring sheet on this page. An example of a completed chart appears a little farther down.
2. For each of the 14 items, compute the average for the five raters and place that number in the "average rating" column.
3. Place your own scores in the "self-rating" column.

Leadership Traits Questionnaire Chart

	Rater 1	Rater 2	Rater 3	Rater 4	Rater 5	Average rating	Self-rating
1. Articulate							
2. Perceptive							
3. Self-confident							
4. Self-assured							
5. Persistent							
6. Determined							

	Rater 1	Rater 2	Rater 3	Rater 4	Rater 5	Average rating	Self-rating
7. Trustworthy							
8. Dependable							
9. Friendly							
10. Outgoing							
11. Conscientious							
12. Diligent							
13. Sensitive							
14. Empathic							

Scoring Interpretation

The scores you received on this questionnaire provide information about how you see yourself and how others see you as a leader. The chart allows you to see where your perceptions are the same as those of others and where they differ. There are no "perfect" scores for this questionnaire. The purpose of the instrument is to provide a way to assess your strengths and weaknesses and to evaluate areas where your perceptions are similar to or different from those of others. While it is confirming when others see you in the same way as you see yourself, it is also beneficial to know when they see you differently. This assessment can help you understand your assets as well as areas in which you may seek to improve.

Example Leadership Traits Questionnaire Ratings

	Rater 1	Rater 2	Rater 3	Rater 4	Rater 5	Average rating	Self-rating
1. Articulate	4	4	3	2	4	3.4	4
2. Perceptive	2	5	3	4	4	3.6	5
3. Self-confident	4	4	5	5	4	4.4	4
4. Self-assured	5	5	5	5	5	5	5
5. Persistent	4	4	3	3	3	3.4	3
6. Determined	4	4	4	4	4	4	4
7. Trustworthy	5	5	5	5	5	5	5

	Rater 1	Rater 2	Rater 3	Rater 4	Rater 5	Average rating	Self-rating
8. Dependable	4	5	4	5	4	4.4	4
9. Friendly	5	5	5	5	5	5	5
10. Outgoing	5	4	5	4	5	4.6	4
11. Conscientious	2	3	2	3	3	2.6	4
12. Diligent	3	3	3	3	3	3	4
13. Sensitive	4	4	5	5	5	4.6	3
14. Empathic	5	5	4	5	4	4.6	3

Summary and interpretation: The scorer's self-ratings are higher than the average ratings of others on articulate, perceptive, conscientious, and diligent. The scorer's self-ratings are lower than the average ratings of others on self-confident, persistent, dependable, outgoing, sensitive, and empathic. The scorer's self-ratings on self-assured, determined, trustworthy, and friendly are the same as the average ratings of others.

Application

2.4 Observational Exercise

Leadership Traits

Purpose

1. To gain an understanding of the role of traits in the leadership process
2. To examine the traits of selected historical and everyday leaders

Directions

1. Based on the descriptions of the historical leaders provided in the chapter, identify the three major leadership traits for each of the leaders listed as follows.
2. Select and briefly describe two leaders in your own life (e.g., work supervisor, teacher, coach, music director, business owner, community leader). Identify the three major leadership traits of each of these leaders.

Historical leaders   The leader's three major traits

Harriet Tubman   1. _____   2. _____   3. _____

Winston Churchill   1. _____   2. _____   3. _____

Mother Teresa   1. _____   2. _____   3. _____

Dr. Anthony Fauci   1. _____   2. _____   3. _____

Oprah Winfrey   1. _____   2. _____   3. _____

LeBron James   1. _____   2. _____   3. _____

Everyday leaders

Leader 1 _____

Brief description

_____
_____
_____
_____

Traits   1. _____   2. _____   3. _____

Leader 2 _____

Brief description

_____

_____

_____

_____

Traits   1. _____   2. _____   3. _____

Questions

1. Based on the leaders you observed, which leadership traits appear to be most important?

2. What differences, if any, did you observe between the historical and everyday leaders' traits?

3. Based on your observations, what one trait would you identify as the definitive leadership trait?

4. Overall, what traits do you think should be used in selecting our society's leaders?

Application

2.5 Reflection and Action Worksheet

Leadership Traits

Reflection

1. Based on the scores you received on the Leadership Traits Questionnaire, what are your strongest leadership traits? What are your weakest traits? Discuss.

2. In this chapter, we discussed six leadership figures. As you read about these leaders, which leaders did you find most appealing? What was it about their leadership that you found remarkable? Discuss.

3. As you reflect on your own leadership traits, do you think some of them are more "you" and authentic than others? Have you always been the kind of leader you are today, or have your traits changed over time? Are you a stronger leader today than you were five years ago? Discuss.

Action

1. If you could model yourself after one or more of the historical leaders we discussed in this chapter, whom would you model yourself after? Identify two of this leader's traits that you could and should incorporate into your own style of leadership.

2. Although changing leadership traits is not easy, which of your leadership traits would you like to change? Specifically, what actions do you need to take to change your traits?

3. All of us have problematic traits that inhibit our leadership but are difficult to change. Which single trait distracts from your leadership? Since you cannot easily change this trait, what actions can you take to "work around" this trait? Discuss.

3

UNDERSTANDING LEADERSHIP STYLES

INTRODUCTION

A common assignment in leadership courses is to have students write a personal paper that describes their own leadership. In addition to giving students insight into how many of the leadership concepts apply to their own leadership, these papers might be used in a student's career portfolio or with job applications to explain to potential employers who the student might be as a leader.

With that in mind, what is your style of leadership? Are you an in-charge type of leader who closely monitors followers? Or are you a laid-back type of leader who gives followers a lot of rein? Whether you are one or the other or somewhere in between, it is important to recognize your personal style of leadership. This style affects how others respond to you, how they respond to their work, and, in the end, how effective you are as a leader.

In this chapter, we will discuss how a person's view of people, work, and human nature forms a personal philosophy and style of leadership. In addition, this chapter will examine how that philosophy is demonstrated in three of the most commonly observed styles of personal leadership: the authoritarian, democratic, and laissez-faire styles. We will discuss the nature of these styles and the implications each has for effective leadership performance. The information in the chapter will be useful in helping you determine and develop your own leadership philosophy and style.

LEADERSHIP PHILOSOPHY EXPLAINED

Each of us approaches leadership with a unique set of values, beliefs, and expectations about the nature of people and the nature of work. This is the basis for our **philosophy of leadership**. For example, some think people are basically good and will happily work if given the chance. Others think people are prone to be a bit lazy and need to be nudged to complete their work. At the same time, the goals and needs of the organization, as well as those of the leader, can influence our expectations of people and work. These values, beliefs, and expectations about people and work have a significant impact on an individual's leadership style and probably come into play in every aspect of their leadership.

Do you think people like work, or do you think people find work unpleasant? This was one of the central questions addressed by Douglas McGregor in his famous book *The Human Side of Enterprise* (1960). McGregor believed that managers need to understand their own core assumptions about human nature and assess how these assumptions relate to their managerial practice.

In particular, McGregor was interested in how managers view the motivations of workers and their attitudes toward work. He believed that understanding these motivations was central to knowing how to become an effective manager. To explain the ways that managers approach workers, McGregor proposed two general theories—Theory X and Theory Y. McGregor believed that by exploring the major assumptions of each of these theories people could develop a better understanding of their own viewpoints on human behavior and the relationship of these viewpoints to their leadership style. The following is a description of both theories. As you read, ask yourself if the assumptions of the theory are consistent or inconsistent with your own philosophy about leadership.

Theory X

Theory X is made up of three assumptions about human nature and human behavior (see Table 3.1). Taken together, these assumptions represent a philosophy of leadership that many leaders exhibit to one degree or another.

TABLE 3.1 ■ Assumptions of McGregor's Theory X
1. People dislike work.
2. People need to be directed and controlled.
3. People want security, not responsibility.

Assumption 1: The average person dislikes work and will avoid it if possible.

This assumption argues that people do not like work; they view it as unpleasant, distasteful, or simply a necessary evil. According to this assumption, if given the chance, people will choose not to work. An example of this assumption is the worker who says, "I only go to work to be P-A-I-D. If I didn't need to pay my bills, I would never work." People with this perspective would avoid work if they could.

Assumption 2: People need to be directed and controlled.

This assumption is derived directly from the first assumption. Since people naturally do not like work, management needs to set up a system of incentives and rewards regarding work that needs to be accomplished because workers are often unwilling or unable to motivate themselves. This assumption says that without external direction and incentives, such as threats, people would be unmotivated to work. An example of this is the high school teacher who persuades students to hand in homework assignments by threatening them with bad grades. The teacher forces students to perform because the teacher thinks that the students are unwilling to do it or incapable of doing it without that force being applied. From the perspective of Theory X, leaders play a significant role in encouraging others to accomplish their work.

Assumption 3: People want security, not responsibility.

The picture this assumption paints is of workers who want their leaders to take care of them, protect them, and make them feel safe. Because it is too difficult to set their own goals, workers want management to do it for them. This can only happen when managers establish the guidelines for workers. An example of this assumption can be observed on a sorting line for an orchard, where the employees only have to focus on completing the specific tasks set before them (e.g., picking out bad fruit, filling boxes with fruit) and are not required to take initiative for decisions on their own. In general, because of the pace and repetitiveness of the work, the sorters are not required to accept many challenging responsibilities. Instead, they are told what to do, and how and when to do it.

So what does it mean if a person's personal leadership philosophy is similar to Theory X? It means these leaders have a tendency to view workers as lazy and uninterested in work because they do not value work. As a result, Theory X leaders tend to be directive and controlling. They supervise followers closely and are quick to both praise and criticize them as they see fit. At times, these leaders remind workers of their goal (e.g., to be P-A-I-D) or threaten them with punishment to persuade them to accomplish tasks. As the person in charge, a Theory X leader sees their leadership role as instrumental in getting the job done. Theory X leaders also believe it is their role to motivate followers because these workers have little self-motivation. Because of this belief, these leaders take on the responsibility for their followers' actions. From the Theory X perspective, it is clear that followers have a *need* for leadership.

Theory Y

Like Theory X, **Theory Y** is based on several specific assumptions about human nature and behavior (see Table 3.2). Taken together, the assumptions of Theory Y present a distinctly different perspective from the ideas set forth in Theory X. It is a perspective that can be observed to a degree in many leaders today.

TABLE 3.2 ■ Assumptions of McGregor's Theory Y
1. People like work.
2. People are self-motivated.
3. People accept and seek responsibility.

Assumption 1: The average person does not inherently dislike work. Doing work is as natural as play.

Rather than viewing work as a burden or bad, this assumption suggests people see work as satisfying and not as a punishment. It is a natural activity for them. In fact, given the chance, people are happy to work. An example of this can be seen in what former U.S. president Jimmy Carter has done in his retirement. He has devoted much of his time and energy to constructing homes throughout the United States and around the world with Habitat for Humanity. Certainly, the former president does not need to work: He does so because work is natural for him. All his life, Carter has been used to making a contribution to the well-being of others. Working with Habitat for Humanity is another opportunity for him to contribute. Some people view work as a natural part of their lives.

Assumption 2: People will show responsibility and self-control toward goals to which they are committed.

As opposed to Theory X, which suggests that people need to be supervised and controlled, Theory Y suggests that people can and will make a conscious choice to work on their own.

People can be committed to the objectives of their work. Consider some examples from the sports world. Successful athletes are often highly committed to their goals and usually do not need to be controlled or supervised closely. Coaches design training plans for these athletes, but the athletes do the work themselves. A successful long-distance runner does not need to be pushed to run 60 training miles a week in preparation for a marathon because the runner is already motivated to run long distances. Similarly, an Olympic swimmer does not need to be forced to do daily 3-mile pool workouts at 5:00 a.m. because the swimmer chooses to do this independently of any coach's urging. These athletes are self-directed because they are committed to their goals. This is the point of Theory Y. When people can find commitment in their work, they will work without needing leaders to motivate or cajole them. Put another way, when people have a passion for their work, they will do it even without outside direction.

Assumption 3: In the proper environment, the average person learns to accept and seek responsibility.

While Theory X argues that people lack ambition, prefer to be directed, and want security, Theory Y assumes that the average person is inherently resourceful and, if given the chance, will seek to take responsibility. If given the chance, people have the capacity to engage in a wide range of goal-setting and creative problem-solving activities. Theory Y argues that, given the opportunity, people will act independently and be productive.

For example, two university students working in the main stacks section of the library were required to complete a checklist whenever they worked to be sure that they correctly carried out various sorting and shelving activities. The checklist was long, cumbersome, and repetitious, however. Frustrated by the checklist, the students took it upon themselves to design an entirely new, streamlined checklist. The new checklist for sorting and shelving was very clear and concise, and was playful in appearance. After reviewing the checklist and giving it a short trial period, management at the library adopted the new checklist and required that it be implemented throughout the entire library. In this example, library management provided an environment where students felt comfortable suggesting a rather major change in how their work was to be completed. In addition, management was willing to accept and adopt a student-initiated work change. It is not unrealistic to imagine that these students will be more confident initiating ideas or taking on new challenges in other work settings in the future.

So if a leader's philosophy of leadership is similar to Theory Y, what does it mean? It means that the leader views people as capable and interested in working. Even though Theory Y leaders may define work requirements, they do not try to control workers. To these leaders, followers are not lazy; on the contrary, they naturally want to work. In addition, these leaders do not think they need to try to motivate followers or make them work since workers are capable of motivating themselves. Using coercion or external reinforcement schemes is not a part of their leadership repertoire. Theory Y leaders are very attuned to helping followers find their passion for what they want to do. These leaders know that when followers are committed to their work, they are more motivated to do the job. Allowing followers to seek and accept responsibilities on their own comes easily for Theory Y leaders. In short, Theory Y leadership means supporting followers without the need to direct or control them.

In the late 1970s and 1980s, a new leadership theory tangentially related to Theory X and Theory Y was developed by William Ouchi (1981). Ouchi contrasted the collectivistic culture of Japanese companies—which had begun to dominate markets, especially in automobiles and electronics—with the individualism stressed in American organizations and developed an approach that was a hybrid of the two called **Theory Z**. A Theory Z organization is one that emphasizes common cultural values, beliefs, and objectives among its members with a focus on communication, collaboration, and consensual decision making. At the same time, some of the individualistic values of American organizations are also incorporated. Theory Z organizations still maintain formal authority structures and an emphasis on individual contributions and recognizing individual achievements. However, the individual decision making of the leader that is found in both Theory X and Theory Y is not a characteristic of a Theory Z organization.

In summary, all of us maintain certain basic beliefs and assumptions about human nature and work that form our leadership philosophy. The next section discusses how that philosophy impacts your behaviors as a leader, or your *leadership style*. Whether a person's philosophy is similar to Theory X or similar to Theory Y, it affects their style of leadership. The challenge is to understand the philosophical underpinnings of your own leadership style.

LEADERSHIP STYLES EXPLAINED

What behaviors do you exhibit as a leader? Do you like to be in control and keep up on the activities of your followers? Or do you believe in a more hands-off approach in leading others, letting them make decisions on their own?

Whatever your behaviors are as a leader, they are indicative of your leadership style. **Leadership style** is defined as the behaviors of leaders, focusing on what leaders do and how they act. This includes leaders' actions toward followers in a variety of contexts. As noted in the previous section, your leadership style is driven by your personal leadership philosophy. In the following section, we discuss the most commonly observed leadership styles associated with Theory X and Theory Y: authoritarian, democratic, and laissez-faire. While none of these styles emerges directly from Theory X or Theory Y, the authoritarian and democratic styles closely mirror the ideas set forth in these theories, respectively.

The primary work on styles of leadership was done by Kurt Lewin and colleagues (1939), who analyzed the impact of various leadership styles on small group behavior. Using groups of 10-year-old boys who met after school to engage in hobby activities, the researchers analyzed what happened when their adult leaders used one of three styles: authoritarian, democratic, or laissez-faire. The groups of boys experienced each of the three styles of leadership for a six-week period.

The outcome of the study by Lewin and colleagues was a detailed description of the nature of the leadership behaviors used for each of the three styles (White & Lippitt, 1968). They also described the impact each of these three styles had on group members.

The following sections describe and elaborate on their findings and the implications of using each of these leadership styles. Be aware that these styles are not distinct entities (e.g., like personality traits). They overlap each other. That is, a leader can demonstrate more than one style in any given situation. For example, a leader may be authoritarian about some issues and democratic about others, or a leader may be authoritarian at some points during a project and democratic at others. As leaders, we may display aspects of all of these styles.

Authoritarian Leadership Style

In many ways, the **authoritarian leadership style** is very similar to Theory X. For example, authoritarian leaders perceive followers as needing direction. The authoritarian leader needs to control followers and what they do. Authoritarian leaders emphasize that they are in charge, exerting influence and control over group members. They determine tasks and procedures for group members but may remain aloof from participating in group discussions. Authoritarian leaders do not encourage communication among group members; instead, they prefer that communication be directed to them. In evaluating others, authoritarian leaders give praise and criticism freely, but it is given based on their own personal standards rather than based on objective criticism.

Recent research on authoritarian leadership distinguishes between autocratic leadership, where authority and power are concentrated in the leader; authoritarian leadership, which uses a domineering style that generally has negative outcomes (House, 1996); and authoritarian followership, which is the psychological mindset of people who seek powerful leaders (Harms et al., 2018). There is also evidence that situational and personality factors can make authoritarian leadership more likely, including uncertain or negative circumstances where strong leadership is perceived to be a solution to problems, such as when a group is performing poorly, under time pressure, or facing an external threat (Harms et al., 2018).

Some have argued that authoritarian leadership represents a rather pessimistic, negative, and discouraging view of others. For example, an authoritarian leader might say something like "Because my workers are lazy, I need to tell them what to do." Or, "My job is to motivate the workers because they tend to lose interest in their tasks."

Others would argue that authoritarian leadership is a much-needed form of leadership—it serves a positive purpose, particularly for people who seek security above responsibility. In many contexts, authoritarian leadership is used to give direction, set goals, and structure work. For example, when employees are just learning a new job, authoritarian leadership lets them know the rules and standards for what they are supposed to do. Authoritarian leaders are very efficient and successful in motivating others to accomplish work. In these contexts, authoritarian leadership is very useful.

What are the *outcomes* of authoritarian leadership? Authoritarian leadership has both pluses and minuses. On the positive side, it is efficient and productive. Authoritarian leaders give direction and clarity to people's work and accomplish more in a shorter period. Furthermore, authoritarian leadership is useful in establishing goals and work standards. On the negative side, it fosters dependence, submissiveness, and a loss of individuality. The creativity and personal growth of followers may be hindered. It is possible that, over time, followers will lose interest in what they are doing and become dissatisfied with their work. If that occurs, authoritarian leadership can create discontent, hostility, and even aggression.

In addition, authoritarian leadership can become abusive leadership, where these leaders use their influence, power, and control for their personal interests or to coerce followers to engage in unethical or immoral activities. For example, a coach who withholds playing time from athletes who openly disagree with his play calls or a boss who requires salaried employees to work up to 20 hours of overtime each week or "be replaced with someone who will" are both examples of the dark side of authoritarian leadership. Historically, we have seen how authoritarian leaders such as Benito Mussolini and Adolf Hitler took advantage of susceptible followers by projecting power, conviction, and control during unstable political times and getting people to go along with their violent schemes.

While the negative aspects of authoritarian leadership appear to outweigh the positive, it is not difficult to imagine contexts where authoritarian leadership would be the preferred style of leadership. For example, in a busy hospital emergency room, it may be very appropriate for the leader in charge of triaging patients to be authoritarian with various types of emergencies. The same could be true in other contexts, such as the chaperone of a middle school canoe trip, who for the sake of student safety needs to establish and enforce clear rules for conduct.

In the 2004 film *Miracle*, based on the 1980 U.S. men's Olympic hockey team's experience, coach Herb Brooks uses an authoritarian style of leadership to prepare his college-age athletes to face the heavily favored Soviet team. Brooks is aggressive and demanding, pushing his players to become more fit and do extra workouts and benching them when they don't give their best. At first, the players don't like Brooks or his coaching method, but under his direction, the team develops confidence and a sense of unity that enables the players to perform at their peak and win the gold medal.

Despite the negatives of authoritarian leadership, this form of leadership is common and necessary in many situations.

Democratic Leadership Style

The **democratic leadership style** strongly resembles the assumptions of Theory Y. Democratic leaders treat followers as fully capable of doing work on their own. Rather than controlling followers, democratic leaders *work with* followers, trying hard to treat everyone fairly without putting themselves above followers. In essence, they see themselves as guides rather than as directors. They give suggestions to others, but never with any intention of changing them. Helping each follower reach personal goals is important to a democratic leader. Democratic leaders do not use "top-down" communication; instead, they speak on the same level as their followers. Making sure everyone is heard is a priority. They listen to followers in supportive ways and assist them in becoming self-directed. In addition, they promote communication between group members and in certain situations are careful to draw out the less-articulate members of the group. Democratic leaders provide information, guidance, and suggestions, but do so without giving orders and without applying pressure. In their evaluations of followers, democratic leaders give objective praise and criticism.

The *outcomes* of democratic leadership are mostly positive. First, democratic leadership results in greater group member satisfaction, commitment, and cohesiveness. Second, under democratic leadership there is more friendliness, mutual praise, and group-mindedness. Followers tend to get along with each other and willingly participate in matters of the group, making more "we" statements and fewer "I" statements. Third, democratic leadership results in stronger worker motivation and greater creativity. People are motivated to pursue their own talents under the supportive structure of democratic leadership. Finally, under a democratic leader group members participate more and are more committed to group decisions. A democratic leadership style is effective for U.S. presidents who appoint highly qualified individuals to their cabinet, each of whom has great responsibility for running their respective government departments. While the president has the final responsibility for making decisions, in cabinet meetings the members can share the newest information, debate policy, brainstorm different scenarios, and make better recommendations together. Abraham Lincoln was a U.S. president known for actively listening to his cabinet members and inviting different viewpoints. At the same time, however, he exhibited autocratic leadership in some decision making while leading the country through the Civil War.

The downside of democratic leadership is that it takes more time and commitment from the leader. Work is accomplished, but not as efficiently as if the leader were authoritarian. For example, running staff meetings has sometimes been likened to "herding cats," because people aren't always controllable; they have their own ideas and opinions and want to voice them, and consensus isn't guaranteed.

Laissez-Faire Leadership Style

The **laissez-faire leadership style** is dissimilar to both Theory X and Theory Y. Laissez-faire leaders do not try to control followers as Theory X leaders do, and they do not try to nurture and guide followers as Theory Y leaders do. Laissez-faire stands alone as a style of leadership; some have labeled it *nonleadership*. The laissez-faire leader is a nominal leader who engages in minimal influence. As the French phrase implies, *laissez-faire* leadership means the leader takes a "hands-off, let it ride" attitude toward followers. These leaders recognize followers but are very laid back and make no attempt to influence their activities. Under laissez-faire leadership, followers have freedom to do pretty much what they want to do whenever they want to do it. Laissez-faire leaders make no attempt to appraise or regulate the progress of followers, which may be due to various reasons, including disinterest, reluctance to take a stand, or limited positional authority. For example, an interim coach, church pastor, or college president may be hired to occupy a short-term role until a full-time replacement is found. The interim may not be expected or empowered to initiate changes or restructure the organization and mainly functions as a stabilizing presence and a "placeholder" for the eventual organizational leader.

Given that laissez-faire leadership involves nominal influence, what are the *effects* of laissez-faire leadership? Laissez-faire leadership tends to produce primarily negative outcomes. The major effect is that very little is accomplished under a laissez-faire leader. Because people are directionless and at a loss to know what to do, they tend to do nothing. In the earlier example, if an interim leader is in a position too long and takes no action on important issues facing an organization, followers may get frustrated. Without a sense of purpose and direction, group members have difficulty finding meaning in their work; they become unmotivated and disheartened.

Giving complete freedom can also result in an atmosphere that most followers find chaotic. Followers prefer some direction; left completely on their own, they become frustrated. As a result, productivity goes down.

Sometimes, however, the lack of leadership from above can result in frustration that spurs followers to act and create positive outcomes. An example of this would be the student survivors of the shootings at Marjory Stoneman Douglas High School in Parkland, Florida, in 2018, who organized a protest movement against gun violence: "March for Our Lives." On their website, they issued the call that "[n]ow is the time for the youth vote to stand up to the gun lobby when no one else will" (March for Our Lives, 2018). The group's mission statement explains, "As a nation, we continue to witness tragedy after tragedy, yet our politicians remain complacent. The Parkland students, along with young leaders of all backgrounds from across the country, refuse to accept this passivity and demand direct action to combat this epidemic" (March for Our Lives Houston, 2020). The group has galvanized youth and others across the country to work to facilitate change through efforts aimed at encouraging voter registration, calling on local leaders around the country to commit to change, and advocating for gun violence prevention through new policies (March for Our Lives, 2019).

In addition, people who are self-starters, who excel at individualized tasks and don't require ongoing feedback, may prefer working under laissez-faire leaders. It gives them the freedom to be themselves.

For example, Angela is the president of a website development company that uses independent contractors from across the globe. In certain respects, you could describe her leadership style as laissez-faire. The programmers who develop the websites' code are in Poland, the designer is in India, the content writer is in the United Kingdom, and Angela is in the United States. When developing a site, Angela maps out and communicates the basic framework for the website and then relies on all of the individual contractors to determine the tasks they need to do for the site's development. Because their tasks can be dependent on another's—for example, the designer needs the programmers to write the code to make the page display graphics and images in a certain way—they do communicate with one another, but because of time zone differences, this is mostly done by email. As their leader, Angela is kept apprised of issues and developments through an electronic project management system they share, but because all of the contractors are experts at what they do and trust the other team members to do what they do best, she lets them problem-solve issues and concerns with one another and rarely gets involved.

While there are a few situations where laissez-faire leadership is effective, in a majority of situations, it proves to be unsuccessful and unproductive.

LEADERSHIP SNAPSHOT

Ridley Scott, Film Director and Producer

AJ Pics / Alamy Stock Photo

You might not know Ridley Scott's name, but chances are you know his work: movies such as *Alien, Blade Runner, Thelma & Louise, Gladiator, Black Hawk Down, The Martian*, and *House of Gucci* or television shows including the hit series *The Good Wife* and *The Man in the High Castle*.

Scott is known for his visual style, attention to detail, and ability to create immersive worlds on screen. His work has been acclaimed for its strong sense of storytelling and his ability to build tension and suspense in his films. Highly regarded as one of the few Hollywood directors who has made movies that are both profitable and critically acclaimed, Scott is considered to have had a significant impact on the entertainment industry in his 45-year career.

But as anyone who has worked with Scott, and Scott himself, will tell you, his cinematic achievements are a result of his strong, mostly autocratic leadership. "I think, at the end of the day, filmmaking is a team, but eventually there's got to be a captain," he says (Turan, 2010).

Born in 1937 in England, Scott grew up in a military family and studied at the Royal College of Art, where he developed his skills as a designer, before beginning his career in film. His early work included directing commercials and music videos, which he has continued to do throughout his career. By the time he made his first feature film, *The Duellists*, in 1977 at the age of 40, which won an award for best debut film at the Cannes Film Festival, he had already made 2,500 commercials. His next film, *Alien*, released in 1979, was a box office smash, as well as widely recognized as one of the most influential and gripping sci-fi horror movies ever made (Cumming, 2019).

From his early days making commercials, Scott developed a reputation for being a stickler for detail and maintaining a strong adherence to his vision for what he is creating.

He tackled each project like a general with a battle plan, storyboarding every single frame of every commercial and controlling all the elements from photography, to design, to direction—a method he continues with every film he directs.

"I was able to be the insane perfectionist, controlling all the elements—photography, design, direction—in one neat capsule," Scott has said. "What I learned from commercials particularly was to trust my intuition—not anybody else's" (Barber, 2002).

"In a way, it's like a benevolent dictatorship," he said of his directing style (Schulman, 2017).

But his micromanagement doesn't thrill everyone, and he has had tense relationships with both the cast and the crew of his films. His persistent scrutiny of the most minute details on the *Alien* set prompted actress Sigourney Weaver to complain that Scott cared "more about his props and sets than he did about his cast" (IMDb, 2023). A self-described "tough nut," Scott is a perfectionist, which often means long, exhausting days of filming. While filming *Blade Runner* in 1981, the cast and crew worked more than 50 nights and at one point 36 hours straight with no break. Department heads who were used to being able to make their own decisions found themselves carrying out orders from Scott instead. "It was a long slog," actor Harrison Ford recalls. "I didn't really find it that physically difficult—I thought it was *mentally* difficult" (Schulman, 2017).

Even before the filming of *Blade Runner* began, Scott secretly had another scriptwriter rewrite Hampton Fancher's original script to incorporate Scott's ever-evolving new ideas. Fancher found out his work had been replaced from one of Scott's aides who handed him the completed script, telling him, "If you don't do what he wants, he'll get someone who will" (Schulman, 2017).

When Scott turned 85 in 2022, he had directed 28 feature films in his career including his latest, *Napoleon*, released in 2023. Despite his long list of hit movies and having been nominated three times in the directing category, he has yet to win an Academy Award for his work. Despite this and his age, one producer says Scott and his work are so respected in Hollywood that studios will keep backing his projects.

"He's so reliable. I'm not sure I've ever seen a bad Ridley Scott movie. Some of them are better than others, and he strikes real magic on a pretty regular basis," says Peter Chernin, who worked with Scott on *Exodus: Gods and Kings* (2014). "If somebody came to you and said, 'The guy who made *The Martian* wants to make this movie,' any studio in the world would say, 'Let's go.' And he's got 15 of those movies on his résumé" (Keegan, 2022).

LEADERSHIP STYLES IN PRACTICE

Each leader has a unique style of leadership. Some are very demanding and assertive while others are more open and participative. Similarly, some leaders could be called micromanagers, while others could be labeled nondirective leaders. Whatever the case, it is useful and instructive to characterize your leadership regarding the degree to which you are authoritarian, democratic, or laissez-faire.

It is important to note that these styles of leadership are not distinct entities; it is best to think of them as occurring along a continuum, from high leader influence to low leader influence (see Figure 3.1). Leaders who exhibit higher amounts of influence are more authoritarian. Leaders who show a moderate amount of influence are democratic. Those

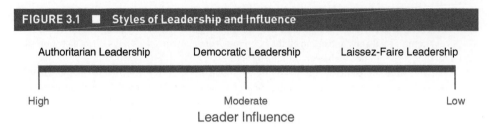

FIGURE 3.1 ■ Styles of Leadership and Influence

Authoritarian Leadership   Democratic Leadership   Laissez-Faire Leadership

High   Moderate   Low
                        Leader Influence

who exhibit little to no influence are laissez-faire. Although we tend to exhibit primarily one style over the others, our personal leadership styles are not fixed and may vary depending on the circumstances.

Consider what your results of the Leadership Styles Questionnaire tell you about your leadership style. What is your main style? Are you most comfortable with authoritarian, democratic, or laissez-faire leadership? If you are the kind of leader who likes to structure work, likes to lay out the ground rules for others, likes to closely supervise your followers, thinks it is your responsibility to make sure followers do their work, wants to be "in charge" or to know what others are doing, and believes strongly that rewarding and punishing followers is necessary, then you are *authoritarian*. If you are the kind of leader who seldom gives orders or ultimatums to followers, instead trying to work with followers and help them figure out how they want to approach a task or complete their work, then you are primarily *democratic*. Helping individual followers reach their own personal goals is important to a democratic leader.

In some rare circumstances, you may find you are showing *laissez-faire leadership*. Although not a preferred style, it is important to be aware when one is being laissez-faire. Laissez-faire leaders take a very low profile to leadership. What followers accomplish is up to them. If you believe that your followers will thrive on complete freedom, then the laissez-faire style may be the right style for you. However, in most situations, laissez-faire leadership hinders success and productivity.

SUMMARY

All of us have a philosophy of leadership that is based on our beliefs about human nature and work. Some leaders have a philosophy that resembles Theory X: They view workers as unmotivated and needing direction and control. Others have a philosophy similar to Theory Y: They approach workers as self-motivated and capable of working independently without strong direct influence from a leader.

Our philosophy of leadership is played out in our style of leadership. There are three commonly observed styles of leadership: *authoritarian, democratic,* and *laissez-faire*. Similar to Theory X, *authoritarian leaders* perceive followers as needing direction, so they exert strong influence and control. Resembling Theory Y, *democratic leaders* view followers as capable of self-direction, so they provide counsel and support. *Laissez-faire leaders* leave followers to function on their own, providing nominal influence and direction.

Effective leadership demands that we understand our philosophy of leadership and how it forms the foundations for our style of leadership. This understanding is the first step to becoming a more informed and competent leader.

KEY TERMS

authoritarian leadership style	philosophy of leadership
democratic leadership style	Theory X
laissez-faire leadership style	Theory Y
leadership style	Theory Z

3.1 Case Study—Several Different Styles

Vanessa Mills was recently hired to work at a branch of Lakeshore Bank as a personal banker. The branch is very busy and has a large staff, including three on-site managers. As a new employee, Vanessa is trying to figure out how to succeed as a personal banker while meeting the expectations of her three very different managers.

Vanessa is paid a salary, but also receives a commission for activities including opening new accounts and selling new services to customers such as credit cards, lines of credit, loans, and stock accounts. Personal bankers are expected to open a certain number of accounts each month and build relationships with customers by exploring their various banking needs and offering services to meet those needs.

Marion Woods is one of the managers at Vanessa's branch. She has worked for Lakeshore Bank for 10 years and prides herself on the success of the branch. Marion openly talks about employees' progress in terms of the number of accounts opened or relationships established, and then commends or scolds people depending on their productivity. Marion stresses to Vanessa the importance of following procedures and using the scripts that Marion provides to successfully convince customers to open new accounts or accept new services with the bank.

As a new banker, Vanessa has not opened many accounts and feels very uncertain about her competence. She is intimidated by Marion, believing that this manager is continually watching and evaluating her. Several times Marion has publicly criticized Vanessa, commenting on her shortcomings as a personal banker. Vanessa tries hard to get her sales numbers up so she can keep Marion off her back.

Bruce Dexter, another manager at Vanessa's branch, has been with Lakeshore Bank for 14 years. Bruce started out as a teller and worked his way up to branch manager. As a manager, Bruce is responsible for holding the bank staff's Monday morning meetings. At these staff meetings, Bruce relays the current numbers for new accounts as well as the target number for new accounts. He also lists the number of new relationships the personal bankers have established. After the meetings, Bruce retreats back into his office where he sits hidden behind his computer monitor. He rarely interacts with others. Vanessa likes when Bruce retreats into his office because she does not have to worry about having her performance scrutinized. However, sometimes when Vanessa is trying to help customers with a problem that falls outside of her banking knowledge, she is stressed because Bruce does not provide her with any managerial support.

The third manager at the branch is Dominque Atwood. Dominque just started at Lakeshore Bank within the last year, but worked for nine years at another bank. Vanessa finds Dominque to be very helpful. She often pops in when Vanessa is with a customer to introduce herself and make sure everything is going well. Dominque also allows Vanessa to listen in when she calls disgruntled customers or customers with complicated requests, so Vanessa can learn how to manage these types of interactions. Dominque trusts her staff and enjoys seeing them grow, encouraging them by organizing games to see who can open the most accounts and offering helpful feedback when customer interactions do not go as planned. Vanessa is grateful for the advice and support she receives from Dominque, and looks up to her because she is competent and kind.

Vanessa is coming up on her three-month review and is very nervous that she might get fired based on her low sales record and the negative feedback she has received from Bruce and Marion regarding her performance. Vanessa decides to talk to Dominque about her upcoming review and what to expect. Dominque assures Vanessa that she is doing fine and shows promise even if her numbers have not reached that of a seasoned banker. Still, Vanessa is concerned about Bruce and Marion. She has hardly had more than two conversations with Bruce and feels intimidated by Marion who, she perceives, manages by running around barking numbers at people.

Questions

1. Based on the assumptions of Theory X and Theory Y, how would you describe each manager's philosophy and style of leadership? In what way do the managers' attitudes about Vanessa affect their leadership?

2. In this type of customer service setting, which leadership style would be most effective for the bank to meet its goals? From the bank's perspective, which (if any) manager exhibits the most appropriate leadership? Discuss.

3. What advice would you give to each of the managers to enhance their leadership skills within the bank?

4. What do you think Vanessa can do to prepare herself for her three-month review?

3.2 Case Study—Leading the Robotics Team

Anders Dahlgren is the mentor for a high school robotics team that has spent the past three months designing, building, and programming a robot for competition. The team is composed of 14 boys and one girl, and the students range from freshmen to seniors. With the first competition in three weeks, Anders needs to designate a team captain so the team can get used to working under a new leader. During the competition, the team captain is often called on to make crucial team decisions.

The robotics team is divided into groups: Mechanical, whose members design and build the robot, and Programming, whose members develop the computer code that tells the robot how to complete its tasks. During competition, the team captain will have to work with both groups to tweak the robot's design and programming on the fly to improve the robot's performance. It can be a high-pressure job for any teenager, and with emotions and stress levels of other team members running on high, the captain will not only need an understanding of both the mechanical and programming aspects, but must also be able to keep 14 other personalities and egos working toward a common goal.

There are three members of the robotics team that Anders is considering for captain:

- Pria is a junior and the only girl on the team. This is her second year on the team, and she is in the Programming group. Anders describes her as being very serious and a whiz at coding, and she has offered some great design ideas. Pria is very organized—after the team's first meeting of the year, she developed a schedule with tasks and deadlines and wrote it on the large whiteboard in the workshop so team members could follow it. Pria doesn't have a lot of patience with teenage boy shenanigans and will admonish her group members to "focus, please" whenever she thinks they've gotten off task, such as when they start talking about TikTok videos or music. Pria is very rule-bound and will point out when team members try to cut corners or haven't adequately followed instructions or the schedule. Anders has noticed that when the other programming group members have a problem or obstacle, they defer to Pria for a solution. He suspects it's partly because they respect her opinion and partly because they know she'll tell them how to fix it regardless. Once, though, when Pria was home sick, Anders overheard several of the boys from both groups call Pria "bossy" and say she "stressed them out" with her deadlines and rigidity.
- Justin, a senior, is also in his second year on the team. An upbeat, congenial kid, Justin is a member of the Mechanical group. He isn't much for planning, however; he has a tendency to pick up a power tool and use it before he has actually thought out what he is going to do with it. The other Mechanical group members call him "MacGyver" because he is great working with his hands and often comes up with fixes to mechanical problems by just fiddling around with different pieces and parts for an hour or so. The group members are also pretty forgiving when Justin makes a mistake because his sense of humor keeps them all laughing and he always finds

a way to fix it. Anders notices that the Mechanical group is the most creative when Justin is at the helm, but that work sessions can devolve into chaos pretty quickly if Anders doesn't step in and set parameters and establish goals.

- Jerome, also a member of the Mechanical group, is quiet, respectful, and polite. He is a senior and has been on the robotics team since his freshman year. He is a veteran of robotics competitions, and what he has learned over the years has informed a lot of the team's efforts this year. He is most happy working on the computer-aided designs for the robot and helping those building it to understand and follow the plans and schematics. When group members question elements of his design, however, he will ask, "How do you think we should do it?" He listens to their ideas, and if the other group members agree, they will implement an idea even when Jerome personally doesn't think it'll work. Jerome's method of allowing for trial and error often slows down progress; when the group realizes an idea won't work, the team members will have to take apart what was built and start over. Anders asked Jerome why he isn't more assertive in defending his plans, and Jerome answered, "How do I know I have all the right answers? We are all supposed to be learning, right?"

Questions

1. How would you describe the individual leadership styles of Pria, Justin, and Jerome?

2. Based on the assumptions of Theory X and Theory Y, how would you describe Pria, Justin, and Jerome's individual philosophies of leadership?

3. The robotics team will be asked to compete in a situation that sounds like it will be intense and stressful. Do you think a democratic leader would be as effective as an authoritarian leader in this situation?

3.3 Leadership Styles Questionnaire

Purpose

1. To identify your style of leadership
2. To examine how your leadership style relates to other styles of leadership

Directions

1. For each of the following statements, circle the number that indicates the degree to which you agree or disagree.
2. Give your immediate impressions. There are no right or wrong answers.

Statements	Strongly disagree	Disagree	Neutral	Agree	Strongly agree
1. Employees need to be supervised closely, or they are not likely to do their work.	1	2	3	4	5
2. Employees want to be a part of the decision-making process.	1	2	3	4	5
3. In complex situations, leaders should let followers work problems out on their own.	1	2	3	4	5
4. It is fair to say that most employees in the general population are lazy.	1	2	3	4	5
5. Providing guidance without pressure is the key to being a good leader.	1	2	3	4	5
6. Leadership requires staying out of the way of followers as they do their work.	1	2	3	4	5

Statements	Strongly disagree	Disagree	Neutral	Agree	Strongly agree
7. As a rule, employees must be given rewards or punishments in order to motivate them to achieve organizational objectives.	1	2	3	4	5
8. Most workers prefer supportive communication from their leaders.	1	2	3	4	5
9. As a rule, leaders should allow followers to appraise their own work.	1	2	3	4	5
10. Most employees feel insecure about their work and need direction.	1	2	3	4	5
11. Leaders need to help followers accept responsibility for completing their work.	1	2	3	4	5
12. Leaders should give followers complete freedom to solve problems on their own.	1	2	3	4	5
13. The leader is the chief judge of the achievements of the members of the group.	1	2	3	4	5
14. It is the leader's job to help followers find their "passion."	1	2	3	4	5

Statements	Strongly disagree	Disagree	Neutral	Agree	Strongly agree
15. In most situations, workers prefer little input from the leader.	1	2	3	4	5
16. Effective leaders give orders and clarify procedures.	1	2	3	4	5
17. People are basically competent and if given a task will do a good job.	1	2	3	4	5
18. In general, it is best to leave followers alone.	1	2	3	4	5

Scoring

1. Sum the responses on items 1, 4, 7, 10, 13, and 16 (authoritarian leadership).
2. Sum the responses on items 2, 5, 8, 11, 14, and 17 (democratic leadership).
3. Sum the responses on items 3, 6, 9, 12, 15, and 18 (laissez-faire leadership).

Total Scores

Authoritarian leadership: _____
Democratic leadership: _____
Laissez-faire leadership: _____

Scoring Interpretation

This questionnaire is designed to measure three common styles of leadership: authoritarian, democratic, and laissez-faire. By comparing your scores, you can determine which styles are most dominant and least dominant in your own style of leadership.

If your score is 26–30, you are in the very high range.
If your score is 21–25, you are in the high range.
If your score is 16–20, you are in the moderate range.
If your score is 11–15, you are in the low range.
If your score is 6–10, you are in the very low range.

Application

3.4 Observational Exercise—Leadership Styles

Purpose

1. To become aware of authoritarian, democratic, and laissez-faire styles of leadership
2. To compare and contrast these three styles

Directions

1. From all of the coaches, teachers, music directors, or managers you have had in the past 10 years, select one who was authoritarian, one who was democratic, and one who was laissez-faire.
   Authoritarian leader (name) _____
   Democratic leader (name) _____
   Laissez-faire leader (name) _____
2. On another sheet of paper, briefly describe the unique characteristics of each of these leaders.

Questions

1. What differences did you observe in how each leader tried to influence you?

2. How did the leaders differ in their use of rewards and punishments?

3. What did you observe about how others reacted to each leader?

4. Under which leader were you most productive? Why?

3.5 Reflection and Action Worksheet—Leadership Styles

Reflection

1. As you reflect on the assumptions of Theory X and Theory Y, how would you describe your own philosophy of leadership?

2. Of the three styles of leadership (authoritarian, democratic, and laissez-faire), what style comes easiest for you? Describe how people respond to you when you use this style.

3. One of the aspects of democratic leadership is to help followers take responsibility for themselves. How do you assess your own ability to help others help themselves?

Action

1. If you were to try to strengthen your philosophy of leadership, what kinds of changes would you have to make in your assumptions and expectations about human nature and work?

2. As you look at your results on the Leadership Styles Questionnaire, what scores would you like to change? What would you have to do to make those changes?

3. List three specific activities you could use to improve your leadership style.

4. If you make these changes, what impact will this have on others?

4 ATTENDING TO TASKS AND RELATIONSHIPS

INTRODUCTION

Most people would agree that good doctors are experts at treating disease *and*, at the same time, care about their patients. Similarly, good teachers are informed about the subject matter *and*, at the same time, are sensitive to the personal lives of their students. In leadership, the same is true. Good leaders understand the work that needs to be done *and*, at the same time, can relate to the people who help them do the job.

When we look at what leaders do—that is, at their behaviors—we see that they do two major things: (1) They attend to tasks, and (2) they attend to their relationships with people. The degree to which leaders are successful is determined by how these two behaviors are exhibited. Situations may differ, but every leadership situation needs a degree of both task and relationship behaviors.

Through the years, many articles and books have been written on how leaders behave (Blake & McCanse, 1991; Kahn, 1956; Misumi, 1985; Stogdill, 1974). A review of these writings underscores the topic of this chapter: The essence of leadership behavior has two dimensions—task behaviors and relationship behaviors. Certain circumstances may call for strong task behavior, and other situations may demand strong relationship behavior, but some degree of each is required in every situation. Because these dimensions are inextricably tied together, it is the leader's challenge to integrate and optimize the task and relationship dimensions in their leadership role.

One way to explore our own task and relationship perspectives on leadership is to explore our **personal styles** in these two areas. All of us have developed unique habits regarding work and play that have been ingrained over many years, probably beginning as far back as elementary school. Rooted in the past, these habits regarding work and play form a very real part of who we are as people and of how we function. Many of these early habits stay with us over the years and influence our current styles.

In considering your personal style, it is helpful to describe in more detail your task-oriented and relationship-oriented behaviors. What is your inclination toward tasks and relationships? Are you more work oriented or people oriented in your personal life? Do you find more rewards in the process of "getting things done" or in the process of relating to people? We all have personal styles that incorporate some combination of work and play. Completing the Task and Relationship Questionnaire can help you identify your personal style. Although these descriptions imply that individuals have either one style or the other, it is important to remember that each of us exhibits both behaviors to some degree.

TASK AND RELATIONSHIP STYLES EXPLAINED

Task Style

Task-oriented people are goal oriented. They want to achieve. Their work is meaningful, and they like things such as to-do lists, calendars, and daily planners. Accomplishing things and doing things is the raison d'être for this type of person. That is, these people's reason for being comes from doing. Their in-box is never empty. On vacations, they try to see and do as much as they possibly can. In all avenues of their lives, they find meaning in doing.

In his book titled *Work and Love: The Crucial Balance* (1980), psychiatrist Jay Rohrlich showed how work can help people organize, routinize, and structure their lives. Doing tasks gives people a sense of control and self-mastery. Achievement sharpens our self-image and helps us define ourselves. Reaching a goal, like running a race or completing a project, makes people feel good because it is a positive expression of who they are.

Some clear examples of task-oriented people include those who use color codes in their daily planners, who have sticky notes in every room of their house, or who, by 10:00 on Saturday morning, have washed the car, done the laundry, and cleaned the apartment. Task-oriented people also are likely to make a list for everything, from grocery shopping to the series of repetitions in their weight-lifting workouts. Common to all of these people is their interest in achieving the goal and accomplishing the work.

In a personal observation paper written for a leadership class, college student Jessica Lembke does a good job detailing how a task-oriented individual behaves:

> I am definitely a task-oriented person. My mother has given me her love of lists, and my father has instilled in me the value of finishing things once you start them. As a result, I am highly organized in all aspects of my life. I have a color-coded planner with all of the activities I need to do, and I enjoy crossing things off my lists. Some of my friends call me a workaholic, but I don't think that is accurate. There are just a lot of things I have to do.

> My roommate Steph, however, is completely different from me. She will make verbal lists for her day, but usually will not accomplish any of them [the items listed]. This drives me crazy when it involves my life. For example, there were boxes all over the place until about a month after we moved into our house. Steph would say every day that she was going to focus and get her room organized that day, but she'd fail miserably most of the time. She is easily distracted and would pass up the opportunity to get unpacked to go out with friends, get on Facebook, or look at YouTube videos.

> No matter how much Steph's life stresses me out, I have learned from it. I'm all about having a good time in the right setting, but I am coming to realize that I don't need to be so planned and scheduled. No matter how carefully you do plan, something will always go awry. I don't know that Steph is the one who has taught me that or if I'm just getting older, but I'm glad I'm learning that regardless.

Relationship Style

Relationship-oriented people differ from task-oriented people because they are not as goal directed. The relationship-oriented person finds meaning in being rather than in doing. Instead of seeking out tasks, relationship-oriented people want to connect with others. They like to celebrate relationships and the pleasures relationships bring.

Furthermore, relationship-oriented people often have a strong orientation in the present. They find meaning in the moment rather than in some future objective to be accomplished. In a group situation, sensing and feeling the company of others is appealing to these people. They have been described by some as "relationship junkies." They are the people who are the last to turn off their cell phones as the airplane takes off and the first to turn the phones back on when the airplane lands. Basically, they are into connectedness.

In a work setting, the relationship-oriented person wants to connect or attach with others. For example, the relationship-oriented person would not be afraid to interrupt someone who was working hard on a task to talk about the weather, sports, or just about anything. When working out a problem, relationship-oriented people like to talk to and be associated with others in addressing the problem. They receive satisfaction from being connected to other people. They value the trust that develops in a group when relationships are strong.

College student Elizabeth Mathews described a relationship-oriented person perfectly in her personal observation paper:

I am an extremely relationship-oriented person. While I know that accomplishing tasks is important, I believe the quality of work people produce is directly related to how they feel about themselves and their leader.

I had the privilege of working with fifth graders in an after-school program. There was a range of issues we dealt with including academic, behavioral, and emotional problems, as well as kids who did not have safe homes (i.e., no running water or electricity, physical and emotional abuse, and drug addictions within the home). The "goal" of our program was to help these kids become "proficient" students in the classroom.

The task-oriented leaders in administration emphasized improving students' grades through repetition of schoolwork, flash cards, and quizzes. It was important for our students to improve their grades because it was the only way statistically to gauge if our program was successful. Given some of the personal trials these young people were dealing with, the last thing in my "relationship-oriented" mind was working on their academics. These young people had so much potential and wisdom that was stifled when they were asked to blindly follow academic assignments. In addition, they did not know how to self-motivate, self-encourage, or get the work done with so many of life's obstacles in their way.

Instead of doing schoolwork, which the majority of my students struggled with and hated, I focused on building relationships with and between the students. We used discussion, role play, dance parties, and leadership projects to build their self-confidence and emotional intelligence. The students put together service projects to improve their school and community including initiating a trash pickup and recycling initiative at the school and making cards for a nearby nursing home. By the end of the year almost every one of my students had improved their grades significantly. More important, at our daily "cheer-for-each-other" meetings, the students would beam with pride for their own and others' successes.

Relationship-oriented leadership is more important to me than task. I much prefer "being" than "doing." I am not an organized, goal-oriented person. I rarely make it out of my house without going back two or three times to grab something I forgot, and my attention span is shorter than that of a fruit fly. However, I feel that my passion for relationships and human connection is what motivates me.

As Elizabeth points out, a relationship-oriented person doesn't find meaning in "doing," but instead derives meaning from "relating" or "being."

TASK AND RELATIONSHIP LEADERSHIP IN PRACTICE

In the previous section, you were asked to consider your *personal* style regarding tasks and relationships. In this section, we are going to consider the task and relationship dimensions of your *leadership* style.

Figure 4.1 illustrates dimensions of leadership along a task–relationship continuum. **Task-oriented leadership**, which appears on the left end of the continuum, represents leadership that is focused predominantly on procedures, activities, and goal accomplishments. **Relationship-oriented leadership**, which appears on the right end of the continuum, represents leadership that is focused primarily on the well-being of followers, how they relate to each other, and the atmosphere in which they work. Most leadership falls midway between the two extremes of task- and relationship-oriented leadership. This style of leadership is represented by the mid-range area, a blend of the two types of leadership.

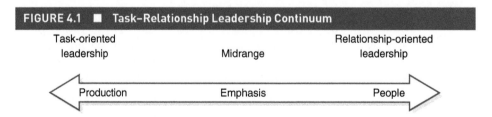

FIGURE 4.1 ■ Task–Relationship Leadership Continuum

Men and women use both styles of leadership. However, they are not perceived the same way by observers when they use these styles. Though the U.S. workplace has become more egalitarian in recent years, social expectations still linger for female leaders to be more relational or communal than task oriented (Eagly & Karau, 2002). In order to be seen as effective leaders, women face the double standard of having to balance these two styles. Wei Zheng and colleagues (2018) found that female leaders balance these styles through seemingly contradictory

LEADERSHIP SNAPSHOT

Ai-jen Poo, President, National Domestic Workers Alliance

Ai-jen Poo is the president of the National Domestic Workers Alliance (NDWA) and codirector of Caring Across Generations. She came to this work after observing the challenges of caregiving for her grandfather, who had suffered a stroke and was placed in a nursing home, sharing a room with six ailing, older people. "The place smelled like mold and death," she wrote in her book, *The Age of Dignity: Preparing for the Elder Boom in a Changing America* (Poo, 2015, p. 2). Her grandfather died three months later. After graduating from Columbia University in 1996, Poo began organizing domestic workers.

As a thought leader and social innovator, Poo sees the future effects of demographic trends such as a burgeoning elder population that will need care in the future. With the population of U.S. residents over the age of 85 expected to double in the next 20 years, more caregiving will be required. Poo sees how interconnected innovative family care solutions are with how we structure our future workplaces, and how the government will resource and regulate elder care.

Everett Collection Inc/Alamy Stock Photo

"Over and over again, at key turning points, we have invested in the infrastructure needed to thrive as a nation and to lead the safe, productive, and fulfilling lives that as individual Americans we expect to live," Poo wrote. "And over and over again, these big ideas, and the momentum behind them, not only transformed our lives but also transformed our economy. In fact, in many cases, these investments *were* our economy, and most certainly saved our economy. An infrastructure for care may seem different from an infrastructure for railroads, highways, electricity, or the Internet. There are no trees to clear or wires to lay. Yet care is among the fundamental building blocks of society. For any of us, thinking about our most basic needs, care always comes first. There's no need for the Internet, or even electricity, if there's no way to feed, bathe, or clothe yourself" (Poo, 2015, p. 143).

In her career, Poo demonstrates both relationship leadership and task leadership. To learn more about the needs of domestic workers, "she spent countless hours in parks, buses, and other gathering places for domestic workers, creating opportunities for these largely isolated women to share their experiences, guiding mistreated workers to appropriate legal channels, articulating the vital economic role of domestic workers, and developing with workers a framework of legal standards for the industry" (MacArthur Foundation, 2014). By listening to and caring about their experiences, Poo shows respect for domestic workers and acknowledges that their work has inherent dignity.

"There are more than 2.5 million women in the United States who make it possible for us to do what we do every day, knowing that our loved ones and homes are in good hands.

They are the nannies that take care of our children, the housekeepers that bring sanity and order to our homes, and the home-care workers that care for our parents and support the independence of our disabled family members," said Poo (Fessler, 2018).

Poo also builds relationships with the domestic workers, learning from them what their needs actually are and connecting them with others in similar situations, to form a larger sense of identity and community. As the president of the NDWA, Poo has built a culture of trust and empowerment for women. Many of the organization's staff work remotely, so twice per year they hold a retreat for all employees where they plan together, laugh together, and share stories. "An important part of the time together is connecting on a personal level, not because we need everyone to be friends, but to know one another's context: Why are you here? What's your story? Our personal journeys are an endless well of inspiration and resilience," Poo explained (Fessler, 2018).

Poo has built her activist work on this foundation of caring for others. Her task leadership is expressed in several ways. First, she has envisioned ways to organize domestic workers into an effective and unified voice for change. As the president of the NDWA, her core responsibility is to help the organization to reach its goals of educating the public about how domestic labor should be viewed and valued, raising the labor standards for all domestic workers, and training new leaders for the labor movement. Poo does this by staying focused on the mission of the organization, developing programs that support that mission, and hiring and equipping employees to assist in this work: "NDWA centers the voice and leadership of women of color in everything we do" (National Domestic Workers Alliance, 2021).

Second, Poo has organized workers to advocate for legislation that acknowledges and protects domestic workers' rights. In 2010, New York enacted the Domestic Workers' Bill of Rights, which entitles workers to overtime pay, one day of rest per week, protection from discrimination, and three days of paid leave per year—after a hard-fought seven-year legislative campaign led by Poo and a dedicated group of workers and advocates. The bill also drew support from an unlikely coalition of domestic workers, their employers, and other unions forged by Poo's ability to leverage common interests across diverse groups (MacArthur Foundation, 2014).

Poo received a "genius" grant from the MacArthur Foundation in 2014, and she was named one of *Time*'s 100 Most Influential People in the World in 2012 and one of *Fortune*'s 50 Greatest Leaders in 2015. While her task leadership has received the most recognition, the behavior Poo most attributes to her success is listening. "The best ideas from our organization have come from listening to our members," she said. "And believe me—when you listen to women, especially to those who have been the least visible in society, you will hear some of the most extraordinary stories that represent the best of who we are as a nation. Listening is a practice; you don't have to be a natural listener to be a good listener, and it's something we can, and should, all learn to do" (Fessler, 2018).

pairs of traits that are directly linked to relationship- and task-oriented behaviors: demanding (task) and caring (relational); authoritative (task) and participative (relational); and distant (task) and approachable (relational). Female leaders will often switch between the behaviors depending on the situation, including first using the relationship style to build trust and then using authoritativeness to accomplish goals. In addition, female leaders seek to reframe a relational orientation not as weakness but as a reflection of their confidence. By bringing relationship and task behaviors into coexistence, women are able to advance their performance, rally others toward common goals, align people's interests, and build leader–follower relationships.

As discussed at the beginning of this chapter, good leaders understand the work that needs to be done, as well as the need to understand the people who will do it. Another student, Sally Johnson, describes how her behavior is often a blend of both task and relationship orientations:

> *The style approach categorizes leaders as being either task oriented or relationship oriented, but I disagree that everyone can be placed concretely into one or the other. When it comes to determining where I stand on each continuum, I'd have to say I'm about even. Not surprisingly, my results of the Task and Relationship Questionnaire reflect these thoughts: I scored a solid 41 in both task- and relationship-oriented styles; I'm equally task and relationship oriented, with each of these styles becoming more prevalent in certain situations.*

> *While I truly enjoy being around other people, making sure everyone is happy and that we all enjoy our time, I'm very focused and goal oriented. If I'm at the movies with my friends, I'm not worrying about a to-do list; alternatively, if I'm working on a group project for school, I'm not as concerned about making friends with the group members.*

> *Completing tasks is very important to me. I have an agenda that I keep with me at all times, partly because without it I would never remember anything, and partly because it provides satisfaction and peace of mind. I make to-do lists for myself: groceries, household chores, homework, and goals. I thrive when I'm busy, but not if I'm disorganized. For example, this semester I'm taking 20 credits, applying to graduate schools, taking the GRE, and working at the bookstore. For me it is comforting to have so many responsibilities. If I have downtime, I usually waste it, and I hate that feeling.*

> *I also feel, however, that I'm very relationship oriented. My task-oriented nature doesn't really affect how I interact with people. I like to make sure people are comfortable and confident in all situations. While I pressure myself to get things done and adhere to a schedule, I'd never think of pushing those pressures onto someone else. If I were the leader of a group that wasn't getting things done, I'd set an example, rather than tell someone what they should be doing.*

> *Whether I am task or relationship focused depends on the situation. While I certainly want to have fun with people, I'm a proponent of the "time and place" attitude, in which people remember when it is appropriate to socialize and when it is appropriate to get a job done.*

The process of "doing" leadership requires that leaders attend to both tasks and relationships. As Sally's observation says, the specific challenge for the leader is to decide how much task orientation and how much relationship orientation is required in a given context or situation.

Task Leadership

Task leadership behaviors facilitate goal accomplishment—they are behaviors that help group members to achieve their objectives. Researchers have found that task leadership includes many behaviors. These behaviors are frequently labeled in different ways, but are always about task accomplishment. For example, some have labeled task leadership as **initiating structure**, which means the leader organizes work, defines role responsibilities, and schedules work activities

(Stogdill, 1974). Others have labeled task leadership as **production orientation**, which means the leader stresses the production and technical aspects of the job (Bowers & Seashore, 1966). From this perspective, the leader pays attention to new product development, workload matters, and sales volume, to name a few aspects. A third label for task leadership is **concern for production** (Blake & Mouton, 1964). It includes policy decisions, new product development, workload, sales volume, or whatever the organization is seeking to accomplish.

In short, task leadership occurs anytime the leader is doing something that assists the group in reaching its goals. This can be something as simple as handing out an agenda for an upcoming meeting or as complex as describing the multiple quality control standards of a product development process. Task leadership includes many behaviors: Common to each is influencing people toward goal achievement.

As you would expect, people vary in their ability to show task-oriented leadership. There are those who are very task oriented and those who are less task oriented. This is where a person's personal style comes into play. Those who are task oriented in their personal lives are naturally more task oriented in their leadership. Conversely, those who are seldom task oriented in their personal lives will find it difficult to be task oriented as a leader.

Task leadership is also critically important in a company or an organization with a large number of newly hired employees or at a charter school with a cadre of new faculty members. It is also called for in an adult fitness class when the instructor is introducing a new exercise. Or, consider the family members of a patient going home after a major heart surgery who have to learn how to change dressings and give medications; they want the health professionals to tell them exactly what to do and how to do it. In situations like these, the followers feel uncertain about their roles and responsibilities, and they want a leader who clarifies their tasks and tells them what is expected of them. In fact, in nearly every group or situation, there are some individuals who want and need task direction from their leader, and in these circumstances, it is paramount that the leader exhibit strong task-oriented leadership.

Whether a person is very task oriented or less task oriented, the important point to remember is that, as a leader, they will always be required to exhibit some degree of task behavior. For certain individuals this will be easy and for others it will present a challenge, but some task-oriented behavior is essential to each person's effective leadership performance.

Relationship Leadership

Relationship leadership behaviors help followers feel comfortable with themselves, with each other, and with the situation in which they find themselves. For example, in the classroom, when a teacher requires each student to know every other student's name, the teacher is demonstrating relationship leadership. The teacher is helping the students to feel comfortable with themselves, with other students, and with their environment.

Researchers have described relationship leadership in several ways that help to clarify its meaning. It has been labeled by some researchers as **consideration behavior** (Stogdill, 1974), which includes building camaraderie, respect, trust, and regard between leaders and followers. Other researchers describe relationship leadership as having an **employee orientation** (Bowers & Seashore, 1966), which involves taking an interest in workers as human beings, valuing their uniqueness, and giving special attention to their personal needs. Another line of research has simply defined relationship leadership as **concern for people** (Blake & Mouton, 1964). Within an organization, concern for people includes building trust, providing good working conditions, maintaining a fair salary structure, and promoting good social relations.

Essentially, relationship leadership behavior is about three things: (1) treating followers with dignity and respect, (2) building relationships and helping people get along, and (3) making the work setting a pleasant place to be. Relationship leadership behavior is an integral part of effective leadership performance.

Many groups or situations will have individuals who want to be affiliated with or connected to others more than they want direction. For example, in a factory, in a classroom, or in a workplace, there are individuals who want the leader to befriend them and relate to them on a personal level. The followers are willing to work, but they are primarily interested in being recognized and feeling related to others. An example would be individuals who are on a high school swim team. They appreciate instruction from their coach, but even more importantly, they want their coach to relate to them. It is similar with individuals who are attending a yoga teacher training session. They want to learn the techniques and methods to be competent yoga instructors from their leader, but they also want the leader to relate to them in a more familiar way, such as sharing their own experiences as a novice teacher and asking them about theirs. Clearly, in these situations, the leader needs to connect with these followers by utilizing relationship-oriented behaviors.

In our fast-paced and very diverse society, the challenge for a leader is finding the time and energy to listen to all followers and do what is required to build effective relationships with each of them. For those who are highly relationship oriented in their personal lives, being relationship oriented in leadership will come easily; for those who are highly task oriented, being relationship oriented in leadership will present a greater challenge. Regardless of your personal style, every leadership situation demands a degree of relationship leadership behavior.

Integrating Task and Relationship Leadership

As discussed earlier in this chapter, task and relationship leadership behaviors are inextricably tied together, and a leader's challenge is to integrate the two in an optimal way while effectively adapting to followers' needs. The U.S. Army has a saying: "Mission first, people always." That means that the leader must nurture interpersonal and team relationships at all times in order to ensure that followers will be motivated to achieve their assigned goals or projects.

In society, the most effective leaders recognize and adapt to followers' needs. Whether they are team leaders, teachers, or managers, they appropriately demonstrate the right degrees of task and relationship leadership. This is no small challenge because different followers and situations demand different amounts of task and relationship leadership. When followers are unclear, confused, or lost, the leader needs to show direction and exhibit task-oriented leadership. At the same time, a leader needs to be able to see the need for affiliation and attachment in followers and be able to meet those needs, without sacrificing task accomplishment.

An important aspect in a leader's ability to be effective is the degree to which followers trust the leader, in both the task and relational realms. Task-oriented trust is developed when followers trust a leader's ability to facilitate the accomplishment of tasks through others as exhibited by the tasks the leader gives attention to in planning, coordinating, and execution. Task-oriented trust in a leader leads to important positive outcomes including improved individual and organizational performance. Relationship-oriented trust develops when followers believe the leader shows concern for and provides support to followers. This trust comes from a leader having an open communication style, showing respect, and listening to followers' needs and providing socioemotional support (Sherwood & DePaolo, 2005).

In the end, the best leader is the leader who helps followers achieve the goal by attending to the task and by attending to each follower as a person. We all know leaders who do this: They are the coaches who force us to do drills until we are blue in the face to improve our physical performance, but who then caringly listen to our personal problems. They are the managers who never let us slack off for even a second, but who make work a fun place to be. They are the professors who clearly outline the assignments and expectations for a class, but also engage personally with students during lectures to ensure they are learning the concepts. The list goes on, but the bottom line is that the best leaders get the job done and care about others in the process.

SUMMARY

Good leaders are both task oriented and relationship oriented. Understanding your personal styles of work and play can provide a better recognition of your leadership. Task-oriented people find meaning in doing, while relationship-oriented people find meaning in being connected to others. Effective leadership requires that leaders be both task oriented and relationship oriented.

KEY TERMS

concern for people

concern for production

consideration behavior

employee orientation

initiating structure

personal style

production orientation

relationship-oriented leadership

task-oriented leadership

4.1 Case Study—From Two to One

Mark Schmidt runs Co-Ed Cleaners, a business that employs college students to clean offices and schools during the night hours. Due to an economic downturn, Co-Ed Cleaners has lost customers, and although Mark has trimmed everywhere he can think of, he has come to the conclusion that he has to cut back further. This will require letting one of his two managers go and consolidating responsibilities under the other manager's leadership.

Dan Cali manages groups of students who clean school buildings. Dan is always on the go, visiting cleaning teams at each school while they are working. His employees describe him as an efficient taskmaster with checklists they are all required to follow and sign off on as they complete each job. Dan initiates most ideas for changing processes based on efficiency. When something goes wrong on a job, Dan insists he be alerted and brought in to solve it. "Dan is a very task-oriented guy," says one of his team members. "There is no one who works harder than he does or knows more about our jobs. This guy gets more done in an hour than most guys do in a day. In the two years I've been here, I don't think I've ever seen him stop and take a break or even have a cup of coffee." Dan's efforts have helped Co-Ed Cleaners be recognized as "The Best Professional Cleaning Service" for three years running.

Asher Roland is the manager of groups of students who clean small offices and businesses. Asher has up to 10 teams working a night and relies on his employees to do their jobs and keep him apprised of problems. He takes turns working alongside his teams to understand the challenges they may face, getting to know each of his employees in the process. Once a month, he takes the teams to a restaurant for a "Great Job Breakfast" where they talk about sports, the weather, politics, their relationships and families, and, when they have time, work issues. One of his employees describes him this way: "Asher is a really good guy. Never had a better boss. If I am having problems, I would go to Asher first. He always advocates for us and listens when we have ideas or problems, but allows us to manage our own jobs the way we think best. He trusts us to do the right things, and we trust him to be fair and honest with us."

Mark likes both Dan and Asher, and in their own way they are both good managers. Mark worries, however, about how each manager's individual style will affect his ability to take on the responsibilities of the manager he replaces. He must let one go, but he doesn't know which one.

Questions

1. Using ideas from the chapter, describe Dan's and Asher's styles of leadership.

2. How will Asher's employees, who are used to being able to manage themselves in their own way, respond to Dan's task-oriented style?

3. How will Dan's employees, who are used to being given clear direction and procedures, respond to Asher's more relationship-oriented style?

4. If you were an employee at Co-Ed Cleaners, would you want Mark to let Dan or Asher go? Explain your choice.

Application

4.2 Case Study—Day and Night

By day, Alice and Heather are the director and assistant director (respectfully) of a human resources (HR) department for a large community college that has 30,000 students at multiple campuses and educational centers. On nights and weekends, Alice and Heather jointly run a local nonprofit organization called Operation D.O.G. (ODOG).

As a member of the executive team for the college, Alice has a leadership role that extends not just to those who report directly to her but to the college overall. Constantly busy with different projects both at work and at home (she owns a small acreage on the outskirts of town where she raises vegetables and cares for geriatric horses), her days are filled with to-do lists. On the rare "girls' weekend away," she is the one who makes up the itinerary, makes the hotel and restaurant reservations, and sees to it that everyone is where she is supposed to be at the designated time. At the college, Alice is responsible for the overall management and day-to-day operations of the HR team, ensuring deadlines are met, projects are completed, and the team meets the needs of its diverse customer base. On an average day, Alice and her team may perform a complex set of tasks, including negotiations, recruiting, regulatory interpretations, compliance and reporting, salary and benefit plan administration, and counseling and advising, as well as navigating personnel issues across the campuses. As a member of the institution's executive team, Alice also participates in strategic planning for the college and is heavily involved with the Board of Education that governs the college. Acutely aware that the development of her team is key to its success, Alice takes a personal interest in each employee, purposefully leading her team members through coaching, empowerment, and trust building.

Heather, who in her 20s survived an aggressive form of cancer, has a strong proclivity for fostering relationships. Her battle with cancer at such a young age heightened her sense of compassion and helped shape her perspective on the importance of connection. While she has many task responsibilities in her role as the assistant director, she, not surprisingly, describes her primary focus as "maintaining the culture" for the team and the college as a whole. This involves developing connections and having ongoing communication with internal and external customers. Heather also guides managers across the college in developing their leadership, conflict resolution, and effective communication skills. She does this through training and in one-on-one consultations with people and modeling the leadership behavior she wants to instill in others.

Alice finds her position to require that she be much more authoritative and task oriented in order to keep on top of all the responsibilities she has and people she must work with. Heather, on the other hand, is the softer side of HR, finding that her relational skills and compassion come into play in most of her daily interactions with other staff and the college community.

Alice and Heather also work closely together outside of the college on the fledgling nonprofit, ODOG. ODOG works with dog owners and rescue organizations to provide financial assistance and case management for dogs suffering from treatable medical conditions in order to either keep them in or find them loving homes.

Alice and Heather share a deeply held belief that every dog deserves a chance at a healthy and happy life. Traditionally, dogs with medical issues are less likely to be adopted from shelters. Often, low-income individuals and families may be forced to euthanize or surrender their pets to a shelter when a pet has a medical issue they cannot afford to treat. Dog rescue organizations take some of these animals, but without outside financial support, they may be reluctant or unable to take on the financial burden.

Each case is considered on an individual basis, requiring that Heather and Alice, currently the only staff of the organization, work directly with owners and their animals. Because they often learn intimate details about people's lives and financial states, both Heather and Alice have to develop relationships of trust with the owners and their pets. At the same time, the pair meets with animal rescues and shelters, veterinarians, and community members to build partnerships and secure treatment. Either Heather or Alice will follow each dog through its medical treatment from beginning to end, assisting with the coordination of care and financial arrangements.

Heather and Alice also oversee the business management functions of the nonprofit including fundraising, raising awareness through advertising and promotions, accounting and reporting, regulatory compliance, negotiating, public speaking, and presenting. Currently, neither Alice nor Heather is paid for her ODOG role; all funds raised go directly to the clients. Both women endeavor to grow the organization and its sphere of influence. They envision serving additional counties and eventually opening a shelter with a dedicated veterinarian clinic that would provide discounted services to low-income individuals and families.

Questions

1. In their roles *for the college*, how would you categorize Alice's and Heather's task and relational leadership behaviors? Using the format in the following grid, rate each woman's predisposition toward each behavior type (on a scale of 1–10, with 10 being high). In the explanation column, support your rating with examples.

Behavior Type		Rank (1–10)	Explanation
Task			
	Alice		
	Heather		
Relationship			
	Alice		
	Heather		

2. Looking at your rankings in question 1, do you feel the two women's leadership styles complement each other? Why or why not?

3. How would you rate the importance of task behaviors vs. relationship behaviors in their leadership of Operation D.O.G.? Is one behavior more important in these roles than the other? Will Alice and Heather be equally as effective in running the nonprofit as they appear to be at the college? Explain your answer.

4.3 Task and Relationship Questionnaire

Purpose

1. To identify how much you emphasize task and relationship behaviors in your life
2. To explore how your task behavior is related to your relationship behavior

Directions

For each of the following items, indicate on the scale the extent to which you engage in the described behavior. Move through the items quickly. Do not try to categorize yourself in one area or another.

Statements	Never	Rarely	Some-times	Often	Always
1. Make a to-do list of the things that need to be done.	1	2	3	4	5
2. Try to make the work fun for others.	1	2	3	4	5
3. Urge others to concentrate on the work at hand.	1	2	3	4	5
4. Show concern for the personal well-being of others.	1	2	3	4	5
5. Set timelines for when the job needs to be done.	1	2	3	4	5
6. Help group members get along.	1	2	3	4	5
7. Keep a checklist of what has been accomplished.	1	2	3	4	5
8. Listen to the special needs of each group member.	1	2	3	4	5
9. Stress to others the rules and requirements for the project.	1	2	3	4	5

Statements	Never	Rarely	Some-times	Often	Always
10. Spend time exploring other people's ideas for the project.	1	2	3	4	5
11. Pay close attention to project deadlines.	1	2	3	4	5
12. Act friendly toward other group members.	1	2	3	4	5
13. Clarify each group member's job responsibilities.	1	2	3	4	5
14. Express support for other group members' ideas.	1	2	3	4	5
15. Emphasize performance standards for the group.	1	2	3	4	5
16. Talk with other group members about their personal concerns.	1	2	3	4	5
17. Keep other group members focused on goals.	1	2	3	4	5
18. Emphasize everyone's unique contributions to the group.	1	2	3	4	5
19. Follow rules and regulations closely.	1	2	3	4	5
20. Express positive feelings toward others in the group.	1	2	3	4	5

Scoring

1. Sum scores for the odd-numbered statements (task score).
2. Sum scores for the even-numbered statements (relationship score).

Total Scores

Task score: _____

Relationship score: _____

Scoring Interpretation

This questionnaire is designed to measure your task-oriented and relationship-oriented leadership behavior. By comparing your scores, you can determine which style is more dominant in your own style of leadership. If your task score is higher than your relationship score, you tend to give more attention to goal accomplishment and somewhat less attention to people-related matters. If your relationship score is higher than your task score, your primary concern tends to be dealing with people, and your secondary concern is directed more toward tasks. If your scores are very similar to each other, it suggests that your leadership is balanced and includes an equal amount of both behaviors.

If your score is 40–50, you are in the high range.

If your score is 31–39, you are in the moderately high range.

If your score is 21–30, you are in the low range.

If your score is 10–20, you are in the very low range.

Application

4.4 Observational Exercise—Task and Relationship

Purpose

1. To understand how leadership includes both task and relationship behaviors
2. To contrast different leaders' task and relationship behaviors

Directions

1. Over the next couple of days, observe the leadership styles of two different leaders (e.g., teacher, athletic coach, choir director, restaurant manager, work supervisor).
2. Record your observations of the styles of each person.

Leader 1 (name) _____

Task behaviors	Relationship behaviors
• _____ _____	• _____ _____
• _____ _____	• _____ _____
• _____ _____	• _____ _____
• _____ _____	
• _____ _____	

Leader 2 (name) _____

Task behaviors	Relationship behaviors
• _____ _____	• _____ _____
• _____ _____	• _____ _____
• _____ _____	• _____ _____
• _____ _____	
• _____ _____	

Questions

1. What differences did you observe between the two leaders?

2. What did you observe about the leader who was most task oriented?

3. What did you observe about the leader who was most relationship oriented?

4. How effective do you think you would be in each of these leadership positions?

Application

4.5 Reflection and Action Worksheet—Task and Relationship

Reflection

1. As you reflect on what has been discussed in this chapter and on your own leadership style, how would you describe your own style in relation to task and relationship orientations? What are your strengths and weaknesses?

2. What biases do you maintain regarding task style and relationship style? How do your biases affect your leadership?

3. One of the most difficult challenges leaders face is to integrate their task and relationship behaviors. Do you see this as a challenge in your own leadership? How do you integrate task and relationship behaviors?

Action

1. If you were to change in an effort to improve your leadership, what aspect of your style would you change? Would you try to be more task oriented or more relationship oriented?

2. Identify three specific task or relationship changes you could carry out.

3. What barriers will you face as you try to make these changes?

4. Given that you believe this change will improve your overall leadership, what can you do (i.e., what strategies can you use) to overcome the barriers you cited in Action Item 3?

5 DEVELOPING LEADERSHIP SKILLS

INTRODUCTION

Whether it is playing the guitar, a video game, or the stock market, most of life's activities require us to have skills if we are to be successful. The same is true of leadership—skills are required. As discussed in the first chapter, leadership skills refer to learned competencies that leaders are able to demonstrate in performance (Katz, 1955). Leadership skills give people the capacity to influence others. They are a critical component in successful leadership.

Even though skills play an essential role in the leadership process, they have received little attention by researchers (Lord & Hall, 2005; T. Mumford et al., 2007). Leadership traits rather than leadership skills have been the focus of research for more than 100 years. However, in the past 20 years a shift has occurred, and leadership skills are now receiving far more attention by researchers and practitioners alike (M. Mumford et al., 2000; Yammarino, 2000).

Although there are many different leadership skills, they are often considered as groups of skills. In this chapter, leadership skills are grouped into three categories: *administrative skills*, *interpersonal skills*, and *conceptual skills* (see Figure 5.1). The next section describes each group of skills and explores the unique ways they affect the leadership process.

ADMINISTRATIVE SKILLS EXPLAINED

While often devalued because they are not glamorous or exciting, **administrative skills** play a primary role in effective leadership. Administrative skills help a leader to accomplish the mundane but critically important aspects of showing leadership. Some would even argue that administrative skills are the most fundamental of all the skills required of a leader.

What are administrative skills? Administrative skills refer to those competencies a leader needs to run an organization in order to carry out the organization's purposes and goals. These involve planning, organizing work, assigning the right tasks to the right people, and coordinating work activities (Mann, 1965).

Administrative Skills in Practice

For purposes of our discussion, administrative skills are divided into three specific sets of skills: (1) managing people, (2) managing resources, and (3) showing technical competence.

FIGURE 5.1 ■ Model of Primary Leadership Skills

Managing People

Any leader of a for-profit or nonprofit organization, if asked what occupies the most time, will reply, "Managing people." Few leaders can do without the skill of being able to manage people. The phrase *management by walking around* captures the essence of managing people. An effective leader connects with people and understands the tasks to be done, the skills required to perform them, and the environment in which people work. The best way to know this is to be involved rather than to be a spectator. For a leader to deal effectively with people requires a host of abilities such as helping employees to work as a team, motivating them to do their best, promoting satisfying relationships among employees, and responding to their requests. The leader also needs to find time to deal with urgent staff matters. Staff issues are a daily fact of life for any leader. Staff members come to the leader for advice on what to do about a problem, and the leader needs to respond appropriately.

A leader must also pay attention to recruiting and retaining employees. In addition, leaders need to communicate effectively with their own board of directors, as well as with any external constituencies such as the public, stockholders, or other outside groups that have a stake in the organization.

Consider the leadership of Nate Parker, the director of an after-school recreation program serving 600 kids in a large metropolitan community. Nate's program is funded by an $800,000 government grant. It provides academic, fitness, and enrichment activities for underserved children and their families. Nate has managers who assist him in running the after-school program in five different public schools. Nate's own responsibilities include setting up and running staff meetings, recruiting new staff, updating contracts, writing press releases, working with staff, and establishing relationships with external constituencies. Nate takes great pride in having created a new and strong relationship between the city government and the school district in which he works. Until he came on board, the relationship between the schools and city government was tense. By communicating effectively across groups, Nate was able to bring the entire community together to serve the children. He is now researching the possibility of a citywide system to support after-school programming.

Managing Resources

Although it is not obvious to others, a leader is often required to spend a significant amount of time addressing resource issues. Resources, the lifeblood of an organization, can include people, money, supplies, equipment, space, or anything else needed to operate an organization. Managing resources requires a leader to be competent in both obtaining and allocating resources. Obtaining resources can include a wide range of activities such as ordering equipment, finding work space, or locating funds for special projects. For example, a middle school cross-country coach wanted to replace the team's outdated uniforms but had no funds to do so. In order to buy new uniforms, the coach negotiated with the athletic director for additional funds. The coach also encouraged several parents in the booster club to sponsor a few successful fundraisers.

In addition to obtaining resources, a leader may be required to allocate resources for new staff or new incentive programs, or to replace old equipment. While a leader may often engage staff members to assist in managing resources, the ultimate responsibility of resource management rests on the leader. As the sign on President Harry S. Truman's desk read, "The buck stops here."

Showing Technical Competence

Technical competence involves having specialized knowledge about the work we do or ask others to do. In the case of an organization, it includes understanding the intricacies of how an organization functions. A leader with technical competence has organizational know-how— they understand the complex aspects of how the organization works. For example, a university president should be knowledgeable about teaching, research, student recruitment, and student retention; a basketball coach should be knowledgeable about the basics of dribbling, passing, shooting, and rebounding; and a sales manager should have a thorough understanding of the product the salespeople are selling. In short, a leader is more effective when they have the knowledge and technical competence about the activities followers are asked to perform.

The importance of having technical competence can be seen in the example of an orchestra conductor. The conductor's job is to direct rehearsals and performances of the orchestra. To do this, the conductor needs technical competence pertaining to rhythm, music composition, and all the many instruments and how they are played. Technical competence gives the conductor the understanding required to direct the many different musicians to perform together successfully.

Technical competence is sometimes referred to as "functional competence" because it means a person is competent in a particular function or area. No one is required to be competent in all avenues of life. So, too, a leader is not required to have technical competence in every situation. But technical knowledge of the functions and activities across levels of an organization is important for a leader. For example, Devonia oversees a large video game development team that includes writers, artists, programmers, and testers. Devonia's background is as a graphic artist, but she must know how each aspect of game development contributes to the end product in order to be able to foresee and solve problems for her team. She doesn't need to be able to write the programming code, but she does need to understand that skill enough to be able to help her coders work out problems.

INTERPERSONAL SKILLS EXPLAINED

In addition to administrative skills, effective leadership requires interpersonal skills. **Interpersonal skills** are people skills—those abilities that help a leader work effectively with followers, peers, and higher-ups to accomplish the organization's goals. While some people downplay the importance of interpersonal skills or disparage them as "touchy-feely" and inconsequential, leadership research has consistently pointed out the importance of interpersonal skills to effective leadership (Bass, 1990; Blake & McCanse, 1991; Katz, 1955).

Interpersonal Skills in Practice

Interpersonal skills are divided into three parts: (1) being socially perceptive, (2) showing emotional intelligence, and (3) managing interpersonal conflict.

Being Socially Perceptive

To successfully lead an organization toward change, a leader needs to be sensitive to how their own ideas fit in with others' ideas. **Social perceptiveness** includes having insight into and awareness of what is important to others, how they are motivated, the problems they face, and how they react to change. It involves understanding the unique needs, goals, and demands of different organizational constituencies (Zaccaro et al., 1991). A leader with social perceptiveness has a keen sense of how employees will respond to any proposed change in the organization. In a sense, you could say a socially perceptive leader has a finger on the pulse of employees on any issue at any time.

Leadership is about change, and people in organizations often resist change because they like things to stay the same. Novel ideas, different rules, or new ways of doing things are often seen as threatening because they do not fit in with how people are used to things being done. A leader who is socially perceptive can create change more effectively if they understand how the proposed change may affect all the people involved.

One example that demonstrates the importance of social perceptiveness is illustrated in the events surrounding the graduation ceremonies at the University of Michigan in the spring of 2008. The university anticipated 5,000 students would graduate, with an expected audience of 30,000. In prior years, the university traditionally held spring graduation ceremonies in the football stadium, which, because of its size, is commonly known as "the Big House." However, because the stadium was undergoing major renovations, the university was forced to change the venue for graduation and decided to hold the graduation at the outdoor stadium of nearby Eastern Michigan University. When the university announced the change of location, the students, their families, and the university's alumni responded immediately and negatively. There was upheaval as they made their strong opinions known.

Clearly, the leadership at the university had not perceived the significance to seniors and their families of where graduation ceremonies were to be held. It was tradition to graduate in the Big House, so changing the venue was offensive to many. Phone calls came into the president's office, and editorials appeared in the press. Students did not want to graduate on the campus of another university. They thought that they deserved to graduate on their own campus. Some students, parents, and alumni even threatened to withhold future alumni support.

To correct the situation, the university again changed the venue. Instead of holding the graduation at Eastern Michigan University, the university spent $1.8 million to set up a temporary outdoor stage in the center of campus, surrounded by the University of Michigan's classroom buildings and libraries. The graduating students and their families were pleased that the ceremonies took place where their memories and traditions were so strong. The university ultimately was successful because it adapted to the deeply held beliefs of its students and their families. Clearly, if the university had been more socially perceptive at the outset, the initial dissatisfaction and upheaval that arose could have been avoided.

Showing Emotional Intelligence

Another important skill for a leader is being able to show emotional intelligence. Although emotional intelligence emerged as a concept less than 25 years ago, it has captivated the interests of many scholars and practitioners of leadership (Bradberry et al., 2009; Caruso & Wolfe, 2004; Goleman, 1995; Mayer & Salovey, 1995). Emotional intelligence is concerned with a person's ability to understand their own and others' emotions, and then to apply this understanding to life's tasks. Specifically, emotional intelligence can be defined as the ability to perceive and express emotions, to use emotions to facilitate thinking, to understand and reason with emotions, and to manage emotions effectively within oneself and in relationships with others (Mayer et al., 2000).

The underlying premise of research on emotional intelligence is that people who are sensitive to their own emotions and the impact their emotions have on others will be more effective leaders. Since showing emotional intelligence is positively related to effective leadership, what should a leader do to enhance their emotional skills? Unlike personality traits, which remain fairly stable over time, emotional intelligence is a skill that can be developed.

LEADERSHIP SNAPSHOT
RUTH BADER GINSBURG, ASSOCIATE JUSTICE OF THE U.S. SUPREME COURT

WDC Photos / Alamy Stock Photo

"Fight for the things that you care about, but do it in a way that will lead others to join you."

This advice, given by Ruth Bader Ginsburg, an associate justice of the U.S. Supreme Court, aptly sums up how the barrier-breaking lawyer approached her career and advocacy work for women's rights and gender equality.

Born in Brooklyn, New York, in 1933, Ginsburg graduated from Cornell University in 1954, where she was one of the few women in her class. She then attended Harvard Law School, where she was one of nine women in a class of 561, and often told the story of how she was asked by the school's then-dean how she justified taking a place in the school that would have gone to a man. She excelled, becoming among the first women to serve on the school's esteemed journal, the *Harvard Law Review*. She transferred to Columbia Law School for her final year after her husband took a job for a New York law firm, graduating in 1959 at the top of her class.

She faced new discrimination as she began her legal career, noting she had "three strikes" against her in trying to get a job: She was Jewish. She was a wife. And she was a mother.

"Getting the first job was hard for women of my vintage," she said. "But once you got the first job you did it at least as well as the men and so the next step was not as hard" (Gresko, 2020).

Throughout her career, Ginsburg focused on fighting gender discrimination and advancing women's rights, inspiring generations of women to break barriers as she helped to pass several laws to achieve gender equality. She cofounded the Women's Rights Project at the American Civil Liberties Union (ACLU) and argued six gender discrimination cases before the Supreme Court, winning five of them. In addition to establishing the legal landscape to challenge gender discrimination in the 1970s, Ginsburg broke a glass ceiling to become the first tenured female professor at Columbia Law School, where she wrote the first textbook on sex discrimination law, *Text, Cases, and Materials on Sex-Based Discrimination*, published in 1974.

Ginsburg was nominated to the Supreme Court by President Bill Clinton in 1993, becoming only the second woman to serve on the Court. During her service, Ginsburg was known for her progressive views and her advocacy for gender equality, reproductive rights, and LGBTQ+ rights. She authored several landmark opinions, including *United States v. Virginia*, which held that the Virginia Military Institute could not exclude women from admission, and *Obergefell v. Hodges*, which legalized same-sex marriage nationwide.

Fellow former Supreme Court associate justice David Souter called Ginsburg a "tiger Justice," praising her initiative, intellect, and emotional stamina (Walsh, 2015). Ginsburg was known for her ability to work collaboratively with other justices, even those with opposing views, by being strategic, patient, and a master of persuasion. She successfully framed gender discrimination arguments as not being about "men vs. women" by substituting the word *gender* for *sex* in her arguments, saying "[*gender*] has a neutral sound and it will ward off distracting associations." She also linked gender discrimination issues to being about "fairness," saying "you needed to persuade men that this was right for society, that it was right for their daughters and granddaughters" (Brady, 2020). At the same time, Ginsburg also sought to break down traditional male/female stereotypes, even challenging laws that privileged women, upholding the notion that any type of gender discrimination was unconstitutional. In 1979, she successfully challenged a Missouri law before the Supreme Court that made jury duty service for women optional.

Ginsburg had a slow, careful, and meticulous communication style, saying "my effort was to speak slowly so that ideas could be grasped" (Gutgold, 2020). She was known for her interpersonal skills, which allowed her to develop a collegiality with her fellow justices that many felt was most typified by her close relationship with fellow Supreme Court justice Antonin Scalia. Ginsburg and Scalia were ideological opposites—he was conservative, she was more liberal—but the two respected each other and, despite their different approaches, bonded over their dedication to the Constitution, the Court, and the country. They were close friends and, with their families, often spent vacations and holidays together.

While her determination and accomplishments made Ginsburg a feminist icon and an exemplar of moral courage in the pursuit of social justice, her traits also helped her overcome a number of daunting personal challenges. In 1999, she was diagnosed with colon cancer, the first of her five bouts with cancer. She underwent surgery, chemotherapy, and radiation therapy without missing a day of service on the bench. Ten years later, she was diagnosed with early-stage pancreatic cancer, and was back in court within 12 days of a successful surgery. She learned in February 2020 that the pancreatic cancer had returned and began receiving treatment, promising to stay on the bench as long as she was able to serve, which she did until she died in September 2020 at the age of 87.

First, leaders need to work on *becoming aware* of their own emotions, taking their emotional pulse, and identifying their feelings as they happen. Whether it is mad, glad, sad, or scared, a leader needs to assess constantly how they are feeling and what is causing those feelings. Each of these core emotional states can range from low to high in intensity. For example, are you feeling content or thrilled? Anxious or terrified? Paying attention to your emotional states and being precise in how you articulate them can affect how you interact with others (Bradberry et al., 2009). For example, a supervisor high in emotional intelligence would monitor their emotional state before delivering feedback to an employee during a performance review in order to ensure the message "sent" was the message "received." A supervisor with less developed emotional intelligence, who might be in a tired or irritated mood, may inadvertently convey a more negative message than intended regarding the objective criteria on which the worker is being evaluated, and cause the worker unnecessary anxiety.

Second, a leader should train to become aware of the emotions of others. A leader who knows how to read others' emotions is better equipped to respond appropriately to these people's wants and needs. Stated another way, a leader needs to have empathy for others. They should understand the feelings of others as if those feelings were their own. For example, when taking on a new role as manager of a team or department, the new leader would be wise to anticipate the varied emotions their direct reports may be feeling, such as uncertainty about the new leader's management style, disappointment that they didn't receive the promotion themselves, or hope that needed changes will finally take place. By taking time to get to know the team and its needs before making changes, the manager can build trust among their workers.

Interestingly, researchers found that people deliver bad news more slowly to others than they do good news, partly to manage their own emotions but also out of a desire to protect the message receiver from embarrassment or hurt. Message senders show empathy when they anticipate the possible responses of the message receivers as they prepare to disclose the news, but it also helps the leader to better manage the outcomes (Dibble & Levine, 2010).

Salovey and Mayer (1990) suggested that empathy is the critical component of emotional intelligence. Empathy, and how to demonstrate it, is discussed further in Chapter 8, "Working With Groups."

Third, a leader needs to learn how to regulate their emotions and put them to good use. Whenever a leader makes a substantial decision, the leader's emotions are involved. Emotions in the workplace are contagious. One person's emotional state can trigger responses in another person's emotional state. Therefore, emotions need to be embraced and managed for the good of the group or organization.

The leader acts as the group's emotional guide. When a leader is sensitive to others and manages their own emotions appropriately, that leader increases the chances that the group's decisions will be effective. For example, in the film *Braveheart*, William Wallace tries to rally a ragged group of Scots to fight against well-equipped English troops. The Scots want to run away because they are outmanned and believe they can't win. Rather than scolding them for cowardice, Wallace acknowledges their fear. He agrees with their claim that running away is an option, and that if they fight they may die. But he also tells them how he, a battle-tested hero, views them: as "Sons of Scotland." They are fighting not just one battle but for the epic cause of freedom. This inspires the men to follow Wallace into battle.

The key point here is that people with emotional intelligence understand emotions and incorporate these in what they do as leaders. To summarize, a leader with emotional intelligence listens to their own feelings and the feelings of others, and is adept at regulating these emotions in service of the common good.

Managing Interpersonal Conflict

A leader also needs to have skill in managing interpersonal conflict. Conflict is inevitable. Conflict creates the need *for* change and occurs as the result *of* change. Conflict can be defined as a struggle between two or more individuals over perceived differences regarding substantive issues (e.g., the correct procedure to follow) or over perceived differences regarding relational issues (e.g., the amount of control each individual has within a relationship). When confronted with conflict, leaders and followers often feel uncomfortable because of the strain, controversy, and stress that accompany conflict. Although conflict is uncomfortable, it is not unhealthy, nor is it necessarily bad. If conflict is managed in effective and productive ways, the result is a reduction of stress, an increase in creative problem solving, and a strengthening of leader–follower and team-member relationships.

Because conflicts are usually very complex, and addressing them is never simple, Chapter 10, "Managing Conflict," provides a more thorough examination of the components of conflict and offers several practical communication approaches that a leader can take to constructively resolve differences.

CONCEPTUAL SKILLS EXPLAINED

Whereas administrative skills are about organizing work, and interpersonal skills are about dealing effectively with people, **conceptual skills** are about working with concepts and ideas. Conceptual skills involve the thinking or cognitive aspects of leadership and are critical to such things as creating a vision or strategic plan for an organization. A leader with conceptual skills is able to conceive and communicate the ideas that shape an organization from its goals and mission to how to best solve problems.

Conceptual Skills in Practice

Conceptual skills for leaders can be divided into three parts: (1) problem solving, (2) strategic planning, and (3) creating vision.

Problem Solving

We all know people who are especially good at problem solving. When something goes wrong or needs to be fixed, they are the first ones to jump in and address the problem. Problem solvers do not sit idly by when there are problems. They are quick to ask, "What went wrong?" and they are ready to explore possible answers to "How can it be fixed?" Problem-solving skills are essential for effective leadership.

What are problem-solving skills? **Problem-solving skills** refer to a leader's cognitive ability to take corrective action in a problem situation in order to meet desired objectives. The skills include identifying the problem, generating alternative solutions, selecting the best solution from among the alternatives, and implementing that solution (see Table 5.1). These skills do not function in a vacuum, but are carried out in a particular setting or context.

Step 1: Identify the problem. The first step in the problem-solving process is to identify or recognize the problem. The importance of this step cannot be understated. Seeing a problem and addressing it is at the core of successful problem solving. All of us are confronted with many problems every day, but some of us fail to see those problems or even to admit that they exist. Others may recognize that something is wrong but then do nothing about it. People with problem-solving skills see problems and address them.

TABLE 5.1 ■   Steps in Problem Solving
1. Identify the problem
2. Generate alternative solutions
3. Select the best solution
4. Implement the solution

Some problems are simple and easy to define, while others are complex and demand a great deal of scrutiny. Problems arise when there is a difference between what is expected and what actually happens. Identifying the problem requires awareness of these differences. The questions we ask in this phase of problem solving are "What is the problem?" "Are there multiple aspects to it?" and "What caused it?" Identifying the exact nature of the problem precedes everything else in the problem-solving process.

Step 2: Generate alternative solutions. After identifying the problem and its cause or causes, the next step in problem solving is to generate alternative solutions where there is more than one possible resolution to the problem. Because problems are often complex, there are usually many different ways of trying to correct them. During this phase of problem solving, it is important to consider as many solutions as possible and not dismiss any as unworthy. For example, consider a person with a major health concern (e.g., cancer or multiple sclerosis). There are often many ways to treat the illness, but before choosing a course of treatment, it is important to consult a health professional and explore all the treatment options. Every treatment has different side effects and different probabilities for curing the illness. Before choosing an option, people often want to be sure that they have fully considered all of the possible treatment options. The same is true in problem solving. Before going forward, it is important to consider all the available options for dealing with a problem.

Step 3: Select the best solution. The next step in problem solving is to select the best solution to the problem. Solutions usually differ in how well they address a particular problem, so the relative strengths and weaknesses of each solution need to be addressed. Some solutions are straightforward and easy to enact, while others are complex or difficult to manage. Similarly, some solutions are inexpensive while others are costly. Many criteria can be used to judge the value of a particular solution as it applies to a given problem. Selecting the best solution is the key to solving a problem effectively.

The importance of selecting the best solution can be illustrated in a hypothetical example of a couple with marital difficulties. Having struggled in their marriage for more than two years, the couple decides that they must do something to resolve the conflict in their relationship. Included in the list of what they could do are attend marital counseling, receive individual psychiatric therapy, separate, date other people even though they are married, and file for divorce. Each of these solutions would have a different impact on what happens to the couple and their marital relationship. While not exhaustive, the list highlights the importance in problem solving of selecting the best solution to a given problem. The solutions we choose have a major impact on how we feel about the outcome of our problem solving.

Step 4: Implement the solution. The final step in problem solving is implementing the solution. Having defined the problem and selected a solution, it is time to put the solution into action. Implementing the solution involves shifting from thinking about the problem to doing something about the problem. It is a challenging step: It is not uncommon to meet with resistance from others when trying to do something new and different to solve a problem. Implementing change requires communicating with others about the change, and adapting the change to the wants and needs of those being affected by the change. Of course, there is always the possibility that the chosen solution will fail to address the problem; it might even make the problem worse. Nevertheless, there is no turning back at this phase. There is always a risk in implementing change, but it is a risk that must be taken to complete the problem-solving process.

To clarify what is meant by problem-solving skills, consider the following example of John and Kristen Smith and their troublesome dishwasher. The Smiths' dishwasher was five years old, and the dishes were no longer coming out clean and sparkling. Analyzing the situation, the Smiths determined that the problem could be related to one of several possible causes: their use of liquid instead of powdered dish detergent, a bad seal on the door of the dishwasher, ineffective water softener, misloading of the dishwasher, or a defective water heater. Not knowing what the problem was, John thought they should implement all five possible solutions at once. Kristen disagreed, and suggested they address one possible solution at a time to determine the cause. The first solution they tried was to change the dish detergent, but this did not fix the problem. Next, they changed the seal on the door of the dishwasher—and this solved the problem. By addressing the problem carefully and systematically, the Smiths were able to find the cause of the dishwasher malfunction and to save themselves a great deal of money. Their problem-solving strategy was effective.

Strategic Planning

A second major kind of conceptual skill is **strategic planning**. Like problem solving, strategic planning is mainly a cognitive activity. A leader needs to be able to think and consider ideas to develop effective strategies for a group or an organization. Being strategic requires developing careful plans of action based on the available resources and personnel to achieve a goal. It is similar to what generals do in wartime: They make elaborate plans of how to defeat the enemy given their resources, personnel, and the mission they need to accomplish. Similarly, athletic coaches take their knowledge of their players and their abilities to create game plans for how to best compete with the opposing team. In short, strategic planning is about designing a plan of action to achieve a desired goal.

In their analysis of research on strategic leadership, Boal and Hooijberg (2000) suggested that strategic leaders need to have the ability to learn, the capacity to adapt, and managerial wisdom. The *ability to learn* includes the capability to absorb new information and apply it toward new goals. It is a willingness to experiment with new ideas and even to accept failures. The *capacity to adapt* is about being able to respond quickly to changes in the environment. A leader needs to be open to and accepting of change. When competitive conditions change, an effective leader will have the capacity to change. Having *managerial wisdom* refers to possessing a deep understanding of the people with whom and the environment in which a leader works. It is about having the good sense to make the right decisions at the right time, and to do so while keeping in mind the best interests of everyone involved.

To illustrate the complexity of strategic planning, consider the following example of how NewDevices, a startup medical supply company, used strategic thinking to promote itself. NewDevices developed a surgical scanner to help surgical teams reduce errors during surgery.

Although there were no such scanners on the market at that time, two companies were developing a similar product. The potential market for the product was enormous and included all the hospitals in the United States (almost 8,000 hospitals). Because it was clear that all hospitals would eventually need this scanner, NewDevices knew it was going to be in a race to capture the market ahead of the other companies.

NewDevices was a small company with limited resources, so management was well aware of the importance of strategic planning. Any single mistake could threaten the survival of the company. Because everyone at NewDevices, including the sales staff, owned stock in the company, everyone was strongly motivated to work to make the company succeed. Sales staff members were willing to share effective sales approaches with each other because, rather than being in competition, they had a common goal.

Every Monday morning, the management team met for three hours to discuss the goals and directions for the company. Much time was spent on framing the argument for why hospitals needed the NewDevices scanner more than its competitors' scanners. To make this even more challenging, the NewDevices scanner was more expensive than the competition, although it was also safer. NewDevices chose to sell the product by stressing that it could save money in the long run for hospitals because it was safer and would reduce the incidence of malpractice cases.

Managers also developed strategies about how to persuade hospitals to sign on to their product. They contacted hospitals to inquire as to whom they should direct their pitch for the new product. Was it the director of surgical nursing or some other hospital administrator? In addition, they analyzed how they should allocate the company's limited resources. Should they spend more money on enhancing their website? Did they need a director of advertising? Should they hire more sales representatives? All of these questions were the subject of much analysis and debate. NewDevices knew the stakes were very high; if management slipped even once, the company would fail.

This example illustrates that strategic planning is a multifaceted process. By planning strategically, however, leaders and their employees can increase the likelihood of reaching their goals and achieving the aims of the organization.

Creating Vision

Similar to strategic planning, creating vision takes a special kind of cognitive and conceptual ability. It requires the capacity to challenge people with compelling visions of the future. To create vision, a leader needs to be able to set forth a picture of a future that is better than the present, and then move others toward a new set of ideals and values that will lead to the future. A leader must be able to articulate the vision and engage others in its pursuit. Furthermore, the leader needs to be able to implement the vision and model the principles set forth in the vision. A leader with a vision has to "walk the walk," and not just "talk the talk." Building vision is an important leadership skill and one that receives extensive discussion in Chapter 7, "Creating a Vision."

SUMMARY

In recent years, the study of leadership skills has captured the attention of researchers and practitioners alike. Skills are essential to being an effective leader. Unlike traits that are innate, leadership skills are *learned* competencies. Everyone can learn to acquire leadership skills. In this chapter, we considered three types of leadership skills: administrative skills, interpersonal skills, and conceptual skills.

Often thought of as unexciting, *administrative skills* play a primary role in effective leadership. These are the skills a leader needs to run the organization and carry out its purposes. These are the skills needed to plan and organize work. Specifically, administrative skills include managing people, managing resources, and showing technical competence.

A second type of skills is *interpersonal skills*, or people skills. These are the competencies that a leader needs to work effectively with followers, peers, and higher-ups to accomplish the organization's goals. Research has shown unequivocally that interpersonal skills are of fundamental importance to effective leadership. Interpersonal skills can be divided into being socially perceptive, showing emotional intelligence, and managing interpersonal conflict.

A leader also needs *conceptual skills*. Conceptual skills have to do with working with concepts and ideas. These are cognitive skills that emphasize the thinking ability of a leader. Although these cover a wide array of competencies, conceptual skills in this chapter are divided into problem solving, strategic planning, and creating vision.

In summary, administrative, interpersonal, and conceptual skills play a major role in effective leadership. Through practice and hard work, we can all become better leaders by improving our skills in each of these areas.

KEY TERMS

administrative skills

conceptual skills

interpersonal skills

problem-solving skills

social perceptiveness

strategic planning

technical competence

5.1 Case Study—Give Me Shelter

Theodore Henderson was an unlikely candidate for the executive director's job at The Ross Center, a day shelter and organization that serves people who are hungry, lonely, or unhoused.

Theo had grown up in a home with six siblings, and his parents barely made enough money to keep their family clothed and fed. Theo's father was critical of him, telling Theo he wasn't smart or strong and didn't work hard enough. Theo became very driven, always trying to prove himself. He would rarely ask for help or support from his parents, his teachers, or any other authority figure.

When Theo became a single dad at 17, his parents told him he had to move out. Theo worked odd jobs to support himself and his very young son, and the pair spent more than one occasion living in a homeless shelter. Through sheer determination, Theo was able to earn a GED and enrolled part-time in community college, where he graduated after five years with an associate's degree in education.

After he graduated, however, he became discouraged, knowing he needed a bachelor's degree to become a teacher but couldn't afford more college. A classmate told him about a new volunteer coordinator position at The Ross Center. The Ross Center provided up to 300 people each day with breakfast and lunch, laundry and shower facilities, and assistance in accessing social services, and its volunteer coordinator would not only recruit and manage volunteers, but also train them.

When Theo interviewed for the job, he was asked what he would do first as the volunteer coordinator. He recalled his own time being homeless and said, "As these folks who come here go about their day out on the streets, no one looks them in the eye or says hi to them. When they come here, every volunteer and staff member should do just that. They have to believe that anybody that walks through these doors is an important, lovable human being, and treat them that way." He was hired.

Theo thrived in the job. The job required a lot of organization, matching volunteers with the needs of the organization and making sure all positions were staffed, as well as developing and implementing plans and procedures for volunteer recruitment and training. Theo, who often shared his own "street" experiences with volunteers, quickly built a successful program and was well liked by volunteers and staff, many of whom admired his ability to get things done.

After a year, the center's director, Linda, told him to find and train his replacement because he was to become the operations manager, overseeing the shelter's day-to-day operations. He balked and said, "I can't do that. How am I going to run the facility and do human resource stuff?" The response was, "You have already been doing it. You got this."

But Theo found the operations job very difficult. He did a lot of what he called "band-aiding"—doing whatever needed to be done in various departments to keep the building going. As a result, Theo found himself torn in many directions. When Linda found Theo on a ladder, tool in hand, trying to repair one of the refrigerators' compressors, she asked him, "Theo, is this the best use of your time? Isn't there someone else whose job this is?" Staff members complained because they felt like Theo was too busy to hear their concerns and suggestions for improvements. In addition, Theo's son was having problems in school, and Theo would need to leave in the middle of the day to pick him up, which he felt put him further behind at work. Despite all the hours and hard work, Theo thought he was failing. He told his boss he needed to find a new job.

Recognizing Theo's concerns, Linda told Theo she had a new job for him: She wanted him to take a leave of absence from the operations job to oversee the effort to build a new facility for The Ross Center. The job would require leading groups of people—committees, contractors, fundraisers, city leaders—to design and build the best possible day shelter. There was no way for one single human being to do it all and make all the decisions; Theo would have to engage in strategic planning and learn to lead others to accomplish the goals.

Once again, Theo didn't believe he was qualified for or deserved the role. "Theo, you have to learn to lead people, not do their work for them," Linda told him. "Being a leader isn't about doing, it's about facilitating others to achieve objectives and goals. Your job will be to lead others in making the decisions to create a building that meets all our needs."

Theo started by listening, meeting with staff, volunteers, and clients to engage in brainstorming sessions to determine what amenities the shelter needed. He established several committees to oversee the budgeting, site selection, and fundraising for the new building. He put together a team of regular clients and volunteers to assist in picking out everything from paint colors to shower tile for the new building. It was through this team that Theo learned that the building needed taller toilets for clients with mobility issues and shorter toilets for the family bathrooms to accommodate children. "I didn't know you could have a three-hour meeting about toilets, but we did," he said, laughing.

When committee or team members developed conflicts or encountered obstacles, Theo resisted his inclination to just go ahead and tell the committees what to do; instead, he let them work to find resolution, and mediated when groups couldn't reach consensus. As the project progressed, Theo did become a key decision maker as contractors, city planners, and vendors required answers that would take too long to reach in a committee. Theo found it a delicate balancing act of being in charge and letting others be in charge.

After the new building opened, Theo went back to being the facility's operations director. Instead of being nervous, Theo approached the job with new confidence. "I have always felt I needed to control things," he admits. "But in working on the new building, I had to learn to give up that control to lead others. It was hard, but it wasn't going to happen otherwise. I see it's the same in the day-to-day operations of the shelter."

Two years later, Theo's boss announced at a board meeting that she would be retiring. The board suggested that it might take a year to do a search to find her replacement, but she shook her head. "You have the perfect person already in place. He knows the organization inside and out, he's committed to the mission, and he has the respect of the staff, volunteers, and clients."

When she told Theo that the board wanted him to apply to be the CEO, he was stunned, but this time he didn't argue. He nodded. "I'm ready," he said.

Questions

1. Based on the Model of Primary Leadership Skills (Figure 5.1), how would you describe Theo's skills? In what skills is he strongest, and in what skills is he weakest?

2. Why do you think Theo was more successful in the role overseeing the new facility's development than he was as the operations director?

3. What skills did Theo exhibit that made Linda think he would be a good operations manager the first time? What skills did he learn and develop that led her to think he would be a good CEO?

4. How do you think Theo's emotional intelligence developed during his career?

5.2 Case Study—Reviving an Ancient Art

Nilda Callañaupa grew up in the Chinchero, a rural, impoverished community nestled high in the Andes of Peru. As a young child, Nilda, a descendant of the Inca and a member of Peru's indigenous Quechua people, shepherded her family's sheep in the highlands near her home, befriending an older shepherdess, Doña Sebastiana. Doña, who was an expert spinner and weaver, taught young Nilda the ancient art of her ancestors. Learning to spin yarn at 5 years old and to weave patterns when she was 6, Nilda quickly became an expert weaver, creating beautiful handiworks in the ancient traditions of her people (WorldStrides, 2019).

The Inca had a rich tradition of textiles, establishing textiles centers throughout their vast empire. Known for their beautiful, brightly colored intricate detail, these textiles often denoted wealth and status in the community and were an integral part of the Inca's social, political, and religious life. The adult female weavers of the Chinchero gathered often to weave and spin together, sharing techniques and ideas. Many, like Nilda's grandmother, sold their textiles to supplement their families' meager farm incomes. In the early 1970s, a small group of these women had become concerned that the young people of their communities were disinterested in the weaving traditions of their people and that if they didn't preserve this native knowledge, an important part of their culture would be lost forever.

They formed a weaving collective where women gathered to study and learn the traditional ways of spinning, weaving, and natural dyeing, reviving the techniques of using handspun yarn and natural fibers from the animals they raised (sheep, alpaca, and llama). The collective hoped to market the women's creations to the growing tourism industry in Peru, helping support the weavers and provide them with an independent income.

This sparked a passion in Nilda, and she sought to glean as much about spinning and weaving as she could from her own mother, her grandmothers, and other Chinchero elders. Though still a girl, she became a leader in the collective. When a young couple from the United States moved to her village in the early 1970s, she befriended them, becoming their weaving teacher. This couple assisted the weaving collective and the young Nilda in securing support to create a community cultural center focused on the spinning and weaving tradition in Chinchero.

Nilda was considered a prodigy; by the time she was 14, she had traveled far from her small Peruvian village, giving weaving demonstrations at the Smithsonian Institution and at the American Museum of Natural History in the United States. She was one of the few girls in Chinchero to attend high school and later the first woman of her community to attend university, weaving to help pay for her education. She earned a master's degree from the National University of San Antonio Abad in Cusco in 1986 and subsequently obtained a grant to study historical textiles in Berkeley, California. Nilda traveled the world teaching, demonstrating, and promoting her art and the products of her community.

During Nilda's absence, the cultural center she helped to found in Chinchero began to falter. In an effort to preserve it, Nilda led the weavers in forming the Centro de Textiles

Tradicionales del Cusco (CTTC) in 1996, a nonprofit dedicated to assisting the communities from the Cusco region to "revive textile traditions and empower weavers, especially women" (CTTC, 2020). Through the many contacts Nilda had made in her travels, she was able to secure significant international and foundational support for this organization and worked with the weavers to revise their goals and set a path forward.

Under Nilda's leadership, the CTTC partnered with several communities, first working with the elders to educate the weavers in 10 communities on weaving designs, techniques, and knowledge and then building centers in each community to provide a place where weavers could gather to work, "free from the distractions of home life and sheltered from the rain" (CTTC, 2020). Each community's weavers work to revive historical unique ancestral designs and traditions, recovering ancient techniques and refining processes for natural dyes. The resulting finely crafted and unique products of the CTTC members have become recognized worldwide and highly valued for their superior workmanship (Van Buskirk & Van Buskirk, 2012b), and to market these, the CTTC opened a store, an office, and a museum in the heart of the city of Cusco, a tourism center of the region.

"The work of the Center is not just to preserve and to study Peruvian textiles, their symbolism and significance, etc. Our goal also is to assist families to create a larger market for their textiles and a new economy for their communities," Nilda says (Van Buskirk & Van Buskirk, 2012b).

Weaving was long considered "women's work" and not highly valued, leaving women economically disadvantaged and reliant on male family members and the meager earnings of agricultural life in the region. The CTTC's efforts to revive an important cultural art form of the Indigenous people of Peru has also provided the weavers and their families with a much-needed source of income. Many of these women are now the primary breadwinners for their families. Empowered and proud, they hold important status in their communities and families.

"Through the sale of their textiles at a fair price, many of the weavers and their families have been able to greatly improve their quality of life. They are able to invest their new income in their children and land. More children are able to complete high school, and now many young people are even going to university or institutes in the city of Cusco. Families can access better health services and improve their homes or even buy more land," says Nilda (Hallum, 2018).

Nilda, now married with two children, is an award-winning author of three books and continues to travel the world sharing the beautiful work, traditions, and techniques of CTTC weavers and educating others on how to re-create the success she spearheaded for her own community high in the Andes.

"I guess you never know what is in your future, especially if you come from a small place," she says. "But it is relationships that make a difference. It doesn't matter what languages we speak, the level of education we have, the society in which we grew up, or the part of the world in which we live. We can do surprising things if we share with each other" (Van Buskirk & Van Buskirk, 2012a).

Questions

1. Based on the Model of Primary Leadership Skills (Figure 5.1), how would you describe Nilda's skills?

2. Which skills do you feel contributed most strongly to Nilda's success leading the CTTC?

3. In what ways do you think Nilda exhibited emotional intelligence?

4. What is your biggest takeaway from this story? What do you find most inspiring?

Application

5.3 Leadership Skills Questionnaire

Purpose

1. To identify your leadership skills
2. To provide a profile of your leadership skills showing your strengths and weaknesses

Directions

1. Place yourself in the role of a leader when responding to this questionnaire.
2. For each of the following statements, circle the number that indicates the degree to which you feel the statement is true.

Statements	Not true	Seldom true	Occasionally true	Somewhat true	Very true
1. I am effective with the detailed aspects of my work.	1	2	3	4	5
2. I usually know ahead of time how people will respond to a new idea or proposal.	1	2	3	4	5
3. I am effective at problem solving.	1	2	3	4	5
4. Filling out forms and working with details come easily for me.	1	2	3	4	5
5. Understanding the social fabric of the organization is important to me.	1	2	3	4	5
6. When problems arise, I immediately address them.	1	2	3	4	5

Statements	Not true	Seldom true	Occasionally true	Somewhat true	Very true
7. Managing people and resources is one of my strengths.	1	2	3	4	5
8. I am able to sense the emotional undercurrents in my group.	1	2	3	4	5
9. Seeing the big picture comes easily for me.	1	2	3	4	5
10. In my work, I enjoy responding to people's requests and concerns.	1	2	3	4	5
11. I use my emotional energy to motivate others.	1	2	3	4	5
12. Making strategic plans for my company appeals to me.	1	2	3	4	5
13. Obtaining and allocating resources is a challenging aspect of my job.	1	2	3	4	5
14. The key to successful conflict resolution is respecting my opponent.	1	2	3	4	5

Statements	Not true	Seldom true	Occasionally true	Somewhat true	Very true
15. I enjoy discussing organizational values and philosophy.	1	2	3	4	5
16. I am effective at obtaining resources to support our programs.	1	2	3	4	5
17. I work hard to find consensus in conflict situations.	1	2	3	4	5
18. I am flexible about making changes in our organization.	1	2	3	4	5

Scoring

1. Sum the responses on items 1, 4, 7, 10, 13, and 16 (administrative skill score).
2. Sum the responses on items 2, 5, 8, 11, 14, and 17 (interpersonal skill score).
3. Sum the responses on items 3, 6, 9, 12, 15, and 18 (conceptual skill score).

Total Scores

Administrative skill: _____

Interpersonal skill: _____

Conceptual skill: _____

Scoring Interpretation

The Leadership Skills Questionnaire is designed to measure three broad types of leadership skills: administrative, interpersonal, and conceptual. By comparing your scores, you can determine where you have leadership strengths and where you have leadership weaknesses.

If your score is 26–30, you are in the very high range.

If your score is 21–25, you are in the high range.

If your score is 16–20, you are in the moderate range.

If your score is 11–15, you are in the low range.

If your score is 6–10, you are in the very low range.

Application

5.4 Observational Exercise—Leadership Skills

Purpose

1. To develop an understanding of different types of leadership skills
2. To examine how leadership skills affect a leader's performance

Directions

1. Your task in this exercise is to observe a leader and evaluate that person's leadership skills. This leader can be a supervisor, a manager, a coach, a teacher, a fraternity or sorority officer, or anyone who has a position that involves leadership.
2. For each of the groups of skills listed as follows, write what you observed about this leader.

Name of leader: _____

Administrative skills	1	2	3	4	5
Managing people	Poor	Weak	Average	Good	Very good
Managing resources	Poor	Weak	Average	Good	Very good
Showing technical competence	Poor	Weak	Average	Good	Very good

Comments:

Interpersonal skills	1	2	3	4	5
Being socially perceptive	Poor	Weak	Average	Good	Very good
Showing emotional intelligence	Poor	Weak	Average	Good	Very good
Managing conflict	Poor	Weak	Average	Good	Very good

Comments:

Conceptual skills	1	2	3	4	5
Problem solving	Poor	Weak	Average	Good	Very good
Strategic planning	Poor	Weak	Average	Good	Very good
Creating vision	Poor	Weak	Average	Good	Very good

Comments:

Questions

1. Based on your observations, what were the leader's strengths and weaknesses?

2. In what setting did this leadership example occur? Did the setting influence the kind of skills that the leader used? Discuss.

3. If you were coaching this leader, what specific things would you tell this leader about how they could improve leadership skills? Discuss.

4. In another situation, do you think this leader would exhibit the same strengths and weaknesses? Discuss.

Application

5.5 Reflection and Action Worksheet—Leadership Skills

Reflection

1. Based on what you know about yourself and the scores you received on the Leadership Skills Questionnaire in the three areas (administrative, interpersonal, and conceptual), how would you describe your leadership skills? Which specific skills are your strongest, and which are your weakest? What impact do you think your leadership skills could have on your role as a leader? Discuss.

2. This chapter suggests that emotional intelligence is an interpersonal leadership skill. Discuss whether you agree or disagree with this assumption. As you think about your own leadership, how do your emotions help or hinder your role as a leader? Discuss.

3. This chapter divides leadership into three kinds of skills (administrative, interpersonal, and conceptual). Do you think some of these skills are more important than others in some kinds of situations? Do you think lower levels of leadership (e.g., supervisor) require the same skills as upper levels of leadership (e.g., CEO)? Discuss.

Action

1. One unique aspect of leadership skills is that they can be practiced. List and briefly describe three things you could do to improve your administrative skills.

2. Leaders need to be *socially perceptive*. As you assess yourself in this area, identify two specific actions that would help you become more perceptive of other people and their viewpoints. Discuss.

3. What kind of problem solver are you? Are you slow or quick to address problem situations? Overall, what two things could you change about yourself to be a more effective problem solver?

6 ENGAGING STRENGTHS

INTRODUCTION

Think of a time or circumstance when you were performing at the peak of your abilities. Now, step back and try to explain why you were so effective in that situation. What was it about *you* or the *way you presented yourself* that made you feel good? What did you *do* that worked so well? Why did others respond to you the way they did? The answers to each of these questions are related to your strengths—the central theme of this chapter.

Every one of us has identifiable leadership strengths, areas in which we excel or thrive. But we often fail to recognize these strengths. As a result, many times our strengths are used ineffectively or not at all. The same is true for the strengths of our coworkers and followers; sometimes their strengths are known, but often they go untapped. The challenge we face as leaders is to identify our own strengths as well as the strengths of others and then use these to make our organizations and followers more efficient, productive, and satisfied.

Identifying individual strengths is a unique challenge because people often feel hesitant and inhibited about acknowledging positive aspects of themselves. In the American culture, expressing positive self-attributes is often seen as boastful or self-serving. In fact, focusing on self is disdained in many cultures, while showing humility and being self-deprecating is seen as virtuous. In this chapter, you will be asked to set aside your inhibitions about identifying your own strengths in an effort to better understand the inextricable role these strengths play in leading and working with others.

Above all, read this chapter because it explains something about yourself that could significantly affect your work and leadership for years to come. The role of strengths is not discussed in many textbooks, but it is a variable that is integral to how we lead and how we accomplish work. Having an appreciation for your own strengths, as well as those of others, can be critically important to you in your personal life and your career.

Our goal in this chapter is to explore how understanding strengths can make one a better leader. First, we will explain the concept by defining *strengths* and describing the *historical background* of strengths-based leadership. We will examine *how to identify strengths*, followed by a description of different *measures* that can be used to assess your strengths. The final section of the chapter will look at the concept of strengths-based leadership in *practice*, including specific strategies that leaders can employ to use strengths to become more effective leaders.

STRENGTHS-BASED LEADERSHIP EXPLAINED

Before discussing the development and principles of strengths-based leadership, we need to clarify what is meant by strengths. A **strength** is *an attribute or quality of an individual that accounts for successful performance.* It is the characteristic, or series of characteristics, we demonstrate when our performance is at its best.

Strengths researchers (Buckingham & Clifton, 2001; Rath, 2007) suggest that strengths are the ability to consistently demonstrate exceptional work. Similarly, Linley (2008) defines strength as a preexisting capacity that is authentic and energizing and enables peak performance.

A strength is an *applied* trait. As mentioned in Chapter 2, traits are characteristics of people that are often inherited; in the case of strengths, these traits are being engaged at their highest level. For example, sociability is considered a leadership trait, but for someone who is very good at establishing and maintaining social relationships, someone we might call a "people person," that trait is a strength.

A strength is also different from a skill. As discussed in Chapter 5, skills are learned competencies; everyone can be taught skills. Strengths are expressions of a preexisting capacity and are unique to each person. A skill can become a strength, however. For example, a person can learn time management and organization, and with application and practice that allow them to become very good at this skill, it can become a strength.

Simply put, strengths are positive features of ourselves that make us effective and help us flourish. For example, Antonio was born with a talent for drawing and design. He worked as a construction laborer for years while he attended a university to study architecture. As a result, when Antonio became an architect, his experiences in building made his design skills stronger because he more fully understood the concepts of actual construction. His clients often comment that one of his strengths is his "construction-friendly" designs.

Historical Background

Studying leadership from the perspective of strengths is a recent area of study, which came to the forefront in the late 1990s as a result of two overlapping research developments. First, researchers at Gallup initiated a massive study that included interviews of over 2 million people to describe what's right with people—that is, their talents and what they are good at—rather than what's wrong with people (Rath, 2007).

Second, academic research scholars began to question the exclusive focus in psychology on the disease model of human problems and started to study mentally and physically healthy people and what accounted for their well-being. From this work, a new field called *positive psychology* emerged (Peterson, 2006; Peterson & Seligman, 2003). Each of these two developments helped to explain the rising popularity of strengths-based leadership.

Gallup

Best known as a public opinion research organization that conducts political polling, **Gallup** also conducts research in other areas of the social sciences. For nearly 40 years, the study of people's strengths has been a major research focus at Gallup. Spearheaded by the late Donald O. Clifton, millions of people were interviewed regarding their performance and human strengths. Based on these interview data, Gallup researchers designed the StrengthsFinder profile, an online assessment of people's talents and potential strengths. Originally titled the Clifton StrengthsFinder in honor of its chief designer, it became StrengthsFinder 2.0 in 2007 and is now known as CliftonStrengths. Later in the chapter, we will discuss more extensively CliftonStrengths and the specific talent-based strengths it measures.

CliftonStrengths is one of the most widely used self-assessment questionnaires in the world and has been completed by nearly 30 million people to date. This assessment has been adopted by many organizations to help individuals identify their strengths, become more engaged, and improve their performance. While Gallup has not published a theory about strengths, the wide use of CliftonStrengths has elevated strengths as a key variable in discussions of factors that account for effective leadership development and performance.

Positive Psychology

At the same time Gallup's CliftonStrengths profile was growing in popularity, a major change was occurring in the discipline of psychology. Researchers were challenging the discipline to expand its focus on not only what is wrong with people and their weaknesses, but also what is right with people and their positive attributes. This expanded focus, which was initiated by Martin Seligman in an address to the American Psychological Association in 1998 (see Fowler et al., 1999), soon became the field of *positive psychology*. Since its inception more than two decades ago, positive psychology has grown exponentially and developed into a credible and important area of psychological research.

Specifically, **positive psychology** can be defined as "the scientific study of what makes life most worth living" (Peterson, 2009, p. xxiii). Rather than study the frailties and flaws of individuals (the disease model), positive psychology focuses on individuals' strengths and the factors that allow them to thrive (Fredrickson, 2001; Seligman, 2002; Seligman & Csikszentmihalyi, 2000). It addresses people's positive experiences, such as their happiness and joy; people's positive traits, such as their characteristics and talents; and people's positive institutions, such as families, schools, and businesses that influence them (Cameron et al., 2003).

Most prominently, positive psychology is devoted to the study of people's positive characteristics—their *strengths*. This makes it invaluable for understanding strengths-based leadership. Positive psychology launched the analysis of people's strengths into the mainstream of scientific research (Linley, 2008). Concepts and theories from the field of positive psychology directly relate to learning how strengths-based leadership works.

Identifying and Measuring Strengths

As indicated in the historical background, most of the research on strengths has been done by scholars connected with Gallup and scholars studying positive psychology. This body of research has produced multiple ways of identifying strengths and a wide-ranging list of individual strengths. This section explores the way strengths have been identified by three major groups: (1) Gallup, (2) VIA Institute on Character, and (3) Centre of Applied Positive Psychology in the United Kingdom. Although there is much overlap in their work, each research group provides a unique perspective on identifying and measuring individual strengths. Collectively, this research provides an extensive list of specific strengths, a clear picture of how strengths can be measured, and an expansive view of how strengths can be used to understand human behavior.

Gallup and the CliftonStrengths Profile

Gallup researchers interviewed an enormous number of executives, salespeople, teachers, doctors, nurses, and other professionals about their strengths and what made them good at what they did. The goal of the interviews was to identify the qualities of high-performing individuals. From these interviews, Gallup researchers extracted 34 patterns or themes that they thought did the best job at explaining excellent performance (see Table 6.1). These 34 items are "the most common themes that emerged from the study of human talent" (Buckingham & Clifton, 2001, p. 12) and have been the benchmark for discussing strengths in the workplace.

It is important to point out that Gallup researchers identified **themes of human talent**, not strengths. Talents are similar to personality traits—they are relatively stable, fixed characteristics that are not easily changed. From talents, strengths emerge. The equation for developing a strength is talent times investment (see Figure 6.1). Strengths are derived from having certain talents and then further developing those talents by gaining additional knowledge, skills, and practice (Rath, 2007). For example, you may have the talent for being able to communicate easily with others. If you were to invest time in learning more about the intricacies of effective communication and practicing it with the help of Toastmasters International, a club that helps individuals develop public speaking skills, you could enhance your communication strength. Similarly, if you were born with talent as an initiator, you could develop it further into one of your strengths by studying how to "think outside of the box" and then practicing this thought process in your organization. To summarize, talents are not strengths, but they provide the basis for developing strengths when they are coupled with knowledge, skills, and practice.

TABLE 6.1 ■ 34 Talent Themes

Executing	Influencing	Relationship Building	Strategic Thinking
Achiever	Activator	Adaptability	Analytical
Arranger	Command	Developer	Context
Belief	Communication	Connectedness	Futuristic
Consistency	Competition	Empathy	Ideation
Deliberative	Maximizer	Harmony	Input
Discipline	Self-Assurance	Includer	Intellection
Focus	Significance	Individualization	Learner
Responsibility	Woo	Positivity	Strategic
Restorative		Relator	

FIGURE 6.1 ■ Strength Equation

Talent (a natural way of thinking, feeling, or behaving)

$\times$

Investment (time spent practicing, developing your skills, and building your knowledge base)

$=$

Strength (the ability to consistently provide near-perfect performance)

How are strengths measured from the Gallup perspective? Gallup's CliftonStrengths is a 177-item questionnaire that identifies "the areas *where you have the greatest potential to develop strengths*" (Rath, 2007, p. 31). After taking this questionnaire, you receive a list of your five strongest talents. You can build on these talents, furthering your personal growth and development. The questionnaire, which takes about 30 minutes to complete, is available through an access code that appears in the back of strengths books published by Gallup. It is also available on the organization's website at www.gallup.com/cliftonstrengths/en/home.aspx. How can leaders use strengths in their leadership? In the book *Strengths Based Leadership*, Rath and Conchie (2008) explain how a leader's scores on the CliftonStrengths profile can be interpreted. They developed a configuration that depicts four domains of leadership strengths (see Table 6.2: executing, influencing, relationship building, and strategic thinking). These domains were derived from information obtained during interviews with thousands of executive teams and from a factor analysis of the Gallup talent data set. Taken together, the four domains represent the four kinds of strengths that help create successful teams.

Effective teams possess broad groupings of strengths and work best when all four domains of leadership strengths are represented on their teams (Rath & Conchie, 2008). Effective teams are generally well rounded and have different group members who fulfill different needs of the group. Leaders bring unique strengths to teams, but leaders do not have to demonstrate strengths in all four domains. Strong and cohesive teams bring into play everyone's strengths to make the team effective.

TABLE 6.2 ■ Four Domains of Leadership Strengths

Executing
Influencing
Relationship Building
Strategic Thinking

For example, Maria Lopez, who has owned a successful bridal shop for 10 years, took the CliftonStrengths profile and found her dominant strengths were in the *strategic thinking* domain. Maria is known for her futuristic thinking and deliberate planning. She is outstanding at forecasting trends in bridal wear and helping her team navigate the constantly changing bridal market. Maria hired Claudia, whose dominant strengths are in *relationship building.* Claudia is the most positive person on the staff and connects with everyone. It is Claudia who treats customers in the store like they are part of "the family." To run the store on a day-to-day basis, Maria brought on Kristen, who is a hard worker and uses her strengths in *executing* to get the job done. She is highly disciplined and motivated to make the bridal shop the best in the city. Lastly, Maria hired Brianna because of her strengths in the domain of *influencing.* Brianna is always out in the community promoting the shop. She is seen as a credible professional by other shop owners because she is self-assured and knowledgeable. In the store, people like Brianna because she is not afraid to be in charge and give directions to others. In summary, Maria, the store's owner, is a leader with strengths in one domain who has the wisdom to hire personnel with strengths in other domains. Collectively, the combined strengths of Maria and her team allow them to have a very successful bridal shop.

VIA Institute on Character and Inventory of Strengths

At the same time the CliftonStrengths profile was gaining prominence, researchers at the VIA Institute on Character, led by Martin Seligman and Christopher Peterson, were engaged in a project to develop a framework for the field of positive psychology that defined and conceptualized character strengths. This classification focused on what is best in people rather than their weaknesses and problems. To develop the classification, they reviewed philosophical and spiritual literature in Confucianism, Buddhism, Hinduism, Judeo-Christianity, Ancient Greece, and Islam to determine whether there were commonalities that consistently emerged across cultures regarding virtues (Peterson & Park, 2009; Peterson & Seligman, 2004). From the review, they identified six universal core virtues—*wisdom, courage, humanity, justice, temperance*, and *transcendence*—around which Seligman and Peterson developed the VIA Classification of Character Strengths (see Table 6.3). The VIA Classification includes 24 strengths organized under these six basic virtues.

As illustrated in Table 6.3, the 24 character strengths identified in the VIA Classification are somewhat different from the strengths identified in Gallup's CliftonStrengths profile (see Table 6.1). For example, "forgiveness" and "gratitude," which are strengths in the VIA Classification, seem more encompassing and virtue oriented than "arranger" and "relator," which are strengths identified in the Gallup 34 Talent Themes. Furthermore, the strengths outlined by CliftonStrengths are more closely tied to the workplace and helping individuals perform better, while the VIA strengths are focused more directly on a person's character and how one can become more virtuous.

From the VIA perspective, character strengths are measured with the VIA Character Strengths Survey, a questionnaire designed to create a profile of your character strengths. It takes about 30 minutes to complete and is available free at www.viacharacter.org. After

TABLE 6.3 ■ VIA Classification of Character Strengths	
Classification	**Strengths**
WISDOM & KNOWLEDGE *Cognitive Strengths*	**1.** Creativity **2.** Curiosity **3.** Judgment **4.** Love of learning **5.** Perspective
COURAGE *Emotional Strengths*	**6.** Honesty **7.** Bravery **8.** Perseverance **9.** Zest
HUMANITY *Interpersonal Strengths*	**10.** Kindness **11.** Love **12.** Social intelligence
JUSTICE *Civic Strengths*	**13.** Fairness **14.** Leadership **15.** Teamwork
TEMPERANCE *Strengths Over Excess*	**16.** Forgiveness **17.** Humility **18.** Prudence **19.** Self-regulation
TRANSCENDENCE *Strengths About Meaning*	**20.** Appreciation of beauty and excellence **21.** Gratitude **22.** Hope **23.** Humor **24.** Spirituality

Source: Adapted from VIA Institute on Character. (2023). *The 24 character strengths.* https://www.viacharacter.org/character-strengths

completing the questionnaire, you will receive reports and feedback identifying your top five character strengths as well as a rank order of your scores on all 24 character strengths.

Centre of Applied Positive Psychology and the Strengths Profile Assessment

Based on the principles of positive psychology, researchers at the Centre of Applied Positive Psychology (CAPP) in the United Kingdom developed an approach to strengths that differs from the approaches used in Gallup's CliftonStrengths and the VIA Character Strengths

Survey. Rather than focusing exclusively on the identification of a specific number of strengths, CAPP researchers created a more dynamic model of strengths that emphasizes the changing nature of strengths (see Figure 6.2). They also examined different kinds of strengths and weaknesses. CAPP argued that strengths are more fluid than personality traits and can emerge over a lifetime through the different situations we experience.

From CAPP's perspective, strengths were conceptualized as "the things that we are good at and that give us energy when we are using them" (Linley & Dovey, 2012, p. 4). The three central elements of this definition became the criteria in CAPP's questionnaire (Strengths Profile) for assessing strengths: (1) performance—how good we are at doing something; (2) energy—how much vitality we get out of it; and (3) use—how often we are able to do it. Therefore, the Strengths Profile assesses 60 strengths in relation to three dimensions of energy, performance, and use. Based on an individual's combined scores across these dimensions, CAPP provides feedback that specifies the individual's realized strengths, unrealized strengths, learned behaviors, and weaknesses. It takes about 20 minutes to complete the Strengths Profile, which is available for a fee at www.strengthsprofile.com.

The CAPP strengths perspective is represented in the Strengths Profile 4M Model (see Figure 6.2). It is divided into quadrants labeled *realized strengths, unrealized strengths, learned behaviors*, and *weaknesses*. As you can see in Figure 6.2, each quadrant lists attributes based on the dimensions of performance, energy generation, and use. Each quadrant characterizes different individual attributes and how they can be put into use.

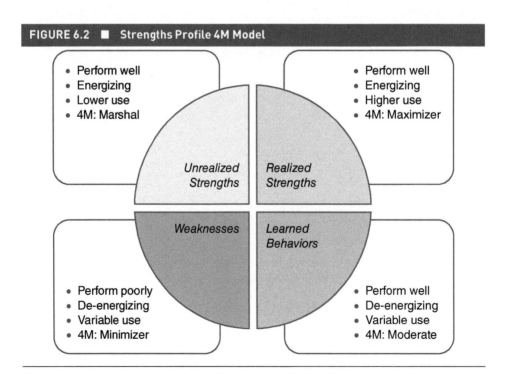

FIGURE 6.2 ■ Strengths Profile 4M Model

- Perform well
- Energizing
- Lower use
- 4M: Marshal

- Perform well
- Energizing
- Higher use
- 4M: Maximizer

Unrealized Strengths

Realized Strengths

Weaknesses

Learned Behaviors

- Perform poorly
- De-energizing
- Variable use
- 4M: Minimizer

- Perform well
- De-energizing
- Variable use
- 4M: Moderate

Source: Centre of Applied Positive Psychology (CAPP), Coventry, UK: CAPP Press.

Realized Strengths. **Realized strengths** are personal attributes that represent our strongest assets. We are energized when we use them because they help us perform well. For example, one of Rachel's strengths is *narrator*. She is a wonderful storyteller and uses these stories to convey her message and express her values. The model suggests that people should make every effort to *maximize* the use of these realized strengths, when it is appropriate to do so.

Unrealized Strengths. **Unrealized strengths** are personal attributes that are less visible. We feel good when we tap into unrealized strengths because they support our efforts and help us achieve our goals. One of Javier's unrealized strengths is *creativity.* He is good at coming up with new ideas and concepts, but more often than not he just goes with the flow and does not express his creativity. The model challenges individuals to become more aware of these strengths and to use them more frequently—thus to *marshal* them as a resource.

Learned Behaviors. **Learned behaviors** represent those ingrained things we have learned throughout our life experience. Although valuable, they do not excite or inspire us. For example, one of Sunil's learned behaviors is *driver*. As the eldest of five, he was driven to graduate from college. Highly self-motivated, Sunil constantly pushes himself to succeed in everything he does, often to the detriment of his own health. Many times Sunil doesn't recognize when his goals are unrealistic, and not succeeding in these leads to feelings of self-doubt and worthlessness. The model suggests limiting, or *moderating*, the use of these behaviors because they are draining and do not energize us.

Weaknesses. **Weaknesses** are our limiting attributes. They often drain our energy and result in poor performance. One of Kaylee's weaknesses is *unconditionality.* She finds it hard to genuinely accept people for who they are, without being judgmental about them and expecting them to change to meet her ideals. As a leader, she is constantly frustrated by others because they don't meet her standards in a number of areas. The model suggests that effective people try to *minimize* their weaknesses so as to make them irrelevant or of less concern.

Unlike the previous approaches to strengths, the CAPP model is prescriptive and pragmatic, suggesting ways people can be more effective by increasing their strengths and minimizing their weaknesses. The model recommends that individuals use their realized strengths when possible, but also intentionally look for ways to increase use of their unrealized strengths. In addition, the model recommends that we try to moderate our use of learned behaviors and minimize our use of our weaknesses. We are energized by our strengths (the top two quadrants), and we lose energy when we express our weaknesses and learned behaviors (the bottom two quadrants).

A good example of using the CAPP model is Tamaria, who has recently taken on the role of project manager for a team that is developing a new website for her company. Tamaria's *realized strength* is her focus on details and organization; her *weakness* is that she isn't as technically skilled as some of the members of her team. As a child, Tamaria struggled in school, and one of her coping mechanisms was to ask a lot of questions so that she thoroughly understood assignments. That has become a *learned behavior* she still employs. Finally, one of Tamaria's *unrealized strengths* is her ability to problem-solve and mediate in conflict.

TABLE 6.4 ■ Approaches to Identifying Strengths

Approach	Purpose	Number of Strengths
Strengths of Competence **Gallup CliftonStrengths**	To identify traits/strengths of peak performers	24
Strengths of Character **VIA Character Strengths Survey**	To identify virtuous/moral character strengths	36
Strengths Fully Realized **CAPP Strengths Profile**	To identify strengths and weaknesses to improve performance	60+

In order for her team to succeed, Tamaria will need to *maximize* the use of her realized strengths of organization and attention to detail in outlining the tasks and deadlines for the project. To deal with her weakness in technical skills, she will need to *minimize* her involvement in the technical development of the website, relying on other team members' technical skills. By employing her learned behavior of asking her team members a lot of questions about what they are doing and why, Tamaria will slow down the team's progress and frustrate team members who may feel she's micromanaging them. In this case, she will need to *moderate* her inquisitiveness, identifying the questions that she really needs answered or finding a way to research the questions on her own. Finally, working within a team can result in disparate opinions and ideas, and Tamaria will need to *marshal* her unrealized strength in mediation and problem solving so the team works smoothly together and meets deadlines while creating a dynamic website.

To summarize, researchers have developed three unique assessment tools to identify strengths: (1) Gallup CliftonStrengths, (2) VIA Character Strengths Survey, and (3) CAPP Strengths Profile (see Table 6.4). Each of these assessments provides a unique approach to strengths, and together they help to define and clarify the meaning of strengths. All of the questionnaires are accessible online, and they are worthwhile self-assessment tools for identifying and exploring your personal strengths.

STRENGTHS-BASED LEADERSHIP IN PRACTICE

How are strengths used in leadership? Although there are no established leadership theories on how to practice leadership from a strengths perspective, many useful applications can be made from strengths research in everyday leadership situations. In this section, we discuss several specific ways to incorporate strengths in your personal and work settings. The steps include (1) discovering your strengths, (2) developing your strengths, (3) addressing your weaknesses, (4) recognizing and engaging the strengths of others, and (5) fostering a positive strengths-based environment around you. Following these steps will not be a panacea for becoming a perfect strengths-based leader, but it will most certainly help you, as a leader, to maximize the use of your strengths as well as those of others.

Discovering Your Strengths

As discussed earlier in this chapter, strengths emerge from our basic personality traits. We all have unique personality traits, and therefore we all have unique strengths. No one is without strengths. As suggested by psychologist Howard Gardner (1997), extraordinary individuals are "distinguished less by their impressive 'raw power' than by their ability to identify their strengths and then exploit them" (p. 15). MacKie (2016) suggests that our leadership capability is enhanced when we are able to discover our fully utilized strengths, underutilized strengths, and weaknesses. The challenge we face is identifying our strengths and then employing them effectively in our leadership and personal lives.

Discovering your strengths requires you to concentrate on your positive attributes and those times when you feel inspired. To do so, you need to pay attention to your successes rather than focusing on your weaknesses or failures. For example, when are you at the top of your game? What is it about you or your interactions with others that contributes to that feeling? What accounts for your best performance? When things are going really well for you, what attributes are behind this success? Answering these questions will help you discover your strengths. They are the first and most important step in practicing strengths-based leadership.

There are several ways you can discover your strengths. First, you can complete one or more of the strengths questionnaires (e.g., CliftonStrengths, VIA Character Strengths Survey, and Strengths Profile) that are available online. Each questionnaire gives a unique snapshot of your greatest strengths. Second, you can fill out the Leadership Strengths Questionnaire that appears in this chapter. This questionnaire will provide you with specific feedback regarding your relative strengths in the areas of implementation, innovation, encouragement, analysis, and mediation. Third, you can complete the Reflected Best Self Exercise (RBSE) (Quinn et al., 2003), which can be found at https://positiveorgs.bus.umich.edu/cpo-tools/rbse/. The RBSE can assist you in identifying unrecognized and unexplored areas of strengths (Roberts et al., 2005). Fourth, you can complete the Reflection and Action Worksheet to discover your strengths. This exercise allows people you know to tell you what they see as your strengths when you are performing at your best. It is a powerful exercise you can use to become more aware of your strengths, and it may help you learn about some you have not recognized. Fifth, you can engage in a self-assessment of what you believe to be your strongest attributes. Intuitively, we all have a sense of what we do well, but taking the time to intentionally contemplate and consider our own strengths leads us to become more fully aware of our strengths.

This myriad of methods for discovering strengths will allow you to painlessly develop a definitive list of your major strengths. One of the benefits of knowing your strengths is the attainment of self-confidence, which has a positive correlation with goal accomplishment. Research by Lockman et al. (2023) of women leaders who participated in a strengths-based training program found that there was a huge gain—from 37% before to 95% after the training—in these leaders' confidence in being able to direct their talents and strengths to accomplish goals. This process is not only enlightening but also a vital first step in developing strengths-based leadership.

Developing Your Strengths

Once you have discovered your strengths, what do you do with that knowledge? How do you make use of this information to be a stronger leader? Developing your strengths is a multi-faceted process that involves several steps. First, you must acknowledge your strengths and be prepared to reveal them to others. As we discussed at the beginning of this chapter, it is often difficult to share our strengths with others because we may feel inhibited about openly and verbally acknowledging positive aspects of ourselves. But expressing our strengths is essential to making others aware of our leadership.

Telling others about our strengths is important because it lets them know how we can be most useful when working or collaborating together, clarifying the unique contributions we can make to others and their work. In essence, disclosing strengths declares "this is what I bring to the table, this is what I am best at, this is what I can do for you," and that allows others to know what they can expect from us. For example, when Tanya lets others know that her strongest quality is that she is an *achiever*, others learn that Tanya is not likely to allow mediocrity in their work. She is going to be demanding and push others toward excellence. Similarly, when Damian tells his staff that his strength is *listening*, his staff learns that Damian will have an open door and be willing to hear their problems or concerns. Putting our strengths out in the open makes us more transparent to others, and this helps others predict how we are going to act and how they might want to act toward us.

People use a variety of ways to reveal their strengths. Some people post their top five strengths on Facebook or LinkedIn, add them to their email signature, or list them on their résumé as a way of making their strengths more visible to others. Several unique examples of how some people share their strengths are illustrated in Figure 6.3. Disclosing our strengths to others does not need to be a daunting or embarrassing task, but can be done in a fairly simple, straightforward manner.

In addition to revealing your strengths, practice working consistently with others based on your strengths. For example, if your strength is being an *innovator*, find ways to be creative in your leadership. For example, do not hesitate to engage in activities like brainstorming or creating a vision for your group or organization. Similarly, if your strength is that you are *deliberative*, place yourself in a position where your strength in providing structure and order to a project can be put to use. Add your well-thought-out perspective by being vigilant and practical when people around you are coming up with ideas that have never been tested. The point is that you should lead from your strengths; your strengths represent the best you have to offer in influencing others. As Anderson (2004) from Gallup has suggested, "The best of the best invent ways of developing and applying strengths in areas where they want to improve, achieve, and become more effective" (p. 7).

FIGURE 6.3 ■ Examples of Ways to Express Strengths

Jane Doe, PhD
Consultant

STRENGTHS
Organized
Empathic
Problem Solver
Discussion Leader
Achiever

John Smith, CPA
Consultant

STRENGTHS
Adaptability
Positivity
Activator
Maximizer
Arranger

A good example of practicing strengths is Warren Buffett, one of the wealthiest people in the world. Buffett is known for his *patience, practicality*, and *trustfulness*, and he used these strengths to make Berkshire Hathaway, a multinational conglomerate, successful (Buckingham & Clifton, 2001). His patience led him to adopt the now famous "20-year perspective" on investing only in companies that he believed would be successful for the long term. His practicality explains how he selected specific companies whose services and products he understood (e.g., American Express). Finally, Buffett's trustfulness allowed him to select senior managers who were reputable and dependable to run his company. Clearly, Buffett recognized his strengths and carved out a role for himself that allowed him to practice these strengths every day (Buckingham & Clifton, 2001).

Addressing Your Weaknesses

Leaders must not only recognize and capitalize on their strengths, but also be able to identify their weaknesses and address them (MacKie, 2016). Harvard leadership professor John P. Kotter states, "Great leadership doesn't mean running away from reality . . . sharing difficulties can inspire people to take action that will make the situation better" (Blagg & Young, 2001).

While some of the models discussed here advocate minimizing your weaknesses, understanding them can allow you to work to improve them and to recognize situations where your weaknesses can be a liability to your leadership. For example, Lisa owns a small business developing e-commerce websites for companies that sell products online. Her strengths are her structural and process-oriented thinking and technical expertise. She is adept at anticipating and managing the many small details for creating a website that is secure and provides a good user experience. However, Lisa can't describe what she does in normal "layperson" terms for clients. In her proposals and presentations, she tends to lose clients with her use of technical language and minutiae of detail. In Lisa's case, it isn't enough that she minimize her weakness—she can't *not* talk to clients because that's how she generates new business. She must find a way to communicate better with her clients.

LEADERSHIP SNAPSHOT
STEVE JOBS, FOUNDER, APPLE INC.

By Matthew Yohe, CC BY-SA 3.0, https://commo
ns.wikimedia.org/w/index.php? curid=10584359

While Steve Jobs was undoubtedly brilliant, he didn't possess the technical abilities to be a computer genius. In fact, Jobs didn't know how to write computer code or program a computer. But he succeeded—twice—in building one of the most successful and profitable computer companies in the world.

Jobs had many notable strengths, including his creativity, team building, strategic vision, and influencing. He had intuitive vision, imagining products and applications of which no one else dared to dream. When he created Apple in 1976 with partner Steve Wozniak, he sought to create an attractive, simple, inexpensive computer marketed as the first home computer. Jobs micromanaged every detail of the computer's creation from its unique operating software to the color of its casing.

Jobs was an influencer, using his indomitable will and charisma to convince himself and others of almost anything. He believed rules were meant to be broken, and in 1984, Apple did just that, introducing a truly revolutionary product, the Macintosh. It used graphics, icons, a mouse, and the point-and-click technology that is still standard. It was innovative and influential.

But Jobs wasn't perfect. He could be confrontational, and this quality eventually resulted in him being booted out of his own company by Apple's board of directors.

Jobs moved on, using his visionary skills and passion for perfection to create NeXT Computer, recognized as a great product that never caught on with consumers.

Undaunted, Jobs branched out into movie animation by acquiring Pixar Animation Studios, bringing his vision, passion, and influencing skills to a new industry. Under his leadership, Pixar revolutionized movie animation and made Jobs a multibillionaire.

His old company, Apple, hadn't done so well. A decade after Jobs exited, Apple was nearly bankrupt. It decided to buy NeXT Computer and the services of Jobs as a consultant. But he would soon take over as CEO. His first move was to employ another of his strengths—focus. He took the two-dozen products Apple was producing—printers, computers, and software—and winnowed them down to only laptop and desktop computers for the professional and home consumer.

Jobs didn't stop there. Over the next 14 years, he dreamt up the iPod, the iPad, and the iPhone. By combining creativity, technology, and feats of engineering, Apple produced new devices that consumers hadn't even thought of or knew they needed. Jobs insisted these devices be intuitive and simple to use and oversaw every detail of design from creating specialized glass for the screens to determining the width of their metal casings.

In the end, Jobs's vision revolutionized seven industries: personal computers, animated movies, music, telephones, tablet computing, digital publishing, and retail stores. When he returned to Apple in 1997, he personally created the company's new ad campaign—"Think Different"—which was as much a statement of his own strengths as a leader as it was a mission statement for Apple.

After losing out on several possible projects, Lisa listened to the feedback of the clients when they said that what she was proposing was "too complicated." Lisa brought in a marketing professional, Julie, to help her develop and pitch proposals to clients. Julie understands enough of the technical parts of Lisa's work to be able to put it in easier-to-understand terms for potential clients. Julie is very strong in communication and social interactions, and Lisa is finding that by observing and working with Julie, she is learning to communicate more effectively with clients.

While making the most of our strengths is important for leaders, recognizing our weaknesses is also important in effective leadership. In the case of Lisa, she had to address her communication problems; there was no way around it. Working to improve on your weaknesses or using them as opportunities for others to contribute their strengths will improve your leadership.

Recognizing and Engaging the Strengths of Others

In addition to employing their own strengths, leaders need to recognize and engage the strengths of their followers. They need to determine what followers are good at doing and help them to do it. Educators who study group dynamics and the roles individuals play in effective groups often say "people do what they do best." What they mean by this is that individuals often become engaged and contribute positively to groups when they are allowed to do what they are good at and feel comfortable doing. Research has shown that when leaders help followers match their strengths with roles and tasks, followers make better use of their abilities (Gist & Mitchell, 1992), leading to better outcomes. In addition, collaboration between group members increases when the leader pairs members who have complementary strengths. This also benefits interactions within the group. In a group setting, being aware of members' strengths and capabilities is vital in the group's performance (van Woerkom et al., 2022). As you'll read in Chapter 8, "Working With Groups," people feel comfortable when they can contribute to the group from their strengths.

A good example of this is the Mary Kay cosmetic company. Mary Kay Ash was a skilled motivator and trainer, who founded her business with five products and a dream to inspire women to transform their lives by empowering women and putting them in control of their own futures (Mary Kay, n.d.). She established the company as a multilevel marketing enterprise specializing in direct sales, where each saleswoman could determine her own sales goals and commitment level. Saleswomen recruited and trained other saleswomen and supported one another in their work. Ash imparted to her salespeople that she imagined everyone wearing a sign that said, "Make me feel important," and made it part of everything she did. Ash connected a community of women who found confidence through encouragement; as a result, Mary Kay is now the sixth-largest network marketing company in the world, with more than $3.25 billion in wholesale volume in 2018 (DSN Staff, 2018).

How do leaders know what people are good at? Sometimes people are very up front and freely express their strengths. Mia, for example, often says when she joins a new work project, "I'm a good notetaker, so you can plan on me to be the record keeper for our meetings." Similarly, Josh often says on the first day of a roofing project, "I am pretty fast with the nail gun, so you might want me on the roof nailing shingles." Clearly, sometimes followers openly inform leaders of their strengths. When this occurs, it is important for leaders to acknowledge the strengths of these individuals if possible and assign them to roles in the work setting that capitalize on these strengths.

While recognizing strengths sounds simple, it is not uncommon for leaders to overlook followers' strengths. Oftentimes, the strengths of followers are not evident to leaders or even to the followers themselves. This becomes a challenging situation, because leaders need to ascertain followers' strengths from what they observe rather than what followers explicitly express to them. Cordelia was a struggling graduate student who was just plodding along, uncertain about her direction and goals. When she received an A++ on a challenging reaction paper, she became excited and was surprised to learn that her strength was *creativity*, particularly in writing. Cordelia and her instructor both became aware of her strengths in writing by the work she did on her assignment.

In another example, Juan is good with solving computer glitches in the office, suggesting his strengths lie in the area of *technology*. When he was assisting a staff member who was having a problem downloading a file from the web, he found that he liked the challenge of solving these problems. Or consider Ashley, who is a good worker, always present, and never oppositional. She is a wonderful team member whose strengths are *consistency*, *kindness*, and being *fun-loving*. She fosters the *esprit de corps* in the athletic center where she works. In each of these examples, an effective leader tries to identify the followers' strengths and then incorporate them into building a more productive team.

However, it is important to note that others' strengths may not always be directly recognizable. Followers may have strengths that are not observable because their situations don't allow for many facets of their overall abilities to emerge. Therefore, it is important to find opportunities outside followers' normal realm of duties or activities that will allow their strengths to emerge. For example, Jeff works on an assembly line at a golf cart manufacturer attaching seats to the chassis of golf carts. The position is very repetitive and structured, and Jeff, like the other assembly line employees, spends most of his workday at his station with limited interaction with other workers. However, with the blessing of his supervisor, Jeff recently organized a softball team made up of other plant workers to play in a local league. Jeff has recruited team members, arranged all the practices, communicated practice and game schedules to the team, organized the purchase of team uniforms, and promoted the team's games in the plant through flyers and the company newsletter. As a result, many individuals who work with Jeff have observed his strengths in *organization*, *inclusion*, and *communication*, which would not be observable through his day-to-day work on the assembly line.

As discussed earlier in this chapter, high-performing teams and work groups possess strengths in four domains: executing, influencing, relationship building, and strategic thinking (see Table 6.2). When leaders become aware of their followers' strengths as well as their own, they can use this information to design work groups that have individuals with strengths representing each of the domains. Knowing followers' unique strengths allows leaders to make work assignments that maximize each individual's contribution to the collective goals of the group (Rath & Conchie, 2008). If a leader is strong on executing and knows how to make new ideas come to fruition, but is not as strong in building relationships, the leader should identify followers with strengths in that area. Or if a leader has strengths in connecting with people and taking command, the leader can identify others who are strong in executing and strategic thinking. Knowledge of followers' strengths is a valuable tool to help leaders to build effective groups.

Fostering a Positive Strengths-Based Environment

A final way to practice strengths-based leadership is to create and promote a positive work environment in which people's strengths play an integral role. Multiple studies by researchers in positive organizational scholarship indicate that companies and organizations that create positive work environments have a positive physiological impact on employees and, in turn, this has an advantageous impact on their performance (Cameron, 2012; Dutton & Ragins, 2007). Similarly, research suggests that when employees have the opportunity to engage their strengths, they are more productive and more loyal, and their companies experience less turnover (Clifton & Harter, 2003). In short, people feel better and work better when the climate in which they work is positive.

In his book *Positive Leadership*, Cameron (2012) argues that leaders who want to create a positive work environment should attend to four areas: *climate, relationships, communication,* and *meaning.* To create a *positive climate,* leaders should foster among their employees virtues such as compassion, forgiveness, and gratitude. When these qualities are present, people feel encouraged and are more productive. Leaders can also promote celebrating people's strengths. Doing so helps people feel valued as individuals and respected for their contribution to the organization. To build *positive relationships,* leaders need to highlight individuals' positive images and strengths rather than their negative images and weaknesses. Acknowledging and building on people's strengths encourages others to do the same, and this results in the development of an environment where positive relationships flourish. To develop *positive communication,* leaders must be supportive, make more positive than negative statements, and be less negatively evaluative of others. Positive communication helps people feel connected and encourages them to capitalize on their strengths. Finally, leaders can foster *positive meaning* in their organizations by emphasizing the connection between employees' values and the long-term impact of their work. Employees who find meaning in their work and see it as valuable are more engaged and productive.

Fostering a positive strengths-based organizational environment is embraced by a multitude of organizations. For example, more than 500 colleges and universities have integrated dimensions of a strengths-based perspective into their student learning, faculty, and culture, including Azusa Pacific University, Baylor University, San José State University, Texas A&M University, Texas Tech University, University of Arkansas, and University of Minnesota. Among the many companies that have adopted strengths as a systematic program are Fortune 500 companies Best Buy, Chick-fil-A, Cisco, Coca-Cola, Facebook, Hilton, Microsoft, and Pfizer.

SUMMARY

Strengths-based leadership has been given much attention in recent years because researchers believe it can have a significant impact on the way leaders choose to lead and on the performance of followers. In this chapter, we explored people's strengths and how leaders can make use of these strengths to become more effective leaders. Although we all have strengths, they often go unrecognized and unused. Understanding strengths can make one a better leader.

A strength is defined as an attribute or quality of an individual that accounts for successful performance. In simple terms, a strength is what we do when we are performing at our best. Strengths often begin with our inborn talents and can be further developed through knowledge, skills, and practice. The equation for developing a strength is *talent times investment* (Rath, 2007).

Strengths-based leadership has come to the forefront in recent years as a result of two research developments. First, spearheaded by Donald O. Clifton, Gallup interviewed millions of people about their strengths and what made them good at what they did. From interviews, Gallup extracted 34 themes that best explained excellent performance. Second, academic scholars created a new field called positive psychology that focused less on the disease model and more on the study of healthy people and what accounted for their well-being. Prominent in this new field is the study of people's positive characteristics—their strengths. Taken together, research at Gallup and in positive psychology explains the rising popularity of strengths-based leadership.

People's strengths have been measured in different ways. The benchmark is Gallup's *CliftonStrengths*, which is a 177-item questionnaire that identifies an individual's five strongest talents across four domains (i.e., executing, influencing, relationship building, and strategic thinking). Strengths can also be measured using the *VIA Character Strengths Survey*, which provides an individual's top five character strengths as well as a rank order of their scores on 24 virtue-derived character strengths. A third measure, CAPP's *Strengths Profile*, assesses 60 strengths in relationship to an individual's energy, performance, and use, and provides feedback on an individual's realized strengths, unrealized strengths, learned behaviors, and weaknesses.

Although there are no established theories about the practice of strengths-based leadership, there are several straightforward ways for individuals to incorporate strengths into their leadership. First, leaders need to discover their own strengths. They can do this through completing questionnaires and other self-assessment activities. The goal is to develop a definitive list of one's strengths. Second, leaders need to be prepared to acknowledge their strengths and reveal them to others. Although we may feel inhibited about disclosing our strengths to others, it is essential for making others aware of our capabilities. We need to make ourselves transparent to others and lead from our strengths. Third, leaders must make a concerted effort to recognize and engage the strengths of others. Because "people do what they do best," leaders have an obligation to help uncover others' strengths and then integrate these strengths into building more productive teams. Finally, leaders can practice strengths-based leadership by fostering work environments in which people's strengths play an integral role. Leaders can do this by creating for their followers a positive climate, positive relationships, positive communication, and positive meaning (Cameron, 2012). Research shows that people feel better and work better when the climate in which they work is positive.

To summarize, strengths-based leadership is a new area of research that offers a unique approach to becoming a more effective leader. Not a panacea, strengths concepts provide an innovative and valuable perspective to add to our leadership toolbox.

KEY TERMS

Gallup

learned behaviors

positive psychology

realized strengths

strengths

themes of human talent

unrealized strengths

weaknesses

6.1 Case Study—Ready to Be CEO?

Christine Jorgens was shocked when the board of Begin the Future Foundation, the non-profit organization she worked for, asked her to apply for the position of CEO of the organization. For 40 years, Begin the Future Foundation had provided programs in a nine-county region to help children living in poverty in urban and rural areas succeed in school and life, and the CEO's job was a big one.

Christine had never aspired to be a CEO. She had grown up on a small farm in a rural area, one of seven children in a family that struggled financially. In high school, she worked at a local restaurant, first as a dishwasher and then as a waitress, continuing to work there while she attended college studying social work.

In her senior year of college, she landed an internship at Begin the Future Foundation overseeing an after-school program for middle school students. Christine ended up working for Begin the Future Foundation for 12 more years, with many of her colleagues joking that she was "the intern who never left." Friendly and approachable, she eagerly took on whatever work the organization had for her to do. She worked as a receptionist, became a grant writer, helped out in public relations and marketing, and then was given a position developing and initiating new programs and working with donors to fund those programs.

She thrived at program development, finding ways to implement community resources that were often overlooked. Her program, Study Buddies, paired up volunteer tutors from a local college with children to meet three times a week for a half-hour of tutoring followed by a half-hour of recreation and games. Christine also initiated Girl Power, a program allowing middle school girls to spend an afternoon each week shadowing a local female professional or businesswoman who worked in a career that they were interested in pursuing.

Christine's enthusiasm was contagious, especially with donors. Her programs were all successfully funded, and potential donors often approached Christine with ideas they had for new initiatives that they were willing to fund.

But despite all her successes, Christine wasn't sure she was CEO material. She saw herself as a local girl who had lucked into some great opportunities. The board had been clear about what credentials a new CEO must have: strategic thinking, experience running a nonprofit organization, ability to work with people on all levels of society from the poorest to the richest, ability to manage people, and a commitment to the organization's mission of helping kids escape poverty. Christine didn't have direct experience overseeing a nonprofit and felt she needed more experience in the day-to-day management of the organization.

At the suggestion of the board members, she took a strengths assessment and learned her strengths were in strategic planning, relationship building, creativity, compassion, and influencing. In addition, the board members pointed out that she had a deep knowledge and commitment to the organization and the children they served. Despite Christine's hesitancy, the board was convinced Christine was the right candidate.

Questions

1. Strengths are considered inborn traits that can be enhanced with experience. What experiences in Christine's background helped her develop her strengths?

2. Of the strengths identified by the assessment, which were directly observable in Christine's work? Were there any that were not?

3. Christine admitted having some weaknesses, especially in day-to-day management of the organization. Which of her strengths could she put into use to help her deal with that, and how?

4. What strengths should Christine seek from others that would complement her own and fill some gaps?

6.2 Case Study—The Strength to Stand Out

Sociologist Dr. Brené Brown is a highly recognized thought leader, acclaimed best-selling author, teacher, researcher, and sought-after speaker who has built a small empire and a very large following around the study of such difficult topics as shame, vulnerability, courage, and empathy.

A Texan who prefers "shit kickers" (cowboy boots), jeans, and clogs to business attire, Brené is a professor of sociology at the University of Houston. She has authored eight number-one *New York Times* best-selling books. Her TED Talk, "The Power of Vulnerability," is one of the top five most-accessed TED Talks ever with more than 61 million views. In 2019, she hosted her first Netflix special, *Brené Brown: The Call to Courage* (Brown, 2023a).

Though Brené is more likely to bill herself as simply a "research professor," she is also an entrepreneur, CEO, mother, and wife. She founded The Daring Way, a training and certification program for helping professionals who want to facilitate her work on vulnerability, courage, shame, and empathy in their practices.

Brené's path to where she is today began when she was a child. Cassandra Brené Brown's family moved several times—from Houston to New Orleans to Houston to Washington, DC, and back to Houston. Fitting in and feeling a sense of belonging was not easy for her. After moving to New Orleans, Brown's parents changed neighborhoods and enrolled her in a Catholic school despite their own Episcopal faith. Later, when Brené was a teenager, her family returned to Houston, and she was once again the new kid in school. Her efforts to fit in fell short, and that feeling of belonging remained elusive. Deepening Brené's feelings of separateness was the disintegration of her parents' marriage during her high school years, shaking the only real sense of belonging she had.

Despite this, Brené was a plucky, curious young girl who grew to be tenacious and outspoken. Reflecting back, she credits these formative years in helping shape her later success.

"I owed my career to not belonging. First as a child, then as a teenager. I found my primary coping mechanism for not belonging in studying people. I was a seeker of pattern and connection. I knew if I could recognize patterns in people's behaviors and connect those patterns to what people were feeling and doing, I could find my way," she said. "I used my pattern recognition skills to anticipate what people wanted, what they thought, or what they were doing. I learned how to say the right thing or show up the right way. I became an expert fitter-in, a chameleon" (Brown, 2017, p. 16).

The years after high school were unsettled years for Brené; she hitchhiked across Europe, bartended, and waitressed, gaining a variety of life experiences and admittedly engaging in an array of self-destructive behaviors. After having dropped out of college earlier, she graduated at 29 at the top of her class with a bachelor's degree in social work from the University of Texas at Austin and immediately entered graduate school at the University of Houston where she completed both a master's and doctoral program.

Through her studies, Brené found a passion for social work and discovered the concept of qualitative research. She became interested in and trained in a methodology known as *grounded theory*, which starts with a topic (rather than a theory) from which, through the process of collecting and analyzing data based on discussions with the study participants, patterns and theories emerge. The grounded theory model fit Brené's gift for storytelling and her ability to connect patterns in her subjects through the listening and observation skills she developed as coping mechanisms in her teens. "I fell in love with the richness and depth of qualitative research," she said. "Storytelling is my DNA, and I couldn't resist the idea of research as storycatching. Stories are data with a soul and no methodology honors that more than grounded theory" (Brown, 2023b).

Unfortunately, the grounded theory model is a departure from traditional academic research, which tends to place higher value on the cleaner, more measurable outcomes of quantitative research. Despite being discouraged by other academics and counseled to not use the methodology for her doctoral dissertation, Brené pushed forward. And like the research method she espouses, Brené allowed the stories emerging from the data to shape her explorations, and she began to study the emotion of shame.

"I didn't sign on to study shame—one of the most (if not the most) complex and multifaceted emotions that we experience. A topic that not only took me six years to understand, but an emotion that is so powerful that the mere mention of the word 'shame' triggers discomfort and avoidance in people," she said. "I innocently started with an interest in learning more about the anatomy of connection. . . . Because the research participants had the courage to share their stories, experiences, and wisdom, I forged a path that defined my career and my life" (Brown, 2023b).

As with her choice of research methodology, Brené was discouraged from studying shame as a topic. But she prevailed, trusting her instincts and the path the data opened to her. Her research would soon extend to other, equally difficult emotions: vulnerability, courage, and belonging. She was willing to study areas that were often difficult to define, very personal, and sometimes painful, not only for her study subjects, but often for herself.

After getting a PhD, Brené accepted a professorship with the University of Houston, teaching and continuing her research. She was often asked by her shame study participants to share her findings. In academia, research findings are usually released as peer-reviewed articles in academic journals. Brené wanted to make her work more widely available and decided to publish it in a more mainstream format. Knowing it would be difficult to balance this ambition with her academic career, she tendered her resignation to the university. When the dean of her department was unwilling to accept Brené's resignation, she then proposed working part-time—which also was rejected as there was no precedent at the university for that type of arrangement. Brené stood firm, ultimately winning the blessing of the dean, the provost, and the university's president. She borrowed money to self-publish her first book, *Women and Shame: Reaching Out, Speaking Truths and Building Connection*, in 2004. The book sold well enough that it attracted a well-known publisher who republished it, launching Brené's career as an author.

Brené sums up her journey in her 2017 book *Braving the Wilderness*: "Was living lock-step really how I wanted to spend my life? No. When I was told I couldn't do a qualitative dissertation, I did it anyway. When they tried to convince me not to study shame, I did it anyway. When they told me I couldn't be a professor and write books that people might actually want to read, I did it anyway" (Brown, 2017, p. 18).

Brené's publishing success created speaking opportunities where her engaging, self-reflective personality and willingness to share her own stories in a brutally (yet warmly) honest way make her highly relatable to others. With her Texas-style no-nonsense wit, she weaves humor and lightness with topics most people find uncomfortable. She is a sought-after speaker, trainer, and facilitator to the tune of $100,000 per engagement. Her work translates to many different fields and encompasses a wide swath of clients including C-suite executives, educators, engineers, mental health professionals, and parents. *Time* magazine even called Brené "one of the leading brainiacs on feelings," adding that "what Brown offers that others don't is a nerd's capacity for qualitative data and grounded theory coupled with enough warmth and humor that she moves people rather than merely training them" (Luscombe, 2018).

As her success has grown, Brené has maintained the down-to-earth authenticity of a woman who knows who she is and presents herself exactly as she is—cuss words and all. She believes strongly in her work and has the willingness and courage to practice it in everyday living, even when it is uncomfortable and requires her to look closely at her own behaviors and responses. Brené has also bumped up against many who challenge her and attempt to corral her into "fitting in" with their ideals of who she should be and what she should discuss. She has been asked by event leaders to dress differently or pare back her discussions to suit the perspective of their audience. She's had business groups ask her not to bring up "faith" and religious groups concerned that she might use cuss words and offend the audience. She opts, instead, to remain true to who she is.

"I can't go on that stage and talk about authenticity and courage when I don't feel authentic or brave. I physically can't do it," she said. "I'm not here so my business-self can talk to their business-selves. I'm here to talk from my heart to their hearts. This is who I am" (Brown, 2017, p. 24).

Exercises/Questions

Brené Brown has achieved considerable success and a loyal following by playing to her own strengths. See Brené in action and acquaint yourself further with her by viewing her two TED Talks:

The Power of Vulnerability (www.ted.com/talks/brene_brown_on_vulnerability)
Listening to Shame (www.ted.com/talks/brene_brown_listening_to_shame)

1. Based on the case study narrative and what you learned about Brené and her work from the TED Talk videos:

   a. Which strengths listed in Table 6.1 do you think are descriptive of Brené Brown? Explain your answer.

   b. Which of the four domains of leadership strengths found in Table 6.2 (executing, influencing, relationship building, or strategic thinking) do you think best apply to Brené? Which domain do you believe is her strongest? Explain.

2. Based on the case study narrative and what you learned about Brené and her work from the TED Talk videos:

   a. Which of the VIA character strengths (Table 6.3) would you attribute to Brené Brown?

   b. On a scale from 1 (*low*) to 5 (*high*), how would you rate Brené in each classification of the VIA (Table 6.3)? Explain your ratings.

3. In applying the CAPP perspective, strengths are defined as "the things that we are good at and that give us energy when we are using them." Based on the definitions for the CAPP categories:

   a. Identify and list Brené Brown's "realized strengths."

   b. What would you consider to be Brené's "unrealized strengths"?

   c. Can you identify any "learned behaviors" as defined by this model?

   d. Can you identify any "weaknesses" as defined by this model?

Application

6.3 Leadership Strengths Questionnaire

Purpose

1. To develop an understanding of your leadership strengths
2. To rank your strengths in selected areas of performance

Directions

1. Please answer the following statements in terms of whether the statement describes *what you are like.*
2. For each of the statements, circle the number that indicates the degree to which *you feel the statement is like you.*

Statements	Very Much Unlike Me	Unlike Me	Neutral	Like Me	Very Much Like Me
1. I am an energetic participant when working with others.	1	2	3	4	5
2. Brainstorming is one of my strengths.	1	2	3	4	5
3. I am good at encouraging coworkers when they feel frustrated about their work.	1	2	3	4	5
4. I want to know "why" we are doing what we are doing.	1	2	3	4	5
5. I look for common ground in opposing opinions of others.	1	2	3	4	5
6. I enjoy implementing the details of projects.	1	2	3	4	5

Statements	Very Much Unlike Me	Unlike Me	Neutral	Like Me	Very Much Like Me
7. I like to explore creative approaches to problems.	1	2	3	4	5
8. I go out of my way to help others feel good about their accomplishments.	1	2	3	4	5
9. Examining complex problems or issues is one of my strengths.	1	2	3	4	5
10. I am a mediator in conflict situations.	1	2	3	4	5
11. I stick with the task until the work is completed.	1	2	3	4	5
12. I can initiate change, if it is needed, when working with others.	1	2	3	4	5
13. I show concern for the personal well-being of others.	1	2	3	4	5
14. I like to consider various options for doing things.	1	2	3	4	5
15. I am effective communicating with people who are inflexible.	1	2	3	4	5
16. I try to follow through with ideas so that the work gets done.	1	2	3	4	5
17. I enjoy creating a vision for a work-related project.	1	2	3	4	5

Statements	Very Much Unlike Me	Unlike Me	Neutral	Like Me	Very Much Like Me
18. I am the "glue" that helps hold the group together.	1	2	3	4	5
19. I like exploring the details of a problem before trying to solve it.	1	2	3	4	5
20. I can draw the best out of people with diverse opinions.	1	2	3	4	5
21. I like making to-do lists so that the work gets completed.	1	2	3	4	5
22. I can "think outside of the box."	1	2	3	4	5
23. Encouraging others comes easily for me.	1	2	3	4	5
24. I like thinking things through before engaging in work projects.	1	2	3	4	5
25. I am good at finding common ground when a conflict is present.	1	2	3	4	5
26. I enjoy scheduling and coordinating activities so the work is completed.	1	2	3	4	5
27. I am good at developing new ideas for others to consider.	1	2	3	4	5
28. I am good at encouraging others to participate on projects.	1	2	3	4	5

Statements	Very Much Unlike Me	Unlike Me	Neutral	Like Me	Very Much Like Me
29. I like to explore problems from many different perspectives.	1	2	3	4	5
30. I am effective at helping coworkers reach consensus.	1	2	3	4	5

Scoring

1. Sum the responses on items 1, 6, 11, 16, 21, and 26 (implementer score).
2. Sum the responses on items 2, 7, 12, 17, 22, and 27 (innovator score).
3. Sum the responses on items 3, 8, 13, 18, 23, and 28 (encourager score).
4. Sum the responses on items 4, 9, 14, 19, 24, and 29 (analyzer score).
5. Sum the responses on items 5, 10, 15, 20, 25, and 30 (mediator score).

Total Scores:

Implementer: _____

Innovator: _____

Encourager: _____

Analyzer: _____

Mediator: _____

Scoring Interpretation

The Leadership Strengths Questionnaire is designed to measure your strengths in the areas of implementation, innovation, encouragement, analysis, and mediation. By assessing the rank order of your scores, you can determine the areas in which you have the greatest strengths and the areas in which you are weaker. A high score in a certain area indicates where you are strong; a low score shows where you are weak. As discussed in this chapter, every person has multiple strengths. In addition to the strengths revealed by the Leadership Strengths Questionnaire, you may wish to complete other strengths assessments to obtain a more complete picture of all of your strengths.

If your score is 26–30, you are in the very high range.

If your score is 21–25, you are in the high range.

If your score is 16–20, you are in the moderate range.

If your score is 11–15, you are in the low range.

If your score is 6–10, you are in the very low range.

Application

6.4 Observational Exercise—Strengths

Purpose

1. To learn to recognize people's strengths
2. To gain an understanding of the role of strengths in the leadership process

Directions

1. In this exercise, your task is to observe a leader *in action*. The leader can be a teacher, a supervisor, a coach, a manager, or anyone who has a position that involves leadership.
2. Based on your observations of the leader in action, identify areas in which the leader has strengths and areas in which the followers have strengths.

Questions

1. Based on the virtue-based strengths listed in Table 6.3, identify two strengths you observed the leader exhibit. How did these strengths affect their followers?

2. Discuss what strengths group members appeared to exhibit and how these strengths may complement or distract from the leader's leadership.

3. Do you think the followers in this situation would feel comfortable expressing their own strengths to others? Discuss.

4. If you were coaching the leader in this situation, what specific things could they do to create a positive environment where the expression of people's strengths was welcomed?

Application

6.5 Reflection and Action Worksheet—Strengths

Reflection

1. For this exercise, you are being asked to interview several people you know about your strengths. Instructions:

   • First, identify three people (e.g., friends, coworkers, colleagues, family members) from whom you feel comfortable asking for feedback about yourself.

   • Second, ask each of these individuals to do the following:

      a. Think of a time or situation when they saw you at your best

      b. Tell a brief story about what you were doing

      c. Describe why they thought you were performing well in this situation

      d. Based on this story, describe what unique benefits you offered others in this situation

   • Third, from the answers the individuals gave, identify two or three recurring themes. These themes represent your strengths.

2. What is your reaction to what others (in Step 1) have identified as your strengths? Are the strengths others identified about you consistent with your own perceptions of your strengths? In what way are they consistent with your scores on the Leadership Strengths Questionnaire?

3. This chapter suggests that it is important for leaders to reveal their strengths to others. As a leader, how do you feel about disclosing your strengths to others? How do you react when others express their strengths to you?

Action

1. Based on the questionnaire in this chapter and your own insights, create a business card for yourself that lists your five signature strengths.

2. Of the four domains of leadership strengths (see Table 6.2), which are your strongest? Describe how you could solicit support from followers to complement these areas of strength.

3. Imagine you are the leader of a classroom group required to do a semester-long service-learning project. Identify and discuss specific things you could do to create a positive climate, positive relationships, positive communication, and positive meaning.

7 CREATING A VISION

INTRODUCTION

An effective leader creates compelling visions that guide people's behavior. In the context of leadership, a vision is a mental model of an ideal future state. It offers a picture of what could be. Visions imply change and can challenge people to reach a higher standard of excellence. At the same time, a vision is like a guiding philosophy that provides people with meaning and purpose. It is important here to distinguish between *vision* and *mission*, terms that are sometimes used interchangeably. A vision is *a mental model* of an ideal future state; it can be generated by an individual leader or crafted by a team working together. A mission is *how to get there.* It is what people do in order to achieve the vision. For example, a company's mission statement may describe what it is currently doing—improving customer satisfaction, developing new products, increasing its use of renewable energy sources—in order to become a global leader in a particular industry (which is its vision).

A leader's challenge is to develop a long-term vision that organizational members can share, of the future they seek to create together. Peter Senge (1990) suggests that leaders sometimes carry with them "entrenched mental models" that limit their ability to see new possibilities in their environments. These could be assumptions about the nature of people, organizational politics, attitudes toward risk-taking, or any number of fixed ideas. For organizations to grow and flourish, leaders need to be able to change and to learn from their followers, their experiences, and the external environment.

In developing a vision, a leader is able to visualize positive outcomes in the future and communicate these to others. Ideally, the leader and the members of a group or an organization share the vision. Although this picture of a possible future may not always be crystal clear, the vision itself plays a major role in how the leader influences others and how others react to their leadership.

For the past 30 years, vision has been a major topic in writings on leadership. Vision plays a prominent role in training and development literature. For example, Covey (1991) suggested that vision is one of seven habits of highly effective people. He argued that effective people "begin with the end in mind" (p. 42); that they have a deep understanding of their goals, values, and mission in life; and that this understanding is the basis for everything they do. Kouzes and Posner (2003), whose Leadership Practices Inventory is a widely used leadership assessment instrument, identified vision as one of the five practices of exemplary leadership. Clearly, vision has been an important aspect of leadership training and development in recent years.

Vision also plays a central role in many of the common theories of leadership (Zaccaro & Banks, 2001). For example, in transformational leadership theory, vision is identified as one of the four major factors that account for extraordinary leadership performance (Bass & Avolio, 1994). In charismatic leadership theories, vision is highlighted as a key to organizational change (Conger & Kanungo, 1998; House, 1977). Charismatic leaders create change by linking their vision and its values to the self-concept of followers. For example, through her charisma, Mother Teresa linked her vision of serving poor and disenfranchised people to her followers' beliefs in personal commitment and self-sacrifice. Some theories are actually titled visionary leadership theories (see Nanus, 1992; Sashkin, 1988, 2004) because vision is their defining characteristic of leadership.

To better understand the role of vision in effective leadership, this chapter will address the following questions: *What are the characteristics of a vision? How is a vision articulated?* and *How is a vision implemented?* In our discussion of these questions, we will focus on how you can develop a workable vision for whatever context you find yourself in as a leader.

VISION EXPLAINED

Given that it is essential for a leader to have a vision, how are visions formed? What are the main characteristics of a vision? Research on visionary leadership suggests that visions have five characteristics: a picture, a change, values, a map, and a challenge (Nanus, 1992; Zaccaro & Banks, 2001).

A Picture

A vision creates a **picture** of a future that is better than the **status quo**. It is an idea about the future that requires an act of faith by followers. Visions paint an ideal image of where a group or an organization should be going. It may be an image of a situation that is more exciting, more affirming, or more inspiring. As a rule, these mental images are of a time and place where people are working productively to achieve a common goal. Although it is easier for followers to comprehend a detailed vision, a leader's vision is not always fully developed. Sometimes a leader's vision provides only a general direction to followers or gives limited guidance to them. At other times, a leader may have only a bare-bones notion of where they are leading others; the final picture may not emerge for a number of years. Nevertheless, when a leader is able to paint a picture of the future that is attractive and inspiring, it can have significant impact on their ability to lead others effectively. Martin Luther King Jr.'s "I Have a Dream" speech, given during the March on Washington in 1963, is the epitome of an ideal future worth striving for: "I have a dream that one day this nation will rise up and live out the true meaning of its creed: 'We hold these truths to be self-evident, that all men are created equal.'"

A Change

Another characteristic of a vision is that it represents a **change** in the status quo and moves an organization or a system toward something more positive in the future. A vision points the way to new ways of doing things that are better than how things were done in the past. It takes the best features of a prior system and strengthens them in the pursuit of a new goal.

Changes can occur in many forms: rules, procedures, goals, values, or rituals, to name a few. Because visions imply change, it is not uncommon for a leader to experience resistance to the articulated vision. Some leaders are even accused of "stirring the pot" when promoting visionary changes. Usually, though, visions are compelling and inspire others to set aside old ways of doing things and to become part of the positive changes suggested by a leader's vision.

For example, at age 15, Greta Thunberg went on a "school strike" to bring attention to the issue of climate change. Instead of attending school each day, Thunberg stood outside the Swedish Parliament holding a sign and calling for leaders to initiate action on climate change. She posted what she was doing on social media, and it soon went viral. She spoke in front of political leaders and assemblies, publicly criticizing them for their failure to address the climate change crisis, recordings of which were seen by millions of people around the globe. Awareness of her efforts spurred other students around the globe to engage in similar protests in their communities, which became a student strike movement called Fridays For Future. In 2019, more than 7 million students from 1,600 cities in 125 countries walked out of school to protest climate change. Thunberg's efforts have brought an aroused awareness of the problem and leaders' inaction across the globe.

Values

A third characteristic of a vision is that it is about *values*, or the ideas, beliefs, and modes of action that people find worthwhile or desirable. To advocate change within a group or an organization requires an understanding of one's own values, the values of others, and the values of the organization. Visions are about changes in those values. For example, if a leader creates a vision that emphasizes that everyone in the company is important, the dominant value being expressed is human dignity. Similarly, if a leader develops a vision that suggests that everyone in the company is equal, the dominant value being expressed is fairness and justice. Visions are grounded in values. They advocate a positive change and movement toward some new set of ideals. In so doing, they must address values.

For example, the city leaders of Kalamazoo, Michigan, began offering benefits to the same-sex domestic partners of its employees in 2004. Five years later, voters in the city approved including sexual orientation and gender identity expression in the city's nondiscrimination ordinance. Both of these are evidence of the community's values of equality and nondiscrimination. So 12 years later, when Southwest Michigan First, the organization that oversees economic development for the area, hired a former state representative with a record of promoting anti-LGBTQ+ efforts to be its CEO, there was a swift, negative reaction by Kalamazoo's elected officials and key community leaders. The city commission and the area's colleges and universities, nonprofit foundations, and several large employers pulled their support for the organization. As a result, the new CEO resigned after a week, and Southwest Michigan First has undergone an extensive evaluation of its diversity, equity, and inclusion policies.

LEADERSHIP SNAPSHOT
INNA BRAVERMAN, FOUNDER AND CEO OF ECO WAVE POWER

Randy Shropshire / Stringer/ via Getty images

When a catastrophic accident and explosion occurred at the Chernobyl nuclear power reactor near her hometown of Cherkasy, Ukraine, causing the largest nuclear disaster in history, Inna Braverman was just 2 weeks old, but that event was pivotal in determining her future.

The accident and its resulting fire released large quantities of radioactive material into the air for 10 days, affecting the health of hundreds of thousands of people who were exposed to the radiation, including Inna.

"My mother found me lifeless in my crib. I suffered respiratory arrest and was clinically dead. Fortunately, my mother, who is a nurse, gave me mouth-to-mouth resuscitation, which saved my life," Braverman said. "My family constantly talked about how special it was that I was given a second chance in life, so I grew up with a strong sense of purpose. My dream was to do something meaningful for the world" (Mathias, 2022; "Queen of the Waves," 2020).

Her family was evacuated from their home and relocated to Acre, Israel, a city on the Mediterranean Sea, where Inna grew up watching waves breaking on the shore, studying the ebb and flow with great interest. After graduating from the University of Haifa with a bachelor's degree in political science and government, her first job was as an English–Hebrew translator at a renewable energy company, which sparked a new passion in her.

"As a little girl, I was impressed by the sea waves," she said. "I wanted to produce energy from the waves. However, no company had been able to make it a reality. I researched day and night to see why wave energy companies had failed."

At the time, wave energy systems were very expensive and complicated to install—most were fixed installations several miles offshore and required ships, divers, and underwater cabling and mooring. The existing wave energy equipment was often exposed to wave heights of 20 meters and higher, which it could not withstand, causing it to break down after a short time. There was also concern about the stations' environmental impact as they were moored to the ocean floor, disturbing the marine environment.

As much as two thirds of the world's population live along coastlines, and according to the World Energy Council, ocean waves can deliver double the amount of electricity needed on the planet today ("Queen of the Waves," 2020).

Even though she had no training in or knowledge of engineering, Inna developed her own ideas for creating wave energy, but without connections or funding, she put the ideas aside as unrealistic. But when she met real estate entrepreneur David Leb, she discovered they both had desired to fight climate change through the renewable, clean source of wave energy and wanted to eliminate the problems hindering the commercialization of that form of power generation. The two formed Eco Wave Power (EWP) in 2011 to make Inna's ideas a reality.

EWP turns water into electricity using uniquely shaped floating devices, which are attached to man-made structures, such as jetties or piers, and rise and fall with the waves' up-and-down motion and changes in water levels. This motion is then transmitted to power stations on land, which convert the energy into fluid pressure used to spin a generator, producing electricity.

Because most of EWP's system is located on land, it is more cost-effective to construct, operate, and maintain than offshore wave energy systems. In addition, the company has developed and patented unique storm protection mechanisms for their system.

"We fix everything on existing marine structures. This way we can avoid the huge costs associated with power transmission, which is one of the areas where offshore systems have failed in the past," she explained ("Queen of the Waves," 2020).

In April 2012, Eco Wave Power tested its technology on two breakwaters in the Black Sea, which is known for its severely stormy weather. The tests proved successful, and EWP installed its first off-grid power station in Israel's Jaffa Port in 2014. The company's first grid-connected commercial project was installed in Gibraltar in 2016 and provides 15% of Gibraltar's electrical capacity. The company now has operating power plants in Gibraltar, China, India, Chile, Mexico, and Israel and has several installations planned in Spain, Portugal, Turkey, Greece, and Los Angeles, California.

Eco Wave Power's innovations have gained worldwide recognition, being recognized as a "Pioneering Technology" by Israel's Ministry of Energy and as an "Efficient Solution" by the Solar Impulse Foundation. The company received the United Nations "Climate Action Award" in 2019 (United Nations Climate Change, 2019) and began trading on the NASDAQ stock exchange the same year, attracting many large institutional investors. For her groundbreaking work in clean energy, Braverman has received many accolades including being featured on MSN's list of the "30 most influential women of the 21st century" alongside Michelle Obama and Oprah Winfrey; included in the *Forbes* "30 Under 30" list in the energy category; and named one of BBC's "100 Women" for her groundbreaking work in clean energy. Braverman has become a prominent voice for renewable energy and climate change advocacy, becoming a sought-after speaker who passionately advocates for the adoption of sustainable energy solutions and the mitigation of climate change.

"Believe in yourself; if you have a great idea and passion—go for it," she advised. "Passion is the greatest source of renewable energy" (Paz-Frankel, 2017).

Another, more positive example illustrates the centrality of values in visionary leadership. Chris Jones was a new football coach at a high school in a small rural community in the Midwest. When Jones started coaching, there were barely enough players to fill the roster. His vision was to have a strong football program that students liked and that instilled pride in the parents and school community. He valued good physical conditioning, self-discipline, skills in all aspects of the game, esprit de corps, and an element of fun throughout the process. In essence, he wanted a top-notch, high-quality football program.

Over a period of five years, the number of players coming out for football grew from 15 to 95. Parents wanted their kids to go out for football because Jones was such a good coach. Players said they liked the team because Coach Jones treated them as individuals. He was very fair with everyone. He was tough about discipline but also liked to have fun. Practices were always a challenge but seldom dull or monotonous. Because of his program, parents formed their own booster club to support team dinners and other special team activities.

Although Coach Jones's teams did not always win, his players learned lessons in football that were meaningful and long lasting. Coach Jones was an effective coach whose vision promoted individual growth, competence, camaraderie, and community. He had a vision about developing a program around these strong values, and he was able to bring his vision to fruition.

A Map

A vision provides a **map**—a laid-out path to follow—that gives direction so followers know when they are on track and when they have slipped off course. People often feel a sense of certainty and calmness in knowing they are on the right course, and a vision provides this assurance. It is also comforting for people to know they have a map to direct them toward their short- and long-term goals. One person who does this effectively is Stephen Ritz, an educator and innovator who founded Green Bronx Machine (2023), an urban food-growing initiative with the slogan "We grow vegetables . . . and students!" Ritz's program helps at-risk students stay in school and succeed in life by giving them practical skills to overcome obstacles such as poverty and food insecurity. In the program's indoor teaching farm, students learn how to set up a grow light system, create energy from bicycles, start seedlings, grow the plants, and harvest them. In its kitchen, chefs teach children how to prepare these homegrown vegetables so they can feed themselves.

At the same time, visions provide a guiding philosophy for people that gives them meaning and purpose. When people know the overarching goals, principles, and values of an organization, it is easier for them to establish an identity and know where they fit within the organization. Furthermore, seeing the larger purpose allows people to appreciate the value of their contributions to the organization and to something larger than their own interests. The value of a vision is that it shows others the meaningfulness of their work.

A Challenge

A final characteristic of a vision is that it **challenges** people to transcend the status quo to do something to benefit others. Visions challenge people to commit themselves to worthwhile causes. In his inaugural address in 1961, President John F. Kennedy challenged the American people by saying, "Ask not what your country can do for you—ask what you can do for your country." This challenge was inspiring because it asked people to move beyond self-interest to work for the greater good of the country. Kennedy's vision for America had a huge impact on the country.

An example of an organization that has a vision with a clear challenge component is the Leukemia and Lymphoma Society's Team In Training program. The primary goal of this program is to raise funds for cancer research, public education, and patient aid programs. As a part of Team In Training, participants who sign up to run or walk a marathon (26.2 miles) are asked to raise money for cancer research in return for the personalized coaching and fitness training they receive from Team In Training staff. Since its inception in the late 1980s, the program has raised more than $600 million for cancer research. A recent participant said of Team In Training, "I was inspired to find something I could do both to push myself a little harder and to accomplish something meaningful in the process." When people are challenged to do something good for others, they often become inspired and committed to the task. Whether it is to improve their own group, organization, or community, people like to be challenged to help others.

To summarize, a vision has five main characteristics. First, it is a mental *picture* or image of a future that is better than the status quo. Second, it represents a *change* and points to new ways of doing things. Third, it is grounded in *values*. Fourth, it is a *map* that gives direction and provides meaning and purpose. Finally, it is a *challenge* to change things for the better.

VISION IN PRACTICE

It is one thing for a leader to have a vision for an organization. But making that vision a reality requires communication and action. In this section, we explore how a leader can articulate a vision to others and what specific actions a leader can take to make the vision clear, understandable, and a reality.

Articulating a Vision

Although it is very important for a leader *to have* a vision, it is equally important for a leader to be able *to articulate*—explain and describe—the vision to others. Although some are better than others at this, there are certain ways all leaders can improve the way they communicate their visions.

First, a leader must communicate the vision by *adapting the vision* to their audience. Psychologists tell us that most people have a drive for consistency and when confronted with the need to change will do so only if the required change is not too different from their present state (Festinger, 1957). A leader needs to articulate the vision to fit within others' latitude of acceptance by adapting the vision to the audience (Conger & Kanungo, 1987). If the vision is too demanding and advocates too big a change, it will be rejected. If it is articulated in light of the status quo and does not demand too great a change, it will be accepted.

For example, in the first decade of the 20th century, motorcars were seen as a frivolous fad for the rich, and most people believed automobiles would never replace the horse. But Henry Ford articulated his vision of the United States becoming a nation where every family would be able to have an automobile. His development of the assembly line process of car production resulted in more affordable cars and kicked off the automobile-centered culture of the world today. Ford's assembly line innovations also led to changing the manufacturing process for industries around the world.

A leader also needs to *highlight the values* of the vision by emphasizing how the vision presents ideals worth pursuing. Presenting the values of the vision helps individuals and group members find their own work worthwhile. It also allows group members to identify with something larger than themselves, and to become connected to a larger community (Shamir et al., 1993).

In the example of Ford, his emphasis on making ownership of an automobile accessible for every family, not just the rich, was a key in energizing workers and supporters in his revolutionized transportation and American industry.

Articulating a vision also requires *choosing the right language.* A leader should use *words and symbols* that are motivating and inspiring (Sashkin, 2004; Zaccaro & Banks, 2001). Words that describe a vision need to be affirming, uplifting, and hopeful, and describe the vision in a way that underscores its worth. The inaugural speech by President Kennedy is an example of how a leader used inspiring language to articulate his vision.

Symbols are often adopted by leaders in an effort to articulate a vision and bring group cohesion. A good illustration of this is how, in 1997, the University of Michigan football team and coaching staff chose to use Jon Krakauer's book *Into Thin Air* and "conquering Mount Everest" as a metaphor for what they wanted to accomplish. Krakauer provided a firsthand account of a team's challenging journey up Mount Everest that was successful, although five climbers lost their lives in the process. One of the Michigan coaches said, "It's amazing how many similarities there are between playing football and climbing a mountain. . . . The higher you get on a mountain, the tougher it gets. The longer you play during the season, the harder it gets to keep playing the way you want to play." Throughout the season, the coaches frequently emphasized that achieving great feats required tremendous discipline, perseverance, strength, and teamwork. In the locker room, real climbing hooks and pitons were hung above the door to remind everyone who exited that the mission was to "conquer the mountain"—that is, to win the title. The imagery of mountain climbing in this example was a brilliant way to articulate the vision the coaches had for that season. This imagery proved to be well chosen: The team won the 1997 National Collegiate Athletic Association championship.

Visions also need to be described to others *using inclusive language* that links people to the vision and makes them part of the process. Words such as *we* and *our* are inclusive and better to use than words such as *they* and *them.* The goal of this type of language is to enlist participation of others and build community around a common goal. Inclusive language helps bring this about.

In general, to articulate a vision clearly requires that a leader *adapt the content* to the audience, emphasize the vision's *intrinsic value,* select *words and symbols* that are uplifting, and use language that is *inclusive.* If a leader is able to do these things, they will increase the chances that the vision will be embraced and the goal achieved.

Implementing a Vision

In addition to creating and articulating a vision, a leader needs to *implement* the vision. Perhaps the real test of a leader's abilities occurs in the implementation phase of a vision. Implementing a vision requires a great deal of effort by a leader over an extended period. Although some leaders can "talk the talk," leaders who implement the vision "walk the walk." Most important, in implementing a vision the leader must model to others the attitudes, values, and behaviors set forth in the vision. The leader is a living example of the ideals articulated in the vision. For example, if the vision is to promote a deeply humanistic organization, the leader needs to demonstrate qualities such as empathy and caring in every action.

Similarly, if the vision is to promote community values, the leader needs to show interest in others and in the common good of the broader community. When a leader is seen *acting out the vision*, they build credibility with others. This credibility inspires people to express the same kind of values.

Implementing a vision also requires a leader to set high performance expectations for others. Setting challenging goals motivates people to accomplish a mission. An example of setting high expectations and worthwhile goals is illustrated in the story of Terry Fox. Fox was diagnosed with bone cancer at the age of 18 and, in an effort to stem it, doctors amputated his right leg 15 centimeters (6 inches) above the knee.

While in the hospital, Fox was so overcome by the suffering of other cancer patients—many of them young children—that he decided to run across Canada to raise money for cancer research. He called his journey the Marathon of Hope.

After 18 months of training, Fox started his run in St. John's, Newfoundland, on April 12, 1980, with little fanfare. Although it was difficult to garner attention in the beginning, enthusiasm soon grew, and the money collected along his route began to mount. He ran 42 kilometers (26 miles) a day through Canada's Atlantic provinces, through Quebec, and through part of Ontario. It was a journey that Canadians never forgot.

On September 1, 1980, after 143 days and 5,373 kilometers (3,339 miles), Fox was forced to stop running outside Thunder Bay, Ontario, because cancer had appeared in his lungs. An entire nation was saddened when he passed away on June 28, 1981, at the age of 22.

Fox had a vision and established an extremely challenging goal for himself and others. He was courageous and determined. Unfortunately, he died before completing his journey, but his vision lives on. A Terry Fox Run to raise money for cancer research is still held annually in Canada and across the world and has brought in more than $850 million (Terry Fox Foundation, 2023).

The process of carrying out a vision does not happen rapidly but takes continuous effort. It is a step-by-step process, and not one that occurs all at once. For this reason, it is imperative for a leader's eyes to stay on the goal. By doing so, the leader encourages and supports others in

The Terry Fox statue in Ottawa, Ontario.

the day-to-day efforts to reach the larger goal. A leader alone cannot implement a vision. The leader must work with others and empower them in the implementation process. It is essential that leaders share the work and collaborate with others to accomplish the goal.

SUMMARY

A competent leader will have a compelling vision that challenges people to work toward a higher standard of excellence. A vision is a mental model of an ideal future state. It provides a *picture* of a future that is better than the present, is grounded in *values*, and advocates *change* toward some new set of ideals. Visions function as a *map* to give people direction. Visions also *challenge* people to commit themselves to a greater common good.

First, an effective leader clearly articulates the vision to others. This requires the leader to adapt the vision to the attitudes and values of the audience. Second, the leader highlights the *intrinsic values* of the vision, emphasizing how the vision presents ideals worth pursuing. Third, a competent leader uses language that is *motivating* and *uplifting* to articulate the vision. Finally, the leader uses *inclusive language* that enlists participation from others and builds community.

A challenge for a leader is to carry out the difficult processes of implementing a vision. To implement a vision, the leader needs to be a living *model* of the ideals and values articulated in the vision. In addition, they must *set high performance expectations* for others, and *encourage and empower* others to reach their goals.

KEY TERMS

challenge	picture
change	status quo
map	vision

Application

7.1 Case Study—A Clean Slate

Nick Gibbons was described by his classmates at Columbia University's prestigious School of Journalism as a "hard-core newshound with ink running in his blood." After working as a beat reporter for 10 years, Nick became city editor of a newspaper in a midsized Midwest town of about 100,000, overseeing a large staff of local reporters and writers.

So when the president of the large media group that owned his newspaper asked Nick to come to its headquarters for a meeting, he was excited . . . until he heard what was said. The company was going to stop printing daily newspapers, instead publishing digital editions. Nick's newspaper would only be printed three days a week; the other days, the news would be delivered in an electronic edition. As a result, 75% of the newspaper's workforce would lose their jobs. As the president witnessed Nick's shock and dismay, he said, "Nick, we think you are the only editor at your newspaper that can make this happen."

On the three-hour drive home, Nick realized that change at the newspaper was inevitable. Newspapers had been losing subscribers and revenue for a decade as readers turned to the internet to get their news. Digital versions of newspapers were cheaper to produce and deliver. Although he did not like the idea of going digital, Nick knew in his heart that he still believed strongly in the importance of reporting the news and informing the community, no matter the format.

To succeed in taking the newspaper to a digital format, Nick was going to have to change an entrenched culture and belief system about newspapers, not only within his staff but among the public as well. To do this, he had to start from the ground up, creating something entirely new. This would require bringing aboard people who were energized about the future and not mourning the past.

His plan employed a three-prong approach. *First*, he informed the entire newspaper staff that they would lose their current jobs in three months and they would have to reapply for new jobs within the newspaper. The first required qualification was a willingness to "forge the future for local journalism and make a contribution to this movement." If you can't let go of the past, he told his coworkers, then you can't move forward. In the end, almost 80% of the new positions were filled by former staffers whom Nick believed to be the "best and brightest" people the newspaper had.

Second, Nick moved the company's offices out of the building they had been in for 120 years to a smaller, very public space on the first floor of a downtown building. The offices were located on a corner completely sided by windows, the inner workings of the newspaper on display to passersby. Nick wanted the newspaper's operations to be very visible so that it didn't seem like they had just "disappeared."

Nick's *third* approach was what he called a "high forgiveness factor." What they were creating was new and untried, and he knew there would be plenty of missteps along the way. He stressed to his new staffers that he expected not perfection, just dedication and determination. For example, one misstep was the elimination of the newspaper's exhaustive list of local events, which resulted in a huge community outcry. To correct this, staffers determined they could satisfy the community's frustrations by creating a dedicated website for a local events calendar with event organizers submitting the information electronically. A staff member would oversee college interns in editing the submissions and updating the website.

When the newspaper announced its change to a digital format, the reaction was harsh: Readers canceled subscriptions, and advertisers dropped away like flies. It's been four years since the change, and the newspaper is slowly gaining back readers and experiencing more visits to its website. The sales staff is starting to be successful teaching advertisers how to create digital ads that can reach the right audiences by using behavioral targeting and social media.

Questions

1. What is Nick Gibbons's vision in this case study? How is it similar to or different from the vision of the owners of the paper? Discuss the unique challenges one leader faces when required to implement another leader's vision.

2. Why do you think Nick wanted to open up the workings of the paper to the public? How is this related to his vision?

3. Visions usually require changing people's values. What desired changes in values are highlighted by this case study?

4. How well did Nick articulate his vision for the paper? If you were in his shoes, how would you articulate your vision in this case?

5. Do you think the newspaper will thrive under Nick's leadership? Why?

7.2 Case Study—Kakenya Ntaiya

At 5, Kakenya Ntaiya's future was decided. The little Maasai girl from Kenya was betrothed to be married when she reached puberty. Early marriage and a family were believed to be the only way to secure a girl's future, and parents in her village married their daughters off young in exchange for highly valued cows. Girls were married once they completed "the ceremony," a much-celebrated event in a Maasai girl's life. The ceremonial procedure that would mark the end of her childhood was never openly discussed. The procedure known in the Western world as female genital mutilation (FGM) is a dangerous and extremely painful cutting done without anesthetic and often in unsanitary conditions.

Until she was 12, Kakenya lived much like any other little Maasai girl, up early and working on the farm, constantly in training to be a mother and wife. From the time she was old enough to walk, she was taught to sweep the house, gather wood, fetch water from the river, and cook for her family.

Only after her chores were completed could Kakenya attend school. She did so at the urging of her mother, who worked hard running the family's farm, growing food and tending the animals so the family could eat. Because women were not allowed to own property, everything belonged to her husband and Kakenya's father, a policeman who worked in a nearby city and returned home only once a year to sell the livestock and produce his wife raised, using the money to drink with his friends.

Kakenya dreamed of becoming a teacher, but knew once "the ceremony" was completed, she would be married, and that dream would vanish. As she neared the end of the eighth grade, she approached her father with a proposal: She would go through the ceremony only if he would postpone her marriage and allow her to return to school. If he didn't, she would run away, thereby shaming her father with the lifelong stigma of "being the father of that girl who didn't go through the ceremony" (Ntaiya, 2012).

Kakenya's father acquiesced to her terms, and she endured the painful procedure, returning to high school three weeks later with a fiercer resolve to become a teacher. She applied to several colleges abroad and was offered a scholarship to attend Randolph-Macon Woman's College in Lynchburg, Virginia. However, she needed money for the airfare and had a new obstacle—her father had suffered a stroke and could not speak for her. In her community, all the men her father's age were also considered her father, and thus, without her own father's blessing, she had to persuade them. This was no easy task, as the general consensus was that this was an opportunity "wasted on a girl" (Gleissner, 2017).

But Kakenya knew that if the village chief said "yes," the others would follow. Employing the traditional Maasai belief "that someone who comes to you before the sunrise will bring to you good news and you must not tell them 'no,'" she visited the chief very early in the morning with her request. She promised to come back and use her education to help her village. The chief consented but directed her to also enlist the support of 15 more men in the village. So early each morning, she visited one, until she gained the support of her entire village, who pooled their resources to purchase the plane fare she needed. She was the first girl to leave the village to go to college (*National Geographic*, 2023).

College opened her world and her awareness. "I learned that the ceremony that I went through when I was 13 years old . . . was called female genital mutilation. I learned that it was against the law in Kenya. I learned that I did not have to trade part of my body to get an education. I learned that my mom had a right to own property. I learned that she did not have to be abused because she is a woman. Those things made me angry. I wanted to do something" (Ntaiya, 2012).

Kakenya earned a degree in international relations and political science and became the first youth adviser to the United Nations Population Fund, traveling the world as an advocate for girls' education and youth. Encouraged by her work and seeking ways to create policies and programs that would "empower children," Kakenya pursued and earned a PhD in education from the University of Pittsburgh.

Haunted by her trips home to her Kenyan village where the practices of FGM and child marriage continued, she reiterated her promise to come back to help and asked what the villagers needed most. "As I spoke to the women, they told me, 'We really need a school for girls.' . . . And the reason they wanted the school for girls is because when a girl is raped when she's walking to school, the mother is blamed for that. If she got pregnant before she got married, the mother is blamed for that, and she's punished. She's beaten. They said, 'We want to put our girls in a safe place'" (Ntaiya, 2012).

After getting the village elders to donate land for a girls' school, Kakenya quickly established one. There were two conditions for admittance to the school: First, the parents had to agree that the girl would not go through FGM. Many opposed the requirement. In response, the school worked to educate the parents on how FGM affected a girl's life to gain their support. Second, the girls would not marry until they at least finished high school.

Kakenya had hoped to enroll 10 girls. When the school opened, 100 came. Unable to accommodate everyone, the school enrolled 30 girls, including some who had been abused or orphaned or were from traditional families who had never before sent a girl to school. The students were determined, but they were also hungry and weary from chores at home and the long walk to the school. They were highly vulnerable to assault, rape, and kidnapping on their way to and from school. To truly succeed, the girls needed to have a boarding school where they would feel safe, rested, and well nourished.

"I came to realize once again . . . that while I could dream or have a dream, I could not make it come true all by myself. So I went back to the elders who helped me more than a decade ago," forming a community board of religious leaders, parents, and teachers (Ntaiya, 2018).

While she still met with resistance to her school from those who clung to traditional ways and from some Western educators who opposed her direct approach to sex education for the girls, she focused on the positives such as that their daughters' attendance at the school had led to a shift in attitude by many traditional men who previously did not believe in the education of girls.

In 2008, she founded Kakenya's Dream (n.d.), an organization with a mission to educate girls, end "harmful traditional practices," and "uplift her community." Kakenya's Dream not only includes boarding schools, but has an alumnae program providing mentoring, scholarships, tutoring, career advice, and assistance with university applications.

The organization provides life skills training to *both* boys and girls from rural communities through weekend and weeklong camps. This important aspect of the organization was inspired by Kakenya's understanding that true change requires educating boys, as well, to think differently about women. As of 2023, nearly 25,000 boys and girls had participated (Kakenya's Dream, n.d.).

"Our program thrives because the community owns it. The community supports it. They are part of it," Kakenya said.

"I think the biggest thing that I learned early on is the importance of those gatekeepers, the custodians of the culture. . . . So I will call the meeting, and they will come . . . And they will turn the conversation to being, 'this is their idea,' and that going forward they will be singing my message. Then it's their message. So they own it, and they run with it. And to me, I'm happy with that" (Harvard T.H. Chan School of Public Health, 2018).

Questions

1. The chapter states "charismatic leaders create change by linking their vision and its values to the self-concept of followers." How did Kakenya Ntaiya accomplish this?

2. How would you describe Kakenya's vision?

    a. According to the text, a vision has five characteristics: a picture, a change, values, a map, and a challenge. How are each of these elements expressed in Kakenya's vision?

b. Discuss the evolution of Kakenya's vision over the course of her life—from the vision she had for herself as a young girl to its more global expression today. Discuss the specific elements of this vision and how they have evolved and scaled over the years.

3. Given the cultural challenges, articulating her vision was a critical component to Kakenya's success. Using the four elements of articulation described in this chapter, what are the challenges Kakenya faced, and how did she address them through articulation?

4. What roles did building credibility, setting high performance standards that motivated others to accomplish the vision, and empowering others play in Kakenya's vision?

Application

7.3 Leadership Vision Questionnaire

Purpose

1. To assess your ability to create a vision for a group or an organization
2. To help you understand how visions are formed

Directions

1. Think for a moment of a work, school, social, religious, musical, or athletic organization of which you are a member. Now, think what you would do if you were the leader and you had to create a vision for the group or organization. Keep this vision in mind as you complete the exercise.
2. Using the following scale, circle the number that indicates the degree to which you agree or disagree with each statement.

Statements	Strongly disagree	Disagree	Neutral	Agree	Strongly agree
1. I have a mental picture of what would make our group better.	1	2	3	4	5
2. I can imagine several changes that would improve our group.	1	2	3	4	5
3. I have a vision for what would make our organization stronger.	1	2	3	4	5
4. I know how we could change the status quo to make things better.	1	2	3	4	5
5. It is clear to me what steps we need to take to improve our organization.	1	2	3	4	5
6. I have a clear picture of what needs to be done in our organization to achieve a higher standard of excellence.	1	2	3	4	5

Statements	Strongly disagree	Disagree	Neutral	Agree	Strongly agree
7. I have a clear picture in my mind of what this organization should look like in the future.	1	2	3	4	5
8. It is clear to me what core values, if emphasized, would improve our organization.	1	2	3	4	5
9. I can identify challenging goals that should be emphasized in my group.	1	2	3	4	5
10. I can imagine several things that would inspire my group to perform better.	1	2	3	4	5

Scoring

Sum the numbers you circled on the questionnaire (visioning ability skill).

Total Score

Visioning ability skill: _____

Scoring Interpretation

The Leadership Vision Questionnaire is designed to measure your ability to create a vision as a leader.

If your score is 41–50, you are in the very high range.
If your score is 31–40, you are in the high range.
If your score is 21–30, you are in the moderate range.
If your score is 10–20, you are in the low range.

| Application |

7.4 Observational Exercise—Leadership Vision

Purpose

1. To understand the way visions are constructed by leaders in ongoing groups and organizations
2. To identify strategies that leaders employ to articulate and implement their visions

Directions

1. For this exercise, select two people in leadership positions to interview. They can be leaders in formal or informal positions at work, at school, or in society. The only criterion is that the leaders influence others toward a goal.
2. Conduct a 30-minute interview with each leader, by phone or in person. Ask the leaders to describe the visions they have for their organizations. In addition, ask, "How do you *articulate* and *implement* your visions?"

Leader 1 (name):
Vision content   Vision articulation   Vision implementation

Leader 2 (name):
Vision content   Vision articulation   Vision implementation

Questions

1. What differences and similarities did you observe between the two leaders' visions?

2. Did the leaders advocate specific values? If yes, what values?

3. Did the leaders use any unique symbols to promote their visions? If yes, what symbols?

4. In what ways did the leaders' behaviors model their visions to others?

Application

7.5 Reflection and Action Worksheet—Leadership Vision

Reflection

1. Stephen Covey contended that effective leaders "begin with the end in mind" (1991, p. 42). These leaders have a deep understanding of their own goals and mission in life. How would you describe your own values and purpose in life? In what way is your leadership influenced by these values?

2. Creating a vision usually involves trying to change others by persuading them to accept different values and different ways of doing things. Are you comfortable influencing people in this way? Discuss.

3. As we discussed in this chapter, effective visions can be articulated with strong symbols. How do you view yourself as being able to do this? Are you effective at generating language and symbols that can enhance a vision and help make it successful?

Action

1. Based on your score on the Leadership Vision Questionnaire, how do you assess your ability to create a vision for a group? Identify specific ways you could improve your abilities to create and carry out visions with others.

2. Good leaders *act out the vision.* Describe what ideals and values you act out or could act out as a leader.

3. Take a few moments to think about and describe a group or an organization to which you belong presently or belonged in the past. Write a brief statement describing the vision you would utilize if you were the leader of this group or organization.

8

WORKING WITH GROUPS

INTRODUCTION

In prior chapters we focused on what it takes to be an effective leader, highlighting the importance of knowing your own traits and styles, identifying your unique leadership strengths, and learning how to develop a compelling vision that people will want to follow. In this chapter, we shift gears and turn our attention to how leaders can bring the best out of group members to help carry out the work of an organization. Because groups are integral to the functioning of nearly every organization, it is imperative that leaders acquire and cultivate an understanding of groups and effective group process.

The appearance of COVID-19 throughout the world in 2020 had an immense and lasting impact on nearly everything we do. In particular, it significantly changed the way we communicate with one another. In an effort to minimize people's risk of getting or transmitting the virus, workplaces closed, and people started working from home, which in many cases became a lasting change because their work went fully remote or they found working from home was a better choice for them personally. To keep people safe, social distancing was encouraged, which resulted in creating more distance in our interpersonal communication. Wearing masks required us to talk and listen in different ways, often making us feel uncomfortable with others. Avoidance of others was the norm rather than working with others.

At the same time that COVID-19 negatively affected face-to-face interpersonal communication, it produced a new emphasis on people meeting virtually using video and audio technologies. This was especially true for groups. College classes were taught online through video platforms, corporate board meetings were held virtually, and many organizational planning meetings were conducted over video. While this form of communication was quite different from many groups' prior interactions, working in groups continued to be essential to the functioning of organizations.

Groups play a major role in our personal lives, our work settings, and society in general. Being a part of groups affects our "identity, belonging, meaning, and achievement" (Levi & Askay, 2021). Groups can provide an opportunity for both marginalized and nonmarginalized individuals to feel that they are a part of the conversation (Miller, 2023). Whether groups meet in person, online, or a hybrid of these, it is critical to understand the nature of groups and how they function. "We have all been in situations where relationships with colleagues make or break success. Thus, teams have the power to either unlock deep potential and creativity, or keep us stuck, insecure, and reacting to patterns of the past" (Hawthorne, 2015, p. 1).

In this chapter, our discussion will be divided into two sections: *Groups Explained* and *Groups in Practice*. The first section, *Groups Explained*, discusses various types of groups, specific stages of group development, the various roles that people play in groups, and the benefits people experience when working in groups. The second section, *Groups in Practice*, describes practical things leaders can do to make their groups more effective, including providing structure, clarifying goals, clarifying norms, building cohesiveness, promoting standards of excellence, and dealing with out-group members. Developing an understanding of how groups work will help you when you are asked to be the leader.

GROUPS EXPLAINED

Groups are so prevalent and fundamental in our day-to-day activities that we often fail to recognize the significant impact they have on our work and well-being. To better understand leadership in relationship to group functioning, we need to explore the nature and complexity of groups. Generally speaking, a **group** refers *to a set of three or more individuals who are in some way interdependent and mutually influence one another in an effort to achieve a common goal* (Levi & Askay, 2021). Various groups abound in our lives, such as a team designing a new software product, a book club discussing a new bestseller, or a cancer support group sharing their common experiences.

In this chapter, the terms *group* and *team* will be used interchangeably, recognizing that the word *team* is more frequently used to describe individuals who have a clearly defined organizational task, specified roles and responsibilities, coordination, and performance results.

Types of Groups

A general way of viewing the numerous types of groups is according to whether they are task-oriented or process-oriented. In task-oriented groups, time is often spent on content such as discussing assignments, projects, and goals. In process-oriented groups, time is spent relating and getting along with people. Typically, most groups have both a content and process component, but groups vary in the degree to which one of these elements is emphasized, as shown in Figure 8.1. The dashed line in Figure 8.1 shows how a group's emphasis on task or process can progress on a continuum, while the colored line shows how that emphasis can fluctuate in

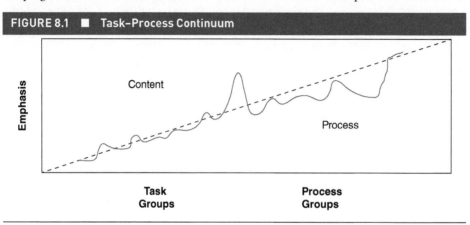

FIGURE 8.1 ■ Task–Process Continuum

Source: Adapted from Loomis, M. E. (1979). *Group process for nurses* (p. 102). Mosby.

a group. It is important when working with groups to know when and how to shift the group's emphasis between task and process communication.

Task Groups

Task groups, which appear on the left end of the continuum in Figure 8.1, focus most of their efforts on substantive content issues such as identifying and meeting the goals of the group, the business or work that the group needs to accomplish, or the procedures the group will follow. In organizations, task groups are involved in a wide range of activities involved in whatever the organization is seeking to accomplish, such as policy decisions, new product development, or establishing a group's mission. Common examples of content-focused task groups include management teams, project teams, school boards, task forces, staff development teams, special-ops military teams, and medical treatment planning meetings. For example, a committee that is formed to revise a company's overtime rules exemplifies a task group that is mainly concerned with content issues. Another type of task group is an accountability group. An accountability group is a small cluster of people who meet regularly to share their goals, report on their progress in meeting those goals, and keep each other accountable about achieving the goals they set for themselves. A group of aspiring and experienced writers who meet regularly to share their manuscripts with one another, get each other's input, and report on their progress in the publication process is an example of an accountability group.

Process Groups

Process groups, which appear on the right end of the continuum in Figure 8.1, focus on group members, how they are related, and how they communicate with one another. Rather than concentrating exclusively on a task to be addressed, process groups direct more attention to individual group members and the interactions between group members. Group dynamics are more evident in these groups as members are very aware of how they treat and respond to each other. Process groups focus more on people's emotional needs, their likes and dislikes, and questions such as who is included and who is not, who is in charge, and who needs support from the group. Members of process groups help one another feel comfortable with themselves, with each other, and with the situation in which they find themselves. A support group for students who have experienced the trauma of a mass shooting is an example of a process group. Other examples include participants in a wellness retreat, a coffee group, a divorce support group, and an Al-Anon family support group.

Groups are never exclusively task-oriented or process-oriented; they are a blend of the two, sometimes being equally task and process, and sometimes being nearly all of one or the other. Characterizing groups along the task–process continuum in Figure 8.1 provides a useful way of differentiating groups and learning how they work.

Stages of Groups

No matter the type they are, most groups go through identifiable stages as they develop and proceed over time. Several models have been proposed to explain the common developmental stages of groups (Bales & Strodtbeck, 1951; Bennis & Shepard, 1956; Fisher, 1974; Schutz, 1958; Tuckman, 1965; Tuckman & Jensen, 2010). Some of these models have been constructed by assessing the various stages in task groups, while others have been constructed by observing the development of process groups. Considered together, this research provides a basis for suggesting that most groups go through similar stages. The stages have characteristics and qualities that make them distinct, but these stages can often overlap and blur into one another (Yalom, 1995). Furthermore, some groups may skip a stage or two, while others may remain in one stage for an extended period.

Generally, most researchers and practitioners agree with Tuckman's model of developmental stages that delineates five stages: *forming, storming, norming, performing,* and *adjourning* (Tuckman, 1965; Tuckman & Jensen, 2010). His research was based on a synthesis of 50 articles on the sequential phases of groups.

Forming

The beginning period in small group development is called the **forming stage**. It is the orientation phase when individuals spend time assessing their purpose for joining the group, attempt to figure out if they fit into the group, and learn what is appropriate and acceptable behavior within the group. The focus of the forming stage is often on questions of "in or out" as members try to determine how included or excluded they are by the group. In the forming stage, members want to know the extent to which they are included in the group as distinct individuals who can retain their unique identity (Schutz, 1958).

Communication between group members during the forming stage is often stereotypical and restricted (Yalom, 1995), remaining at a superficial level with little self-disclosure until members gain more trust in one another and feel more secure in the group setting. As a result, members frequently introduce safe topics of conversation, such as the weather or mutual acquaintances, that allow them to size up others and determine how others respond to them. In some groups, talk of "safe" topics can dominate for long periods of time and hinder the group's movement toward the next stages.

Leadership in the forming stage is directed toward helping group members feel safe and satisfying their needs for belonging. It requires helping members to feel part of the group but also to feel a sense of privacy, trust, and independence. An effective leader provides a degree of structure and social support for the group as a whole and helps individual group members understand group norms. If the leader can help members move through some of the discomfort in the forming stage, the work of the group members in subsequent stages becomes easier.

Storming

The second stage in the development of groups is the **storming stage**, also identified by some as the "conflict phase." During this stage members become less interested in inclusion issues, such as how they fit into the group, and more interested in control issues, such as how they influence the group. During this stage, members weigh options more carefully and consider how changes will affect them personally.

This stage is called storming because of the intragroup conflicts that typically occur during this period. In this stage, the focus is on issues of "top or bottom"—that is, who will have more influence in the group (top position) and who will have less influence (bottom position). Personal insecurities are sometimes below the surface and sometimes on full display.

Conflicts resulting from struggles for control are common as a group develops and are always present in this stage. Struggles for control may occur between the leader and group members or between group members. This can result in the emergence of subgroups as a way for members to express their needs for control (Bennis & Shepard, 1956; Yalom, 1995).

Leadership during the storming stage is directed toward helping the group members accept and work through group conflicts because conflict over even small issues may impede the group from getting to bigger issues. Group members often fear that conflict and criticism will harm cohesiveness and that group squabbles and indecision are symptomatic of poor group functioning. Leaders can help members realize that increased conflict is normal during this stage and that group decisions take time. Learning to work through their differences nearly always helps groups to make high-quality decisions later on. In this stage, members learn how to bond together even though they have different ideas and interests. Leaders can also help group members satisfy their needs for control or influence within the group. For example, a leader could give a special assignment to a member who wants more influence while allowing other members with less desire for control to maintain lower profiles in the group. The value of the storming stage is knowing that regardless of differences, group members can work together as a group. Hawthorne (2015) states, "As team members become more and more themselves, and foster genuine relationships, stronger connections emerge between them, fear and power dynamics lessen, creativity flourishes, and the collective potential of the team improves" (p. 2).

Norming

The third stage in the development of groups, the **norming stage**, usually follows on the heels of the control struggles and conflicts of the storming stage. In the norming stage, group cohesion develops as members begin feeling connected to one another. This stage can emerge for a variety of reasons. For example, members of a task group may become aware of time pressures and realize that they need to achieve consensus to meet their objectives. Members of a process group may become more understanding and accepting of one another's differences. Often, members may observe the splits and factions of the storming stage and feel the need to move closer rather than farther away from others.

Essentially, members want to develop unity during the norming stage; they focus on issues of "close or far" (Schutz, 1958). Group members want to maintain close, positive relationships with each other while retaining their individuality and independence. As group members start feeling more positive about each other and the group, they become more secure expressing their opinions, believing now that others will listen and support them. This stage often results in increased morale among members as their trust in one another builds (Yalom, 1995). It is not unusual during this stage for group members to suppress negative comments and feelings for the sake of group unity.

For example, competitors from the same industry are on the board of a trade association that seeks to influence important legislation that could negatively affect the industry. Because achieving solidarity as a group is critical to having influence over the issue, the board members put aside their rivalries and listen to one another's concerns and ideas in order to reach consensus on the best strategies to implement. As a result, they come to value the others' respective opinions and, rather than competitors, see one another as teammates with the same goal.

Because of the positive feelings and the unified sense of direction of the group, leadership during the norming stage faces fewer challenges than during other stages. The leader can assume a nondominant role, putting the group on "automatic pilot" as members work in harmony on group objectives, providing guidance and direction only as needed.

Performing

The fourth stage of group development is the **performing stage**. This stage is similar to the norming stage, but involves more time, greater depth, and increased disclosure among group members. The performing stage is so named because in this phase members now perform the work they have set out to do. They feel secure to express both positive and negative emotions in task groups, yet communication usually remains positive, even to the point of members joking and praising each other. The group spirit and the feeling of unity among members are often high during the performing stage.

There can be considerable variability in this stage from one type of group to another. In long-established groups, this stage can take a couple of months to develop. In some short-term task groups, a distinct performing phase may never be clearly observable; the work of this stage may be carried out as part of the forming or norming stages.

During the performing stage, little directive leader behavior is needed, since group members are actively solving problems and working with one another in goal-directed activity. Because interpersonal structures are established, the leader can be less hands-on during this stage as well.

Adjourning

The last stage in group development is the **adjourning stage**. This usually occurs when the goals of a group have been fulfilled or the allotted time has run out and the members begin considering the implications of ending the group. During the adjourning, or termination, stage, individuals experience a range of emotions depending on their prior experiences with adjourning a group. Group members can feel a sense of loss at the end of a group. Although relationships between group members can continue and memories of it remain, "the group," as the members know it, cannot be reconvened and will be gone forever (Yalom, 1995).

Groups often go through a cycle during adjournment that is the *reverse* of what a group experiences during its formative stages (Schutz, 1958). Leaders need to summarize the work of the group, emphasize the goals that have been achieved, and help group members find a sense of closure as they confront their feelings about the approaching end of group meetings and the members' relationships. Each group member will confront adjourning in a unique way, and the leader can help the group by being sensitive to these differences. Finally, leaders need to express their own feelings about the group coming to an end.

In summary, most groups progress through five stages: forming, storming, norming, performing, and adjourning. Table 8.1 summarizes the communication that often occurs during each stage, although at times there is overlap between the stages. By being aware of these stages and the issues that can surface in each phase, leaders can increase members' capacities to work effectively in groups.

Group Stages	Forming	Storming	Norming	Performing	Adjourning
Kinds of Communication	Safe topics	Disagreements, debates	Supportive comments	Positive comments	Summary discussions
	Superficial and restricted	Rules and procedures	Increased self-disclosure	Consensus statements	Expression of feelings
	"In or out" discussions	"Top or bottom" discussions	"Close or far" discussions	In-depth self-disclosure	Closure statements

TABLE 8.1 ■ Typical Kinds of Communication in Different Stages of Groups

Individual Group Roles

While the role a leader plays in effective groups is important, the roles members play are also essential. Too often the roles of group members are overlooked or considered of minor importance to group functioning. For example, it is not uncommon to hear employees blame a boring staff meeting entirely on a supervisor. In so doing, the employees overlook the way in which their own behavior (e.g., failing to participate, looking at their phones under the table during the meeting) contributes to the ineffective and boring meeting. Effective group functioning is influenced by *both* leader and group member behavior; it is a shared responsibility.

It is informative and important to know the roles individuals can play in groups. Early work on member roles in small groups was conducted by Benne and Sheats (1948), who classified the roles of group members into three broad categories: (1) *group task roles*, (2) *group-building and maintenance roles*, and (3) *individual roles*. Benne and Sheats believed that group members often fulfill more than one role in a particular group and that the various roles can be played by either the leader or individual group members. Although their work was some of the earliest done in this field, the role categories they identified are still recognized as useful in understanding group functioning, especially in task groups.

Group Task Roles

The first category, **group task roles**, are members' roles that contribute to the group's ability to perform its task. These roles are concerned primarily with how individuals obtain and share information to solve problems.

Benne and Sheats (1948) identified 12 group task roles and what they encompass (Table 8.2). As you read about these, think about a group you've been a part of and which of these task roles you played and which you would have liked to fulfill:

Initiator-contributor: Suggests new ideas or different ways of approaching group problems or tasks, initiates discussions, and often gets the group to explore new areas.

TABLE 8.2 ■ Benne and Sheats *Task Roles*		
Initiator-contributor	Opinion giver	Evaluator-critic
Information seeker	Elaborator	Energizer
Opinion seeker	Coordinator	Procedural technician
Information giver	Orienter	Recorder

Information seeker: Determines what information is missing about an issue or problem and will ask for clarification or seek additional information.

Opinion seeker: Asks for clarification of the values, attitudes, and opinions made by others in the group to make sure different perspectives are given.

Information giver: Offers facts or personal experiences related to the issue or problem being discussed and is often seen as an authority on the subject.

Opinion giver: States their personal opinions and beliefs that are pertinent to the discussion, often in terms of what the group "should" do.

Elaborator: Expands on ideas being discussed using examples, relevant facts, and data and looks at the consequences of proposed ideas and actions.

Coordinator: Pulls together ideas and suggestions of others, often explaining the relationships between ideas, and helps coordinate group activities.

Orienter: Keeps discussion focused on the task and questions if it becomes misdirected, often suggesting how the group can get back on target.

Evaluator-critic: Considers the practicality or logic of suggestions and ideas of the group.

Energizer: Concentrates the group's efforts on forward movement, stimulating the group toward action or decision.

Procedural technician: Assists group movement by carrying out routine tasks such as determining where meetings are to take place and what supplies are needed by the group.

Recorder: Records and keeps track of suggestions or activities decided on by the group.

Sometimes, a group member may think they are performing one role or another, but other group members think differently. For example, a person may believe they are an initiator-contributor when they make suggestions, but by framing it in terms of "what we should do," they are working in the role of an opinion giver. It is important for members to get feedback from the others in the group and the group's leader to gain an understanding of what role they are playing in a group.

Group-Building and Maintenance Roles

The second category, **group-building and maintenance roles**, are those roles that promote cohesiveness among members and enhance their ability to work together as a group (Table 8.3). These roles focus more on developing good working relationships among the members rather than on the task or work of the group.

TABLE 8.3 ■ Benne and Sheats *Group-Building and Maintenance Roles*		
Encourager	Gatekeeper	Follower
Harmonizer	Standard setter	
Compromiser	Group observer	

The specific roles in this category are as follows:

Encourager: Affirms, supports, and praises other group members' contributions and displays a positive attitude in meetings.
Harmonizer: Mediates the differences among group members seeking ways to reduce tension and diffuse conflict.
Compromiser: Offers to modify their own position to maintain group harmony.
Gatekeeper: Regulates the flow of communication, facilitates less-involved members' contributions, and limits comments from members who dominate the discussion.
Standard setter: Reminds group members of the standards they are trying to achieve.
Group observer: Provides feedback on various aspects of the group process, enabling members to be more aware of how well they are functioning as a group.
Follower: Goes along with the movement of the group; seen as a listener, not a contributor.

In which of these group-building and maintenance roles have you engaged in your group experiences? Which of these roles are you the most comfortable playing, and which are you the most uncomfortable fulfilling?

Individual Roles

The final category of group roles is individual roles (Table 8.4). Unlike the categories of group task and group-building and maintenance roles, which facilitate the effective functioning of groups, individual roles do not. **Individual roles** are used by group members to satisfy their own needs, desires, and agendas and are generally nonfunctional and unhelpful to the group. These roles do not help the group accomplish its task or facilitate relationships between members and can disrupt the group's progress and weaken its cohesion. They are negative, dysfunctional roles rather than positive, functional roles.

TABLE 8.4 ■ Benne and Sheats *Individual Roles*		
Aggressor	Self-confessor	Help-seeker
Blocker	Playboy-playgirl	Special interest pleader
Recognition-seeker	Dominator	

Aggressor: Attacks or disapproves of others' suggestions, feelings, or values, using personal attacks in an attempt to decrease other group members' status.

Blocker: Resists, without good reason, or becomes very negative to others' suggestions, but refuses to make their own suggestions. Often causes the group to stall in its progress.

Recognition-seeker: Fears being placed in an "inferior" position and diverts the group's attention from its focus by repeatedly calling attention to their own accomplishments. Sometimes behaves in ways like acting silly or childish that directs members away from the task at hand.

Self-confessor: Uses the group's time to express personal, non-group-oriented feelings and issues and may relate group actions to their own personal life. Often does so in the guise of relevance to the group such as saying, "That reminds me of a time when. . . ."

Playboy-playgirl: Uses group meetings as fun time and a way to get out of doing work and displays behaviors, such as telling jokes or playing games on their phone, that indicate they are not involved in the group process.

Dominator: Tries repeatedly to assert their authority by trying to control the conversation and interrupting other group members, often exaggerating their own knowledge and claiming to have better solutions than anyone else.

Help-seeker: Tries to elicit sympathy from other group members by expressing feelings of inadequacy. Acts helpless, self-deprecating, and unable to contribute.

Special interest pleader: Speaks for a particular group or person but is really using the group to meet personal needs and to cloak personal biases or opinions. Often uses stereotypical positions, such as saying, "The management won't like that idea."

Which of these individual roles have you encountered in your group settings? Did these individuals impede the group's progress? How did the group leader address these problems?

How, then, can knowledge of these three categories of group member roles be helpful to leaders interested in facilitating group process? First, these categories remind us that group members can influence group functioning through the type of role that they assume in the group. Second, these categories can serve as a useful self-assessment tool to help group members become aware of the positive and negative roles they play in the group and the roles that they need to use more often. Third, these categories can help leaders diagnose group problems. For example, if a weekly staff meeting is repeatedly unable to achieve the task of clarifying rules regarding required overtime, group members (either alone or as a group) can analyze the roles in the group that are counterproductive and concentrate on initiating different roles that will increase group productivity.

Group members will often fulfill a variety of these roles so that they can meet the group's needs at various points in time. Some roles will be more helpful to a particular group at one time and less useful at another time. For example, a newly formed task group may have a higher need for someone to be in the initiator-contributor role than that of an evaluator-critic. The evaluator-critic role may be more helpful later when members start to weigh the pros and cons of various alternatives.

These role categories do not prescribe or offer a formula for determining which roles at what time will ensure optimal group functioning but do provide a view of how various roles assumed by group members can influence group process and functioning.

Benefits of Group Work

Many educational institutions and professional development programs offer courses titled Group Problem Solving or Group Discussion because they recognize the prevalence of groups in society and how important groups are to accomplishing a task. In addition to accomplishing tasks, there are many other benefits that individuals can gain from working in groups (Yalom, 1995).

A primary benefit of small groups is the *recognition* members receive from both the leader and the fellow group members. In a well-functioning group, each individual feels acknowledged in three ways: that "I exist," "I am of value," and "I have agency." As a part of a group, the other members often welcome you, call you by name, and accept your presence. Second, when you talk in the group, group members typically listen to what you have to say and acknowledge your contributions (e.g., "That's interesting" or "I like that idea"). Third, the group provides members with the opportunity to affect others. Having influence provides a sense of competency and self-worth. In other words, you are "not nothing" but someone who can say something valuable and influence others and the flow of the group. The importance for all of us being fully recognized by a group cannot be understated.

It has been said, "By the group are you sickened, and by the group are you healed"; the benefits of groups are in the healing. Groups let us know we are recognized and have value, that there is hope in our circumstances, that we can help others and learn from others, and that we are not "in the boat" alone.

GROUPS IN PRACTICE

In first half of the chapter, we discussed the nature of groups and how they function. We described different types of groups, the stages most groups go through, the roles people play in groups, and the benefits derived from group work. Now we will discuss the *fundamentals* that will allow people to be effective as members or leaders of a group.

Through our careers and personal lives, we will experience a multitude of groups, nearly all of which require that we participate in some way. Individuals who understand the fundamentals of working in groups can participate more effectively as members of a group and also lead groups more successfully. These fundamentals are to *establish a constructive climate, provide structure, clarify goals, clarify group norms, build cohesiveness, promote standards of excellence,* and *address out-group members.* This part of the chapter explains these fundamentals, providing a sort of "how-to guide" for being a better leader when working with groups.

Establish a Constructive Climate

If you have ever participated in a music group, sports team, family project, or college class that you considered to be really good or had a close set of friends, you know the feeling of being in a group with a **constructive climate**. A good climate is a positive atmosphere that makes people want to attend and participate in the group. It makes doing the business of the group easier.

Climate is defined as people's shared perceptions of the way things are in an organization (Reichers & Schneider, 1990). This includes people's thoughts and feelings about the activities, procedures, and assumptions of a group, which may fluctuate. In general, a positive climate is shaped by the degree to which people feel they are supported, appreciated, and encouraged for their roles and behaviors within the group. For example, a new group member may get the sense that "This is a laid-back place. People aren't rushing around; they're willing to stop and answer questions if you need help with a project." The opposite of this is a harsher climate where an individual might think, "This seems like an unfriendly place. People aren't making eye contact with me or each other and rarely smile. You hardly hear any real conversations taking place." A constructive climate is just that: an atmosphere that promotes each group member's satisfaction so that they can achieve their personal best. By creating a constructive climate, leaders help group members perform at their highest levels of excellence (Larson & LaFasto, 1989).

Climate is similar to an organization's culture, which is created by the beliefs, values, and traditions that are widespread in the organization (Schein, 2017). An organization's culture develops over longer periods from the many interactions that occur within the group or organization. A culture is reinforced by organizational members who have developed patterns of working together over time to cope with challenges and coordinate efforts that work well for them. These values and assumptions are then often observed by newcomers as "the way things are done around here."

Provide Structure

Because working in groups can be uplifting or chaotic and challenging, it is helpful when a leader provides a sense of **structure** for group members. Reyes and colleagues (2019) analyzed a large body of literature on effective team leaders and identified "initiating and enabling structure" as a key factor. Providing structure is like giving group members an architectural blueprint for their work, providing form and meaning to the purpose of the group's activities. Instilling structure into an organization provides people with a sense of security, direction, and stability and helps them to understand where they fit in and what goals they need to accomplish. For example, it would be frightening, and dangerous, to be part of a team climbing Mount Everest if the other members did not know their roles and did not follow a clear plan for the ascent. Working in a group *without* structure is more difficult for everyone involved and often results in low production and low satisfaction for all concerned.

To provide structure to a group, the leader must first help the group members understand the group's goals, communicating these clearly and sometimes frequently, as things change over time. When a leader gives a clear picture of assignments and responsibilities, group members gain a better sense of direction. For example, soldiers in the military are given orders to carry out a specific mission. The mission describes the assigned task, outlines the goals that they are working toward, and provides organization to their activities. Another example is a leader providing an agenda for a group meeting so that members know what is to be discussed and worked on by the group.

A leader also provides structure by identifying the unique ways that each individual group member can contribute, helping followers understand their roles within the group and how to be productive group members. Effective groups that use the talents of each individual can accomplish a great deal. This is known as **synergy,** and it occurs when the group outcome is greater than the sum of the individual contributions. The challenge for a leader is to discover how individual group members can contribute to the group's mission, and to encourage the group to recognize these contributions. For example, some people are good at generating ideas, while others are skilled at building consensus. Additionally, some people are good at setting agendas, and others are adept at making sure the proper supplies are available at meetings. Recognizing individuals' positive capacities gives structure to the entire group. (See Chapter 6, "Engaging Strengths," for an extended discussion of how leaders can help followers capitalize on their strengths.)

Clarify Goals

Every group needs a reason for its existence, or else there would be no need for individuals to come together. Goals often provide the rationale and motivation for people to form a group. In a broad analysis of 75 teams from diverse organizations including major corporations, hospitals, and sports teams, Larson and LaFasto (1989) found that, without exception, the teams that functioned most effectively had a very clear understanding of their objectives.

Typically, two types of goals operate in groups: *individual goals* and *group goals. Individual goals* are based on the particular needs and desires of each group member, which may or may not be related to the goals of the group. For example, an individual who wants to improve their skills in a certain sport like pickleball may join a league that plays regularly. *Group goals,* on the other hand, are shared (to some extent) by group members and involve some element of interdependence among the members. In the pickleball example, the group goal may be to provide fun, recreational play for players of all skill levels. Both individual and group goals often operate simultaneously within a group.

It is not uncommon for members to be unclear or confused about the group's goal. Sometimes the goal is not known, is obscure, or is hidden among a tangle of competing goals. When goals are not clearly articulated by the leader and understood by members, groups are less likely to be successful in achieving them. Furthermore, group members will be less excited about their work and less gratified about their accomplishments.

The leader needs to make goals clear and understandable. Just as leaders need to provide a map in articulating their vision (see Chapter 7, "Creating a Vision"), they must help group members see the end toward which everything is being directed. All members of a group need a clear picture of where their efforts are being directed. When the goal is vague, the leader needs to clarify it. Similarly, if the goal is embedded in a complex set of related goals, the leader needs to identify a specific goal for group members and explain how it fits with all the other goals.

The following are examples of leaders expressing clear goals. While not glamorous, they exemplify working together as a team based on guidance provided by good leadership.

> *Football coach to team*: "OK, defensive team, your job is to sack the opposing quarterback two times each half!"
> *Orchestra conductor to musicians*: "Our upcoming rehearsals are going to be difficult because the pieces we are playing are really challenging. To get it right, we are going to have to go over each piece two times every practice."

Staff supervisor at a facility for aging adults to volunteer staff: "Our laundry costs are skyrocketing. If you are willing, we need all of you to spend two hours of your shift folding laundry."

In each of these examples, the leader is helping individuals identify and clarify the goals of their work. The individuals doing the work will be more effective and more satisfied as a result of knowing their goals.

Clarify Group Norms

In addition to clarifying goals, a leader needs to clarify group norms. **Norms** are the rules of behavior that are established and shared by group members. Social psychologists have argued for years that norms play a major role in the performance and effectiveness of groups (Cartwright & Zander, 1968; Harris & Sherblom, 2018; Napier & Gershenfeld, 2004). Norms are like a map for navigating how we are supposed to behave, telling us what is appropriate or inappropriate, what is right or wrong, and what is allowed or not allowed (Schein, 2017). Norms do not emerge on their own—they are the outcome of people interacting with each other and with the leader. As norms develop, the leader can reinforce those norms that fall within the general purposes of the organization. For example, in a daylong training seminar, the participants and seminar leader might mutually decide that they will turn off their cell phones and not leave early. Or staff members in an insurance agency might determine that a "business casual" dress code is appropriate during the week and jeans are OK on Fridays. Norms emerge as a result of how leaders treat followers and how followers treat each other.

Norms are important because they have a strong impact on how a group functions and whether the group is successful or not. For example, a weekly staff meeting where people are allowed to constantly whisper with the person next to them will create an atmosphere that lacks cohesiveness and most likely be very unproductive. On the positive side, if in a small business setting a norm develops of workers helping one another if someone falls behind, it can be very useful and inspiring. Leaders need to be aware that norms always exist, and even when they are subtle or not verbally expressed, they impact the productivity of the group.

Norms develop early in a group and are sometimes difficult to change. A leader can impact group norms by paying close attention to norm development and helping to shape constructive norms that will maximize group effectiveness. The following example shows that when a leader brings about constructive norms, it can have a positive effect on the entire group. Home from college for the summer, Matt Smith was asked to take over as coach of his little brother's baseball team because the previous coach was leaving. Before taking over as coach, Matt observed several practices and the norms operating on the team. He observed that team members frequently arrived 15 to 30 minutes late for practice, often came without their baseball shoes or gloves, and goofed off a lot during drills. Overall, Matt observed that the players did not seem to care about the team or have much pride in what they were doing.

After Matt had coached for a few weeks, the team's norms gradually changed. Matt continually stressed the need to start practice on time, encouraged the players to "bring their stuff" to practice, and praised them when they worked hard during drills. By the end of the summer, they were a different team. The players grew to enjoy the practice sessions, worked hard, and performed well. Most importantly, they thought their baseball team was "the greatest."

In this situation, the norms the players were operating under with the old coach interfered with the team and its goals. Under Matt's leadership, the players developed new norms that enabled them to function better.

Build Cohesiveness

A fourth fundamental of leading a group is building cohesiveness. **Cohesiveness** is described as a sense of "we-ness," the cement that holds a group together, or the *esprit de corps* that exists within a group. Cohesiveness allows group members to express their personal viewpoints, give and receive feedback, accept opinions different from their own, and feel comfortable doing meaningful work (Corey et al., 2017). When a group is cohesive, members identify with the group and its goals and find satisfaction in being accepted as part of the group, feeling a connection with each other and the group as a whole. Members appreciate the group and, in turn, are appreciated by the group.

Cohesiveness has been associated with many positive outcomes for groups (see Figure 8.2) (Cartwright & Zander, 1968; Shaw, 1981). First, high cohesiveness is frequently associated with

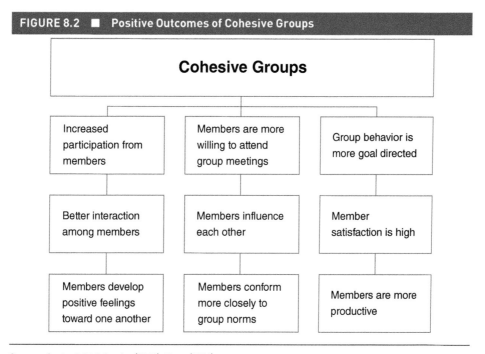

FIGURE 8.2 ■ Positive Outcomes of Cohesive Groups

Cohesive Groups

- Increased participation from members
- Members are more willing to attend group meetings
- Group behavior is more goal directed
- Better interaction among members
- Members influence each other
- Member satisfaction is high
- Members develop positive feelings toward one another
- Members conform more closely to group norms
- Members are more productive

Sources: Cartwright & Zander (1968); Shaw (1981).

increased participation and *better interaction* among members. People tend to talk more readily and listen more carefully in cohesive groups. They also are more likely to express their own opinions and be open to listening to the opinions of others.

Second, in highly cohesive groups, membership tends to be more *consistent*. Members *develop an understanding of each other and positive feelings toward one another* and *are more willing to attend* group meetings. For example, in a weight loss group that is cohesive, members often express strong support for each other, and attendance at meetings is very consistent.

Third, highly cohesive groups can exert a *strong positive influence* on group members. When members feel a part of the group, they usually *conform more closely to group norms* and *engage in more goal-directed behavior* for the group.

Fourth, when members *feel high levels of satisfaction* in cohesive groups, they tend to feel more secure and find enjoyment participating in the group. Think of the best class you have ever been in as a student. It was probably very cohesive, and you probably worked harder and enjoyed it so much that you were sorry when the semester ended.

Finally, members of a cohesive group usually are *more productive* than those of a less cohesive group. Members of groups with greater cohesion can direct their energies toward group goals without spending a lot of time working out interpersonal issues and social conflicts. For example, when a project team is cohesive, there usually are no social loafers (group members who are inclined to work below their capacity). Everyone is together in pursuit of the team goals, and some members may even pick up the slack of a less capable member.

While cohesive groups are what many organizations strive for, in certain instances, highly cohesive groups also can be problematic. First, when group members become extremely close, they can develop a closed-mindedness called *group think*, which values unanimity over critical appraisal of alternate ideas or viewpoints. Group members may be afraid to "rock the boat" and question the group's decision. Instead, both the leader and members go along with an idea perceived to be favored by other group members, even though they may feel that the idea may not turn out well in the long run. It is always helpful for a group to have one or two members who pay attention to the tendency of some members to become closed off to outside input and ideas.

Ways to Build Group Cohesion

Group cohesiveness does not develop instantaneously but is created gradually over time. A leader can assist a group to build cohesiveness by incorporating the following actions in their role as leader:

- Help group members create a climate of trust in one another that allows the free expression of divergent viewpoints

- Encourage passive or withdrawn members to become involved

- Listen and accept group members for who they are

- Help group members to achieve their individual goals

- Allow group members to share the leadership responsibilities

- Foster and promote member-to-member interaction instead of only leader-to-follower interaction (Corey et al., 2017)

When a leader takes some of these actions and supports team members to do the same, it increases the chance that the group will build a sense of cohesiveness.

Promote Standards of Excellence

Leaders of very high-functioning teams also promote **standards of excellence**. In a classic study, Larson and LaFasto (1989) analyzed the characteristics of 75 highly successful teams and found that standards of excellence were a crucial factor associated with team success.

Standards of excellence are the expressed and implied expectations for performance that exist within a group or an organization. To establish standards of excellence, group members need to know all of the following:

1. The skills they need to acquire

2. How much initiative and effort they need to demonstrate

3. How they are expected to treat one another

4. The importance of deadlines

5. The goals they [group members] need to achieve

6. The consequences if they achieve or fail to achieve these goals (Larson & LaFasto, 1989, p. 95)

A good example of standards of excellence can be seen in the slogan (see Figure 8.3) of The Upjohn Company (now Pfizer), a pharmaceutical manufacturing firm in Kalamazoo, Michigan. Founded in 1885, Upjohn was known for revolutionizing the drug industry through its invention of the "friable pill," which can crumble under the pressure of a person's thumb. In addition to this innovation, Upjohn made many other drug discoveries, becoming one of the largest pharmaceutical companies in the world. For many years, the internal slogan promoted throughout the company was "Keep the quality up."

FIGURE 8.3 ■ Standards of Excellence Slogan

Source: Used as Courtesy of the WMU Archives and Regional History Collections.

"Keep the quality up" captures what standards of excellence are all about. This slogan is clear, direct, and forceful. It puts responsibility on employees to work toward maintaining quality—a standard of excellence—and work consistently toward this standard over time. In addition, "Keep the quality up" stresses a positive expectation that has value for both employees and the company; quality is also the valued benchmark of the company's desired performance for its employees.

To influence performance and promote standards of excellence, a leader must stress the "three *Rs*": (1) *Require* results, (2) *Review* results, and (3) *Reward* results (LaFasto & Larson, 2001).

Require Results

A leader needs to articulate clear, concrete expectations for team members. Working together, a leader and group members should establish mutual goals and identify specific objectives for achieving the results associated with those goals. Requiring results is the critical first step in managing performance (LaFasto & Larson, 2001).

Review Results

In addition to requiring results, a leader needs to review results and encourage all group members to acknowledge the importance of quality results. According to LaFasto and Larson (2001), a leader does this by (1) *giving constructive feedback* and (2) *resolving performance issues.*

Giving constructive feedback is a must for a leader if they are going to help group members maintain standards of excellence. **Constructive feedback** is honest and direct communication about a group member's performance. It helps group members know if they are doing the right things, in the right way, at the right speed. It is not mean-spirited or paternalistic, nor is it overly nice or patronizing. Although it is not easy to do, providing constructive feedback is a skill that can be learned and involves five simple communication methods:

1. *Address behaviors.* Use facts to describe the behavior that is problematic, rather than focusing on personal traits. For example, a leader might say, "Jane, I have noticed that you have been late for the past three mornings. Can you explain why?" rather than "Why aren't you able to arrive on time?"

2. *Describe specifically what you have observed.* Observations are what you have seen occur; an interpretation is your analysis or opinion of what has occurred. Observations are more factual and less judgmental. For example, a leader might say, "Dan, there were several factual and grammatical errors in the report you submitted," rather than "Dan, all these mistakes make me wonder if you were doing this report at the last minute."

3. *Use "I" language.* Using "I" statements rather than "you" statements will help reduce the other person's defensiveness. For example, if you say, "Joe, because our cubicles are so close together, I have a hard time concentrating when you play music on your computer," rather than "It is really inconsiderate of you to play music when other people are trying to work," you are more likely to elicit the change you would like.

4. *Give feedback in calm, unemotional language.* Avoid "need to" phrases (e.g., "You need to improve this . . .") or using a tone that implies anger, frustration, or disappointment. Rather than saying, "If you'd just learn the software, you'd do a better job," a leader could say, "I am sure you will be much faster when you understand how to use this software."

5. *Check to ensure clear communication has occurred.* Solicit feedback from the other person to ensure they understand what you have been trying to communicate to them. For example, a leader might say, "Ann, do you know the procedure for ordering the supplies? Can you go over it to be sure I covered everything?" rather than "Ann, you got all that, didn't you?"

When done correctly, constructive feedback allows group members to look at themselves honestly and know what they need to maintain or improve (LaFasto & Larson, 2001).

Resolving performance issues is the second part of reviewing results. LaFasto and Larson (2001) found that a distinguishing characteristic of effective leaders is their willingness to confront and resolve inadequate performance by team members. Working in groups is a collective effort—everyone must be involved and share responsibility for achieving group goals. When some members do not pull their own weight, it affects everyone in the group. If the leader fails to address the inadequate performance of any group members, contributing group members will feel angry and slighted, as if their work does not really matter.

Confronting inadequate performance by group members is a challenging and emotionally charged but necessary part of leadership (LaFasto & Larson, 2001). An effective leader is proactive and confronts problems when they occur. In problem situations, a leader must explain to low-performing group members how their behaviors hinder the group from meeting its goals and what needs to be done differently. After the needed changes have been clearly identified, the leader must monitor the behaviors of the low-performing group members. If the group members make satisfactory changes, they can remain in the group. If a group member refuses to change, the leader needs to counsel them about leaving the group. When a leader addresses behavioral problems in a timely fashion, it is beneficial both to the person with the performance problem and to the entire group.

It is important to recognize, however, that the feedback process can involve power differences and potential bias. For example, in professional settings such as law, medicine, and business, this power difference has been shown to disproportionately affect women and people of color being evaluated (Casad & Bryant, 2016; Dayal et al., 2017; Williams et al., 2018). In a study funded by the American Bar Association, female attorneys (white and of color) and male attorneys of color reported that they go "above and beyond" to get the same recognition and respect as their white male colleagues (Williams et al., 2018). In the technology sector, a comparison of performance reviews of male and female employees showed that while both men and women were given constructive suggestions, the women's reviews were more likely to include critical feedback, and only the women were advised to be less assertive (Snyder, 2014). When evaluations of women and people of color include suggestions that their behavior is somehow "counter-normative," their receptivity to that feedback is diminished (Casad & Bryant, 2016;

Williams et al., 2018). Thus, it is important for leaders to be aware of potential bias when giving feedback, and to ensure equal standards for all, so that they don't promote discrimination.

Reward Results

Finally, an effective leader rewards group members for achieving results (LaFasto & Larson, 2001).

In their well-known consulting work on leadership effectiveness, Kouzes and Posner (2023) identified rewarding results as one of the five major practices of exemplary leaders. They argued that a leader needs to recognize the contributions of group members and express appreciation for individual excellence. This includes paying attention to group members, offering them encouragement, and giving them personalized appreciation. These expressions can be dramatic, such as a dinner celebration, or simple, such as a short email of praise. When a leader recognizes group members and gives encouragement, members feel valued, and there is a greater sense of group identity and community spirit.

Address Out-Group Members

A final group factor that is fundamental to leading groups is *addressing out-group members*. Out-group members are often a common occurrence whenever people come together to solve a problem or accomplish a task. Despite the negativity that may be associated with out-groups, out-groups are not "evil," and leaders have a responsibility to listen to them and "bring them in" to the efforts of the larger group. In fact, the truly serious and effective leader will do everything in their power to bring all group members together to address the common good.

The term **out-group members** refers to those individuals in a group or an organization who do not identify themselves as part of the larger group. They are individuals who are disconnected and not fully engaged in working toward the goals of the group. They may be in opposition to the will of a larger group or simply disinterested in the group's goals. They may be unaccepted, alienated, and even discriminated against. In addition, they may believe they are powerless because their potential resources have not been fully accepted by the larger group.

Out-groups come in many forms: They can be people of color in predominantly white organizations whose voices are not being heard or people whose ideas are unappreciated. Sometimes out-group members are social loafers or simply do not identify with the leader or other members of the group. In short, out-group members sense themselves to be at odds with the larger group. For example, the single male nurse on an all-female nursing staff might feel as if he is an "outsider" because he perceives that the other team members do not appreciate his male perspective on issues regarding patients or include him when they meet together outside of work.

Responding to out-group members may seem daunting, but there are six straightforward, strategies a leader can use to more effectively manage out-group members—*listening, showing empathy, recognizing their unique contributions, helping them feel included, creating special relationships with them*, and *giving them voice and empowering them to act*.

Strategy 1: Listen to Out-Group Members

More than anything else, out-group members want to be heard. Whether they perceive themselves to be powerless, alienated, or discriminated against, out-group members have ideas, attitudes, and feelings that they want to express. When they believe they have not been able to or will not be able to express these, they pull away and disassociate from the group.

Listening is one of the most important ways that a leader can respond to out-group members. Listening is both a simple and a complex process that demands concentration, open-mindedness, and tolerance. It requires that a leader set aside their own biases in order to allow out-group members to express their viewpoints freely.

Jane Addams, who founded the social settlement Hull House in Chicago in 1889, is an example of a gifted listener. In response to problems created by industrialization, immigration, and overcrowding in cities, Addams established a live-in community called a settlement house, where trained workers provided resources for newly arrived immigrants to help them acculturate to the United States. It always began with listening to these immigrants' needs—for housing, for child care, for jobs, for language courses, and so on. By listening first, Addams and her associates created a bond of trust that transcended language and cultural barriers and made newcomers to the country feel welcome and want to invest in their new communities (Metzger, 2009).

When out-group members believe that the leader has heard them, they feel confirmed and more connected to the larger group. Clearly, listening should be a top priority of a leader.

Strategy 2: Show Empathy to Out-Group Members

A leader also needs to show empathy to out-group members to help these individuals feel less on the outside. Empathy is a process in which the leader suspends their own feelings in an effort to understand the feelings of the out-group member. It requires a leader to try "standing in the shoes" of out-group members, to see the world as the out-group member does.

Father Greg Boyle, the founder of Homeboy Industries in Los Angeles, the largest gang intervention, rehabilitation, and reentry program in the world, is an example of an empathetic leader. In response to the spike in gang killings in L.A. in the late 1980s and early '90s, Father Boyle started meeting with gang members, listening to their stories, understanding their varied reasons for joining gangs, and treating them as human beings, rather than as social problems to be controlled. With a team of dedicated workers and mentors, he created rehabilitation and job-training programs for these men based on their expressed needs, helping them find hope again in a society where they felt they had no place (Homeboy Industries, 2019).

Strategy 3: Recognize the Unique Contributions of Out-Group Members

Like all of us, out-group members want to know that their ideas matter and that they are important to the group. Out-group members become more motivated when a leader or an active group member acknowledges their contributions. Sometimes, peer feedback from a group member is received more soundly than "feedback from the boss." Expectancy theory

(Vroom, 1964) tells us that the first step in motivating others is to let them know they are competent to do their jobs.

Because it is common for out-group members to believe others do not recognize their strengths, it is important for a leader to identify out-group members' unique abilities and assets (see Chapter 6, "Engaging Strengths") and to integrate these into the group process. For example, if an out-group member suggests a radical but ultimately successful approach to accomplish a difficult task, the leader should express appreciation to the out-group member and let them know that the idea was creative and worthwhile. A leader needs to let out-group members know that what they do matters—that it is significant to the larger group.

An example that helps illustrate the importance of recognizing the unique contributions of out-group members is the team in a small group communication class that chose to build a wheelchair ramp for an older woman in the community as its service learning project. In the initial stages of the project, morale in the group was low because one group member (Alissa) would not participate. Alissa said she was quite uncomfortable using hand tools, and she chose not to do manual labor. The other team members wanted to proceed without her help. As a result, Alissa felt rejected and soon became isolated from the group, criticizing the project's purpose and the personalities of the other team members.

At that point, one of the group's leaders decided to start being more attentive to Alissa and what she was saying. After carefully listening to many of her concerns, the leader figured out while Alissa could not work with her hands, she had two talents: She was good with music, and she made wonderful lunches.

Once the leader found this out, things started to change in the group. Alissa started to participate. Her input into the construction of the ramp consisted of playing each group member's and the older woman's favorite music for 30 minutes each while the other group members worked on the ramp. In addition, Alissa provided wonderful sandwiches and drinks that accommodated each of the group members' unique dietary interests. Alissa felt so included by the group, and was so often praised for providing great food, that on the last day, she helped with the manual labor by raking up trash around the ramp site.

Although Alissa's talents had nothing to do directly with constructing a ramp, she made a real contribution to building a successful team. Everybody was included and useful in a community-building project that could have turned sour if one out-group member's talents had not been identified and utilized.

Strategy 4: Help Out-Group Members Feel Included

William Schutz (1966) pointed out that, in small group situations, one of our strongest interpersonal needs is to know whether we belong to the group. Are we "in" or "out"? The very nature of out-groups implies that their members are on the sidelines and peripheral to the action. Out-group members do not feel as if they belong, are included, or are "in." Schutz suggested that people have a need to be connected to others, to be in a group and to belong, but not so much that they lose their sense of self.

A leader can help out-group members be more included by paying attention to the communication cues given by out-group members and respond in appropriate ways. For example, if a person sits at the edge of the group, the leader can put the chairs in a circle and invite the person to sit in the circle. If a person does not follow the group norms (e.g., does not go outdoors with everyone else during breaks), the leader can personally invite the out-group member to join the others outside. Similarly, if a group member is quiet and has not contributed, a leader can ask for that group member's opinion. Although there are many ways to help out-group members to be included, the bottom line is that a leader needs to be sensitive to out-group members' needs and try to respond to them in ways that help the out-group members know that they are part of the larger group.

Strategy 5: Create a Special Relationship With Out-Group Members

The most well-known study on out-groups was conducted by a group of researchers who developed a theory called *leader–member exchange (LMX) theory* (Dansereau et al., 1975; Graen & Uhl-Bien, 1995). The major premise of this theory is that a leader should create a special relationship with each follower. Special relationships with out-group members are built on good communication, respect, and trust. They are often initiated when a leader recognizes the out-group members who are willing to step out of scripted roles and take on different responsibilities. These relationships can also develop when a leader challenges out-group members to be engaged and try new things. If an out-group member accepts these challenges and responsibilities, it is the first step in forging an improved relationship between the leader and the out-group member. The result is that the out-group member feels validated and more connected to everyone else in the group.

An example of how special relationships benefit out-group members can be seen in the following example. Margo Miller was the school nurse at Central High School. She was also the unofficial school counselor, social worker, conflict mediator, and all-around friend to students. Margo noticed that there were several students who were not part of any of the groups at school, so she invited some of these students and others to exercise with her at the track after school. For some of them, it was the first time they had ever taken part in an extracurricular school program. The students and Margo called themselves the Breakfast Club because, like the characters in the movie by the same name, they were a motley crew. At the end of the semester, the group sponsored a school-wide 5K run/walk that was well attended. One girl who finished the 5K said that Margo and the Breakfast Club were the best thing that had ever happened to her. Clearly, it was the special relationships that Margo created with the out-group students that allowed them to become involved and feel good about their involvement in the high school community.

Strategy 6: Give Out-Group Members a Voice and Empower Them to Act

Giving out-group members a voice by giving credence to their ideas and actions lets them be on equal footing with other members of the group. When out-group members have a voice, they know their interests are being recognized and that they can have an impact on the leader and the group. It is quite a remarkable process when a leader is confident enough in their own leadership to let out-group members express themselves and have a voice in the affairs of the group.

LEADERSHIP SNAPSHOT
PROJECT ARISTOTLE

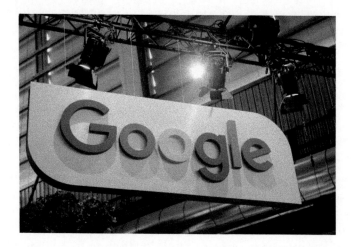

In 2012, Google embarked on an initiative—code-named Project Aristotle—to study hundreds of work teams at its company to determine why some teams stumbled and others soared.

To do so, they started out by reviewing more than 50 years of academic studies on how teams work. They then turned their gaze internally, looking at more than 250 attributes of 180-plus active Google teams. They drew diagrams to show how members overlapped in different groups and which groups had exceeded their departments' goals. They studied how long teams stuck together and if gender balance seemed to have an impact on a team's success.

All these data led to one conclusion: There was no evidence that *the composition* of a team made any difference. What did matter was how the team members interacted, structured their work, and viewed their contributions.

"We had lots of data, but there was nothing showing that a mix of specific personality types or skills or backgrounds made any difference. The 'who' part of the equation didn't seem to matter," said Abeer Dubey, a manager in Google's People Analytics division (Duhigg, 2016).

These researchers identified five key factors of successful teams:

Psychological safety: Creating a safe culture in which team members feel "safe" enough to take interpersonal risks, voice their opinions, and be vulnerable in front of others without being viewed as disruptive, disrespectful, or incompetent.

Dependability: Members see their fellow teammates as accountable, reliable, and trustworthy.

Structure and clarity: The goals, roles, and execution plans for the team are clear, and members understand their function, purpose, expectations, and performance objectives.

Meaning of work: Team members are working on something that is personally important for each of them whether it be pride in the final product, creating financial security, supporting one's family, helping the team succeed, or exhibiting self-expression.

Impact of work: Team members believe that the work they are doing matters and is creating value and impact for others such as those who will utilize the products or services the team creates. Impact of work also refers to how the team's work helps advance the organization's overall goals, mission, and impact.

Of all these factors, however, one—psychological safety—was shown to be the most critical in making a team successful. The Google researchers found that individuals on teams with higher psychological safety were less likely to leave the company, were more likely to harness the power of diverse ideas from their teammates, brought in more revenue, and achieved effective ratings twice as often by executives (re:Work, n.d.).

So, for Google, an organization where decisions are made based on data and analytics and employees are techie types who tend to be introverted and avoid talking about feelings, implementing psychological safety and the concepts of communication and empathy was not going to be easy.

"There's a famous saying at Google," says Matt Sakaguchi, a Google site reliability manager. "Engineering is easy, people are hard" (UC Riverside Staff Assembly, 2019).

To address these findings, Google created a tool called the "gTeams exercise," which starts with a 10-minute check on the five dynamics followed by a report that summarizes how the team is doing. This report is used to facilitate an in-person discussion among the team of the results with suggestions and resources provided to help teams improve. More than 3,000 employees across 300 teams at Google have used the tool. Of those, the teams that adopted a new group norm—like kicking off every team meeting by sharing a risk taken in the previous week—improved their ratings in psychological safety and structure and clarity. Team members said that having a framework around team effectiveness and a function that forced them to talk about these dynamics was the most impactful part of the experience (Rozovsky, 2015). Research also showed that psychological safety has an impact on the bottom line: Google sales teams with high ratings for psychological safety brought in more revenue, exceeding their sales targets by 17%. Teams with low psychological safety fell short by up to 19% (Tamiru, 2023).

"By putting things like empathy and sensitivity into charts and data reports, it makes them easier to talk about," Sakaguchi says. "It's easier to talk about our feelings when we can point to a number" (Duhigg, 2016). But all data and algorithms aside, in the end, Project Aristotle proved that the equation put forth by the Greek philosopher for which the project was named was undeniably true: "The whole is greater than the sum of its parts."

Empowering others to act means a leader allows out-group members to be more involved, independent, and responsible for their actions. True empowerment requires that a leader relinquish some control, giving out-group members more control, which is why empowerment is such a challenging process for a leader. It includes letting out-group members participate in the workings of the group (e.g., planning, decision-making).

It is important to note here that out-group members don't always want to be included. According to LMX theory, followers will become part of the in-group or out-group based on how well they work with the leader and the leader works with them (Northouse, 2022). In work situations, in-group members will often take on extra roles and tasks to help the group or department. In turn, these workers receive more attention and support from the leader and experience greater motivation and job satisfaction at work (Malik et al., 2015). Other workers may be less compatible with the leader, may not like the leader, or may not be interested in expanding their role responsibilities or involvement in the organization and so become part of the out-group, receiving less attention and support from the leader. These could be part-time workers, a busy parent who has obligations and responsibilities outside of work, or someone close to retirement who is mainly interested in getting their required tasks done and going home at the end of the day. Not all out-group members "mind" being in the out-group.

In short, a leader needs to make a concerted effort to include group members and help them feel as if they belong. Good group process requires that a leader attends to the interests, needs, and proclivities of *all* group members, listening to out-group members' perspectives and understanding the reasons that some members may become part of an out-group. By providing empathy to out-group members, giving them a voice, and empowering these members to act, the leader can create a special relationship with out-group members that makes those members feel validated and more connected to the group.

SUMMARY

This chapter is about groups and how leaders can more effectively lead groups. Because groups are integral to all aspects of our lives, it is imperative to understand the nature of groups and the dynamics of group process.

There are two major types of groups. *Task groups* focus primarily on content issues and accomplishing goals, while *process groups* focus primarily on interpersonal relationships and how individual group members communicate with one another. Both types of groups typically proceed through five stages. The *forming stage* is an orientation time when members try to figure out how included or excluded they are by the group. The *storming stage*, sometimes called the conflict phase, occurs when members are concerned about how much influence and control they have in the group. In the *norming stage*, group members begin feeling more cohesive and connected to each other. In the *performing stage*, group members have feelings of unity and perform the work they have set out to do. The *adjourning stage* occurs when members disengage from one another and contemplate what it will be like without the group.

The individual roles group members play in a group are critical. Researchers have identified twelve *task roles* (e.g., opinion giver, energizer) that have a positive impact on how groups work and seven *group-building and maintenance roles* (e.g., encourager, compromiser) that assist groups in developing good working relationships. On the negative side, researchers found eight *individual roles* (e.g., aggressor, dominator) that can disrupt the group's progress and weaken group cohesion.

Though not often discussed, group work can provide very real benefits to individual group members. Groups can help us feel recognized and valued by others. They also help us learn from others, feel connected to others, and increase our sense that we are not "in the boat" alone. When groups are run effectively, they are often healing to group members.

The second half of the chapter lays out seven prescriptions for how to be a better group leader. These include *establishing a constructive climate, providing structure, clarifying group goals and norms, building group cohesiveness, promoting standards of excellence*, and *helping out-group members*.

To summarize, groups play a central role in most everything people do. The challenge for leaders is to understand the complexity of groups and to try to help them to become maximally effective. In the end, when groups function well, group members can feel a sense of belonging and significance, and there is a positive effect on goal accomplishment.

KEY TERMS

adjourning stage

cohesiveness

constructive climate

constructive feedback

forming stage

group

group-building and maintenance roles

group task roles

individual roles

norming stage

norms

out-group members

performing stage

process groups

standards of excellence

storming stage

structure

synergy

task groups

Application

8.1 Case Study—Remote Teamwork

A week before Bristol County Community College was shut down for the COVID-19 pandemic in March 2020, Brenna Taggart had been hired to oversee a project to integrate a new software system that handled all the college's human resource functions such as payroll, benefits, and hiring. To implement the new system, she would be working with teams in two departments—Human Resources and Information Technology. Brenna had the perfect background for the job; she was experienced in both computer software development and human resource management and had helped two other colleges implement the same new software system that Bristol CCC was going to use.

Despite the pandemic, the project had a looming deadline; the old software system the college was using was no longer supported by the company that developed it and was going to be obsolete in a year. Brenna had been warned by the college president that the two departments she was working with had a prickly relationship. For years, the IT staff had been "cobbling together" fixes for the existing software system by writing their own code and were proud that they had been able to keep it functional and save the college money. They resented that the HR department had bought a new, third-party software without IT's input and that the IT staff was now expected to integrate it into the college's existing IT systems. The HR staff thought the IT team was difficult to work with and arrogant, believing that the IT group members would only say what couldn't be done and deliberately talk down to others, using "techno-speak" that others didn't understand.

As all the college's employees were, Brenna began her new job remotely, working from home without having met any of the team members in person. She jumped right in, drafting a project plan that outlined the goals and tasks each team needed to take to implement the new system. She scheduled regular video meetings for each team two days a week and a several-hour joint meeting of both teams once a week. She communicated frequently every day with individual team members, choosing to do so via video and by phone when possible, rather than through email. She quickly developed a strong rapport with each group: the IT team appreciated her knowledge and background in their area and that she understood their "techno-speak." The HR team members were energized by Brenna's affirmation that the new system they had chosen would automate many of their tasks, saving them time and making their jobs easier. But in all her interactions with the individual teams, it was apparent that the separate teams didn't respect each other or believe the other team to be competent.

Before the first joint meeting of the two teams, Brenna paired up individuals from the HR team with members of the IT team and had them interview each other. She gave them a list of suggested questions such as asking about one another's backgrounds, activities outside of work, families, pets, favorite restaurants, and movies or shows they were watching during the pandemic. In the joint meeting, each pair introduced one another to the group, reporting what they had learned about each other. Members of both teams discovered commonalities: Several were avid bicyclists, some had gone to the same college, some had children the same age, and some took their dogs to the same dog park. They shared favorite restaurants and shows. Two even discovered they lived three doors from each other in the same apartment complex.

Toward the end of the meeting, Brenna asked the group to establish "rules of engagement" to foster a positive communication environment for future meetings. After much back and forth, they came up with the following rules: (1) Team members needed to listen respectfully to one another without interrupting; (2) group members could and should express divergent viewpoints as long as they did so in a respectful manner; (3) verbally attacking one another was not acceptable; and (4) team members would use constructive feedback methods during discussion. In addition, the group developed a mission statement for the project that outlined its goals and expected impact and agreed that these would be the guiding principles for the team's interactions and work going forward.

The initial team meetings were rocky. The video platform made it hard for people to speak openly; it aired only the audio of the person speaking. One IT staffer, who had worked at the college the longest, would often "hold the floor," explaining that what the team was trying to do "had been tried before and failed." When other team members would speak, he would interrupt or talk over them so that the audio switched back to him and he could continue talking. An HR team member refused to use her computer's camera so that only her name appeared on the screen, and she rarely said anything during the meetings, leading other group members to wonder if she was even participating. When another HR team member, who also rarely spoke in the meetings, was asked to give their opinion, they would reply that they "didn't know anything about technology and shouldn't even be part of the group." An IT team member told the group that they had it on good authority that the college's president wanted to merge the HR and IT departments and that this joint implementation project was to cross-train staff so that the administration could eliminate positions.

Initially, Brenna would redirect these conversations by reminding the group of their mission statement and guiding principles and ask how what they were contributing would help to forward those. Brenna also enforced the rules of engagement, telling the team members that unless they were speaking, their microphones needed to be on mute so they could listen to the others. If they wanted to speak, they would use the "raise hand" feature of the video platform, allowing her to call upon members in order.

Slowly, interactions within the team began to change. One team member took the initiative to record the meetings and sent out summaries to members of the issues discussed and tasks assigned. Another member encouraged the group to discuss and debate different alternatives by making suggestions, starting with "What would happen if we tried . . . ?" The IT team member who initially dominated the conversations was unable to do so with the raise hand feature and, wanting to be included, began offering his experiences and knowledge in terms of how it could help the transition from the old system to the new one. The team member who claimed to not know anything about technology started asking for clarification and additional information from IT members when they used techno-speak, ultimately helping the whole team to understand the technological aspects of the project better. Two group members realized that the team member who wasn't appearing on-screen or talking much was extremely introverted, and they learned to ask her for her opinion in a way that didn't make her feel anxious.

As the pandemic wore on and the deadline got closer, the two teams found that they needed to meet more often. They suggested to Brenna that the whole group meet twice a week and change the individual department team meetings to only once a week. When Brenna came down with COVID-19 and was unable to lead the meetings for several weeks, a member from each department took turns running the joint meetings and reporting the group's progress back to Brenna.

The team worked together remotely for almost a year, hashing out the minute details and complexities of the implementation. A month before the college reopened its doors to in-person learning, the software system went live, and the team continued working via video, email, and phone to work out the kinks and bugs. When the college's faculty and staff returned to campus, they only saw the new, smooth-running system in place, oblivious to the teamwork that occurred behind the scenes to make it happen.

Questions

1. What fundamentals of group leadership (establish a constructive climate, provide structure, etc.) did Brenna implement? Give examples.

2. What was the intention of having the group establish and observe "rules of engagement"? Did these have a positive or negative impact on the group communication?

3. Discuss, with examples, how the group proceeded through the stages of group development.

4. What methods were used to build group cohesion? Were these methods different from what might have been used if the team was meeting in person and not digitally?

5. What individual, task, and group-building and maintenance roles were evident in this group?

6. Was there an out-group component to this team? How did the leader address any out-group issues?

8.2 Case Study—"Moving Their Cheese"

Miriam is a vice president and national underwriting manager for BMC, a large mortgage company. She has had a long and successful career in mortgage banking, working for several large banks before coming to BMC. In her current position, she oversees all of the underwriting across the country, which includes a leadership team of seven managers and more than 350 employees. The average tenure of the employees at the company is 20 years.

Miriam replaced a man who had been the company's national underwriting manager for 10 years, during which the employees who worked for him became used to his hands-off style of leadership. He was the kind of manager who would walk past his staff in the morning without saying hello and delegated many of his responsibilities to the managers under him, rarely interacting with the employees who reported to his managers.

But that was *not* Miriam's style. For several months before BMC announced Miriam's new role, she worked as an underwriter at the company. She gained an understanding of what the people in the underwriting department did, from the processes and systems they used to the culture and norms of the department and company. So, when it was announced that she would be the new vice president, she knew what norms to keep because they were enabling and what norms needed to be changed because they were restrictive.

Miriam says she knew instilling new norms in an already established group wouldn't be easy. "When they announced my new role, it moved their cheese big time," she says with a laugh, referring to the classic business book *Who Moved My Cheese?* "I knew that the most important thing to do was to create relationships with them that would create bonds and trust between us."

That proved to be a real challenge because Miriam started in early 2021 during the COVID-19 pandemic. Because employees were working from home, her initial meetings with people were done remotely via video and phone.

"As a new person managing groups, I wanted to be engaged. I spent the first year focused on listening and learning, building trust, and establishing relationships so that they knew who I was. I needed to figure out who they were, too, their strengths and their weaknesses," she recalls. "And I did that not only by having weekly meetings to get to know my managers but by going down several levels as well, and contacting the people that report to those managers. I called every single one of them and said, 'Give me three things that are working really well here and three opportunities that we have.'"

Miriam also worked on establishing a safe environment for employees so they could and would share their opinions with her and in group meetings. To help them understand her leadership style, Miriam told her employees a story about how she had been working at a large bank where the culture had become very cutthroat and people acted in negative ways. She found that she was getting sucked into that culture and losing the attributes that she felt had made her a successful leader. "You had to adapt to the environment of the company if you wanted to be successful but at the risk of becoming somebody different. There, I was supposed to be this tough woman who acted strong and confident like the men did. And when you didn't act this way, you were seen as weak. In that company, they didn't care about the people, and that did not match my leadership style." Despite her success and the lucrative financial benefits of the job, she made the choice to leave to find a company that put people first. She also admitted that she spent a year working with an executive coach to "train myself away" from her prior employer's culture.

"Early on at BMC I shared my story with them and made sure they knew that I wanted to hear from them, too," she says. "When they do give me suggestions, I respond to them. I personally thank them and follow up, letting them know if we decided to implement their ideas. Even though it's a large group, I get in front of all 350 team members two times a month and I try to be transparent. In the last two years, they've come to know who I am."

Miriam said she realized that she had succeeded in building trust with her group members when a woman several levels below reached out to her to share that several of the male managers she worked with had been acting inappropriately. "She was very uncomfortable with the incidents, and because I had been vulnerable and shared my experiences, she trusted me enough to tell me," Miriam says. "That trust is critical because there are people out there who are afraid to say anything. She was very afraid and kept saying, 'I need my job, I need my job.' And I told her, 'You have no worry about retaliation here.'

"If you don't have that trust, the risk of things going haywire several layers down is much higher."

BMC had established a "people-first" company culture when it began 30 years ago, but Miriam found that the larger and more successful the company became, that culture wasn't always enacted by those in her group. While sitting in on several video meetings, Miriam observed that one manager was consistently rude and condescending to her own staff, other managers, and even a regional president. Miriam talked with the employee about her attitude, imparting to her that it was important she be more collaborative and work across departmental lines.

"Her attitude on camera in these meetings was curt and rude, and you could tell from her facial expressions that she was irritated or annoyed when she didn't need to be. She would justify it by saying she was upset about another issue going on outside the meeting. But she did this repeatedly," Miriam explains. "In this company you have to be collaborative, work across all lines, work together, and support each other. And she wasn't." The employee continued to act rudely and, after multiple warnings, Miriam was forced to terminate her.

Another change that Miriam implemented within her group was to provide a more consistent structure, especially when it came to meetings. "There had been a lot of leaders in my career who would schedule meetings and then cancel those, or they didn't ensure the meetings were purposeful and had good content," she says. "But I made a point with my leaders to keep consistency, to have those meetings every week where I start off by just engaging them on a personal level, asking about what they did over the weekend, what's going on with their families, and so on. And then we get to the business aspect of what we need to get done."

Miriam also worked with her leaders to implement new controls, policies, and procedures for the department. She initially received pushback from some who questioned why they had to do things that they hadn't done before. "They would say, 'Well, we never had to do this before, so why do we have to do this now? We don't need them.' I had to show them that there were issues and that we needed these new controls to address those issues."

After BMC went through an extensive outside audit, one of Miriam's senior leaders told her he now understood. "The auditors asked to see our policies and procedures and if we hadn't had those robust procedures and policies in place and been adhering to them, our department would have been in jeopardy of being put on an 'action plan,' which is not a positive thing," Miriam explains. "I have to respect the fact that many of the employees have been here for a long time and are used to the way things have historically been done. When you are trying to change a culture, you can't just say 'this is how we are doing things.' It's about helping them to understand *why* we are trying to do what we are trying to do. It's not just because we feel like it; there's a reason for it. You have to show them the 'whys' and bring them along."

Now that the pandemic has abated, Miriam makes a point of traveling across the country to meet with her employees in person to reinforce the bonds she worked to create remotely. She'll be in Chicago one month, Seattle the next, Minneapolis the next, Florida after that, and so on. But the hectic schedule is worth it to bolster the relationships within her group.

"I have their trust right now and I'm in a good spot with them," she says. "On one trip I had a senior manager tell me, 'I just love working for you. I love your style.' And I'm getting more and more of that type of feedback.

"I just really enjoy helping people grow."

Questions

1. Miriam's "style" of leadership is mentioned several times. How would you describe her overall style? How would you describe her style when it comes to leading groups?

2. Describe how Miriam implemented the following fundamentals of leading groups:
   a. Establish a constructive climate
   b. Provide structure
   c. Clarify goals
   d. Clarify group norms
   e. Build cohesiveness
   f. Promote standards of excellence
   g. Address out-group members

3. While Miriam took over leading established groups, the groups still went through many of the stages of group development. Describe these stages and what occurred during these stages.

4. How did Miriam address the out-group members in her department? How did she employ the strategies outlined in the chapter for working with out-group members?

Application

8.3 Group Leadership Questionnaire

Purpose

1. To explore how you, as a leader, respond to members of your group
2. To obtain an assessment of the relative importance you give to different components of group leadership

Directions

1. Think of yourself as a group leader in responding to this questionnaire.
2. For each of the following statements, circle the number that indicates the degree to which you agree or disagree.

As a leader:

Statements	Strongly disagree	Disagree	Neutral	Agree	Strongly agree
1. I am bothered when group members bring up unusual ideas that hinder or block group progress.	1	2	3	4	5
2. Helping people feel comfortable while working in their groups is especially important to me.	1	2	3	4	5
3. I help group members know their individual roles in order to reduce disorganization and uncertainty in the group.	1	2	3	4	5
4. I make it a high priority to encourage withdrawn members to become involved in the group.	1	2	3	4	5
5. I let group members deal with their own disagreements when they occur.	1	2	3	4	5

Statements	Strongly disagree	Disagree	Neutral	Agree	Strongly agree
6. I focus on bringing out the best talents and abilities of group members.	1	2	3	4	5
7. I help group members see the value of working in teams.	1	2	3	4	5
8. I try to create a positive group atmosphere when people disagree with each other.	1	2	3	4	5
9. Trying to reach consensus (complete agreement) among group members is often a waste of my time.	1	2	3	4	5
10. I spend time helping each group member know their roles and responsibilities.	1	2	3	4	5
11. Trying to help people feel positive about attending group meetings is a high priority to me.	1	2	3	4	5
12. Making sure the goals of the group are clear to members is important to me.	1	2	3	4	5
13. A major purpose of leading groups is trying to understand and shape group norms.	1	2	3	4	5

Statements	Strongly disagree	Disagree	Neutral	Agree	Strongly agree
14. Setting standards of excellence in group work is an important part of my role.	1	2	3	4	5
15. A major responsibility of my leadership is to help group members work with each other.	1	2	3	4	5
16. I consistently stress the specific outcomes that I expect my group to accomplish.	1	2	3	4	5
17. Identifying the purpose of group meetings is often a waste of time.	1	2	3	4	5
18. Providing an agenda for group meetings is a high priority for me.	1	2	3	4	5
19. I try to allow others to share in the leadership responsibilities.	1	2	3	4	5
20. Helping everyone feel part of the group is a central focus of my leadership.	1	2	3	4	5
21. It is not important to help group members develop group norms.	1	2	3	4	5
22. I clearly state the specific expectations for group members.	1	2	3	4	5

Statements	Strongly disagree	Disagree	Neutral	Agree	Strongly agree
23. When groups develop bad habits, I do not try to change them.	1	2	3	4	5
24. Trying to create positive group norms is a major aspect of leading groups.	1	2	3	4	5
25. Having good relationships with group members is important to me.	1	2	3	4	5
26. It is essential for me to emphasize the overall mission of the group.	1	2	3	4	5
27. I make a practice of rewarding group members whose performance meets group expectations.	1	2	3	4	5
28. When group members feel left out, it is usually their own fault.	1	2	3	4	5

Scoring

1. Reverse the score value of your responses on items 1, 5, 9, 14, 17, and 21 (i.e., change 1 to 5, 2 to 4, 4 to 2, and 5 to 1, with 3 remaining unchanged).
2. Sum the score values of all the numbered items including the converted values items. This total is your group leadership score.

Total Score

Group leadership score: _____

Scoring Interpretation

This questionnaire is designed to measure your leadership style and effectiveness in leading a variety of small groups. A higher score on the questionnaire indicates that you are likely to be a very effective group leader and suggests that as a leader, you try to help individuals feel included and a part of the whole group. You are likely to listen to people with different points of view and to know that hearing a minority position can be of value to the success of the group. You are most likely concerned about creating a positive climate for a group and a place where group members most likely would feel appreciated. As a group leader, you most likely would clarify group member roles, clarify the goals of the group, and help group members develop productive group habits. Above all, you try to help the group work together as a team, and you stress standards of excellence.

If your score is 118–140, you are in the very high range.
If your score is 96–117, you are in the high range.
If your score is 73–95, you are in the moderate range.
If your score is 51–72, you are in the low range.
If your score is 28–50, you are in the very low range.

Application

8.4 Observational Exercise—Group Leadership

Purpose

1. To develop an understanding of the components of groups and how groups work
2. To identify factors that contribute to effective group leadership

Directions

1. For this exercise, you will make observations about a group of which you are a member presently or were a member in the recent past. For example, it could be a class project group, an employee group, a fraternity or sorority council, a coffee group, or any social group.
2. Name and describe briefly the group and its purpose. For each of the questions that follow, write down what you have observed in your experiences with the group.

Questions

1. Based on the descriptions of task- and process-oriented groups in this chapter, what did you observe the orientation of your group to be? Based on your own preferences, how would describe the way the group functioned along the task–process continuum?

2. What stage of group development (i.e., forming, storming, norming, performing, or adjourning) would you say the group is in? Explain and defend your observation.

3. What roles did you typically play in the group? Give examples of and describe two task roles and two group-building and maintenance roles you played.

4. What did you observe regarding the participation level of group members? Did you observe some group members to be less included than others? How did you respond to them? How did the group leader respond? Discuss.

Application

8.5 Reflection and Action Worksheet—Group Leadership

Reflection

1. Based on the score you received on the Group Leadership Questionnaire, how would you describe your group leadership? Briefly discuss what the questionnaire suggests about your strengths and weaknesses.

2. Considering all the groups in your life to which you have contributed, which group did you like the best, and why did you enjoy participating in it?

3. Because we are all human, it is normal to get frustrated when a leader of a group does not provide the amount of task and process leadership we want or think we need. Reflecting on yourself, describe what others might find as most frustrating and unhelpful regarding your group leadership.

Action

1. This chapter lists several individual roles that disrupt a group's progress (dominator, blocker, recognition seeker, etc.). When you are in a group, which of the individual roles mentioned in the chapter do you most commonly assume? Explain your answer. How can you teach yourself to avoid these roles?

2. What do you think is meant by the phrase "By the group are you sickened, and by the group are you healed?" What is your reaction to this statement? Discuss how groups accept you, acknowledge your contributions, give you a sense of competency, and let you know that you are not in the boat alone.

3. Imagine for a moment that you are doing a class project with six other students. After an extended and contentious discussion, the group has decided by taking a vote to do a fundraising campaign for the local Big Brothers Big Sisters program. However, two people in the group have indicated they are not enthused about the project and would rather do something for any organization other than Big Brothers Big Sisters. While the group is moving forward with the agreed-upon project, the two people who did not like the idea start missing meetings, and when they do attend, they are very negative. As a leader, list five specific actions you could take to assist and engage these two out-group members.

9 EMBRACING DIVERSITY AND INCLUSION

INTRODUCTION

Leadership requires skill, a clear vision, and a strong commitment to bringing the best out of group members. It also requires that leaders understand diversity and inclusion, and the essential role these play in organizational outcomes.

Issues regarding diversity and inclusion have come to the forefront in recent years, especially within the United States. While many of the leadership concepts discussed in this text so far (e.g., task behavior, goal setting, and strengths) involve rather straightforward leadership efforts, addressing diversity and inclusion is a multilayered process that requires a wider range of leadership practices. While diversity and inclusion is a global topic, much of the research thus far conducted in the area has been done by Western researchers in Europe and the United States and represents diversity concerns of those cultures.

Although the terms *diversity* and *inclusion* seem to represent distinctly different concepts, they are actually interrelated processes, and while not usually discussed as core leadership concepts, diversity and inclusion play a seminal role in effective leadership.

In this chapter, we explore how embracing diversity and inclusion can make you a more effective leader. First, we define *diversity* and *inclusion* and discuss common usages for these terms. Next, we provide a brief history of how these concepts have become more important in society over time. Additionally, we provide a framework to conceptualize inclusion and a model of inclusive practices. Last, we discuss communication practices to improve inclusion and the barriers that can be encountered when trying to embrace diversity and inclusion.

DIVERSITY AND INCLUSION EXPLAINED

Diversity and *inclusion* are general terms that represent complex processes. A closer look at each of the terms will help explain why they are closely related and why leaders need to be aware of both concepts when addressing diversity within their group or organization.

Diversity

In the most general sense, **diversity** is about variety or difference. Diversity matters because we live in an increasingly globalized world that has become widely interconnected (Hunt et al., 2015). Researchers have defined diversity in a multitude of ways (Mor Barak, 2014). For example, *diversity* is often used to refer to the mixture of racial identities, genders, or religions represented in a group of people. Harrison and Sin (2006) define diversity as "the collective amount of differences among members within a social unit" (p. 196). Ferdman (2014), a diversity scholar, suggests that diversity is the representation of multiple groups of individuals with different identities and cultures within a group or an organization. Similarly, Herring and Henderson (2015) suggest that diversity refers to policies and practices that are designed to include people who are different in some way from the traditional group members. From this perspective, diversity means creating an organizational culture that embraces the values and skills of all of its members. Herring and Henderson contend that diversity is about more than valuing differences between groups; it includes addressing issues of parity, equity, and inequality. We will say more about equity later in this chapter.

According to a study by Deloitte and the Billie Jean King Leadership Initiative (Dishman, 2015), of 3,700 individuals from a variety of backgrounds, Millennials (born 1980–2000) define diversity differently than Boomers (born 1946–1964) and Gen-Xers (born 1965–1979). Millennials look at diversity as the mixing of different backgrounds and perspectives within a group. Boomers and Gen-Xers, on the other hand, see diversity as a process of fairness and protection for all group members, regardless of gender, race, religion, ethnicity, or sexual orientation. Millennials are more likely than non-Millennials to focus on the unique experiences of individuals, teamwork, and collaboration rather than issues of justness. The Pew Research Center (2018) reports that Gen-Zers (born after 2000) are the most racially and ethnically diverse group yet in the United States; almost 48% come from communities of color. Gen-Zers are expected to have a more inclusive perspective on diversity in the workplace because they have been exposed to different racial groups and cultures at a younger age.

In this chapter, we define diversity *as the amount of difference among members of a group or an organization*. As set forth by Loden (1996), the core dimensions of diversity include age, gender, race, mental and physical abilities, ethnicity, and sexual orientation (see Table 9.1). These are elsewhere referred to as **social identities**—the parts of our self-concept that come from our

TABLE 9.1   ■   Dimensions of Diversity

Primary Dimensions	Secondary Dimensions
Age	Geographic Location
Gender	Military and Work Experience
Race	Family Status
Mental and Physical Abilities	Income
Ethnicity	Religion
Sexual Orientation	Education
Communication and Work Style	First Language
	Organizational Role and Level

Source: Based on Loden (1996).

group memberships (Tajfel & Turner, 1986). Secondary dimensions include geographic location, military and work experience, family status, income, religion, education, first language, organizational role and level, and communication and work style. The primary dimensions of diversity are more powerful and less changeable, while the secondary dimensions can change, are less visible, and are less influential in how they impact our lives.

Inclusion

Inclusion is the process of incorporating differing individuals into a group or an organization. It is creating an environment where people who are different feel they are part of the whole. For example, inclusion is represented by making accommodations so that a student with disabilities can feel involved and accepted in regular school classes. Similarly, inclusion is about the *majority* incorporating the opinions of the *minority* and giving voice to the people who are seldom heard. Booysen (2014) suggests that when inclusion exists in a workplace, "all people from diverse backgrounds will feel valued, respected, and recognized" and "no one will feel that [they do] not have a place in the organization; no one will ask: 'What about me?'" (p. 299). Furthermore, Ferdman (2014) suggests that people experience inclusion not only when they feel they are treated well individually but also when groups of people who share their identity are respected and valued.

The underpinnings of inclusion are described in the work of Schutz (1958), who posited that inclusion (along with control and affection) is a basic human need that people experience in their interpersonal relationships. It is our need to belong, feel accepted, and be connected to others, but not to the extent that we lose a sense of ourselves as unique individuals. Inclusion means feeling like you are a full member of the group but at the same time maintaining your own identity. It requires a balance between belonging and uniqueness (Shore et al., 2011).

Schutz (1958) argued that we express our need to be included by how we communicate with others, and we experience less anxiety if our need to be "in the group" matches the degree to which we want others to "include us." This suggests that leaders should open their arms to include others, but not so much that the individual differences of others get smothered or lost.

Equity

One additional consideration in this process is **equity**, recognizing the historic inequalities that have kept some groups, particularly racial minorities, from having the same access to programs, financial resources, and jobs as others have. Equity recognizes that not all individuals start from the same place. Equity is not the same as *equality*, which aims to ensure that all people receive equal resources; equal access to education, health care, and jobs; and equal treatment from the very beginning (Streitmatter, 1994). An equality perspective doesn't recognize the discrimination and systemic inequalities that have created the social disparities in our society.

In the arts, for example, equity embodies the values, policies, and practices that ensure that all people—especially those underrepresented based on race/ethnicity, age, disability, sexual orientation, gender, gender identity, socioeconomic status, geography, citizenship status, or religion—are represented in the development of arts policy; accessible, thriving venues for expression; and support of artists, which includes the fair distribution of programmatic, financial, and informational resources (Americans for the Arts, n.d.).

In short, diversity focuses on recognizing differences, inclusion is concerned with embracing those differences, and equity aims to provide equal access to resources for historically disadvantaged people. As Myers (2012) aptly suggests, diversity is about "being invited to the party," and inclusion is about "being asked to dance" (p. 13). To continue the same metaphor, equity ensures everyone has the opportunity to take dance lessons. Leaders often recognize the value of diversity but struggle with creating supportive, inclusive environments. It is one thing to have a diverse group or organization, but another to make sure each individual is included in the group or organization in a positive manner, and equipped to contribute fully.

There is a current emphasis in organizational consulting of emphasizing belonging as part of diversity and inclusion work. **Belonging** "is working to help employees be their 'whole selves' at work by ensuring no one feels left out." At a time when national divisions are creeping into the workplace, leaving people feeling anxious and defensive, belonging focuses on "relating" and "building bridges." This focus may even include helping "old timers" in the organization who feel marginalized by the current emphasis on diversity and inclusion (Miller, 2023). Later in the chapter, we provide an inclusion framework to help leaders understand how to approach diversity in different settings.

Approaches to Diversity

To better understand the complexity of diversity, it is useful to briefly describe how diversity has been addressed in the past, and then to discuss how these descriptions influence the meaning of diversity today. Addressing issues of diversity is not unique; it has been a central challenge for leaders of every generation.

In the United States, diversity was at the foundation of the country's democratic system. The United States was originally formed by people seeking to escape religious persecution elsewhere. This ideal of seeking freedom drove many groups of immigrants to the United States, all of whom had different values, traditions, and religions. As the country evolved, diversity also came to mean addressing the needs of people who are marginalized in the United States, including African Americans whose ancestors originally came to the country through the trans-Atlantic slave trade as well as Native Americans who were already living here. Even today, the diversity of the country continues to shift and change as waves of newcomers enter the United States and continue to alter its social landscape (Healey & Stepnick, 2017). Building a democratic nation is only possible by acknowledging and addressing issues of diversity.

While a lot has been written on **multiculturalism**, intergroup relations, and diversity in society, much of the information we present in this chapter comes from diversity and inclusion research as it has occurred in the realm of the workplace. While this research may be workplace specific, it is salient to leaders of any organization. This is especially true of the research on the historical development of workplace diversity in the United States as it reflects how perspectives on diversity evolved in wider society. Harvey (2015) suggests that the approach to diversity in the workplace has changed and evolved over three periods: the early years of diversity (1960s and 1970s), the era of valuing diversity (1980s and 1990s), and diversity management and inclusion in the 21st century (2000 to present) (see Table 9.2).

TABLE 9.2 ■ Changing Perspectives on Diversity

Time Period	Perspective	Metaphor	Emphasis
1960s and 1970s	Government Addresses Inequalities	Melting Pot	Assimilation
1980s and 1990s	Advantages of Accepting Differences Recognized	Salad	Differentiation (Multiculturalism)
2000 to present	Different Opinions and Insights Valued	Smorgasbord	Inclusion (Integration)

Sources: Adapted from Harvey, C. P. (2015). Understanding workplace diversity: Where have we been and where are we going? In C. P. Harvey & M. J. Allard (Eds.), *Understanding and managing diversity: Readings, cases, and exercises* (pp. 1–7). Pearson; Thomas, D. A., & Ely, R. J. (1996, September–October). Making differences matter: A new paradigm for managing diversity. *Harvard Business Review.*

Early Years—1960s and 1970s

This was the period of the civil rights movement in the United States. During this time, Black American activists fought to end discrimination and to secure their legal rights as spelled out in the U.S. Constitution. It was also a time when the federal government passed a series of landmark equal employment opportunity laws: (1) the *Equal Pay Act* (1963), which stated that women and men must receive equal pay for equal work; (2) the *Civil Rights Act* (1964), which prohibited discrimination in employment based on race, sex, national origin, religion, and color; (3) the *Executive Orders* (1961–1965), which required organizations that accepted federal funds to submit affirmative action plans that demonstrated their progress in hiring and promoting groups of people who had been discriminated against previously; and (4) the *Age Discrimination Act* (1975), which protected workers over 40 years of age from being discriminated against at work because of their age.

During these early years, the focus of diversity was on "righting the wrongs" experienced by people who were perceived as different because of their race or gender (Harvey, 2015) and who were also the targets of discrimination and exclusion. It was also a time when the government began forcing organizations to confront inequities between individuals and groups in the workplace. Thomas and Ely (1996) contend that these early years were focused on discrimination and fairness. Because of prejudice, certain demographic groups were not treated the same as other groups. To comply with federal mandates, it was important for organizations to ensure that all people were treated equally and that no one was given an unfair advantage over another person.

It was common during the early years to think of diversity using the term **melting pot**, a metaphor for a blending of many into one, or a heterogeneous society becoming homogeneous. Sociologically, diversity was thought of as an assimilation process where those from different cultures were expected to adapt to and, in many cases, adopt the customs of the majority group (Blaine, 2013). **Assimilation** focused on the process of making people from diverse cultures come together to create one American culture. Healey and Stepnick (2017) point out that while assimilation is often thought of as a gradual and fair blending of diverse cultures, in fact it requires different cultures to blend in with the predominant English language and British cultural style. Although assimilation helps bring diverse individuals together, it requires that those in the minority culture give up many, if not most, of their own values and traditions in order to adopt the dominant culture.

A key example of this can be seen in how, from 1819 to 1969, hundreds of thousands of Native American children were taken from their families and forced to attend government- or church-operated boarding schools throughout the United States. At these schools, the children were forbidden to speak their native languages, wear their traditional clothing, engage in their traditional religious practices, or use their given names, being assigned new English ones instead. These children were taught that their native cultures were inferior to the American culture, causing many to become ashamed of their Indigenous heritage. The phrase "Kill the Indian in him and save the man" was often quoted as justification for this forced assimilation. By the 1970s, these assimilation efforts had ended, most of these schools had been closed, and the remaining schools were being run under Indigenous leadership.

Era of Valuing Diversity—1980s and 1990s

This period was marked by a new approach to diversity that emphasized the acceptance and celebration of differences (Thomas & Ely, 1996). The approach to diversity at this time broadened beyond an emphasis on race and gender to include many dimensions (sexual orientation, age, physical and mental abilities, etc. [see Table 9.1]). In addition to stressing fairness and equality, organizations recognized that society was becoming more multicultural and that supporting diversity in the workforce could have competitive advantages. Research focused on how diversity in the workplace was related to positive outcomes for an organization, such as reduced turnover, better creative thinking, enhanced problem solving, and improved decision making. Organizations found that diversity was not just about fairness; it made economic sense (Thomas & Ely, 1996).

Rather than a melting pot, the metaphor for diversity during this time was more of a salad composed of different ingredients, made by mixing different individuals or cultures and their unique characteristics together. A multicultural approach acknowledges and accepts differences. The emphasis was on the individual unique contributions that each person or culture brings to an organization, rather than blending ("melting") differences into a single whole (Harvey, 2015). Furthermore, diversity during this period emphasized **pluralism**, the recognition that people of different cultures did not need to sacrifice their own traditions and values to become a part of one society. Pluralism means that people of all racial groups, classes, religions, and backgrounds can coexist in one society without giving up their identities, customs, or traditions. A pluralistic society appreciates and celebrates differences.

Diversity Management and Inclusion in the 21st Century—2000 to Present

Diversity during this period continues to be a major concern for organizations and society in general. Inequities between individuals and groups in regard to differences in race, gender, ethnicity, sexual orientation, and other dimensions remain unresolved. The laws of the 1960s and

1970s still occupy an important role in trying to achieve diversity in the workplace. At the same time, multiculturalism is more widely accepted and celebrated today.

What is new in the last 20 years regarding diversity is an emphasis on creating inclusive organizations. Harvey (2015) points out that people today are recognizing that both organizations and individuals can benefit from diversity. Furthermore, she points out that diversity today is broader in scope and harder to manage because of a changing composition of workers, the need to acknowledge multiple social identities, and the challenge of trying to establish and maintain an inclusive organizational culture. The new way of approaching diversity acknowledges differences among people and values those differences, integrating them into the organization. People feel they are all on the same team because of their differences, not despite their differences (Thomas & Ely, 1996).

As opposed to being like a melting pot that blends many into one or a salad that mixes differences together, diversity today can be thought of as a smorgasbord that celebrates the unique qualities of a variety of different dishes. Diversity from this perspective means that people's unique qualities are accepted and enjoyed, and that people do not need to downplay their own unique characteristics for the benefit of others. It also means that people do not need to deny their own cultural identities to be a part of the larger group or organization. Diversity means that an organization is composed of many unique elements and, when taken together, these elements make the organization unique.

Diversity has a positive impact on organizational outcomes. Komives and associates (2016) found that "diverse groups can be more productive, make higher quality and more creative decisions, are better at adapting to changing conditions, and are less prone to groupthink than are groups with homogeneous membership" (p. 118; see also Johnson & Johnson, 2009).

To that point, a McKinsey study of hundreds of international organizations found that those with a more diverse leadership team experienced better financial performance. "The companies in the top quartile of gender diversity were 15 percent more likely to have financial returns that were above their national industry median. Companies in the top quartile of racial/ethnic diversity were 35 percent more likely to have financial returns above their national industry median" (Hunt et al., 2015, p. 1). This relationship is a correlation, not a causal link. But the research shows "that more diverse companies are better able to win top talent, and improve their customer orientation, employee satisfaction, and decision making, leading to a virtuous cycle of increasing returns" (Hunt et al., 2015, p. 1).

While our perspectives on diversity have changed over the last 50 years, society's need to address matters of diversity has remained constant. For example, in 2021 only 36% of leadership roles in professional and technical fields globally were filled by women (World Economic Forum, 2022). In the United States, people of color, who constitute more than 40% of the U.S. population, accounted for only 14% of the CEOs in Fortune 500 companies in 2021, while less than 1% of Fortune 500 CEOs identified as LGBTQ+ (Wilkie, n.d.).

For many years, progress in the areas of diversity and inclusion has been gauged in terms of numbers and whether or not more people from underrepresented groups are attaining leadership and employment opportunities. But the current approach to diversity places the *inclusion process* at center stage of the pathway to addressing concerns about diversity. Inclusion means allowing people with different cultural characteristics to have a voice and feel integrated and connected with others (Ferdman, 2014). In the next section, we describe a framework for understanding the inclusion process.

INCLUSION FRAMEWORK

Social psychologist Marilynn Brewer (1991) argued that individuals have two opposing needs in regard to being a part of a group. First, they have a desire to assimilate and be included; second, they have a need to differentiate themselves from the group. Similar to Schutz's (1958) early work on inclusion, people seek an optimal balance between inclusion and differentiation.

To better understand how people balance these needs, Shore and colleagues (2011) developed an inclusion framework. The framework, depicted in Table 9.3, illustrates how varying levels of belongingness (i.e., the desire to be included) interact with uniqueness (i.e., the desire to maintain one's own identity) and result in the four quadrants shown.

The *Exclusion quadrant* (top left) represents individuals in a group or an organization who feel left out and excluded; they do not feel a part of things, and they do not feel valued. Exclusion occurs when organizations fail to see and value the unique qualities of diverse employees and fail to accept them as organizational insiders. An example might be a female vice president of a bank whose ideas are discounted by her male counterparts and who is seldom invited to corporate planning meetings. In effect, exclusion represents a complete failure to deal with matters of diversity.

TABLE 9.3 ■ Inclusion Framework	Low Belongingness	High Belongingness
Low Value in Uniqueness	**Exclusion** Individual is not treated as an organizational insider with unique value in the work group, but there are other employees or groups who are insiders.	**Assimilation** Individual is treated as an insider in the work group when they conform to organizational/dominant culture norms and downplay uniqueness.
High Value in Uniqueness	**Differentiation** Individual is not treated as an organizational insider in the work group, but their unique characteristics are seen as valuable and required for group/organization success.	**Inclusion** Individual is treated as an insider and also allowed/encouraged to retain uniqueness within the work group.

Source: Shore, L. M., Randel, A. E., Chung, B. G., Dean, M. A., Holcombe Ehrhard, K., & Singh, G. (2011). Inclusion and diversity in work groups: A review and model for future research. *Journal of Management, 37*(4), 1266.

The *Differentiation quadrant* (lower left) describes individuals who feel unique and respected but who also feel left out and not a part of the in-group. Differentiation occurs when organizations accept and value the unique qualities of members who are different but then fail to let these individuals become full members of the organization. For example, this might occur when a customer service center hires several Spanish-speaking representatives because the center is working with more Spanish-speaking customers. But those representatives are not asked for their input on organizational issues such as the scripting they use for complaint calls. In terms of diversity, differentiation goes halfway—it recognizes different individuals, but does not fully accept them.

The *Assimilation quadrant* (top right) represents people who feel they are insiders and in the organizational in-group but whose unique characteristics are not really valued by the organization. An example of assimilation could be a Native American college student who is 100% involved and accepted in the classroom but whose unique heritage is not acknowledged by the other students, who expect him to not express that heritage to blend into the dominant group. In terms of diversity, assimilation represents an attempt by organizations to open their arms and bring everyone in; however, the same organizations can be faulted for failing to acknowledge the uniqueness of their members—they accept different individuals, but do not fully value them.

The *Inclusion quadrant* (lower right) describes individuals who feel they belong and are valued for their unique beliefs, attitudes, values, and background. This quadrant represents the optimal way to address diversity. It means, in short, accepting others and at the same time valuing them for who they are without requiring them to give up valued identities or cultural features (Ferdman, 1992). For example, inclusion occurs when students at a small rural high school welcome three new students who are Afghan refugees whose families have been relocated to the community. The students establish an "international club" where they discuss each other's cultures. The American students learn about the many different native languages spoken by the Afghanis from the new students while helping the Afghan students with their English. The social sciences teacher has incorporated a research project on Afghanistan for all his students based on a presentation that one of the Afghan students gave about his experiences. Another of the Afghan students is a gifted singer and is in the choir, and the choir teacher has asked her to pick out a song from her native country that the choir is learning to sing for its winter program. Most important of all, students at the school feel accepted, engaged, and comfortable. The camaraderie they have has produced a new sense of community.

The inclusion framework presented in Table 9.3 is useful for understanding ways to address diversity because it illustrates inclusion as an integration of two factors: (1) an individual's connectedness (i.e., belonging) to others and (2) a person's individuality (i.e., uniqueness). In addition, the inclusion framework is helpful because it underscores that *differentiation* focuses primarily on people's differences and *assimilation* focuses primarily on people's connectedness to the whole.

LEADERSHIP SNAPSHOT

Damien Hooper-Campbell, Chief Impact Officer, StockX

David Livingston / Contributor/via Getty images

After a 20-plus-year career working in diversity and inclusion (D&I), one would think Damien Hooper-Campbell would be an expert on the topic. Hooper-Campbell, who has led the design and implementation of strategies to implement diversity and inclusion for such companies as Zoom, eBay, Uber, Google, and Goldman Sachs and is now chief impact officer for online marketplace StockX, says that he never stops learning.

"The definition of D&I and what it means to be a chief diversity officer (CDO) is always evolving. Just when you think you've mastered a concept, a new element is added. Just when you think you understand the scope of the role, your job description expands," he says. "This work is extremely complex, at times ambiguous and often misunderstood" (Goldman Sachs Group, 2023).

Each step in his career, which has included working as a front-of-the-house manager at an organic Chinese food restaurant in Harlem, recruiting students for Harvard Business School, and key CDO roles at some of the globe's largest tech companies, Hooper-Campbell says one thing is constant: Diversity is about "everything."

"Oftentimes, this conversation narrows to be about only race and gender. While, yes, race and gender are very important aspects, diversity goes well beyond them. It absolutely should include them, but goes even further into hundreds of attributes," he says (The Review, n.d.).

As a case in point, Hooper-Campbell was diagnosed with attention deficit hyperactivity disorder (ADHD) well into his adulthood and career and has learned to manage his condition, including being upfront with his employers about the condition and how he can work best individually and on teams. Now he is helping reshape workplace misconceptions about ADHD, including how companies can utilize neurodivergent employees.

"The best way to establish an inclusive culture is to lead by example," he says. "As executive leaders, it's important for us to be real human beings who do not always show up like everything's perfect. One of the first times I brought [my ADHD] up in a company-wide all-hands meeting, I was traveling around the world to the company's different global locations. I misplaced my luggage and was without my medication for four days. I got up on stage in front of 300 employees and I said, 'Look, I'm here with you but if you see me rambling a little bit, just know, it's because I have ADHD.' And told them the story of losing my bags and meds. After that session I had an employee come up to me and say they really appreciated that I shared my story because they had never seen a leader do that publicly" (Billboard Staff, 2022).

Hooper-Campbell says that while D&I work is often approached in qualitative terms—measured by the increase in numbers of BIPOC employees, for example—the work is about more than data.

"D&I is human-centered . . . At its core, it is an aspiration to help all of us unpack all that we've learned (the good, bad and ugly) and to figure out what is reality and what is perception. When given a voice and a real seat at the table, this role can help with innovations in hiring, culture development, product design, and community citizenship, to name a few," he says (Goldman Sachs Group, 2023).

Literally at the heart of D&I, says Hooper-Campbell, is "the heart." When helping others to understand the concept of inclusion, he has them remember a time when they were excluded and use adjectives to describe how it made them feel.

"This could be from when you were four-years-old and you didn't get picked for the kick-ball team. This could be from earlier today when you realized that people at your company held a meeting and didn't invite you. It doesn't matter what it is, these answers won't just be responses—they'll be stories of the human condition," he says. "There will be adjectives like 'insecure, fear, lonely, crippled, demotivated.' These adjectives aren't mutually exclusive to any one category of people" (*The Review*, n.d.).

Then Hooper-Campbell will ask those same people to acknowledge how many of them have ever been responsible—intentionally or unintentionally—for excluding someone else.

"That's what you want to fix at your organization. I'm not asking you to start with a training. I'm not asking you to take money and throw it at the problem. I'm asking you to simply start with a human conversation and a commitment to use your positions of leadership to never knowingly—either directly or indirectly—allow anyone in your sphere of influence to feel the adjectives of the excluded," says Hooper-Campbell.

"Diversity can be likened to being invited to the dance party. We all open up our texts or email and have received an invitation to the party. So fast forward and now we're all standing around at the party and there's tons of diversity in the room. Awesome. But that's only part of the equation. What if only people of a certain weight are dancing? Or only certain people who are close enough friends to be invited to the wedding who are dancing? Or only people of a certain age who are dancing? Or only people who speak a certain language who are dancing? Or only people who are cool enough from the soccer team who are dancing? Inclusion is getting asked to dance when you're at the dance party" (*The Review*, n.d.).

The message is that diversity alone isn't sufficient. "As leaders, it's great if you're trying to recruit people from diverse backgrounds. But I challenge you all to get rid of the noise that focuses all of this conversation on recruiting and statistics alone," he says. "A diverse workforce helps with profits and business because many of our customers and end users reflect a broad array of diversity. But what about the workplace? How do you actually feel when you're there? Have you only been invited to the dance or are you also being invited to dance when you're actually in the workplace?" (*The Review*, n.d.).

DIVERSITY AND INCLUSION IN PRACTICE

Model of Inclusive Practices

Since inclusion is essential for integrating everyone into a group or an organization, the next question is, how does the inclusion process work in practice?

To understand this process, Ferdman (2014) suggests treating inclusion as a multilevel process centered on each individual's experience of inclusion. Simply put, inclusion exists when individuals experience it. This occurs as a result of inclusion practices on many levels, including interpersonal, group, leader, organizational, and societal (see Figure 9.1). Ferdman's framework illustrates how inclusion at one level is related to the way inclusion is practiced at other levels.

As shown at the top of the model in Figure 9.1, the way a society or community thinks about and addresses inclusion affects the way an individual experiences it. For example, if the city commission in a community such as Dearborn, Michigan, which has a large percentage of Muslims, were to promote the recognition of the Muslim holy month of Ramadan, then Muslim Dearborn residents might feel that their heritage is being valued and recognized.

Moving down the model, organizational policies and practices also influence the inclusion experience. For instance, if a new employee training program at a retail store fosters acceptance of customers who are LGBTQ+, it may help these customers feel welcome shopping at the store.

At the leadership level, which is indispensable to promoting inclusion at all levels, leaders need to set the tone for inclusion and hold followers accountable for inclusion practices. For example, if, during a staff meeting of a department that is predominantly male, the department head gives a female staff member time to voice her opinions to the others, that staff member will feel that her opinions matter. It will also model to the group's members how to listen to others and value their opinions, even if those opinions are different from their own.

Another form of inclusion occurs at the group level. If group members do not actively recognize that "individuals with different values, perspectives, and working and learning styles may come to a group with different ideas of what is important and different notions of how groups should function, and value different styles of communication," then group members can experience misunderstandings that will create barriers to group effectiveness (Komives et al., 2016, p. 119).

Groups promote inclusion when they establish enabling norms that give everyone in the group an equal chance to voice their opinion, acknowledge and respect individuals' differences, promote collaborative work on tasks, and address conflicts productively. As discussed in Chapter 8, "Working With Groups," there is an axiom regarding people in groups: "By the group are you sickened, by the group are you healed." When a group is functioning inclusively, it is positive to group members, not toxic. The members feel accepted, comfortable, unique, valued, and inspirited. This is the strength of inclusive group practices.

The interpersonal level is perhaps the most common place where inclusive practices are played out. Through our interpersonal communication with others, we let them know our need to be included, our willingness to include others, and our willingness to have others include us. For example, a first-year international student living on campus may want her roommate to

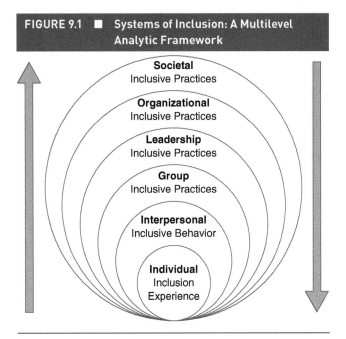

FIGURE 9.1 ■ Systems of Inclusion: A Multilevel Analytic Framework

Source: Adapted from Ferdman, B. M. (2014). The practice of inclusion in diverse organizations. In B. M. Ferdman & B. R. Deane (Eds.), *Diversity at work: The practice of inclusion* (pp. 3–54). Wiley.

invite her to parties, but when the roommate does invite her, the student makes an excuse for not being able to attend. The student expresses a need to be included, but when she is included, the student becomes uncomfortable and wants to pull back. Interpersonal inclusion happens when we ask others for their opinions and are interested in who they are, but still enable them to maintain their personal space as individuals.

The individual inclusion experience is the foundation of the framework illustrated in Figure 9.1. Ferdman et al. (2009) describe this experience "as the degree to which individuals feel safe, trusted, accepted, respected, supported, valued, fulfilled, engaged, and authentic in their working environment, both as individuals and as members of particular identity groups" (p. 6). The experience of individual inclusion is affected by the inclusion practices at other levels, and individual inclusion can also impact these other levels (see Figure 9.1).

To understand how the different levels of inclusion in the framework can influence the other levels, consider, for example, in the United States, same-sex marriage has been legalized, giving same-sex couples the same legal rights as those in heterosexual marriages. This can influence other inclusive practices down the line. At the organizational level, this new legal status allows same-sex couples the same benefits as heterosexual couples, such as health insurance and family leave. In 2020, the United States joined 81 other countries around the globe to provide protections to LGBTQ+ employees from workplace discrimination. But even with these legal protections, more than 50% of LGBTQ+ Americans remain closeted in the workplace, according to a 2021 report (Sears et al., 2021) for reasons from fear of being stereotyped or making people feel uncomfortable to possibly losing connections or relationships with cowork-ers. However, if the leader of an organization engages in inclusive practices, such as encouraging LGBTQ+ couples to openly attend organizational events with their partners and inviting them to dinner with other staff members and their spouses, that leader is modeling inclusive behavior for followers. At the group level, the coworkers of an LGBTQ+ employee host a baby shower when their colleague welcomes a child into their family. On the interpersonal level, coworkers will talk with an LGBTQ+ employee about their partner. Finally, you can see how this inclu-sion would lead to an LGBTQ+ employee feeling that their sexual orientation and marriage are accepted and respected by their coworkers. These inclusive practices may be helpful in allowing other LGBTQ+ people in the organization to feel more comfortable sharing their sexual orien-tation and gender identity with their coworkers. Inclusion comes from the top down—starting with society and community and ending with the individual.

As shown in Figure 9.1, Ferdman's framework also identifies that the influence of inclu-sion travels back up the levels from individual to societal. The same-sex-couple example also works to show this upward influence of inclusion. When LGBTQ+ employees feel accepted and respected, they may be more likely to engage in inclusive behaviors with others who are different from them. If a group's majority is engaged in inclusive behaviors, it can influence its leaders to adopt those same inclusive practices. As a result, the organization overall becomes an accept-ing work environment for LGBTQ+ individuals, and the community in which the company operates is influenced by the company's inclusive practices. Because of the company's inclusive practices, more LGBTQ+ employees may choose to join the company, which will bring more LGBTQ+ people into the community. As LGBTQ+ people become engaged in the community as neighbors, friends, and community members, the society around them will become more accepting and respecting of LGBTQ+ people and relationships.

While this example shows that inclusion can and should happen at many levels, as a leader, the challenge is to foster that sense of inclusion among one's followers as well as influence the organization's approach to diversity and inclusion. In the next section, we discuss some practices leaders can engage in that help to do just that.

Leader Practices That Advance Diversity and Inclusion

A questionnaire to measure inclusion in work groups developed by Ferdman and his colleagues (Ferdman, 2014; Ferdman et al., 2009; Hirshberg & Ferdman, 2011) identified six key com-ponents of the experience of inclusion (see Table 9.4). Components are like the ingredients of inclusion. When followers experience these components, they feel included. These components provide a good blueprint for actions and behaviors and communication that leaders should engage in to provide inclusion for others.

1. Feeling Safe

To help individuals feel safe, it is important for leaders to treat followers in nonthreatening ways. In situations where one person feels different from others, the leader plays a fundamental role in letting that person know that they will not be hurt physically or psychologically if their

TABLE 9.4 ■ Components of the Inclusion Experience	
Components	**Examples**
1. **Feeling Safe**	• Do I help others feel physically and psychologically safe? • Do I help others feel like they are a full member of the group? • Do I help others express opposing opinions without fear of negative repercussion?
2. **Feeling Involved and Engaged**	• Do I treat others as full participants—as insiders? • Do I give others access to information and resources to do their work? • Do I help others feel like they are part of our team?
3. **Feeling Respected and Valued**	• Do I treat others as I would like to be treated myself? • Do I let others know I trust and care about them? • Do I treat others like they are a valued group member?
4. **Feeling Influential**	• Do I let others' ideas and perspectives influence the group? • Do I let others participate in decision making? • Do I listen to others' perspectives on substantive issues?
5. **Feeling Authentic and Whole**	• Do I allow others to be truly themselves in the group? • Do I let others know they can be completely open with the group? • Do I encourage others to be honest and transparent?
6. **Recognizing, Attending to, and Honoring Diversity**	• Do I treat everyone fairly without discrimination? • Do I let others know I trust and care about them? • Do I encourage others to be honest and transparent?

Source: Adapted from Ferdman, B. M. (2014). The practice of inclusion in diverse organizations. In B. M. Ferdman & B. R. Deane (Eds.), *Diversity at work: The practice of inclusion* (pp. 3–54). Wiley.

ideas differ from others and that they will not be ridiculed or criticized for expressing these ideas. Even if a person's opinions go directly against the majority opinion, that individual can feel safe that they will not experience negative repercussions. This is especially important in situations of alleged harassment, where targets may hesitate to report the behavior for fear of not being believed by a supervisor, having no action taken against the perpetrator, or being regarded as a "troublemaker." Leaders need to communicate with each of their followers in such a way that all of them feel they are a part of the whole. It is a safe feeling for individuals to know they will not be rejected by the group for their uniqueness.

2. Feeling Involved and Engaged

In addition to a feeling of safety, inclusion comes from feeling involved and engaged. Helping followers find this feeling is a challenge for leaders, but worthwhile because engaged and involved followers are more productive and satisfied. It is inspiriting to be around them. Cultural differences may affect how followers are perceived by others in the group. For example, employees from some cultures may be less likely to speak up or contribute to group projects, and so may be overlooked or regarded as weaker members of a diverse team. If they come from a culture with a strong politeness norm, where disagreeing openly is seen as disrespectful, or where women are expected to defer to men, they may feel uncomfortable with sharing ideas, being assertive, or disagreeing with a group's thinking.

Leaders must find ways to help individuals become involved and immersed in the larger group's efforts. When an individual likes their work, participates freely in it, and enjoys being a part of the team, they are more likely to feel involved and engaged. As discussed in Chapter 6, "Engaging Strengths," recognizing people's strengths is a wonderful way for leaders to help followers feel engaged. In addition, leaders should treat followers as if they are insiders, as people who are important and deserve to know what is going on within the organization. Leaders need to share information freely so that followers feel like full participants in the workings of the group or organization. People feel involved and engaged when they know they are full-fledged group members and that their participation matters.

3. Feeling Respected and Valued

Practicing the Golden Rule—"Treat others as you would like to be treated"—is at the core of how leaders can help followers feel respected and valued. When leaders put themselves in the shoes of their followers, they can get in touch with what it means to be well thought of, worthy, and wanted. None of us like to be judged, stereotyped, ridiculed, singled out, disconfirmed, ignored, or belittled. Followers want to feel that they belong and are connected to the group, that the leader trusts and cares about them, and that they are intrinsic to the group.

4. Feeling Influential

Another component contributing to the inclusion experience is a feeling of having influence. All of us have unique ideas and positions on issues. When people express their ideas and are heard, they feel like they exist and that they are meaningful. When an individual is in a staff meeting and others listen to their ideas, it makes that individual feel significant. If that person's comments influence the direction of the group, it really makes the person feel significant. We all want to be influential, to put our stamp on things, to touch the world and have our efforts mean something.

It is critically important for leaders to recognize that followers have a need to have an impact—to express themselves in a way that affects others. Effective leaders help followers feel influential when they recognize that followers want to be heard and have an impact. Letting followers participate in important organizational discussions and acknowledging their comments and suggestions as substantive and valuable makes those followers feel influential. Another way of allowing followers to feel influential is by including them in the decision making of a group. When followers are able to participate in decisions, they feel a sense of significance; they feel agency. To have agency is to affect the process, to feel alive, to feel influential. It is having agency that helps followers feel included.

5. Feeling Authentic and Whole

In any group or organization, there is always a certain amount of pressure to assimilate to that group or organization's mission, norms, and values. This pressure creates tension within individuals because in order to be accepted with the larger group, they often find it necessary to hide or downplay unique characteristics of themselves or the group with which they identify. For example, to be accepted as an autoworker at a Ford plant in Detroit, an individual might try to hide the fact that they drive a foreign-made car. Or, if your partner's parents are quite liberal and against the National Rifle Association's stance on gun rights, you might not want to disclose to them that you are an avid hunter and longtime NRA member.

This tension between wanting to be yourself and wanting to be a part of the group can be counterproductive to feeling authentic and whole. Leaders can address this tension for followers by creating an atmosphere where individuals feel free to be as honest and transparent as they are comfortable being. To be transparent and authentic, followers need to feel trust from the leader. Leaders need to establish environments where being fully transparent with one another is rewarded and not punished. When you are in this kind of group or organization, you feel unique and connected at the same time. It is a situation where assimilating to the larger entity does not require losing your own sense of self.

For example, Angie is a multiracial college student at a small private university who, because of her very light skin color, knows that most of her fellow students assume she is white. Even though she is very involved in campus activities, the topic of her racial identity rarely comes up, and Angie doesn't feel a need to discuss it with other students. However, she often wants to speak up when she hears students making racist comments, but doesn't do so. The college's president recently asked Angie to join the school's antiracism committee representing students of color on the campus. Angie is hesitant to do so because it would mean being open about her racial identity, which could change how some of the other students treat her. However, she also knows that she would be more true to herself if she did participate on the committee, because she could effect change in some of the racist attitudes on campus. The president has talked with her at length about the importance of being acknowledged by others for her unique multiracial perspective, encouraging her to be authentic and transparent with others. He has expressed that he believes because she is already a very respected and active member of the campus community, she would be influential in helping the other students to embrace change regarding racism.

6. Recognizing, Attending to, and Honoring Diversity

The last component of the inclusion experience is directly related to leaders and diversity. In any group or organization, people want to be treated fairly; they do not want to be discriminated against because of their social identity or the identity of their social groups. Research shows the importance of validating the social identities of diverse group members when bringing them together for collaborative work. Workers should be able to talk about their social identities openly (race, nationality, gender identification, etc.), celebrate their identities and the unique perspectives they provide, and discuss together ways in which the group members' diverse backgrounds and skill sets can be mutually beneficial (Hofhuis et al., 2016; Ospina & Foldy, 2010).

Having leadership that understands and embraces diversity in the organization can be critical for innovation. "When leadership lacks innate or acquired diversity or fails to foster a 'speak up' culture, fewer promising ideas make it to market. Ideas from women, ethnic minorities, LGBTQ individuals, and members of Generation Y are less likely to win the endorsement they need to go forward because 56 percent of leaders don't value ideas they don't personally see a need for. This thinking can exert a stranglehold on an organization if its leaders are predominantly white, male, and heterosexual, for example, or come from similar educational and socioeconomic backgrounds. In short, the data strongly suggests that homogeneity stifles innovation" (Hunt et al., 2015, p. 13).

As a leader, each of us has the responsibility to be fair-minded and open-minded toward all of our followers. But dealing with diversity is not just about fairness. It is also about acknowledging differences and fully embracing them even if it produces conflict. Leaders need to work through conflicts related to differences. Last, leaders need to be attentive to recognizing the ways people differ and honoring the individuality of each of them.

Barriers to Embracing Diversity and Inclusion

Unfortunately, in the effort to successfully embrace diversity and inclusion, a leader can run into five common barriers—both on an individual level and on an organizational level—that can hinder this: ethnocentrism, prejudice, unconscious bias, stereotypes, and privilege. Leaders must confront these barriers head-on in order to effectively address diversity and develop inclusion in their organization.

Ethnocentrism

As the word suggests, **ethnocentrism** is the tendency for individuals to place their own group (ethnic, racial, or cultural) at the center of their observations of others and the world. Ethnocentrism is the perception that one's own culture is better or more natural than the culture of others. Because people tend to give priority and value to their own beliefs, attitudes, and values over and above those of other groups, they often fail to recognize the unique perspectives of others. Ethnocentrism is a universal tendency, and each of us is ethnocentric to some degree.

Ethnocentrism is a perceptual window through which people make subjective or critical evaluations of people from cultures other than their own (Porter & Samovar, 1997). For example, some Americans think that the democratic principles of the United States are superior to the political beliefs of other countries; they often fail to understand the complexities of other cultures. Ethnocentrism accounts for our tendency to think our own cultural values and ways of doing things are right and natural (Gudykunst & Kim, 1997).

Ethnocentrism can be a major obstacle to effective leadership because it prevents people from fully understanding or respecting the viewpoints of others. For example, if a person's culture values individual achievement, it may be difficult for that person to understand someone from a culture that emphasizes collectivity (i.e., people working together as a whole). Similarly, if a person believes strongly in respecting authority, that person may find it difficult to understand someone who challenges authority or does not easily defer to authority figures. The more ethnocentric we are, the less open or tolerant we are of other people's cultural traditions or practices.

A skilled leader cannot avoid issues related to ethnocentrism. A leader must recognize their own ethnocentrism, as well as understand—and to a degree tolerate—the ethnocentrism of others. In reality, it is a balancing act for leaders. On the one hand, leaders need to promote and be confident in their own ways of doing things; on the other, they need to be sensitive to the legitimacy of the ways of other cultures. Skilled leaders are able to negotiate the fine line between trying to overcome ethnocentrism and knowing when to remain grounded in their own cultural values.

Prejudice

Closely related to ethnocentrism is prejudice. **Prejudice** is a largely fixed attitude, belief, or emotion held by an individual about another individual or group that is based on faulty or unsubstantiated data. Prejudice refers to judgments we make about others based on previous decisions or experiences and involves inflexible generalizations that are resistant to change or evidence to the contrary (Ponterotto & Pedersen, 1993).

Prejudice often is thought of in the context of race or ethnicity (e.g., European American vs. African American), but it also applies in areas such as gender, age, sexual orientation, and other independent contexts. Although prejudice can be positive (e.g., thinking highly of another culture without sufficient evidence such as "the Swiss are the best skiers"), it is usually negative (e.g., "women are too emotional").

As with ethnocentrism, we all hold prejudices to some degree. Sometimes our prejudices allow us to keep our partially fixed attitudes undisturbed and constant. Sometimes prejudice can reduce people's anxiety because it gives them a familiar way to structure their observations of others. One of the main problems with prejudice is that it is self-oriented rather than other-oriented. It helps us to achieve balance for ourselves at the expense of others. Moreover, attitudes of prejudice inhibit understanding by creating a screen that limits our ability to see multiple aspects and qualities of other people. Prejudice is often expressed in crude or demeaning comments that people make about others. Both ethnocentrism and prejudice interfere with our ability to understand and appreciate the human experience of others.

In addition to fighting their own prejudices, leaders face the challenge of dealing with the prejudice of their followers. These prejudices can be toward the leader or the leader's culture. Furthermore, it is not uncommon for a leader to have followers who represent several culturally different groups that have their own prejudices toward each other. Prejudice can result in advantages for some groups over others and in **systemic discrimination**, which occurs when patterns of discriminatory behavior, policies, or practices become a part of an organization and continue to perpetuate disadvantage to those being discriminated against. Systemic discrimination can have a broad impact on an industry, a profession, or a geographic area.

A skilled leader needs to think about, recognize, and address when systemic discrimination exists within their organization and find ways to create inclusion with followers and groups who exhibit a multitude of differences.

Unconscious Bias

Also called *implicit bias*, **unconscious bias** is the term used to describe when we have attitudes toward people or associate stereotypes with them without our conscious knowledge that we are doing so. Thoughts and feelings are "implicit" if we are unaware of them or mistaken about their nature. Sometimes these attitudes actually contradict our own explicit beliefs (Devine, 1989). Research suggests that unconscious bias occurs automatically and is triggered by the brain making quick judgments and assessments of people and situations that are influenced by our own personal background, experiences, memories, and cultural environment (Byyny, 2017). Unconscious bias can result in some people benefiting while others are penalized.

For example, in screening potential candidates for a job, you may unconsciously choose to interview candidates who are similar to you in age, gender, ethnicity, or other ways, such as having lived in the same region, having attended the same schools, or having similar work experience. One of the most common examples of unconscious bias is seen in studies that show that white people will frequently associate criminality with Black people without even realizing they're doing it (Oliver, 1999).

As discussed in the preceding section on prejudice, it is very important for leaders to recognize not only their own unconscious biases, but those of their followers as well. One way to identify implicit bias is through an assessment instrument like the Implicit Association Test (IAT) developed by Greenwald et al. (Project Implicit, n.d.). The IAT measures an individual's implicit biases in several areas including race, weapons, body weight, age, gender, career, and skin tone. The IAT is available to take online for free at the Harvard Project Implicit website (https://implicit.harvard.edu/implicit/).

Another way to learn and address unconscious biases is to have discussions with others, especially those from socially dissimilar groups. Sharing your biases can help others feel more secure about exploring their own biases. Facilitated discussions and training sessions promoting bias literacy have been proven effective in minimizing bias, and providing unconscious bias training can reduce the impact of bias in the workplace (Carnes et al., 2012).

Unconscious bias is malleable and can be changed by devoting intention, attention, and time to developing new associations. It requires taking the time to consciously think about possible biases prior to acting or making decisions. There is evidence that even minimal interventions in reducing stereotyping and discrimination can be effective (Byyny, 2017).

Stereotypes

A **stereotype** is a fixed belief held by an individual that classifies a group of people with a similar characteristic as alike. Stereotypes allow people to respond to complex information and make meaning from it by either generalizing it or putting a blanket category around it. It is a way of processing information quickly.

Stereotypes label a group of individuals as the same at the expense of recognizing the uniqueness of each individual. Labeling everyone the same results in assuming things about some individuals that are not true. Stereotypes provide a way to generalize information, but during the process, individuals may get labeled with characteristics or qualities that do not apply to them. For example, if you say, "Nightshift workers are lazy," you are characterizing every worker who works that shift as lazy, when in fact it may be only one or two workers. If you stereotype the members of a certain ethnic or cultural group based on perceptions or information you have, you will be making incorrect assumptions about them. Additionally, many stereotypes about marginalized groups are deeply flawed, negative, and harmful.

In a small way, stereotypes can be useful. Stereotypes can reduce uncertainty in some situations because they provide partial information to us about others. For example, if you see some people wearing jerseys for the New England Patriots and you are also a Patriots fan, you will feel comfortable sitting next to them at a Patriots football game. You already assume, based on their clothing, that they have beliefs similar to yours. Similarly, if you tell your parents, who are of Dutch heritage, that they'll like your new partner because she is a "good Dutch woman," you are using a positive stereotype that will give your parents some information about your partner. This kind of stereotype provides limited information and begs to be challenged with phrases such as "What else can you tell me about this person?" Each individual is much more than a label can communicate, so we must constantly challenge our mental assessments to look for the unique qualities of every person.

For leaders, stereotypes are a barrier to diversity and inclusion because stereotypes categorize individual followers into a single classification, which prevents the leader from seeing each individual's unique merits and qualifications. Because stereotypes are a mental shortcut, leaders can avoid thinking more deeply about individual followers. For example, if a college instructor who teaches three classes labels one class as "a good class" and the other two as "bad classes" based on experiences he has had with some students in those classes, the stereotype will prevent him from seeing the many good qualities of individuals in the "bad" classes and also the negative qualities of the students in the "good" class.

Stereotypes have a significant impact on how leaders treat followers. To include followers and embrace them fully, leaders need to be attentive and open to the individual nuances of each of their followers. For Jane Doe to be included requires more than recognition of her gender. It requires understanding that she is a single mom with four kids, a part-time college student, a wife who lost her husband in the Iraq War, and a woman who is struggling with breast cancer. Calling Jane Doe a woman classifies her, but fails completely in accurately describing the uniqueness of her situation. When leaders stereotype followers, they box them in and trap them under simplistic and empty labels.

Privilege

A final barrier to inclusion is privilege. **Privilege** is an advantage held by a person or group that is based on age, race, ethnicity, gender, class, or some other cultural dimension, which gives those who have it power over those who don't. Privilege has been described as an unearned advantage that some people have in comparison to others (Harvey & Allard, 2015). In situations where it exists, privilege excludes others and puts them at a disadvantage. For example, in many countries around the world, privileged people in the ruling class have political, economic, and social power over people living in poverty, who are exploited and lack opportunities to transcend their circumstances. Or, to consider another example, during the Jim Crow period in the United States, privileged white citizens had power over Black citizens, and as a result, Black citizens suffered tremendously on all levels from employment and economics to education. Privilege is something that often goes unrecognized by those who have it, but usually is very apparent to those who do not have it.

Because privilege is a barrier to inclusion, leaders need to be introspective and determine if they are privileged in some way in comparison to others, including their followers. Because leadership involves a power differential between the leader and followers, leaders can often be blinded to the privilege they have. In addition, privilege can be very difficult for those without it to address because leaders may deny they have privilege or not acknowledge it because they do not want to weaken their power.

Those with privilege sometimes argue that the status and power they have is *not* privilege. Rather, they believe it is the result of their hard work, competence, and experience. For example, individuals who are born to affluent parents and go to elite schools are likely to land high-paying, prestigious jobs when they graduate from college (Rivera, 2015). If one were to challenge privileged individuals about their privilege, they might say they obtained a good job because they worked hard and put in long hours. Rivera (2015) points out that it is often the connections that privileged individuals have with others of influence that lead them to find better jobs. Ultimately, privilege and hard work are not mutually exclusive, and both an individual's circumstances and their efforts can contribute to their success.

Unfortunately, those with privilege are many times unaware of how that privilege makes their lives different from the lives of those without privilege. Some people may believe that those in poverty are lazy and undeserving because they have not worked hard enough to pull themselves out of their circumstances. They may not be aware that poverty is a difficult condition to transcend. For example, imagine being the mother of two children, and as the result of a car accident, your spouse has developed a chronic health condition that keeps him from working and requires he have constant care. His medical bills wipe out any extra money you have. Even with the benefits of Temporary Assistance for Needy Families and disability income, it's a struggle to make rent and utility payments and buy enough food to feed your family. You want to work, but you can only work during school hours on weekdays when your children are in school. You do not have a car, so you must walk or take public transportation, which limits how far away your job can be from your home. Any small thing can upset the fragile balance you have established: a trip to the doctor, an unexpected bill, an increase in expenses. The road out of poverty for this mother and her family seems nearly impossible. Her situation seems so intractable that no amount of motivation or hard work could resolve it.

Having privilege blinds individuals to the experience of the underprivileged. Without the ability to understand, without judgment, individuals and their unique situations, leaders end up excluding rather than including them.

Collectively, the barriers to embracing diversity and inclusion (i.e., ethnocentrism, prejudice, unconscious bias, stereotypes, and privilege) underscore the difficulty in accepting and confirming those who are different from ourselves. Leaders must not only address these barriers as they occur with their followers but must also take a critical look at their own biases regarding diversity and work to eliminate these barriers in their own lives. As we have learned from Ferdman's framework, inclusion is a fluid process and must occur at the individual as well as societal level.

SUMMARY

This chapter discusses how leaders can embrace diversity and inclusion in their organizations. *Diversity* plays a seminal role in effective leadership; it is defined as the *differing individuals in a group or an organization. Inclusion* is defined as the process of *incorporating others who are different into a group or an organization* in a way that allows them to feel they are part of the whole. Diversity focuses on recognizing differences, and inclusion is concerned with embracing those differences.

The historical development of workplace diversity in the United States has emerged over three periods. The *early years* (1960s and 1970s), which included the creation of landmark equal employment laws, focused on discrimination and fairness. Second, the *era of valuing diversity* (1980s and 1990s) emphasized pluralism and the competitive advantages of diversity in the workplace. Third, the *era of diversity management and inclusion in the 21st century* (2000 to present) emphasizes acknowledging, valuing, and integrating people's differences into the organization and places inclusion at center stage in addressing concerns about diversity.

An inclusion framework was developed by researchers to describe how the process of inclusion works. This framework illustrates inclusion as an interaction of an individual's levels of belongingness (i.e., the desire to be connected) and uniqueness (i.e., the desire to maintain one's own identity). For leaders, managing diversity is about managing the tension followers experience between connectedness and individuality. The individual experience of inclusion occurs as a result of inclusion practices on many levels, including interpersonal, group, leader, organizational, and societal. Inclusion travels from the societal level down to the individual and back up the levels from the individual to societal.

Researchers have identified six components of the inclusion experience that provide a blueprint of how leaders should behave and communicate to provide inclusion for followers. To help followers *feel safe*, leaders need to treat them in nonthreatening ways. To help followers *feel involved and engaged*, leaders should recognize followers' strengths and let them know they are full-fledged members of the organization. To help followers *feel respected and valued*, leaders should practice the Golden Rule and show trust and care for followers. To help followers *feel influential*, leaders should recognize followers' need to have an impact on others and enable them to participate in decision making. To help followers feel *authentic and whole*, leaders should create an atmosphere where followers can feel free to be as honest and transparent as they are comfortable being. Finally, to help followers feel *recognized, attended to, and honored*, leaders should exhibit open-mindedness toward all followers, honoring the individuality of each of them.

Barriers that can inhibit leaders and followers from embracing diversity are *ethnocentrism, prejudice, unconscious bias, stereotypes*, and *privilege*. The challenge for leaders is to remove or mitigate these barriers. Although addressing diversity is an interactive process between leaders and followers, the burden of effectively addressing diversity and building inclusion rests squarely on the shoulders of the leader. Effective leaders recognize the importance of diversity and make it a focal point of their leadership.

KEY TERMS

assimilation

belonging

diversity

equity

ethnocentrism

inclusion

melting pot

multiculturalism

pluralism

prejudice

privilege

social identities

stereotype

systemic discrimination

unconscious bias

9.1 Case Study—What's in a Name?

Springfield High School's athletic teams have been called the Redskins since the school opened in 1944. The small town of 7,000, which is roughly 95% white, is located in an area of the Midwest that once had thriving Native American tribes, a fact the community is proud to promote in its tourism brochures. So when the members of a local family with Native American ancestry came before the school board to ask that the name of Springfield High School's athletic teams be changed because they found the use of the word *Redskins* to be offensive, it created a firestorm in the town.

The school's athletic teams had competed as Redskins for 70 years, and many felt the name was an integral part of the community. People personally identified with the Redskins, and the team and the team's name were ingrained in the small town's culture. Flags with the Redskins logo flew outside homes and businesses, and decals with the image of the smiling Redskins mascot adorned many car windows.

"Locals would come before the board and say, 'I was born a Redskin and I'll die a Redskin,'" recalls one board member. "They argued that the name was never intended to be offensive, that it was chosen for the teams before 'political correctness' was a thing, and that it honored the area's relatively strong Native American presence."

But several other local Native American families and individuals also came forward in support of changing the name. One pointed out that "the use of the word *Redskin* is essentially a racial slur, and as a racial slur, it needs to be changed." The issue drew national attention, and speakers came in from outside the state to discuss the negative ramifications of Native American mascots.

However, the opposition to change was fierce. T-shirts and bumper stickers started appearing around town sporting the slogans "I'm a Redskin and Proud" and "Don't tell me I'm not a Redskin." At board meetings, those in favor of keeping the name would boo and talk over those speaking in favor of changing it, and argue that speakers who weren't from Springfield shouldn't even be allowed to be at the board meetings.

The board ultimately approved a motion, 5–2, to have the students at Springfield High School choose a new name for their athletic teams. The students immediately embraced the opportunity to choose a new name, developing designs and logos for their proposed choices. In the end, the student body voted to become the Redhawks.

There was still an angry community contingent, however, that was festering over the change. They began a petition to recall the school board members and received enough signatures for the recall to be put up for an election.

"While the kids are going about the business of changing the name and the emblem, the community holds an election and proceeds to recall the five members of the board who voted in favor of it," one of the recalled board members said.

The remaining two board members, both of whom were ardent members of the athletic booster organization, held a special meeting of the board (all two of them) and voted to change the name back to the Redskins.

That's when the state Department of Civil Rights and the state's Commission for High School Athletics stepped in. They told the Springfield School Board there could not be a reversal of the name change and that the high school's teams would have to go for four years without one, competing only as Springfield.

Over the course of those four years, new school board members were elected, and the issue quieted down. At the end of that period, the students again voted to become the Springfield Redhawks. "You know, the kids were fine with it," says one community member. "It's been 10 years, and there's an entire generation of kids who don't have a clue that it was ever different. They are Redhawks and have always been Redhawks.

"It was the adults who had the problem. There's still a small contingent today that can't get over it. A local hardware store still sells Springfield Redskins T-shirts and other gear. There is just this group of folks who believe there was nothing disrespectful in the Redskins name."

Questions

1. Do you agree with the assertion the athletic team name should be changed?

2. Describe how Ferdman's model of inclusion practices (Table 9.4) worked in this case. Did the influence for inclusive practices travel both up and down the model?

3. What barriers to embracing diversity and inclusion did the school board and community experience in this case?

4. Using the inclusion framework in Table 9.3, where would you place the Native American residents in the town of Springfield? What about Native American students at Springfield High School?

5. By changing the name of the athletic teams, do you believe the school board was showing inclusive practices? If so, which ones?

6. What role does privilege play in the resistance of community members to change the athletic teams' name?

Application

9.2 Case Study—Symbolic Progress

New Orleans mayor Mitch Landrieu wanted to observe the 300th anniversary of his city in 2018 in a way that would "build something that would make us better" (Winfrey, 2018).

The city was still rebuilding and recovering from the devastation of a recession, a major oil spill, and four hurricanes when Landrieu was approached by a friend with the idea of removing the Robert E. Lee statue, one of four prominently placed statues around the city memorializing the Southern Confederacy and its leaders. The 2015 massacre by a white supremacist gunman of nine Black parishioners at the Mother Emanuel African Methodist Episcopal Church in Charleston, South Carolina, had sparked a national conversation about removing public monuments and flags and renaming schools, parks, roads, and other public works that pay homage to the Confederacy (Southern Poverty Law Center [SPLC], 2022).

Born and raised in New Orleans, the son of white parents, Landrieu grew up in a diverse neighborhood surrounded by the richness of the culture of New Orleans. His father, a member of the Louisiana legislature, was one of the only people to vote against segregation-ist laws in the 1960s. Initially, Landrieu shied away from the proposal to remove the statues, but started researching the history of the monuments—who had constructed them and to what purpose. Realizing this was an opportunity to heal a significant wound at an impor-tant time in the city's history, he decided all four of the statues should be removed. After almost two years of effort, significant controversy, and difficulty, the last statue came down on May 19, 2017. On that day, Mayor Landrieu delivered the following speech explaining why he felt this was so important for the City of New Orleans and its people:

Thank you for coming.

The soul of our beloved city is deeply rooted in a history that has evolved over thousands of years; rooted in a diverse people who have been here together every step of the way—for both good and for ill. It is a history that holds in its heart the stories of Native Americans—the Choctaw, Houma Nation, the Chitimacha. Of Hernando De Soto, Robert Cavelier, Sieur de La Salle, the Acadians, the Islenos, the enslaved people from Senegambia, Free People of Color, the Haitians, the Germans, both the empires of France and Spain. The Italians, the Irish, the Cubans, the south and central Americans, the Vietnamese and so many more.

You see—New Orleans is truly a city of many nations, a melting pot, a bubbling cauldron of many cultures. There is no other place quite like it in the world that so eloquently exemplifies the uniquely American motto: *e pluribus unum*—out of many we are one. But there are also other truths about our city that we must confront. New Orleans was America's largest slave market: a port where hundreds of thousands of souls were bought, sold and shipped up the Mississippi River to lives of forced labor, of misery, of rape, of torture. America was the place where nearly 4,000 of our fellow citizens were lynched, 540 alone in Louisiana; where the courts enshrined "separate but equal"; where Freedom Riders coming to New Orleans were beaten to a bloody pulp. So when people say to me that the monuments in question are history, well what I just described is real history as well, and it is the searing truth.

And it immediately begs the questions, why there are no slave ship monuments, no prominent markers on public land to remember the lynchings or the slave blocks; nothing to remember this long chapter of our lives; the pain, the sacrifice, the shame . . . all of it happening on the soil of New Orleans. So for those self-appointed defenders of history and the monuments, they are eerily silent on what amounts to this historical malfeasance, a lie by omission. There is a difference between remembrance of history and reverence of it.

For America and New Orleans, it has been a long, winding road, marked by great tragedy and great triumph. But we cannot be afraid of our truth. As President George W. Bush said at the dedication ceremony for the National Museum of African American History & Culture, "A great nation does not hide its history. It faces its flaws and corrects them." So today I want to speak about why we chose to remove these four monuments to the Lost Cause of the Confederacy, but also how and why this process can move us towards healing and understanding of each other. So, let's start with the facts.

The historic record is clear, the Robert E. Lee, Jefferson Davis, and P.G.T. Beauregard statues were not erected just to honor these men, but as part of the movement which became known as The Cult of the Lost Cause. This "cult" had one goal—through monuments and through other means—to rewrite history to hide the truth, which is that the Confederacy was on the wrong side of humanity. First erected over 166 years after the founding of our city and 19 years after the end of the Civil War, the monuments that we took down were meant to rebrand the history of our city and the ideals of a defeated Confederacy. It is self-evident that these men did not fight for the United States of America, they fought against it. They may have been warriors, but in this cause they were not patriots. These statues are not just stone and metal. They are not just innocent remembrances of a benign history. These monuments purposefully celebrate a fictional, sanitized Confederacy; ignoring the death, ignoring the enslavement, and the terror that it actually stood for.

After the Civil War, these statues were a part of that terrorism as much as a burning cross on someone's lawn; they were erected purposefully to send a strong message to all who walked in their shadows about who was still in charge in this city. Should you have further doubt about the true goals of the Confederacy, in the very weeks before the war broke out, the Vice President of the Confederacy, Alexander Stephens, made it clear that the Confederate cause was about maintaining slavery and white supremacy. He said in his now famous "cornerstone speech" that the Confederacy's "cornerstone rests upon the great truth, that the negro is not equal to the white man; that slavery—subordination to the superior race—is his natural and normal condition. This, our new government, is the first, in the history of the world, based upon this great physical, philosophical, and moral truth."

Now, with these shocking words still ringing in your ears . . . I want to try to gently peel from your hands the grip on a false narrative of our history that I think weakens us. And make straight a wrong turn we made many years ago—we can more closely connect with integrity to the founding principles of our nation and forge a clearer and straighter path toward a better city and a more perfect union.

Last year, President Barack Obama echoed these sentiments about the need to contextualize and remember all our history. He recalled a piece of stone, a slave auction block engraved with a marker commemorating a single moment in 1830 when Andrew Jackson and Henry Clay stood and spoke from it. President Obama said, "Consider what this artifact tells us about history . . . on a stone where day after day for years, men and women . . . bound and bought and sold and bid like cattle on a stone worn down by the tragedy of over a thousand bare feet. For a long time the only thing we considered important, the singular thing we once chose to commemorate as history with a plaque were the unmemorable speeches of two powerful men."

A piece of stone—one stone. Both stories were history. One story told. One story forgotten or maybe even purposefully ignored. As clear as it is for me today . . . for a long time, even though I grew up in one of New Orleans' most diverse neighborhoods, even with my family's long proud history of fighting for civil rights . . . I must have passed by those monuments a million times without giving them a second thought. So I am not judging anybody, I am not judging people. We all take our own journey on race.

I just hope people listen like I did when my dear friend Wynton Marsalis helped me see the truth. He asked me to think about all the people who have left New Orleans because of our exclusionary attitudes. Another friend asked me to consider these four monuments from the perspective of an African American mother or father trying to explain to their fifth-grade daughter who Robert E. Lee is and why he stands atop of our beautiful city. Can you do it? Can you look into that young girl's eyes and convince her that Robert E. Lee is there to encourage her?

Do you think she will feel inspired and hopeful by that story? Do these monuments help her see a future with limitless potential? Have you ever thought that if her potential is limited, yours and mine are too? We all know the answer to these very simple questions. When you look into this child's eyes is the moment when the searing truth comes into focus for us. This is the moment when we know what is right and what we must do. We can't walk away from this truth.

And I knew that taking down the monuments was going to be tough, but you elected me to do the right thing, not the easy thing, and this is what that looks like. So relocating these Confederate monuments is not about taking something away from someone else. This is not about politics, this is not about blame or retaliation. This is not a naïve quest to solve all our problems at once.

This is, however, about showing the whole world that we as a city and as a people are able to acknowledge, understand, reconcile and, most importantly, choose a better future for ourselves making straight what has been crooked and making right what was wrong. Otherwise, we will continue to pay a price with discord, with division and, yes, with violence.

To literally put the Confederacy on a pedestal in our most prominent places of honor is an inaccurate recitation of our full past. It is an affront to our present, and it is a bad prescription for our future. History cannot be changed. It cannot be moved like a statue. What is done is done. The Civil War is over, and the Confederacy lost and we are better for it. Surely we are far enough removed from this dark time to acknowledge that the cause of the Confederacy was wrong.

And in the second decade of the 21st century, asking African Americans—or anyone else—to drive by property that they own; occupied by reverential statues of men who fought to destroy the country and deny that person's humanity seems perverse and absurd. Centuries-old wounds are still raw because they never healed right in the first place. Here is the essential truth. We are better together than we are apart.

Indivisibility is our essence. Isn't this the gift that the people of New Orleans have given to the world? We radiate beauty and grace in our food, in our music, in our architecture, in our joy of life, in our celebration of death; in everything that we do. We gave the world this funky thing called jazz, the most uniquely American art form that is developed across the ages from different cultures. Think about second lines, think about Mardi Gras, think about muffaletta, think about the Saints, gumbo, red beans and rice. By God, just think.

All we hold dear is created by throwing everything in the pot; creating, producing something better; everything a product of our historic diversity. We are proof that out of many we are one—and better for it! Out of many we are one—and we really do love it! And yet, we still seem to find so many excuses for not doing the right thing. Again, remember President Bush's words, "A great nation does not hide its history. It faces its flaws and corrects them."

We forget, we deny how much we really depend on each other, how much we need each other. We justify our silence and inaction by manufacturing noble causes that marinate in historical denial. We still find a way to say "wait"/not so fast, but like Dr. Martin Luther King Jr. said, "wait has almost always meant never." We can't wait any longer. We need to change. And we need to change now.

No more waiting. This is not just about statues, this is about our attitudes and behavior as well. If we take these statues down and don't change to become a more open and inclusive society, this would have all been in vain. While some have driven by these monuments every day and either revered their beauty or failed to see them at all, many of our neighbors and fellow Americans see them very clearly. Many are painfully aware of the long shadows their presence casts; not only literally but figuratively. And they clearly receive the message that the Confederacy and the Cult of the Lost Cause intended to deliver.

Earlier this week, as the Cult of the Lost Cause statue of P.G.T. Beauregard came down, world-renowned musician Terence Blanchard stood watch, his wife Robin and their two beautiful daughters at their side. Terence went to a high school on the edge of City Park named after one of America's greatest heroes and patriots, John F. Kennedy. But to get there he had to pass by this monument to a man who fought to deny him his humanity.

He said, "I've never looked at them as a source of pride . . . it's always made me feel as if they were put there by people who don't respect us. This is something I never thought I'd see in my lifetime. It's a sign that the world is changing." Yes, Terence, it is, and it is long overdue. Now is the time to send a new message to the next generation of New Orleanians who can follow in Terence and Robin's remarkable footsteps.

A message about the future, about the next 300 years and beyond; let us not miss this opportunity, New Orleans, and let us help the rest of the country do the same. Because now is the time for choosing. Now is the time to actually make this the City we always should have been, had we gotten it right in the first place.

We should stop for a moment and ask ourselves—at this point in our history— after Katrina, after Rita, after Ike, after Gustav, after the national recession, after the BP oil catastrophe and after the tornado—if presented with the opportunity to build monuments that told our story or to curate these particular spaces . . . would these monuments be what we want the world to see? Is this really our story?

We have not erased history; we are becoming part of the city's history by righting the wrong image these monuments represent and crafting a better, more complete future for all our children and for future generations. And unlike when these Confederate monuments were first erected as symbols of white supremacy, we now have a chance to create not only new symbols, but to do it together, as one people. In our blessed land we *all* come to the table of democracy as equals. We have to reaffirm our commitment to a future where each citizen is guaranteed the uniquely American gifts of life, liberty and the pursuit of happiness.

That is what really makes America great, and today it is more important than ever to hold fast to these values and together say a self-evident truth that out of many we are one. That is why today we reclaim these spaces for the United States of America. Because we are *one* nation, not two; indivisible with liberty and justice for all . . . not some. We all are part of one nation, all pledging allegiance to one flag, the flag of the United States of America. And New Orleanians are in . . . all of the way. It is in this union and in this truth that real patriotism is rooted and flourishes. Instead of revering a four-year brief historical aberration that was called the Confederacy we can celebrate all 300 years of our rich, diverse history as a place named New Orleans and set the tone for the next 300 years.

After decades of public debate, of anger, of anxiety, of anticipation, of humiliation and of frustration. After public hearings and approvals from three separate community led commissions. After two robust public hearings and a 6–1 vote by the duly elected New Orleans City Council. After review by 13 different federal and state judges. The full weight of the legislative, executive and judicial branches of government has been brought to bear and the monuments in accordance with the law have been removed. So now is the time to come together and heal and focus on our larger task. Not only building new symbols, but making this city a beautiful manifestation of what is possible and what we as a people can become.

Let us remember what the once exiled, imprisoned and now universally loved Nelson Mandela said after the fall of apartheid. "If the pain has often been unbearable and the revelations shocking to all of us, it is because they indeed bring us the beginnings of a common understanding of what happened and a steady restoration of the nation's humanity." So before we part let us again state the truth clearly.

The Confederacy was on the wrong side of history and humanity. It sought to tear apart our nation and subjugate our fellow Americans to slavery. This is the history we should never forget and one that we should never again put on a pedestal to be revered. As a community, we must recognize the significance of removing New Orleans' Confederate monuments. It is our acknowledgment that now is the time to take stock of, and then move past, a painful part of our history.

Anything less would render generations of courageous struggle and soul-searching a truly lost cause. Anything less would fall short of the immortal words of our greatest President Abraham Lincoln, who with an open heart and clarity of purpose calls on us today to unite as one people when he said: "With malice toward none, with charity for all, with firmness in the right, as God gives us to see the right, let us strive on to finish the work we are in, to bind up the nation's wounds . . . to do all which may achieve and cherish—a just and lasting peace among ourselves and with all nations." (Time Staff, 2017)

By 2022, 377 Confederate symbols had been removed in the United States according to the SPLC (2022). Most of these occurred as the result of tragedies involving hate crimes, including 200 removals that were spurred by killing of George Floyd, a Black man, by white police officers in Minneapolis, Minnesota, in 2020. According to the SPLC (2022), however, more than 1,747 such symbols still remain.

Questions

1. Some people argue that leadership has a moral dimension that moves people toward the common good. Do you think Mayor Mitch Landrieu's speech has a moral dimension? If yes, what values is Mayor Landrieu promoting? What are the obstacles to his advocacy?

2. By removing the statues and through his speech, Mayor Landrieu takes a strong stand against dignifying symbols of the Confederacy. Do you feel his actions fostered a stronger sense of inclusion within the city of New Orleans? Discuss how different perceptions of the statues and their inherent messages may have affected different groups within the community.

3. The chapter discussed five barriers to diversity and inclusion: ethnocentrism, prejudice, unconscious bias, stereotypes, and privilege. In what ways were these statues symbolic of these barriers?

4. Table 9.2 describes different metaphors for diversity during different time periods. What is the metaphor and emphasis of Mayor Landrieu's speech, and what are the implications of this approach for diversity and inclusion?

5. Consider the various symbols in your community, school, or workplace that you see every day. Select one or two and discuss the possible perceptions of each symbol to different members of your community.

Application

9.3 Cultural Diversity Awareness Questionnaire

Purpose

1. To identify your attitudes and perspectives regarding cultural diversity
2. To help you become aware of and understand your prejudices and biases
3. To help you understand the potential consequences of your approach to diversity in the workplace

Directions

1. Read each statement and circle the number that best describes your belief or behavior.
2. Be as candid as possible with your responses; there are no right or wrong answers.

	Never	Almost Never	Some-times	Almost Always	Always
1. I am aware of my own biases and how they affect my thinking.	1	2	3	4	5
2. I can honestly assess my strengths and weaknesses in the area of diversity and try to improve myself.	1	2	3	4	5
3. I assume good intent and ask for clarification when I don't understand what was said or implied.	1	2	3	4	5
4. I challenge others when they make racial/ethnic/sexually offensive comments or jokes.	1	2	3	4	5
5. I speak up if I witness another person being humiliated or discriminated against.	1	2	3	4	5

	Never	Almost Never	Some-times	Almost Always	Always
6. I do not participate in jokes that are derogatory to any individual group.	1	2	3	4	5
7. I don't believe that my having a friend of color means that I'm culturally competent.	1	2	3	4	5
8. I understand why a lack of diversity in my social circle may be perceived as excluding others.	1	2	3	4	5
9. I realize that people of other cultures have a need to support one another and connect as a group.	1	2	3	4	5
10. I do not make assumptions about a person or individual group until I have verified the facts on my own.	1	2	3	4	5
11. I have multiple friends from a variety of ethnicities and abilities.	1	2	3	4	5
12. I connect easily with people who look different from me and am able to communicate easily with them.	1	2	3	4	5
13. I'm interested in the ideas and beliefs of people who don't think and believe as I do, and I respect their opinions even when I disagree.	1	2	3	4	5

	Never	Almost Never	Some-times	Almost Always	Always
14. I work to make sure people who are different from me are heard and accepted.	1	2	3	4	5
15. I recognize and avoid language that reinforces stereotypes.	1	2	3	4	5
16. I know others' stereotypes associated with my ethnicity.	1	2	3	4	5
17. I encourage people who are culturally different from myself to speak out on their issues and concerns, and I validate their issues and concerns.	1	2	3	4	5
18. I avoid assuming that others will have the same reaction as I do when discussing or viewing an issue.	1	2	3	4	5
19. I understand that I'm a product of my upbringing and believe there are valid beliefs other than my own.	1	2	3	4	5
20. I do not take physical characteristics into account when interacting with others or when making decisions about others' competence or ability.	1	2	3	4	5

	Never	Almost Never	Some-times	Almost Always	Always
21. I recognize that others stereotype me, and I try to overcome their perceptions.	1	2	3	4	5
22. I include people who are culturally different from myself in team decision-making processes that impact them.	1	2	3	4	5
23. I actively seek opportunities to connect with people who are different from me and seek to build rapport with them.	1	2	3	4	5
24. I believe "color blindness" is counterproductive and devalues a person's culture or history.	1	2	3	4	5
25. I avoid generalizing behaviors or attitudes of one individual in a group to others.	1	2	3	4	5
26. I actively convey that employees or students of varying backgrounds are as skilled and competent as others.	1	2	3	4	5
27. I do not try to justify acts of discrimination to make the victim feel better. I validate their assessment of what occurred.	1	2	3	4	5

	Never	Almost Never	Some- times	Almost Always	Always
28. I try to learn about and appreciate the richness of other cultures and honor their holidays and events.	1	2	3	4	5
29. I believe there are policies and practices in place that negatively impact people outside the majority culture.	1	2	3	4	5
30. I understand the definition of internalized racism and how it impacts people of color.	1	2	3	4	5
31. I recognize that race is a social construct, not a scientific fact.	1	2	3	4	5
32. I know and accept that people's experiences and background impact how they interact with and trust me.	1	2	3	4	5

Source: Adapted from Special Populations and CTE Illinois Leadership Project. (2016). *Cultural Diversity Self-Assessment.* http://illinoiscte.org/index.php/resources/cultural-competency-module

Scoring

Sum the numbers you circled on the questionnaire. This number is your cultural diversity awareness score.

Total Score

Cultural diversity awareness score: _____

Scoring Interpretation

This self-assessment is designed to measure your beliefs and behavior regarding cultural diversity and inclusion. A *higher score* on the assessment indicates that you are acutely aware of prejudice and bias, and that you are very aware of the impact of your behavior on others. Individuals who score high relate to others in ways that value diversity. A *lower score* on the assessment suggests that you are unaware of prejudice and bias, and that you are not fully aware of the impact of your biased behavior on others. Individuals who score low communicate with others in ways that do not value diversity.

If your score is 130–160, you are in the very high range.
If your score is 100–129, you are in the high range.
If your score is 70–99, you are in the moderate range.
If your score is 40–69, you are in the low range.
If your score is 0–39, you are in the very low range.

9.4 Observational Exercise—Diversity and Inclusion

Purpose

1. To become aware of the dimensions of diversity and inclusion
2. To develop an understanding of how leaders address diversity and inclusion in the workplace

Directions

1. Your task in this exercise is to interview a leader about their views on diversity and inclusion. The individual you interview should have a formal position of authority in a company (e.g., supervisor, manager), a school (e.g., teacher, principal), or the community (e.g., director of social work, bank vice president, small business owner).
2. Conduct a 30-minute semistructured interview with this individual by phone or in person.
3. Develop your own interview questions. If necessary, you may incorporate ideas from the following questions:
   - Tell me about your job. How long have you held this position, and how did you get it?
   - What comes to your mind when you hear the word *diversity*? How is diversity addressed within your organization? How important do you think diversity is in your place of work? Why?
   - Are there areas within your organization that have less diversity than other areas? Do you think the organization should address this?
   - What challenges do you face regarding diversity among those whom you supervise?
   - How do you treat employees/followers who are different from others? Do you allow everyone to participate in decision making?
   - What is the best way to make an employee/follower who is a member of a marginalized group feel genuinely included with others?

Questions

1. Based on your observations, how important is diversity and inclusion to the leader you interviewed?

2. Which metaphor in Table 9.2 (i.e., melting pot, salad, or smorgasbord) would you use to describe the way the leader approaches their followers? Give examples to illustrate this metaphor.

3. Do you think the leader holds any stereotypes about others? In what way do these affect their leadership?

4. In what way does the leader try to make individuals who are different from the group feel a part of the organization? Give specific examples where relevant.

5. Do you think privilege is in any way related to how this person leads? Defend your answer.

9.5 Reflection and Action Worksheet—Diversity and Inclusion

Reflection

1. What is your response to the word *diversity*? Explain your thoughts on diversity.

2. Reflect on the seven primary dimensions of cultural diversity shown in Table 9.1 (i.e., age, gender, race, mental and physical abilities, ethnicity, sexual orientation, and communication and work style). Which type of diversity is easiest for you to embrace, and why? Explain your answers.

3. One way to explore the concept of *inclusion* is to reflect on your own personal feelings about inclusion. In a group situation, how much do you want to be included by others? Using a personal example, discuss a time when you were in a group or on a team when you felt included by others and a time when you felt excluded. Why did you feel included in one situation and not the other? Elaborate and discuss.

4. Think about what circumstances got you to where you are today. Do you have a past that some would describe as privileged? Or, would you say you are not privileged? Do you see your colleagues or coworkers as having privilege? Discuss your thoughts on privilege.

Action

1. Explore your answers on the Cultural Diversity Awareness Questionnaire. Select three items on which you chose *almost never* or *never*. Based on your responses to these items, discuss what you could do in your own leadership to be more inclusive toward others.

2. Imagine for a moment that you have been selected to lead a group service learning project. What will you say to make others in your group feel psychologically safe? In what way will you let them participate in decision making? How will you encourage those individuals who are most different from the group to feel like insiders yet still unique? Discuss.

3. As discussed in the chapter, stereotypes often get in the way of including others who differ from us. What common stereotypes do you sometimes attribute to others (e.g., a white male police officer, a Muslim woman wearing a hijab, or a transgender man)? How can you change these stereotypes? What messages will you give yourself to eliminate these stereotypes? Discuss.

10 MANAGING CONFLICT

INTRODUCTION

Conflict is inevitable in groups and organizations, and it presents both a challenge and a true opportunity for every leader. In the well-known book *Getting to Yes*, Fisher and Ury (1981) contend that handling conflict is a daily occurrence for all of us. "People differ, and they use negotiation to handle their differences" (Fisher et al., 1991, p. xvii). *Getting to Yes* asserts that mutual agreement is possible in any conflict situation—if people are willing to negotiate in authentic ways.

When we think of conflict in simple terms, we think of a struggle between people, groups, organizations, cultures, or nations. Conflict involves opposing forces pulling in different directions. Many people believe that conflict is disruptive, causes stress, and should be avoided.

As we stated in Chapter 5, while conflict can be uncomfortable, it is not unhealthy, nor is it necessarily bad. Conflict will always be present in leadership situations, and surprisingly, it often produces positive change. When leaders handle conflict effectively, problem solving increases, interpersonal relationships become stronger, and stress surrounding the conflict decreases.

Communication plays a central role in handling conflict. Conflict is an interactive process between two or more parties that requires effective human interaction. By communicating effectively, leaders and followers can successfully resolve conflicts to bring positive results.

This chapter will emphasize ways to handle conflict. First, we will define conflict and describe the role communication plays in conflict. Next, we will discuss different kinds of conflict, followed by an exploration of Fisher and Ury's (1981) ideas about effective negotiation as well as other communication strategies that help resolve conflict. Last, we will examine styles of approaching conflict and the pros and cons of these styles.

CONFLICT EXPLAINED

Conflict is a charged word. By its very definition, it has negative connotations: disagreement, argument, incompatibility, clash. Although conflict can be uncomfortable, it is not necessarily unhealthy, nor is it necessarily bad. Conflict is inevitable in groups and organizations, and it can present an opportunity for people to learn and grow. Working through conflict can result in new perspectives and understandings and better solutions, ideas, and innovations.

When addressing conflict, the question is not "How can people *avoid* conflict and *eliminate* change?" but rather "How can people *manage* conflict and produce *positive* change?"

Conflict has been studied from multiple perspectives, including *intra*personal, *inter*personal, and societal. Intrapersonal conflict refers to the discord that occurs *within an individual*. It is a topic often studied by psychologists and personality theorists who are interested in the dynamics of personality and factors that predispose people to inner conflicts. Interpersonal conflict refers to the disputes that arise *between individuals*. This is the type of conflict we focus on when we discuss conflict in organizations. Societal conflict refers to clashes *between societies and nations*. Studies in this field focus on the causes of international conflicts, war, and peace. The continuing crisis between the Israelis and the Palestinians is a good example of societal conflict. This chapter focuses on conflict as an interpersonal process that plays a critical role in effective leadership.

The following definition, based on the work of Wilmot and Hocker (2011), best describes conflict. **Conflict** is a felt struggle between two or more interdependent individuals over perceived incompatible differences in beliefs, values, and goals, or over differences in desires for esteem, control, and connectedness. This definition emphasizes several unique aspects of conflict.

First, conflict is a *struggle*; it is the result of opposing forces coming together. For example, there is conflict when a leader and a senior-level employee oppose each other on whether or not all employees must work on weekends. Similarly, conflict occurs when a school principal and a parent disagree on the type of sex education program that should be adopted in a school system. In short, conflict involves a clash between opposing parties.

Second, there needs to be an element of *interdependence* between parties for conflict to take place. If leaders could function entirely independently of each other and their followers, there would be no reason for conflict. Everyone could do their own work, and there would be no areas of contention. However, leaders do not work in isolation. Leaders need followers, and followers need leaders. This interdependence sets up an environment in which conflict is more likely.

When two parties are interdependent, they are forced to deal with questions such as "How much influence do I want in this relationship?" and "How much influence am I willing to accept from the other party?" Because of our interdependence, questions such as these cannot be avoided. In fact, Wilmot and Hocker (2011) contend that these questions permeate most conflicts.

Third, conflict always contains an *affective* element, the "felt" part of the definition. Conflict is an emotional process that involves the arousal of feelings in both parties of the conflict (Brown & Keller, 1979). When our beliefs or values on a highly charged issue (e.g., the right to strike) are challenged, we become upset and feel it is important to defend our position. When our feelings clash with others' feelings, we are in conflict.

The primary emotions connected with conflict are not always anger or hostility. Rather, an array of emotions can accompany conflict. Hocker and Wilmot (1995) found that many people report feeling lonely, sad, or disconnected during conflict. For some, interpersonal conflict creates feelings of abandonment—that their human bond to others has been broken. Feelings such as these often produce the discomfort that surrounds conflict.

Fourth, conflict involves *differences* between individuals that are perceived to be incompatible. Conflict can result from differences in individuals' beliefs, values, and goals, or from differences in individuals' desires for control, status, and connectedness. The opportunities for conflict are endless because each of us is unique with particular sets of interests and ideas. These differences are a constant breeding ground for conflict.

In summary, these four elements—struggle, interdependence, feelings, and differences—are critical ingredients of interpersonal conflict. To further understand the intricacies of managing conflict, we'll look at the role of communication in conflict and examine two major kinds of conflict.

Communication and Conflict

When conflict exists in leadership situations, it is recognized and expressed through communication. Communication is the means that people use to express their disagreements or differences. Communication also provides the avenue by which conflicts can be successfully resolved, or worsened, producing negative results.

To understand conflict, we need to understand communication. When human communication takes place, it occurs on two levels. One level can be characterized as the *content dimension* and the other as the *relationship dimension* (Watzlawick et al., 1967). The **content dimension** of communication involves the objective, observable aspects such as money, weather, and land; the **relationship dimension** refers to the participants' perceptions of their connection to one another. In human communication, these two dimensions are always bound together.

To illustrate the two dimensions, consider the following hypothetical statement made by a supervisor to an employee: "Please stop texting your friends while at work." The *content* dimension of this message refers to rules and what the supervisor wants the employee to do. The *relationship* dimension of this message refers to how the supervisor and the employee are affiliated—to the supervisor's authority in relation to the employee, the supervisor's attitude toward the employee, the employee's attitude toward the supervisor, and their feelings about one another. It is the relationship dimension that implicitly suggests how the content dimension should be interpreted, since the content alone can be interpreted in different ways. The exact meaning of the message to the supervisor and employee is interpreted as a result of their interaction. If a positive relationship exists between the supervisor and the employee, then the content "please stop texting your friends while at work" will probably be interpreted by the employee as a friendly request by a supervisor who is honestly concerned about the employee's job performance. However, if the relationship between the supervisor and the employee is superficial or strained, the employee may interpret the content of the message as a rigid directive, delivered by a supervisor who enjoys giving orders. This example illustrates how the meanings of messages are not in words alone but in individuals' interpretations of the messages in light of their relationships.

The content and relationship dimensions provide a lens for looking at conflict. As illustrated in Figure 10.1, there are two major kinds of conflict: conflict over content issues and conflict over relationship issues. Both kinds of conflict are prevalent in groups and organizational settings.

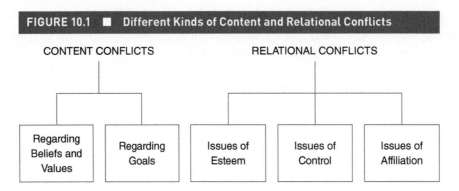

FIGURE 10.1 ■ Different Kinds of Content and Relational Conflicts

Conflict on the Content Level

Content conflict involves struggles between leaders and others who differ on issues such as policies and procedures. Debating with someone about the advantages or disadvantages of a particular rule is a familiar occurrence in most organizations. Sometimes these debates can be very heated (e.g., an argument between two employees about surfing the internet while working). These disagreements are considered conflicts on the content level when they center on differences in (1) beliefs and values or (2) goals and ways to reach those goals.

Conflict Regarding Beliefs and Values

Each of us has a unique system of beliefs and values that constitutes a basic philosophy of life. We have had different family situations as well as educational and work experiences. When we communicate with others, we become aware that others' viewpoints are often very different from our own. If we perceive what another person is communicating as incompatible with our own viewpoint, a conflict in beliefs or values is likely to occur.

Conflicts arising from differences in beliefs can be illustrated in several ways. For example, members of PETA (People for the Ethical Treatment of Animals) are in conflict with researchers in the pharmaceutical industry who believe strongly in the advantages of using animals to test new drugs. Another example of a conflict of beliefs can occur when teachers or nurses believe they have the right to strike because of unfair working conditions, while others feel that these kinds of employees should not be allowed to withhold services for any reason. In each of these examples, conflict occurs because one individual feels that their *beliefs* are incompatible with the position taken by another individual on the issue.

Conflicts can also occur between people because they have different *values*. When one person's values come into conflict with another's, it can create a difficult and challenging situation. To illustrate, consider the following example of an issue between Emily, a first-generation college student, and her mother. At the beginning of her senior year, Emily asks her mother if she can have a car to get around campus and to get back and forth to work. In order to pay for the car, Emily says she will take fewer credits, work more often at her part-time job, and postpone her graduation date to the following year. Emily is confident that she will graduate and thinks it is "no big deal" to extend her studies for a fifth year. However, Emily's mother does not feel the

LEADERSHIP SNAPSHOT

Humaira Bachal, Pakistani Educator

Humaira Bachal is a 33-year-old woman who has a dangerous passion: She wants to educate children, especially girls, in her home country of Pakistan where only 57% of the children ever enter primary school.

It's hard not to worry about Bachal in the wake of the 2012 shooting of Malala Yousafzai, a teenage Pakistani girl attacked by the Taliban for speaking out in support of girls' education. But she's not afraid.

When Bachal was in ninth grade, she looked around her village of Moach Goth and saw children playing in the

Photo courtesy of Humaira Bachal

streets instead of being in school or studying, and at all of 14, she thought that was wrong. There were no private or government schools in her neighborhood, and Bachal had received education only because her mother had sewn clothing or sold bundles of wood for 2 cents apiece to send her children to schools elsewhere.

Bachal knew what it meant to have to fight to be educated. Her father did not want her to go to school, saying that she "was only going to get married and have children" (Bachal, 2020).

But her mother had other ideas. She wasn't educated, but believed her children should be. She labored to pay for her daughter's education herself and had to sneak her off to school, hiding Bachal's whereabouts from her father. When he found out Bachal was going to take her ninth-grade entrance exams, he became furious and beat her mother, breaking her arm. Despite this, her mother gathered her daughter's school bag and sent her on her way to the exam, which she passed.

"My mother's support at that critical moment was essential in making me who I am today," Bachal says (Faruqi & Obaid-Chinoy, 2013).

That same year while she was still being educated, Bachal started recruiting students in her neighborhood to come to a small, private school she had opened. She even went door-to-door to convince parents to send their children to the school. More than once she had a door slammed in her face and her life threatened.

"Education is a basic need and fundamental right for every human being," she says. "I want to change the way my community looks at education and I will continue to do this until my last breath" (Temple-Raston, 2013).

Pakistan has had a dismal education rate. In 2013, it spent half as much as neighboring India on education, and if you were a young girl in rural Pakistan, you were unlikely to ever see the inside of a classroom. In 2013, there were more than 32 million girls under the age of 14 in Pakistan; fewer than 13 million of them went to school (Faruqi & Obaid-Chinoy, 2013).

In 2003, Bachal and five friends created their school, the Dream Foundation Trust Model Street School, in a two-room building with mud floors. In two decades, the Model Street School has grown into a formal school with 41 teachers and nearly 1,000 students. The school includes computer classes, a class for "labour boys" who work all day and attend classes in the evening, and adult literacy classes for men and women (Dream Foundation Trust, 2023).

But Bachal and the school were specifically interested in educating girls. Bachal would often visit fathers at their workplaces to convince them to send their daughters to school. She asked why, when the girls become teenagers, they stop coming to school. The fathers talked about honor and culture and how the girls are looked at by men as they go to school, and the men say things about them. Bachal can relate; at one point the men in her village called her immoral for becoming educated, and her brothers and father wanted to relocate to put an end to their shame (Faruqi & Obaid-Chinoy, 2013).

Bachal also reached out to mothers to make them allies in her crusade, asking them if they wanted their daughters to be treated as unjustly as they had been and urged the women to help their daughters have better lives by insisting that they get an education.

Bachal's mother has no regrets about the sacrifices she made to ensure her daughters were educated, saying, "Education is essential for women. They [her daughters] have reached this potential because of their education. Otherwise they would have been slaving away for their husbands somewhere" (Bachal, 2020).

Since its founding, the Dream Model Street School has seen its emphasis shift to providing free education for all children, boys *and* girls, with the aim of helping those impoverished children who not only cannot afford school tuition, but whose families would prefer the children work and contribute to the family's income. While still focused on providing education, the organization's mission now includes advocacy and awareness campaigns toward issues such as child marriage, domestic violence, and child abuse in order to "improve mutual understanding as well as mobilising communities and the whole society to bring about the necessary change in attitudes and behavior" (Dream Foundation Trust, n.d.).

same. She doesn't want Emily to have a car until after she graduates. She thinks the car will be a major distraction and get in the way of Emily's studies. Emily is the first person in her family to get a college degree, and it is extremely important to her mother that Emily graduates on time. Deep down, her mother is afraid that the longer Emily goes to school, the more student loan debt Emily will have to pay back when she finishes.

The value conflict between Emily and her mother involves Emily's desire to have a car. In this case, both individuals are highly interdependent of one another: To carry out her decision to get a car, Emily needs her mother's agreement; to have her daughter graduate in four years, Emily's mother needs cooperation from Emily. Both individuals perceive the other's values as incompatible with their own, and this makes conflict inevitable. Clearly, the conflict between Emily and her mother requires interpersonal communication about their different values and how these differences affect their relationship.

Conflict Regarding Goals

A second common type of content-related conflict occurs in situations where individuals have different *goals* (see Figure 10.1). Researchers have identified two types of conflict that occur regarding group goals: (1) procedural conflict and (2) substantive conflict (Knutson et al., 1976).

Procedural conflict refers to differences between individuals with regard to the approach they wish to take in attempting to reach a goal. In essence, it is conflict over the best means to an agreed-upon goal; it is not about what goal to achieve. Procedural conflicts can be observed in many situations such as determining how to best conduct job interviews, choose a method for identifying new sales territories, or spend advertising dollars. In each instance, conflict can occur when individuals do not agree on how to achieve a goal.

Substantive conflict occurs when individuals differ with regard to the substance of the goal itself, or what the goal should be. For example, two board members of a nonprofit human service agency may have very different views regarding the strategies and scope of a fundraising campaign. Similarly, two owners of a small business may strongly disagree about whether or not to offer their part-time employees' health care benefits. These illustrations by no means exhaust all the possible examples of substantive conflict; however, they point out that conflict can occur as a result of two or more parties disagreeing on what the goal or goals of a group or an organization should be.

Conflict on the Relational Level

Have you ever heard someone say, "I don't seem to get along with them; we have a personality clash"? The phrase *personality clash* is another way of describing a conflict on the relational level. Sometimes we do not get along with another person, not because of *what* we are talking about (conflict over content issues) but because of *how* we are talking about it. **Relational conflict** refers to the differences we feel between ourselves and others concerning how we relate to each other. For example, at a staff meeting, a manager interrupts employees and talks to them in a critical tone. The employees begin texting on their phones, ignoring the manager. A conflict erupts because both the manager and the employees feel unheard and disrespected. It is typically caused by neither one person nor the other, but arises in their relationship. Relational conflict is usually related to incompatible differences between individuals over issues of (1) esteem, (2) control, and (3) affiliation (see Figure 10.1).

Relational Conflict and Issues of Esteem

The need for esteem and recognition has been identified by Maslow (1970) as one of the major needs in the hierarchy of human needs. Each of us has needs for esteem—we want to feel significant, useful, and worthwhile. We desire to have an effect on our surroundings and to be perceived by others as worthy of their respect. We attempt to satisfy our esteem needs through what we do and how we act, particularly in how we behave in our relationships with our coworkers.

When our needs for esteem are not being fulfilled in our relationships, we experience relational conflict because others do not see us in the way we wish to be seen. For example, an administrative assistant can have repeated conflicts with an administrator if the assistant perceives that the administrator fails to recognize their unique contributions to the overall goals of the organization. Similarly, older employees may be upset if newer coworkers do not give them respect for the wisdom that comes with their years of experience. So, too, younger employees may want recognition for their innovative approaches to problems but fail to get it from coworkers with more longevity who do not think things should change.

At the same time that we want our own esteem needs satisfied, others want their esteem needs satisfied as well. If the supply of respect we can give each other seems limited (or scarce), then our needs for esteem will clash. We will see the other person's needs for esteem as competing with our own or taking that limited resource away from us. To illustrate, consider a staff meeting in which two employees are actively contributing insightful ideas and suggestions. If one of the employees is given recognition for their input but the other is not, conflict may result. As this conflict escalates, the effectiveness of their working relationship and the quality of their communication may diminish. When the amount of available esteem (validation from others) seems scarce, a clash develops.

All of us are human and want to be recognized for the contributions we make to our work and our community. When we believe we're not being recognized or receiving our "fair share," we feel slighted and conflicted on the relational level with others.

Relational Conflict and Issues of Control

Struggles over issues of control are very common in interpersonal conflict. Each one of us desires to have an impact on others and the situations that surround us. Having control, in effect, increases our feelings of potency about our actions and minimizes our feelings of helplessness. Control allows us to feel competent about ourselves. However, when we see others as hindering us or limiting our control, interpersonal conflict often ensues.

Interpersonal conflict occurs when a person's needs for control are incompatible with another's needs for control. In a given situation, each of us seeks different levels of control. Some people like to have a great deal, while others are satisfied (and sometimes even more content) with only a little. In addition, our needs for control may vary from one time to another. For example, there are times when a person's need to control others or events is very high; at other times, this same person may prefer that others take charge. Relational conflict over control issues develops when there is a clash between the needs for control that one person has at a given time (high or low) and the needs for control that others have at that same time (high or low). If, for example, a friend's need to make decisions about weekend plans is compatible with yours, no conflict will take place; however, if both of you want to control the weekend planning and your individual interests are different, then you will soon find yourselves in conflict. As struggles for control ensue, the communication among the participants may become negative and challenging as each person tries to gain control over the other or undermine the other's control.

A graphic example of a conflict over relational control is provided in the struggle between Natalia Alvarez, a college sophomore, and her parents, regarding what she will do on spring break. Natalia has an opportunity to go to the Gulf Coast of Florida with some friends to relax from the pressures of school. Her parents do not want her to go. Natalia thinks she deserves to go because she is doing well in her classes and the trip will cost her very little since they will be staying for free at the vacation home of one of the friends' relatives. Her parents think spring break at the beach in Florida is just a "big party" and nothing good will come of it. As another option, her parents offer to pay Natalia's expenses to visit her grandparents, who have invited

Natalia to their home in California. Natalia is adamant that she "is going" to Florida. Her parents, who help pay their daughter's college expenses, threaten that if she goes to Florida, they will no longer provide her with funding for college.

Clearly, in this example, both parties want to have control over the outcome. Natalia wants to be in charge of her own life and make the decisions about what she does or does not do. At the same time, her parents want to direct her into doing what they think is best for her. Natalia and her parents are interdependent and need each other, but they are conflicted because they each feel that the other is interfering with their needs for control of what Natalia does on spring break.

Conflicts over control are common in leadership situations. Like the parents in the example, the role of leader brings with it a certain inherent level of control and responsibility. When leaders clash with one another over control or when control issues exist between leaders and followers, interpersonal conflicts occur. Later in this chapter, we present some conflict management strategies that are particularly helpful in coping with relational conflicts that arise from issues of control.

Relational Conflict and Issues of Affiliation

In addition to wanting relational control, each of us has a need to feel included in our relationships, to be liked, and to receive affection (Schutz, 1966). If our needs for closeness are not satisfied in our relationships, we feel frustrated and experience feelings of conflict. Of course, some people like to be very involved and very close in their relationships, while others prefer less involvement and more distance. In any case, when others behave in ways that are incompatible with our own desires for warmth and affection, feelings of conflict emerge.

Relational conflict over affiliation issues is illustrated in the following example of a football coach, Terry Hinkle, and one of his players, Calvin Larson. Calvin, a starting quarterback, developed a strong relationship with Coach Hinkle during his junior year in high school. Throughout the year, Calvin and Coach Hinkle had many highly productive conversations inside and outside of school about how to improve the football program. In the summer, the coach employed Calvin in his painting business, and they worked side by side on a first-name basis. Both Calvin and Terry liked working together and grew to know each other quite well. However, when football practice started in the fall, difficulties emerged between the two. During the first weeks of practice, Calvin acted like Coach Hinkle was his best buddy. He called him Terry rather than Coach Hinkle, and he resisted the player–coach role. As Coach Hinkle attempted to withdraw from his summer relationship with Calvin and take on his legitimate responsibilities as a coach, Calvin experienced a sense of loss of closeness and warmth. In this situation, Calvin felt rejection or a loss of affiliation, and this created a relational conflict.

Relational conflicts—whether they are over esteem, control, or affiliation—are seldom overt. Due to the subtle nature of these conflicts, they are often not easy to recognize or address. Even when they are recognized, relational conflicts are often ignored because it is difficult for many individuals to openly communicate that they want more recognition, control, or affiliation.

According to communication theorists, relational issues are inextricably bound to content issues (Watzlawick et al., 1967). This means that relational conflicts will often surface during the discussion of content issues. For example, what may at first appear to be a conflict between two leaders regarding the *content* of a new employee fitness program may really be a struggle over which one of the leaders will ultimately receive credit for developing the program. As we mentioned, relational conflicts are complex and not easily resolved. However, when relational conflicts are expressed and confronted, it can significantly enhance the overall resolution process.

MANAGING CONFLICT IN PRACTICE

Communication is central to managing different kinds of conflict in organizations. Leaders who are able to keep channels of communication open with others will have a greater chance of understanding others' beliefs, values, and needs for esteem, control, and affiliation. With increased understanding, many of the kinds of conflict discussed in the earlier part of this chapter will seem less difficult to resolve and more open to negotiation.

In this section, we will explore three different approaches to resolving conflict: Fisher and Ury's principled negotiation; the communication strategies of differentiation, fractionation, and face saving; and the Kilmann–Thomas styles of approaching conflict. As we discussed previously, conflict can be multifaceted and complex, and while there is no magic bullet for resolving all conflicts, knowing different approaches can help a leader employ the effective strategies for solving conflict.

The Fisher and Ury Approach to Conflict

One of the most recognized approaches of conflict negotiation in the world was developed by Roger Fisher and William Ury. Derived from studies conducted by the Harvard Negotiation Project, Fisher and Ury (1981) provide a straightforward, step-by-step method for negotiating conflicts. This method, called **principled negotiation**, emphasizes deciding issues on their merits rather than through competitive haggling or through excessive accommodation. Principled negotiation shows you how to obtain your fair share decently and without having others take advantage of you (Fisher & Ury, 1981).

As illustrated in Figure 10.2, the Fisher and Ury negotiation method comprises four principles. Each principle directly focuses on one of the four basic elements of negotiation: people, interests, options, and criteria. Effective leaders frequently understand and utilize these four principles in conflict situations.

FIGURE 10.2 ■ Fisher and Ury's Method of Principled Negotiation			
Separate the **People** From the Problem	Focus on **Interests** Not Positions	Invent **Options** for Mutual Gains	Insist on Using Objective **Criteria**

Source: Adapted from Fisher, R., & Ury, W. (1981). *Getting to yes: Negotiating agreement without giving in.* Penguin Books, p. 15.

Principle 1: Separate the People From the Problem

In the previous section of this chapter, we discussed how conflict has a content dimension and a relationship dimension. Similarly, Fisher and Ury (1981) contend that conflicts comprise a *problem factor* and a *people factor*. To be effective in dealing with conflicts, both of these factors need to be addressed. In particular, Fisher and Ury argue that the people factor needs to be separated out from the problem factor.

Separating people from the problem during conflict is not easy because the two are entangled. For example, if a supervisor and an employee are in a heated conversation over the employee's negative performance review, it is very difficult for the supervisor and the employee to discuss the review without addressing their relationship and personal roles. Our personalities, beliefs, and values are intricately interwoven with our conflicts. However, principled negotiation says that people and the problem need to be disentangled. By separating people from the problem, we enable ourselves to recognize others' uniqueness. Everyone has their own distinct thoughts and feelings in different situations. Because we all perceive the world differently, we have diverse emotional responses to conflict. By focusing directly on the *people aspect* of the problem, we become more aware of the personalities and idiosyncratic needs of those with whom we are in conflict.

Perhaps most important, separating people from the problem encourages us to be attentive to our relationships during conflict. Conflicts can strain relationships, so it is important to be cognizant of how one's behavior during conflict affects the other party. Rather than "beat up" on each other, it is useful to work together, alongside each other, and mutually confront the problem. When we separate people from the problem, we are more inclined to work with others to solve problems. Fisher and Ury (1981) suggest that people in conflict need to "see themselves as working side by side, attacking the problem, not each other" (p. 11). Separating the people from the problem allows us to nurture and strengthen our relationships rather than destroy them.

Consider the earlier example of the supervisor and employee conflict over the negative performance review. In order to separate the people from the problem, both the supervisor and the employee need to discuss the negative review by focusing on performance criteria and behavior issues rather than personal attributes. The review indicated that the employee didn't meet performance objectives—the boss could say, "You didn't get your work done," but in separating the people from the problem, the boss would instead explain how the employee was unable to meet the requirements ("The number of contacts you made was below the required number"). The employee, on the other hand, may feel the objectives were unrealistic. Rather than telling their boss it was the boss's fault ("You set unobtainable objectives"), the employee should make their point by providing facts about how these standards are not realistic ("The economic downturn wasn't considered when these objectives were developed"). By focusing on the problem in this way, the employer and the employee are maintaining their relationship but also confronting directly the performance review issues.

Principle 2: Focus on Interests, Not Positions

The second principle, which is perhaps the most well known, emphasizes that parties in a conflict must focus on interests and not just positions. *Positions* represent our stand or perspective in a particular conflict. *Interests* represent what is behind our positions. Stated another way, positions are the opposing points of view in a conflict while interests refer to the relevant needs and values of the people involved. Fisher and Ury (1981) suggest that "your position is something you have decided upon. Your interests are what caused you to so decide" (p. 42).

Focusing on interests expands conflict negotiation by encouraging individuals to explore the unique underpinnings of the conflict. To identify interests behind a position, it is useful to look at the basic concerns that motivate people. Some of our concerns include needs for security, belonging, recognition, control, and economic well-being (Fisher & Ury, 1981). Being attentive to these basic needs and helping people satisfy them is central to conflict negotiation.

Concentrating on interests also helps opposing parties to address the "real" conflict. Addressing both interests *and* positions helps to make conflict negotiation more authentic. In his model of authentic leadership, Robert Terry (1993) advocates that leaders have a moral responsibility to ask the question "*What is really, really going on* in a conflict situation, and what are we going to do about it?" Unless leaders know what truly is going on, their actions will be inappropriate and can have serious consequences. Focusing on interests is a good way to find out what is at the heart of a conflict.

Consider the following conflict between a college professor, Dr. Smith, and his student, Erin Crow, regarding class attendance. Dr. Smith has a mandatory attendance policy but allows for two absences during the semester. A student's grade is lowered 10% for each additional absence. Erin is a very bright student who has gotten As on all of her papers and tests. However, she has five absences and does not want to be penalized. Based on the attendance policy, Dr. Smith would lower Erin's grade 30%, from an A to a C. Erin's position in this conflict is that she shouldn't be penalized because she has done excellent work despite her absences. Dr. Smith's position is that the attendance policy is legitimate and Erin's grade should be lowered.

In this example, it is worthwhile to explore some of the interests that form the basis for each position. For example, Erin is very reticent and does not like to participate in class. She is carrying 18 credit hours and works two part-time jobs. On the other hand, Dr. Smith is a popular professor who has twice received university-wide outstanding teaching awards. He has 20 years of experience and has a strong publication record in the area of classroom learning methodology. In addition, Dr. Smith has a need to be liked by students and does not like to be challenged.

Given their interests, it is easy to see that the conflict between Erin and Dr. Smith over class attendance is more complex than meets the eye. If this conflict were to be settled by negotiating positions alone, the resolution would be relatively straightforward, and Erin would most likely be penalized, leaving both parties unsatisfied. However, if the interests of both Erin and Dr. Smith were fully explored, the probability of a mutually agreeable outcome would be far more likely. Dr. Smith is likely to recognize that Erin has numerous obligations that impact her attendance but are important for her economic well-being and security. On the other hand, Erin may come to realize that Dr. Smith is an exemplary teacher who fosters cohesiveness among students by expecting them to show up and participate in class. His needs for control and recognition are challenged by Erin's attendance and lack of class participation.

The challenge for Erin and Dr. Smith is to focus on their interests, communicate them to each other, and remain open to unique approaches to resolving their conflict.

Principle 3: Invent Options for Mutual Gains

The third strategy in effective conflict negotiation presented by Fisher and Ury (1981) is to invent options for mutual gains. This is difficult to do because humans naturally see conflict as an either-or proposition. We either win or lose; we get what we want, or the other side gets what it wants. We feel the results will be favorable either to us or to the other side, and we do not see any other possible options.

However, this tendency to see conflict as a fixed choice proposition needs to be overcome by inventing new options to resolve the conflict to the satisfaction of both parties. The method of principled negotiation emphasizes that we need to brainstorm and search hard for creative solutions to conflict. We need to expand our options and not limit ourselves to thinking there is a single best solution.

Focusing on the interests of the parties in conflict can result in this kind of creative thinking. By exploring where our interests overlap and dovetail, we can identify solutions that will benefit both parties. This process of fulfilling interests does not need to be antagonistic. We can help each other in conflict by being sensitive to each other's interests and making it easier, rather than more difficult, for both parties to satisfy their interests. Using the earlier example of Dr. Smith and Erin, Erin could acknowledge Dr. Smith's need for a consistent attendance policy and explain that she understands that it is important to have a policy to penalize less-than-committed students. She should make the case that the quality of her papers indicates she has learned much from Dr. Smith and is as committed to the class as she can be, given her other obligations. Dr. Smith should explain that he is not comfortable ignoring her absences and that it is unfair to other students who have also been penalized for missing class. They could agree that Erin's grade will be lowered to a B, rather than a C. While neither party would be "victorious," both would feel that the best compromise was reached given each person's unique interests.

Principle 4: Insist on Using Objective Criteria

Finally, Fisher and Ury (1981) say that effective negotiation requires that objective criteria be used to settle different interests. The goal in negotiation is to reach a solution that is based on principle and not on pressure. Conflict parties need to search for objective criteria that will help them view their conflict with an unbiased lens. Objective criteria can take many forms, including

- *precedent*, which looks at how this issue has been resolved previously;
- *professional standards*, which determine if there are rules or standards for behavior based on a profession or trade involved in the conflict;
- *what a court would decide*, which looks at the legal precedent or legal ramifications of the conflict;
- *moral standards*, which consider resolving the conflict based on ethical considerations or "doing what's right";

- *tradition*, which looks at already established practices or customs in considering the conflict; and

- *scientific judgment*, which considers facts and evidence.

For example, if an employee and their boss disagree on the amount of a salary increase the employee is to receive, both the employee and the boss might consider the raises of employees with similar positions and work records. When criteria are used effectively and fairly, the outcomes and final package are usually seen as wise and fair (Fisher & Ury, 1981).

In summary, the method of principled negotiation presents four practical strategies that leaders can employ in handling conflicts: separate the people from the problem; focus on interests, not positions; invent options for mutual gains; and insist on using objective criteria. None of these strategies is a panacea for all problems or conflicts, but used together they can provide a general, well-substantiated approach to settling conflicts in ways that are likely to be advantageous to everyone involved in a conflict situation.

Communication Strategies for Conflict Resolution

Throughout this chapter, we have emphasized the complexity of conflict and the difficulties that arise in addressing it. There is no universal remedy or simple path. Schmidt and Tannenbaum (1960) pointed out that there is no right way to deal with differences: "Under varying circumstances, it may be most beneficial to avoid differences, to repress them, to sharpen them into clearly defined conflict, or to utilize them for enriched problem solving." (p. 108). In fact, except for a few newsstand-type books that claim to provide quick cures to conflict, only a few sources give practical techniques for resolution. In this section, we describe several practical communication approaches that play a major role in the conflict resolution process: differentiation, fractionation, and face saving. Using these communication strategies can lessen the angst of the conflict, help conflicting parties to reach resolution sooner, and strengthen relationships.

Differentiation

Differentiation describes a process that occurs in the early phase of conflict; it helps participants define the nature of the conflict and clarify their positions with regard to each other. It is very important to conflict resolution because it establishes the nature and parameters of the conflict. Differentiation requires that individuals explain and elaborate their own position, frequently focusing on their differences rather than their similarities. It is essential to working through a conflict (Putnam, 2010). Differentiation represents a difficult time in the conflict process because it is more likely to involve an escalation of conflict rather than a cooling off. During this time, fears may arise that the conflict will not be successfully resolved. Differentiation is also difficult because it initially personalizes the conflict and brings out feelings and sentiments in people that they themselves are the cause of the conflict (Folger et al., 1993).

The value of differentiation is that it defines the conflict. It helps both parties realize how they differ on the issue being considered. Being aware of these differences is useful for conflict resolution because it focuses the conflict, gives credence to both parties' interests in the issue that is in conflict, and, in essence, depersonalizes the conflict. Consistent with Fisher and Ury's (1981) method of negotiation, differentiation is a way to separate the people from the problem.

An example of differentiation involves a group project. Members of the group have complained to the instructor that one member, Rico, seldom comes to meetings; when he does come, he does not contribute to the group discussions. The instructor met with Rico, who defended himself by stating that the group constantly sets meeting times that conflict with his work schedule. He believes they do so on purpose to exclude him. The teacher arranged for the students to sit down together, and then had them explain their differing points of view to one another. The group members said that they believed that Rico cared less about academic achievement than they did because he did not seem willing to adjust his work schedule to meet with them. Rico, on the other hand, said he believed the others did not respect that he had to work to support himself while going to school, and that he was not in total control of his work schedule.

In this example, differentiation occurred among group members as they attempted to assess the issues. It was a difficult process because it demanded that each participant talk about their feelings about why the group was having conflict. Both sides ultimately understood the other's differing viewpoints. The group and Rico set aside a definite time each week when they would meet, and Rico made sure his supervisor did not schedule him to work at that time.

Fractionation

Fractionation refers to the technique of breaking down large conflicts into smaller, more manageable pieces (Fisher, 1971; Wilmot & Hocker, 2011). Like differentiation, fractionation usually occurs in the early stages of the conflict resolution process. It is an intentional process in which the participants agree to "downsize" a large conflict into smaller conflicts and then confront just one part of the larger conflict. Fractionating conflict is helpful for several reasons. First, fractionation reduces the conflict by paring it down to a smaller, less complex conflict. It is helpful for individuals to know that the conflict they are confronting is not a huge amorphous mass of difficulties, but rather consists of specific and defined difficulties. Second, it gives focus to the conflict. By narrowing down large conflicts, individuals give clarity and definition to their difficulties instead of trying to solve a whole host of problems at once. Third, downsizing a conflict helps to reduce the emotional intensity of the dispute. Smaller conflicts carry less emotional weight (Wilmot & Hocker, 2011). Last, fractionation facilitates a better working relationship between participants in the conflict. In agreeing to address a reduced version of a conflict, the participants confirm their willingness to work with one another to solve problems.

An example of fractionation at work involves Malcolm Stedman, an experienced director of a private school that was on the verge of closing due to low enrollment. School board members were upset with Malcolm's leadership and the direction of the school, and Malcolm was disappointed with the board. The school had been running on a deficit budget for the previous three years and had used up most of the endowment money it had set aside. The school's board members saw the problem one way: The school needed more students. Malcolm knew it was not that simple. There were many issues behind the low enrollment: the practices for recruitment of students, retention of students, fundraising, marketing, and out-of-date technology at the school, as well as bad feelings between the parents and the school. In addition to these concerns, Malcolm had responsibility for day-to-day operations of the school and decisions regarding the education of students. Malcolm asked the board members to attend a weekend retreat where, together, they detailed the myriad problems facing the school and narrowed the long list down to three difficulties that they would address together. They agreed to work on an aggressive recruitment plan, fundraising efforts, and internal marketing toward parents so they would keep their children at the school.

In the end, the retreat was beneficial to both Malcolm and the board. The big conflict of "what to do about the school" was narrowed down to three specific areas they could address. In addition, the school board developed an appreciation for the complexity and difficulties of running the school, and Malcolm softened his negative feelings about the school board and its members' input. As a result of fractionating their conflict, Malcolm Stedman and the school board developed a better working relationship and confirmed their willingness to work on problems in the future.

Face Saving

A third skill that can assist a leader in conflict resolution is face saving. **Face saving** refers to communicative attempts to establish or maintain one's self-image in response to threat (Folger et al., 1993; Goffman, 1967; Lulofs, 1994). Face-saving messages help individuals establish how they want to be seen by others. The goal of face-saving messages is to protect one's self-image.

In conflict, which is often threatening and unsettling, participants may become concerned about how others view them in regard to the positions they have taken. This concern for self can be counterproductive to conflict resolution because it shifts the focus of the conflict away from substantive issues and onto personal issues. Instead of confronting the central concerns of the conflict, face-saving concerns force participants to deal with their self-images as they are related to the conflict.

Interpersonal conflicts can be made less threatening if individuals communicate in a way that preserves the self-image of the other. Conflict issues should be discussed in a manner that minimizes threat to the participants. By using face-saving messages, such as "I think you are making a good point, but I see things differently," one person acknowledges another's point of view without making the other person feel stupid or unintelligent. The threat of conflict is lessened if participants try to support each other's self-image rather than to damage it just to win an argument. It is important to be aware of how people want to be seen by others, how conflict can threaten those desires, and how our communication can minimize those threats (Lulofs, 1994).

In trying to resolve conflicts, face saving should be a concern to participants for two reasons. First, if possible, participants should try to avoid letting the discussions during conflict shift to face-threatening issues. Similar to Fisher and Ury's (1981) principle of separating the people from the problem, this can be done by staying focused on content issues and maintaining interactions that do not challenge the other person's self-image. Second, during the later stages of conflict, face-saving messages can actually be used to assist participants in giving each other validation and support for how they have come across during conflict. Face-saving messages can confirm for others that they have handled themselves appropriately during conflict and that their relationship is still healthy.

The following example illustrates how face saving can affect conflict resolution. At a large university hospital, significant disruptions occurred when 1,000 nurses went on strike after contract negotiations failed. The issues in the conflict were salary, forced over-time, and mandatory coverage of units that were short-staffed. There was much name-calling and personal attacks between nurses and administrators. Early negotiations were inhibited by efforts on both sides to establish an image with the public that what *they* were doing was appropriate, given the circumstances. As a result, these images and issues of right and wrong, rather than the substantive issues of salary and overtime, became the focus of the conflict. If the parties had avoided tearing each other down, perhaps the conflict could have been settled sooner.

Despite these difficulties, face-saving messages did have a positive effect on this conflict. During the middle of the negotiations, the hospital ran a full-page advertisement in the local newspaper describing its proposal and why it thought this proposal was misunderstood. At the end of the ad, the hospital stated, "We respect your right to strike. A strike is a peaceful and powerful means by which you communicate your concern or dissatisfaction." This statement showed that the administration was trying to save face for itself, but also it was attempting to save face for nurses by expressing that their being on strike was not amoral, and that the hospital was willing to accept the nurses' behavior and continue to have a working relationship with them. Similarly, the media messages that both parties released at the end of the strike included affirmation of the other party's self-image. The nurses, who received a substantial salary increase, did not try to claim victory or point out what the hospital lost in the negotiations. In turn, the hospital, which retained control of the use of staff for overtime, did not emphasize what it had won or communicate that it thought the nurses were unprofessional because they had gone out on strike. The point is that these gentle face-saving messages helped both sides to feel good about themselves, reestablish their image as effective health care providers, and salvage their working relationships.

All in all, there are no shortcuts to resolving conflicts. It is a complex process that requires sustained communication. By being aware of differentiation, fractionation, and face saving, leaders can enhance their abilities and skills in the conflict resolution process.

The Kilmann and Thomas Styles of Approaching Conflict

There's no doubt that people have different ways of handling conflict and that these different styles affect the outcomes of conflict. A **conflict style** is defined as a patterned response or behavior that people use when approaching conflict. One of the most widely recognized models of conflict styles was developed by Kilmann and Thomas (1975, 1977), based on the work of Blake and Mouton (1964), and is the basis for our Conflict Style Questionnaire (Application 10.3).

The Kilmann–Thomas model identifies five conflict styles: (1) avoidance, (2) competition, (3) accommodation, (4) compromise, and (5) collaboration. This model (see Figure 10.3) describes conflict styles along two dimensions: assertiveness and cooperativeness. *Assertiveness* refers to attempts to satisfy one's own concerns, while *cooperativeness* represents attempts to satisfy the concerns of others. Each conflict style is characterized by how much assertiveness and how much cooperativeness an individual shows when confronting conflict.

In conflict situations, a person's individual style is usually a combination of these five different styles. Nevertheless, because of past experiences or situational factors, some people may rely more heavily on one conflict style than on others. Understanding these styles can help you select the conflict style that is most appropriate to the demands of the situation.

Avoidance

Avoidance is both an unassertive and an uncooperative conflict style. Those who favor the avoidance style tend to be passive and ignore conflict situations rather than confront them directly. They employ strategies such as denying there is a conflict, using jokes as a way to deflect conflict, or trying to change the topic. Avoiders are not assertive about pursuing their own interests, nor are they cooperative in assisting others to pursue theirs.

FIGURE 10.3 ■ Styles of Approaching Conflict

Source: Reproduced with permission of authors and publisher from Kilmann, R. H., & Thomas, K. W. Interpersonal conflict-handling behavior as reflections of Jungian personality dimensions. *Psychological Reports*, 1975, *37*, 971–980. © *Psychological Reports*, 1975.

Advantages and Disadvantages. Avoidance as a style for managing conflict is usually counterproductive, often leading to stress and further conflict. Those who continually avoid conflict bottle up feelings of irritation, frustration, anger, or rage inside themselves, creating more anxiety. Avoidance is essentially a static approach to conflict; it does nothing to solve problems or to make changes that could prevent conflicts.

However, there are some situations in which avoidance may be useful—for example, when an issue is of trivial importance or when the potential damage from conflict would be too great. Avoidance can also provide a cooling-off period to allow participants to determine how to best resolve the conflict at a later time. For example, if Jan is so angry at her girlfriend that she throws her cell phone at the wall, she might want to go for a ride in her car or take a walk and cool down before she tries to talk to her girlfriend about the problem.

Competition

Competition is a conflict style of individuals who are highly assertive about pursuing their own goals but uncooperative in assisting others to reach theirs. These individuals attempt to resolve a struggle by controlling or persuading others in order to achieve their own ends. A competitive style is essentially a win-lose conflict strategy. For example, when Wendy seeks to convince Chris that he is a bad person because he habitually shows up late for meetings, regardless of his reasons for doing so, it is a win-lose conflict style.

Advantages and Disadvantages. In some situations, competition can produce positive outcomes. It is useful when quick, decisive action is needed. Competition can also generate creativity and enhance performance because it challenges participants to make their best efforts.

Generally, though, competitive approaches to conflict are not the most advantageous because they are more often counterproductive than productive. Resolution options are limited to one party "beating" another, resulting in a winner and a loser. Attempts to solve conflict with dominance and control will often result in creating unstable situations and hostile and destructive communication. Finally, competition is disconfirming; in competition, individuals fail to recognize the concerns and needs of others.

Accommodation

Accommodation is an unassertive but cooperative conflict style. In accommodation, an individual essentially communicates to another, "You are right, I agree; let's forget about it." An approach that is "other directed," accommodation requires individuals to attend very closely to the needs of others and ignore their own needs. Using this style, individuals confront problems by deferring to others.

Advantages and Disadvantages. Accommodation allows individuals to move away from the uncomfortable feelings that conflict inevitably produces. By yielding to others, individuals can lessen the frustration that conflict creates. This style is productive when the issue is more important to one party than the other or if harmony in the relationship is the most important goal.

The problem with accommodation is that it is, in effect, a lose-win strategy. Although accommodation may resolve conflict faster than some of the other approaches, the drawback is that the accommodator sacrifices their own values and possibly a higher-quality decision in order to maintain smooth relationships. It is a submissive style that allows others to take charge. Accommodators also lose because they may fail to express their own opinions and feelings and their contributions are not fully considered.

For example, Andi's boyfriend is a sports fanatic and always wants to stay home and watch televised sports while Andi would like to go to a movie or to a club. But to make him happy, Andi stays home and watches football.

Compromise

As Figure 10.3 indicates, **compromise** occurs halfway between competition and accommodation and involves both a degree of assertiveness and a degree of cooperativeness. Many see compromise as a "give and take" proposition. Compromisers attend to the concerns of others as well as to their own needs. On the diagonal axis of Figure 10.3, compromise occurs midway between the styles of avoidance and collaboration. This means that compromisers do not completely ignore confrontations, but neither do they struggle with problems to the fullest degree. This conflict style is often chosen because it is expedient in finding middle ground while partially satisfying the concerns of both parties.

Advantages and Disadvantages. Compromise is a positive conflict style because it requires attending to one's goals as well as others'. Compromise tends to work best when other conflict styles have failed or aren't suitable to resolving the conflict. Many times, compromise can force an equal power balance between parties.

Among the shortcomings of the compromise style is that it does not go far enough in resolving conflict and can become "an easy way out." In order to reach resolution, conflicting parties often don't fully express their own demands, personal thoughts, and feelings. Innovative solutions are sacrificed in favor of a quick resolution, and the need for harmony supersedes the need to find optimal solutions to conflict. The result is that neither side is completely satisfied. For example, Pat wants to go on a camping vacation, and Mike wants to have a "staycation," hanging around the house. In the end, they agree to spend their vacation taking day trips to the beach and the zoo.

Collaboration

Collaboration, the most preferred style of conflict, requires both assertiveness and cooperation. It is when both parties agree to a positive settlement to the conflict and attend fully to the other's concerns while not sacrificing or suppressing their own. The conflict is not resolved until each side is reasonably satisfied and can support the solution. Collaboration is the ideal conflict style because it recognizes the inevitability of human conflict. It confronts conflict, and then uses conflict to produce constructive outcomes.

Advantages and Disadvantages. The results of collaboration are positive because both sides win, communication is satisfying, relationships are strengthened, and negotiated solutions are frequently more cost-effective in the long run.

Unfortunately, collaboration is the most difficult style to achieve. It demands energy and hard work among participants as well as shared control. Resolving differences through collaboration requires individuals to take time to explore their differences, identify areas of agreement, and select solutions that are mutually satisfying. This often calls for extended conversation in which the participants explore entirely new alternatives to existing problems. For example, residents of a residential neighborhood seek to have an adult entertainment facility in their midst close or leave. The owner refuses. The residents work with city officials to find an alternative location to relocate the facility, and the city gives the facility's owner tax breaks to move.

The five styles of approaching conflict—avoidance, competition, accommodation, compromise, and collaboration—can be observed in various conflict situations. Although there are advantages and disadvantages to each style, the conflict-handling style that meets the needs of the participants while also fitting the demands of the situation will be most effective in resolving conflict.

SUMMARY

For leaders and followers alike, interpersonal conflict is inevitable. Conflict is defined as a felt struggle between two or more individuals over perceived incompatible differences in beliefs, values, and goals, or over differences in desires for esteem, control, and connectedness. If it is managed in appropriate ways, conflict need not be destructive but can be constructive and used to positive ends.

Communication plays a central role in conflict and in its resolution. Conflict occurs between leaders and others on two levels: content and relational. Conflict on the content level involves differences in beliefs, values, or goal orientation. Conflict on the relational level refers to differences between individuals with regard to their desires for esteem, control, and affiliation in their relationships. Relational conflicts are seldom overt, which makes them difficult for people to recognize and resolve.

One approach to resolving conflicts is the method of principled negotiation by Fisher and Ury (1981). This model focuses on four basic elements of negotiation—people, interests, options, and criteria—and describes four principles related to handling conflicts: Principle 1—Separate the People From the Problem; Principle 2—Focus on Interests, Not Positions; Principle 3—Invent Options for Mutual Gains; and Principle 4—Insist on Using Objective Criteria. Collectively, these principles are extraordinarily useful in negotiating positive conflict outcomes.

Three practical communication approaches to conflict resolution are differentiation, fractionation, and face saving. Differentiation is a process that helps participants to define the nature of the conflict and to clarify their positions with one another. Fractionation refers to the technique of paring down large conflicts into smaller, more manageable conflicts. Face saving consists of messages that individuals express to each other in order to maintain each other's self-image during conflict. Together or singly, these approaches can assist leaders in making the conflict resolution process more productive.

Finally, researchers have found that people approach conflict using five styles: (1) avoidance, (2) competition, (3) accommodation, (4) compromise, and (5) collaboration. Each of these styles characterizes individuals in terms of the degree of assertiveness and cooperativeness they show when confronting conflict. The most constructive approach to conflict is collaboration, which requires that individuals recognize, confront, and resolve conflict by attending fully to others' concerns without sacrificing their own. Managing conflicts effectively leads to stronger relationships among participants and more creative solutions to problems.

KEY TERMS

accommodation

avoidance

collaboration

competition

compromise

conflict

conflict style

content conflict

content dimension

differentiation

face saving

fractionation

principled negotiation

relational conflict

relationship dimension

10.1 Case Study—Office Space

The five members of the web programming department at a marketing company are being relocated to a new space in their building. The move came as a big surprise; the head of the company decided to cut costs by leasing less space, and with just a few days' notice, the department was relocated.

The new space is a real change from what the programmers are used to. Their old space was a big open room with one wall of floor-to-ceiling windows. Their desks all faced each other, which allowed them to easily talk and collaborate with one another. The new office space has a row of five cubicles along a wall in a long, narrow room. Four of the cubicles have windows; the fifth, which is slightly larger than the others, is tucked into a window-less corner. The cubicle walls are 6 feet tall, and when they are at their desks working, the programmers can no longer see one another.

The team leader, Martin, assigned the cubicles that each programmer has moved into. He put himself in the first cubicle with Rosa, Sanjay, and Kris in the next three cubicles with windows. Bradley was given the larger cubicle in the corner.

Bradley is the first to complain. When he sees his new space, he goes to Martin and asks for a different cubicle, one with a window. He argues that he has been employed there longer than the other programmers and should get to choose his cubicle rather than be told where he is going to be. Because he and Martin work very closely on a number of projects, Bradley feels he should be in the cubicle next to Martin, rather than the one farthest away.

Sanjay is also upset. He is in the middle cubicle with Rosa and Kris on either side of him. Rosa and Kris used to have desks next to each other in the bigger space and would banter back and forth with one another while working. Now that they are in the row of cubicles, they still try to chat with one another, but to do so, they more or less shout to each other over Sanjay's space. When Martin offers to let him trade places with Bradley as a solution, Sanjay says he doesn't want to give up his window.

Martin leaves everyone where they are. He hasn't told them, but he purposely put Sanjay between Rosa and Kris in order to discourage their constant chatting, which he viewed as a time-wasting activity. Martin also felt like the larger cube was better for Bradley because he has more computer equipment than the other programmers.

During the next two months, the web programming department starts to experience a lot of tension. Sanjay seems to be in a bad mood on a daily basis. When Rosa and Kris start chatting with each other over the cubicles, he asks them loudly, "Will you please just work and stop shouting to each other?" or says sarcastically, "I'm trying to work here!" As a result, either Rosa or Kris will leave her cubicle to walk down to the other's space to chat, having conversations that last longer than their old bantering back and forth used to.

Bradley stays in his corner cubicle and avoids talking to the other programmers. He believes that Martin purposely gave him what Bradley perceives is the worst cubicle but doesn't know what he did to deserve being treated this way. He is resentful of the other staff members who have windows in their cubicles and feels like Martin must think more highly of Rosa, Kris, and Sanjay than he does of Bradley. As Bradley observes Rosa and Kris spending more time talking and less time working and the crabbiness from Sanjay, he becomes very upset with Martin. It seems Martin is rewarding the programmers who behave the worst!

Bradley becomes even more reclusive at work and avoids talking to the other programmers, especially Martin. He communicates with them mainly by email messages, even though he's only a few yards away from some of them. He no longer collaborates closely with Martin; instead he tries to work on projects without involving Martin. Unfortunately, if he encounters a problem that he needs Martin's help for, Bradley will try to solve it himself. Often, Martin won't even know there is a problem that needs to be solved until Bradley realizes he can't solve it alone and the problem becomes a crisis.

The only time all five of the programmers actually see one another is in weekly staff meetings, which are held in a conference room with a large table and a dozen chairs. In their old space, they didn't have weekly meetings because they were able to talk about projects and schedules with each other whenever it was needed. In their new staff meetings, it seems like Martin is doing all the talking. Rosa and Kris sit on one side of the table and try to ignore Sanjay who sits by himself across from them. Bradley sits at the far end of the table at least two chairs away from everyone else.

After another unproductive staff meeting where no one spoke or looked at one another, Martin sits at the head of the conference table after the other programmers have left with his head in his hands. He doesn't know what has happened to the cohesive team he used to lead and why things changed. It seems absolutely ridiculous to him that this is all about space.

Questions

1. How would you describe the conflict that has arisen between the members of the web programming department?

2. Is the conflict a relational conflict? If so, what type of relational conflict? Is there a content dimension to this conflict?

3. Using Fisher and Ury's method of principled negotiation, how would you separate the people from the problem? What do you think is really, really going on in this conflict?

4. Using the Kilmann and Thomas conflict styles, how would you characterize Sanjay's conflict style? What about Bradley's? Do Rosa and Kris have a style as well?

5. How could Martin use fractionation and face saving in attempting to resolve this conflict?

10.2 Case Study—High Water Mark

Alcott Lake, a lakeside community, is having a crisis. For the past four years, the water level on the lake has increased each year and is at a record high level. As a result, about 18% of the 250 homes located on the lake are in danger of flooding, while the rest are on higher ground and not directly affected by the high water. Many of the structures in danger are cottages that were built nearly 80 years ago and have been in the same families for years. These cottages, which once had huge lawns separating them from the lake, now have water a few yards from their doors.

The board of directors for the Alcott Lake Homeowners' Association has been working for the last year to find a solution to the high water levels. To directly address the problem, they asked the state's department of natural resources and county officials to allow them to pump water from the lake into a nearby stream. That appeal was rejected because land downstream is also experiencing high water levels and it would further endanger those properties. As the summer season approaches, and the lake promises to get busy with boaters, the board is scrambling to find a resolution to the problem.

To avoid more damage to their properties, the owners of the endangered cottages have created a petition asking the homeowners' association to institute a no-wake policy on the lake for a year. The wakes created by motorized boats cause large waves that crash up against the shore, causing erosion, and could push the water into the endangered cottages. A no-wake policy would require motorized watercraft to run at low speeds, which would eliminate any wakeboarding, tubing, or waterskiing on the lake. The petition also seeks to prohibit personal watercraft (such as jet skis) and large-wake-producing power boats from running on the lake. In order to be considered by the association's board, the petition needed signatures from 25% of the lake's property owners; it garnered support from 35%.

At the meeting, the board heard resident after resident speak either for or against the no-wake policy. Some said that the high water was a result of climate change and a long-term solution is needed, not a short-term one. Others said that those who own rental property are going to lose revenue, while others argued that the owners of endangered cottages were going to lose everything. When one property owner asked why those with water problems didn't install seawalls to protect their property like he was, another responded angrily, saying that those owning the "big McMansions on the hill" can afford to build expensive seawalls, but most people on the lake don't have that kind of money.

One homeowner asked the board who would enforce the no-wake policy if it was passed, to which another owner responded, "Me and my rifle."

The homeowners' association doesn't take the man's threat lightly; the directors know this is a highly charged situation and that whatever they decide isn't going to make everyone happy. Making a policy that satisfies everyone seems like an impossible task.

Questions

1. Describe this conflict using the different elements of the conflict definition—struggle, interdependence, feelings, and differences.

2. What is the content dimension of this conflict? What is the relational dimension?

3. Would Fisher and Ury's method of principled negotiation be a good approach for the homeowners' association to use to resolve the conflict? Why or why not?

4. How could the association board use the communication strategies of differentiation and fractionation to deal with this conflict? What about face saving?

Application

10.3 Conflict Style Questionnaire

Purpose

1. To identify your conflict style
2. To examine how your conflict style varies in different contexts or relationships

Directions

1. Think of two different situations (A and B) where you have a conflict, a disagreement, an argument, or a disappointment with someone, such as a roommate or a work associate. Write the name of the person for each of the following situations.
2. According to the scale that follows, fill in your scores for Situation A and Situation B. For each question, you will have two scores. For example, on Question 1 the scoring might look like this: 1. 2 | 4
3. Write the name of each person for the two situations here:
   - Person A _____
   - Person B _____

1 = never, 2 = seldom, 3 = sometimes, 4 = often, 5 = always

Person A	Person B	
1. ____|____		I avoid being "put on the spot"; I keep conflicts to myself.
2. ____|____		I use my influence to get my ideas accepted.
3. ____|____		I usually try to "split the difference" in order to resolve an issue.
4. ____|____		I generally try to satisfy the other's needs.
5. ____|____		I try to investigate an issue to find a solution acceptable to both of us.
6. ____|____		I usually avoid open discussion of my differences with the other.
7. ____|____		I use my authority to make a decision in my favor.
8. ____|____		I try to find a middle course to resolve an impasse.
9. ____|____		I usually accommodate the other's wishes.
10. ____|____		I try to integrate my ideas with the other's to come up with a decision jointly.
11. ____|____		I try to stay away from disagreement with the other.
12. ____|____		I use my expertise to make a decision that favors me.
13. ____|____		I propose a middle ground for breaking deadlocks.

Person A	Person B	
14. ____|____		I give in to the other's wishes.
15. ____|____		I try to work with the other to find solutions that satisfy both our expectations.
16. ____|____		I try to keep my disagreement to myself in order to avoid hard feelings.
17. ____|____		I generally pursue my side of an issue.
18. ____|____		I negotiate with the other to reach a compromise.
19. ____|____		I often go with the other's suggestions.
20. ____|____		I exchange accurate information with the other so we can solve a problem together.
21. ____|____		I try to avoid unpleasant exchanges with the other.
22. ____|____		I sometimes use my power to win.
23. ____|____		I use "give and take" so that a compromise can be made.
24. ____|____		I try to satisfy the other's expectations.
25. ____|____		I try to bring all our concerns out in the open so that the issues can be resolved.

Source: Adapted from "Confirmatory Factor Analysis of the Styles of Handling Interpersonal Conflict: First-Order Factor Model and Its Invariance Across Groups," by M. A. Rahim and N. R. Magner, 1995, *Journal of Applied Psychology, 80*(1), 122–132. In W. Wilmot and J. Hocker (2011), *Interpersonal Conflict* (pp. 146–148). Published by the American Psychological Association.

Scoring

Add up your scores on the following questions:

A | B	A | B	A | B	A | B	A | B
1. ___|___	2. ___|___	3. ___|___	4. ___|___	5. ___|___
6. ___|___	7. ___|___	8. ___|___	9. ___|___	10. ___|___
11. ___|___	12. ___|___	13. ___|___	14. ___|___	15. ___|___
16. ___|___	17. ___|___	18. ___|___	19. ___|___	20. ___|___
21. ___|___	22. ___|___	23. ___|___	24. ___|___	25. ___|___
___|___ A|B Avoidance Totals	___|___ A|B Competition Totals	___|___ A|B Compromise Totals	___|___ A|B Accommodation Totals	___|___ A|B Collaboration Totals

Scoring Interpretation

This questionnaire is designed to identify your conflict style and examine how it varies in different contexts or relationships. By comparing your total scores for the different styles, you can discover which conflict style you rely most heavily upon and which style you use least. Furthermore, by comparing your scores for Person A and Person B, you can determine how your style varies or stays the same in different relationships. Your scores on this questionnaire are indicative of how you responded to a particular conflict at a specific time and therefore might change if you selected a different conflict or a different conflict period. The Conflict Style Questionnaire is not a personality test that labels or categorizes you; rather, it attempts to give you a sense of your more dominant and less dominant conflict styles.

Scores from 21 to 25 are representative of a very strong style.
Scores from 16 to 20 are representative of a strong style.
Scores from 11 to 15 are representative of an average style.
Scores from 6 to 10 are representative of a weak style.
Scores from 0 to 5 are representative of a very weak style.

Application

10.4 Observational Exercise—Managing Conflict

Purpose

1. To become aware of the dimensions of interpersonal conflict
2. To explore how to use Fisher and Ury's (1981) method of principled negotiation to address actual conflict

Directions

1. For this exercise, you are being asked to observe an actual conflict. Attend a public meeting at which a conflict is being addressed. For example, you could attend a meeting of the campus planning board, which has on its agenda changes in student parking fees.
2. Take notes on the meeting, highlighting the positions and interests of all the people who participated in the meeting.

Questions

1. How did the participants at the meeting frame their arguments? What positions did individuals take at the meeting?

2. Identify and describe the interests of each of the participants at the meeting.

3. Discuss whether the participants were able to be objective in their approaches to the problem. Describe how the people involved were able to separate themselves from the problem.

4. In what ways did the participants seek to find mutually beneficial solutions to their conflict?

Application

10.5 Reflection and Action Worksheet—Managing Conflict

Reflection

1. How do you react to conflict? Based on the Conflict Style Questionnaire, how would you describe your conflict style? How has your past history influenced your conflict style?

2. This chapter describes three kinds of relational conflict (i.e., esteem, control, affiliation). Of the three kinds, which is most common in the conflicts you have with others? Discuss.

Action

1. Briefly describe an actual conflict you had with a family member, roommate, or coworker in the recent past. Identify the positions and interests of both you and the other person in the conflict. (Note: Individuals' positions may be easier to identify than their interests. Be creative in detailing your interests and the other person's.)

2. Describe how you could fractionate the conflict.

3. Using Fisher and Ury's (1981) methods, describe how you could separate the person from the problem and how you could work together to address the conflict. During your discussions, how could you help the other party in the conflict save face? How could the other party help you save face?

11 ADDRESSING ETHICS IN LEADERSHIP

INTRODUCTION

Leadership has a moral dimension because leaders influence the lives of others. Because of this influential dimension, leadership carries with it an enormous ethical responsibility. Hand in hand with the authority to make decisions is the obligation a leader has to use their authority for the common good. Because the leader usually has more power and control than followers have, leaders have to be particularly sensitive to how their leadership affects the well-being of others.

In recent years, there have been an overwhelming number of scandals in the public and private sectors. Accounting and financial scandals have occurred at some of the largest companies in the world, including Adelphia, Enron, Tyco International, and WorldCom. In addition, there have been stories of sexual abuse in the Catholic Church, sexual assaults within the U.S. military, and a multitude of sexual scandals in the lives of public figures including governors, U.S. senators, and mayors, to name but a few. As a result of such high-profile scandals, people are becoming suspicious of public figures and what they do. The public strongly seeks moral leadership.

As mentioned in Chapter 1, "Understanding Leadership," the overriding purpose of this book is to discover what it takes to be a leader. Closely related to this question, and perhaps even more important, is what it takes to be an *ethical* leader. That query is the focus of this chapter. This means our emphasis will be on describing how people act when they show ethical leadership. While it is always intriguing to know whether one is or is not perceived by others to be ethical, our emphasis will not be directed toward whether you are or are not ethical, but rather we will focus on the properties and characteristics of ethical leadership. The assumption we are making is that if you understand the nature of ethical leadership, you will be better equipped to engage in ethical leadership.

Before we discuss the factors that account for ethical leadership, you may want to go to the end of the chapter and take the Ethical Leadership Style Questionnaire. It will help you understand your own ethical leadership style and at the same time introduce you to the ideas we will be discussing in this chapter.

LEADERSHIP ETHICS EXPLAINED

To begin, it is important to define ethical leadership. In the simplest terms, *ethical leadership* is the influence of a moral person who moves others to do the right thing in the right way for the right reasons (Ciulla, 2003). Put another way, ethical leadership is a process by which a good person rightly influences others to accomplish a common good: to make the world better, fairer, and more humane.

Ethics is concerned with the kind of values and morals an individual or society finds desirable or appropriate. In leadership, ethics has to do with what leaders do and the nature of leaders' behavior, including their motives. Because leaders often have control, power, and influence over others, their leadership affects other individuals and organizations. Because of this, it is the leader's ethics—through their behavior, decisions, and interactions—that establish the ethical climate for an organization.

LEADERSHIP ETHICS IN PRACTICE

Leadership ethics is a complex phenomenon with multiple parts that overlap and are interconnected. When trying to practice ethical leadership, there are six factors (see Figure 11.1) that should be of special importance to leaders. Each of these factors plays a role in who leaders are and what they do when they are engaged in ethical leadership.

FIGURE 11.1 ■ Factors Related to Ethical Leadership

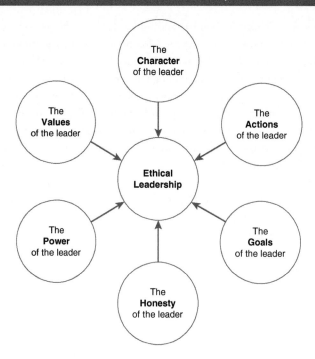

The Character of the Leader

The **character** of the leader is a fundamental aspect of ethical leadership. When it is said that a leader has strong character, that leader is seen as a good and honorable human being. The leader's character refers to their qualities, disposition, and core values. More than 2,000 years ago, Aristotle argued that a moral person demonstrates the virtues of courage, generosity, self-control, honesty, sociability, modesty, fairness, and justice (Velasquez, 1992). Today, all these qualities still contribute to a strong character.

Character is something that is developed. In recent years, the nation's schools have seen a growing interest in character education. Misbehavior of public figures has led to mistrust of public figures, which has led to the public demanding that educators do a better job of training children to be good citizens. As a result, most schools today teach character education as part of their normal curriculum. A model for many of these programs was developed by the Josephson Institute (2008) in California, which frames instruction around six dimensions of character: *trustworthiness, respect, responsibility, fairness, caring*, and *citizenship* (see Table 11.1). Based on these and similar character dimensions, schools are emphasizing the importance of character and how core values influence an individual's ethical decision making.

Although character is clearly at the core of *who you are* as a person, it is also something you can learn to strengthen and develop. A leader can learn good values. When practiced over time, from youth to adulthood, good values become habitual, and a part of people themselves. By telling the truth, people become truthful; by giving to people living in poverty, people become charitable; and by being fair to others, people become just. Your virtues, and hence your character, are derived from your actions.

An example of a leader with strong character is Nobel Peace Prize winner Nelson Mandela (see "Leadership Snapshot" in Chapter 2, "Recognizing Your Traits"). Mandela was a deeply moral man with a strong conscience. When fighting to abolish apartheid in South Africa, he was unyielding in his pursuit of justice and equality for all. When he was in prison and was offered the chance to leave early in exchange for denouncing his viewpoint, he chose to remain incarcerated rather than compromise his position. In addition to being deeply concerned for others, Mandela was a courageous, patient, humble, and compassionate man. He was an ethical leader who ardently believed in the common good.

Mandela clearly illustrates that character is an essential component of moral leadership. Character enables a leader to maintain their core ethical values even in times of immense adversity. Character forms the centerpiece of a person's values, and is fundamental to ethical leadership.

The Actions of the Leader

In addition to being about a leader's character, ethical leadership is about the **actions** of a leader. Actions refer to the ways a leader goes about accomplishing goals. Ethical leaders use moral means to achieve their goals. The way a leader goes about their work is a critical determinant of whether they are an ethical leader. We may all be familiar with the Machiavellian

TABLE 11.1 ■ The Six Pillars of Character

Trustworthiness

Trustworthiness is the most complicated of the six core ethical values and concerns a variety of qualities like honesty, integrity, reliability, and loyalty.

- Be honest
- Be reliable: do what you say you'll do
- Have the courage to do the right thing
- Don't deceive, cheat, or steal
- Build a good reputation

Respect

While we have no ethical duty to hold all people in high esteem, we should treat everyone with respect.

- Be tolerant of differences
- Use good manners
- Be considerate of others
- Work out disagreements

Responsibility

Ethical people show responsibility by being accountable, pursuing excellence, and exercising self-restraint. They exhibit the ability to respond to expectations.

- Do your job
- Persevere
- Think before you act
- Consider the consequences
- Be accountable for your choices

Fairness

Fairness implies adherence to a balanced standard of justice without relevance to one's own feelings or indications.

- Play by the rules
- Be open-minded
- Don't take advantage of others
- Don't blame others

Caring

Caring is the heart of ethics and ethical decision making. It is scarcely possible to be truly ethical and yet unconcerned with the welfare of others. This is because ethics is ultimately about good relations with other people.

- Be kind
- Be compassionate
- Forgive others
- Help people in need

Citizenship

The good citizen gives more than they take, doing more than their "fair" share to make society work, now and for future generations. Citizenship includes civic virtues and duties that prescribe how we ought to behave as part of a community.

- Share with your community
- Get involved
- Stay informed: vote
- Respect authority
- Protect the environment

Source: © 2008 Josephson Institute. The definitions of the Six Pillars of Character are reprinted with permission. www.charactercounts.org

phrase "the ends justify the means," but an ethical leader keeps in mind a different version of this and turns it into a question: "Do the ends justify the means?" In other words, the actions a leader takes to accomplish a goal need to be ethical. They cannot be justified by the necessity or importance of the leader's goals. Ethical leadership involves using morally appropriate actions to achieve goals.

To illustrate the importance of ethical actions, consider what happened at the Abu Ghraib prison in Iraq in 2004. Because of the atrocities on 9/11, national security and intelligence gathering became a high priority. Rules and standards of interrogation were expanded, and harsh interrogation methods were approved. The government's goal was to obtain information for purposes of national security.

Problems at the prison became evident when the media reported that prisoners were being sexually abused, humiliated, and tortured by prison personnel and civilian contract employees. Gruesome photographs of demeaning actions to prisoners appeared in the media and on the internet. To obtain intelligence information, some U.S. Army soldiers used means that violated military regulations and internationally held rules on the humane treatment of prisoners of war established by the Geneva Convention in 1948.

In the case of the Abu Ghraib prison, the goal of maintaining national security and intelligence gathering was legitimate and worthwhile. However, the means that were used by some at the prison were considered by many to be unjustified and even ruled to be criminal. Many believe that the goals did not justify the means.

In everyday situations, a leader can act in many different ways to accomplish goals; each of these actions has ethical implications. For example, when a leader rewards some employees and not others, it raises questions of fairness. If a leader fails to take into consideration an employee's major health problems and instead demands that a job be completed on short notice, it raises questions about the leader's compassion for others. Even a simple task such as scheduling people's workload or continually giving more favorable assignments to one person over another reflects the ethics of the leader. In reality, almost everything a leader does has ethical overtones.

Given the importance of a leader's actions, what ethical principles should guide how a leader acts toward others? Ethical principles for leaders have been described by many scholars (Beauchamp & Bowie, 1988; Ciulla, 2003; Johnson, 2005; Kanungo, 2001; Kanungo & Mendonca, 1996). These writings highlight the importance of many ethical standards. In addition, there are three principles that have particular relevance to our discussion of the *actions* of ethical leaders: (1) showing respect, (2) serving others, and (3) showing justice.

1. ***Showing respect.*** To show respect means to treat others as unique human beings and never as means to an end. It requires treating others' decisions and values with respect. It also requires valuing others' ideas and affirming these individuals as unique human beings. When a leader shows respect to followers, followers become more confident and believe their contributions have value.

2. ***Serving others.*** Clearly, serving others is an example of altruism, an approach that suggests that actions are ethical if their primary purpose is to promote the best interest of others. From this perspective, a leader may be called on to act in the interest of others, even when it may run contrary to their self-interests (Bowie, 1991). In the workplace, serving others can be observed in activities such as mentoring, empowering others, team building, and citizenship behaviors (Kanungo & Mendonca, 1996). In practicing the principle of service, an ethical leader must be willing to be follower centered. That is, the leader tries to place others' interests foremost in their work, and act in ways that will benefit others.

3. ***Showing justice.*** Ethical leaders make it a top priority to treat all of their followers in an equal manner. Justice demands that a leader place the issue of fairness at the center of decision making. As a rule, no one should receive special treatment or special consideration except when a particular situation demands it. When individuals are treated differently, the grounds for different treatment must be clear, reasonable, and based on sound moral values.

In addition, justice is concerned with the Golden Rule: Treat others as you would like to be treated. If you expect fair treatment from others, then you should treat others fairly. Issues of fairness become problematic because there is always a limit on goods and resources. As a result, there is often competition for scarce resources. Because of the real or perceived scarcity of resources, conflicts often occur between individuals about fair methods of distribution. It is important for a leader to establish clearly the rules for distributing rewards. The nature of these rules says a lot about the ethical underpinnings of the leader and the organization.

The challenge of treating everyone fairly is illustrated in what happened to Richard Lee when he coached his son's Little League baseball team. His son, Eric, was an outstanding pitcher with a lot of natural ability. During one of the games, Eric became frustrated with his performance and began acting very immaturely, throwing his bat and kicking helmets. When Richard saw Eric's inappropriate behavior, he immediately took his son out of the game and sat him on the bench. The player who replaced Eric in the lineup was not as good a pitcher, and the team lost the game.

After the game, Richard received a lot of criticism. In addition to Eric being mad at him, the parents of the other players were very angry. Some of the parents came to Richard and told him that he should not have pulled his son out of the game because it caused the team to lose.

In this example, the other players' parents failed to recognize what Richard was doing as a coach. Richard made a strong effort to be fair to all the players by treating his son the way he would treat any player who acted out. He set a standard of good sportsmanship; when his own son violated the rules, he was disciplined. Richard's actions were ethical, but coaching the team as he did was not easy. He did the right thing, but there were repercussions.

This example underscores the importance of the *actions* of a leader. A leader's actions play a significant role in determining whether that leader is ethical or unethical.

LEADERSHIP SNAPSHOT
YVON CHOUINARD, PATAGONIA

When Yvon Chouinard, an avid climber and outdoors enthusiast, realized that iron pitons, the metal spikes permanently placed into rock by climbers, were damaging the very mountains they were made to ascend, he developed reusable steel pitons that could be removed from the rock. And when he determined that even those pitons were a hazard to the environment, his company, Chouinard Equipment, created an aluminum chock that could be wedged into the rock by hand rather than hammered in, birthing a new style of climbing called "clean climbing."

ZUMA Press, Inc. / Alamy Stock Photo

These were the first of many business decisions Chouinard, whose company would become Patagonia, a major retailer of outdoor apparel and gear for climbing, surfing, snowboarding, skiing, and other adventure sports, would make in the name of environmental soundness and human well-being.

"I never wanted to be a businessman. I started as a craftsman, making climbing gear for my friends and myself, then got into apparel. As we began to witness the extent of global warming and ecological destruction, and our own contribution to it, Patagonia committed to using our company to change the way business was done. If we could do the right thing while making enough to pay the bills, we could influence customers and other businesses, and maybe change the system along the way" (Chouinard, 2023).

From the beginning, Chouinard was determined that his company would prioritize employees' welfare and sustainability over profits. Patagonia employees can work flexible hours so they can surf when the waves are right, attend educational courses, or pick their kids up from school "as long as the work gets done with no negative impacts on others" (Dean, 2022). After staff began bringing their young babies into the company's California headquarters, Patagonia opened a subsidized on-site child care center in 1984, when there were only 120 other such centers in the United States. Patagonia was also an early adopter of paid maternity and paternity leave.

Chouinard is an avid environmentalist and has brought those values to his company as well. He created the company with a mission to "build the best product, cause no unnecessary harm, use business to inspire and implement solutions to the environmental crisis" (Sonsev, 2019). Patagonia has also become a certified B Corporation (see Case Study 11.2 for more information on B Corporations) and assesses every aspect of its business for its environmental impact. Chouinard is quoted as saying, "What we take, how and when we make, what we waste, is in fact a question of ethics" (McKinsey & Company, 2023).

In 1996, after determining that traditional methods of growing cotton were too damaging to the environment, Patagonia switched to using only organic cotton even though it reduced the profit margin on those garments. Three years later, it began making its fleece jackets from Synchilla, a fabric woven from recycled soda bottles.

In an industry where 85% of all clothing ends up in a landfill (Environmental Protection Agency, 2022), Patagonia's business model rejects fast fashion, opting to create high-quality, long-lasting products in order to reduce consumption. It offers a lifetime guarantee on its products and offers services to repair its products and trade them in for recycling. Stating that buying less is one step shoppers can take to reduce their own eco footprint, Patagonia even engaged in a "Don't Buy This Jacket" advertising campaign to discourage customers from purchasing too many of its products.

"It would be hypocritical for us to work for environmental change without encouraging customers to think before they buy," the company said about the campaign (Patagonia, 2023).

Patagonia also actively addresses its carbon footprint through its energy consumption. All of the company's electricity usage in the United States comes from renewable sources. The company also has a "drive less" program, paying employees who commute by bike, carpool, or public transit and reserving the best spots in its parking lots for fuel-efficient cars.

But Chouinard is also willing to put his profits where his mouth is. In 2002, he founded 1% for the Planet, an international organization whose members contribute at least 1% of their annual revenue to causes to protect the environment. Patagonia was the first business to commit to the cause, and the nonprofit now has 5,000 members worldwide (1% for the Planet, 2023) and generated nearly $1.503 million in grants to environmental organizations since 1985 (Balch, 2023).

"We can't delude ourselves into thinking that anything we or any other business does is 'sustainable.' The best we can do is minimize the harm we do to the planet," said Chouinard. "We'll do what we can to clean up our own house and convince other businesses and suppliers to use cleaner energy and more responsible materials, but it's a never-ending summit. The work is never done.

"Building the best product while causing the least harm is at the heart of what we do" (McKinsey & Company, 2023).

Chouinard left the helm of day-to-day operations of Patagonia in 1999, but the ethically oriented culture he created at the company is strongly entrenched and has been furthered by successive leaders. In 2018, the company changed its purpose to "We're in business to save our home planet."

Then, in 2022, Chouinard announced that he, his wife, and his children were giving away the company, valued at $3 billion, to fight climate change. Chouinard and his family transferred their voting stock to the newly established Patagonia Purpose Trust, which will ensure that Patagonia maintains its commitment to corporate responsibility and donating its profits. The rest of the company, about 98% of its shares, was donated to the Holdfast Collective, a nonprofit organization that will receive all of the company's profits, roughly $100 million a year, and use them to fight climate change (Ding, 2022).

"Earth is now our only shareholder," Chouinard (2023) said in announcing the transfer.

And while some could claim that making this donation may be due to the potential $1 billion in U.S. taxes that the Chouinards will save in doing so, the Chouinards will still pay $17.5 million in gift taxes for transferring their 2% voting stock to the trust. However, they won't pay an estimated $700 million in capital gains taxes for the accrued value of the stocks or pay anything on the other shares they donated to the Holdfast Collective they created. But one expert says focusing on the tax savings is "missing the forest through the trees."

"Their intent was much bigger than tax savings. They were going to have to work on saving taxes no matter what they did, so I look at the tax issue and say, that's a structure of the law. They worked to minimize that, but they're going to do some good for, hopefully, humanity" (Northeastern Global News, 2022).

The Goals of the Leader

The **goals** that a leader establishes are the third factor related to ethical leadership. How a leader uses goals to influence others says a lot about the leader's ethics. For example, Adolf Hitler was able to convince millions of people that the eradication of the Jews was justified. It was an evil goal, and he was an immoral leader. On the positive side, Mother Teresa's goal to help people experiencing extreme poverty was moral. Similarly, Habitat for Humanity's goal to build houses for people in need of affordable housing is moral. All of these examples highlight the significant role that goals play in determining whether leadership is ethical. The goals a leader selects are a reflection of the leader's ethics.

Identifying and pursuing just and worthy goals are the most important steps an ethical leader will undertake. In choosing goals, an ethical leader must assess the relative value and worth of their goals. In the process, it is important for the leader to take into account the interests of others in the group or organization and, in some cases, the interests of the community and larger culture in which they work. An ethical leader tries to establish goals on which all parties can mutually agree. An ethical leader with ethical goals will not impose their will on others.

Jacob Heckert, president of a regional health insurance company, is an example of a leader who used his leadership for worthwhile goals. Jacob believed in community service and advocated, but did not demand, that his employees engage in community service as well. Because he had several friends with diabetes and two of his employees had died of end-stage renal disease, Jacob was particularly interested in supporting the National Kidney Foundation. To promote his cause, he urged his entire company of 4,000 employees to join him in raising money for the National Kidney Foundation's 5K. Each employee who signed up was responsible for raising $100. Everyone who participated received a free water bottle and T-shirt.

On the day of the rally, Jacob was surprised when more than 1,800 employees from his company showed up to participate. The rally was a great success, raising more than $180,000 for the National Kidney Foundation. The employees felt good about being able to contribute to a worthy cause, and they enjoyed the community spirit that surrounded the event. Jacob was extremely pleased that his goals had been realized.

The Honesty of the Leader

Another major factor that contributes to ethical leadership is **honesty**. More than any other quality, people want their leaders to be honest.

When we were children, we were frequently told by grown-ups to "never tell a lie." To be good meant telling the truth. For leaders, the lesson is the same. To be an ethical leader, a leader needs to be honest.

Dishonesty is a form of lying, a way of misrepresenting reality. Dishonesty may bring with it many negative outcomes, the foremost of which is that it creates distrust. When a leader is not honest, others come to see that leader as undependable and unreliable. They lose faith in what the leader says and stands for, and their respect for this individual is diminished. As a result, the leader's impact is compromised because others no longer trust and believe what they say.

Dishonesty also has a negative effect on a leader's interpersonal relationships. It puts a strain on how the leader and followers are connected to each other. When a leader lies to others, the leader in essence is saying that manipulation of others is acceptable. For example, when a boss does not come forth with a raise as promised, an employee will begin to distrust the boss. The long-term effect of this type of behavior, if ongoing, is a weakened relationship. Dishonesty, even when used with good intentions, contributes to the breakdown of relationships.

But being honest is not just about the leader telling the truth. It also has to do with being open with others and representing reality as fully and completely as possible. This is not an easy task because there are times when telling the complete truth can be destructive or counterproductive. The challenge for a leader is to strike a balance between being open and candid and at the same time monitoring what is appropriate to disclose in a particular situation.

An example of this delicate balance can be seen in a story about Jamal Johnson. Jamal was hired to work as an executive with a large manufacturing company. The new job required Jamal and his family to leave the small Michigan community they lived in, giving up jobs and friends, to move to Chicago. The family put its house on the market and began looking for a new home and jobs in Chicago. A few days after Jamal started, his boss, Don Godfrey, took him aside and told him that he should not sell his Michigan house at that time.

Don suggested that Jamal postpone his move by using his wife's job as an excuse when people inquired why the family had not moved to Chicago. Don could not tell him any more, but Jamal knew something major was about to happen. It did. The company announced a merger a few months later, and Jamal's job in Chicago was eliminated. Don was required to keep the merger news quiet, but if he had not confided the little information that he did, members of Jamal's family would have uprooted their lives only to have them uprooted again. They would have experienced not only financial losses but emotional ones as well.

This example illustrates that it is important for a leader to be authentic. At the same time, it is essential that leaders be sensitive to the attitudes and feelings of others. Honest leadership involves a wide set of behaviors, which includes being truthful in appropriate ways.

The Power of the Leader

Another factor that plays a role in ethical leadership is **power**. Power is the capacity to influence or affect others. A leader has power because they have the ability to affect others' beliefs, attitudes, and courses of action. Religious leaders, managers, coaches, and teachers are all people who have the potential to influence others. When they use their potential, they are using their power as a resource to effect change in others.

The most widely cited research on power is French and Raven's (1959) work on the bases of social power. French and Raven identified five common and important bases of power: referent power, expert power, legitimate power, reward power, and coercive power (see Table 11.2). Each of these types of power increases a leader's capacity to have an impact on others, and each has the potential to be abused.

Since power can be used in positive ways to benefit others or in destructive ways to hurt others, a leader needs to be aware of and sensitive to how they use power. How a leader uses power says

TABLE 11.2 ■ Five Bases of Power		
1. Referent power	Based on followers' identification and liking for the leader	Example: A college professor who is highly admired by students
2. Expert power	Based on followers' perceptions of the leader's competence	Example: A person with strong knowledge about a software program
3. Legitimate power	Associated with having status or formal job authority	Example: A judge who presides over a court case
4. Reward power	Derived from having the capacity to provide benefits to others	Example: A supervisor who can give bonuses to employees
5. Coercive power	Derived from being able to penalize or punish others	Example: A teacher who can lower a student's grade for missing class

Source: Based on French and Raven (1959).

a great deal about that leader's ethics. Power is not inherently bad, but it can be used in negative ways.

As discussed in Chapter 12, "Exploring Destructive Leadership," there is a dark side of leadership where a leader uses their influence or power for personal ends. Unfortunately, there are many examples in the world of such leaders.

One example is Kim Jong-un, ruler of North Korea. Kim became the country's leader in 2011 at the age of 27 after the death of his father, Kim Jong-il. Like his father before him, the younger Kim is seen as a brutal dictator who has proven he will eliminate anyone he perceives as threatening. He ordered the executions of hundreds of rivals, bureaucrats, and military officers, as well as his own uncle and older half-brother Kim Jong-nam. Human Rights Watch (2021), based in New York, charged that Kim has "expanded invasive surveillance and repression of North Koreans, denied people their freedom of movement within the country and across borders, and responded to the COVID-19 pandemic with heightened food insecurity that threatens widespread starvation." Kim has poured nearly $1.6 billion into the development of the nation's nuclear weapons and weapons of mass destruction while the country's economy has faltered (Suzuki, 2022). Because of this, nations around the globe have instituted economic sanctions against North Korea, further isolating the country and affecting its ability to import products, including food. The United Nations estimated that between 2019 and 2021, 42% of North Koreans were malnourished and experiencing food insecurity.

Another example of a leader using power in unethical and destructive ways is Jim Jones, an American who set up a religious cult in the country of Guyana, and who led more than 900 of his followers to commit suicide by drinking cyanide-laced punch. While these are extreme examples, power can also be abused in everyday leadership. For example, a supervisor who forces an employee to work every weekend by threatening to fire the worker if they do not comply is being unethical in the use of power. Another example is a high school cross-country track coach who is highly admired by his runners, but who requires them to take costly health food supplements even though the supplements are not proven effective by standard medical guidelines.

There are many ways that power can be abused by a leader. From the smallest to the largest forms of influence, a leader needs to try to be fair and caring in their leadership.

The key to not misusing power is to be constantly vigilant and aware of the way one's leadership affects others. An ethical leader does not wield power or dominate, but instead takes into account the will of the followers, as well as the leader's own will. An ethical leader uses power to work with followers to accomplish their mutual goals.

The Values of the Leader

A final factor that contributes to understanding ethical leadership is **values**. Values are the ideas, beliefs, and modes of action that people find worthwhile or desirable. Some examples of values are peace, justice, integrity, fairness, and community. A leader's ethical values are demonstrated in everyday leadership.

Scholar James MacGregor Burns suggested that there are three kinds of leadership values: ethical values, such as kindness and altruism; modal values, such as responsibility and accountability; and end values, such as justice and community (Ciulla, 2003). **Ethical values** are similar to the notion of character discussed earlier in this chapter. **Modal values** are concerned with the means or actions a leader takes. **End values** describe the outcomes or goals a leader seeks to achieve. End values are present when a person addresses broad issues such as liberty and justice. These three kinds of values are interrelated in ethical leadership.

In leadership situations, both the leader and the follower have values, and these values are seldom the same. A leader brings their own unique values to leadership situations, and followers do the same. The challenge for the ethical leader is to be faithful to their own leadership values while being sensitive to the followers' values.

For example, a leader in an organization may value community and encourage their employees to work together and seek consensus in planning. However, the leader's followers may value individuality and self-expression. This creates a problem because these values are seemingly in conflict. In this situation, an ethical leader needs to find a way to advance their own interests in creating community without destroying the followers' interests in individuality. There is a tension between these different values; an ethical leader needs to negotiate through these differences to find the best outcome for everyone involved. While the list of possible conflicts of values is infinite, finding common ground between a leader and followers is usually possible, and is essential to ethical leadership.

In the social services sector, where there are often too few resources and too many people in need, leaders constantly struggle with decisions that test their values. Because resources are scarce, a leader has to decide where to allocate the resources; these decisions communicate a lot about the leader's values. For example, in mentoring programs such as Big Brothers Big Sisters, the list of children in need is often much longer than the list of available mentors. How do administrators decide which child is going to be assigned a mentor? They decide based on their values and the values of the people with whom they work. If they believe that children from single-parent households should have higher priority, then those children will be put at the top of the list. As this example illustrates, making ethical decisions is challenging for a leader, especially in situations where resources are scarce.

CULTURE AND LEADERSHIP ETHICS

The world today is globally connected in ways it never has been before. Through your life-time, you will undoubtedly be exposed to and work with individuals from cultures very different from your own. As a leader, it is important to recognize that not every culture shares the same ethical ideals as yours. Different cultures have different rules of conduct, and as a result, leadership behaviors that one culture deems ethical may not be viewed the same way by another culture.

For example, Resick and colleagues (2006) found that Nordic European cultures such as Denmark and Sweden place more importance on a leader's character and integrity—defined as a leader behaving in a manner that is just, honest, sincere, and trustworthy—than Middle Eastern cultures such as those in Egypt, Turkey, and Qatar.

Another example is the use of bribery in business practices. Bribery (offering money or gifts in exchange for favorable treatment or influence) to obtain business is forbidden for U.S. companies, no matter where on the globe they are doing business, and offenders can face jail terms and large fines. However, in some countries, bribery is a norm, and business can't be transacted without it. In China, for example, it is expected in business relationships that there will be the giving of carefully chosen gifts to convey respect and that the business relationship is valued by the giver. It is considered a matter of business etiquette (Pitta et al., 1999). And, until 1999, bribes were tax-deductible and seen as a necessary part of conducting business in Germany.

SUMMARY

There is a strong demand for ethical leaders in our society today. This chapter answers the question "What does it take to be an ethical leader?" Ethical leadership is defined as a process in which a good person acts in the right ways to accomplish worthy goals. There are six factors related to ethical leadership.

First, *character* is fundamental to ethical leadership. A leader's character refers to who the leader is as a person and their core values. The *Six Pillars of Character* are trustworthiness, respect, responsibility, fairness, caring, and citizenship.

Second, ethical leadership is explained by the *actions* of the leader—the means a leader uses to accomplish goals. An ethical leader engages in showing respect, serving others, and showing justice.

Third, ethical leadership is about the *goals* of the leader. The goals a leader selects reflect their values. Selecting goals that are meaningful and worthwhile is one of the most important decisions an ethical leader needs to make.

Fourth, ethical leadership is concerned with the *honesty* of the leader. Without honesty, a leader cannot be ethical. In telling the truth, a leader needs to strike a balance between openness and sensitivity to others.

Fifth, *power* plays a role in ethical leadership. A leader has an ethical obligation to use power for the influence of the common good of others. The interests of followers need to be taken into account, and the leader needs to work *with* followers to accomplish mutual ends.

Finally, ethical leadership is concerned with the *values* of the leader. An ethical leader has strong values and promotes positive values within their organization. Because leaders and followers often have conflicting values, a leader needs to be able to express their values and integrate these values with others' values.

In summary, ethical leadership has many dimensions. To be an ethical leader, you need to pay attention to who you are, what you do, what goals you seek, your honesty, the way you use power, and your values.

KEY TERMS

actions	honesty
character	modal values
end values	power
ethical values	values
goals	

Application

11.1 Case Study—The Write Choice

Each semester, community college professor Julia Ramirez requires her students to do a 10-hour community service project at a nonprofit agency of their choice and write a paper about the experience. In the paper, they are to discuss their volunteer experience and incorporate concepts presented in class into this reflection. This is the sixth semester that Professor Ramirez has used this assignment, and she has always received positive feedback about the benefits of the assignment from her students and the nonprofits.

The community college that Professor Ramirez works at is making an effort to be "green" and, in order to cut down on paper usage, requests that faculty and staff utilize online tools for giving and receiving assignments and providing feedback to students. Professor Ramirez takes advantage of these green initiatives, requiring her community learning papers to all be turned in electronically at noon on the last Friday before exams. She likes having the papers turned in electronically because it has significantly cut down on late papers and it is now very easy to check student work for plagiarism.

That day has arrived, and Professor Ramirez downloads her student papers from the class webpage and begins to grade them. The papers are informal in nature, written in first-person narrative as if the students were talking directly to Professor Ramirez. After grading a number of papers, Professor Ramirez comes to the paper written by student Kelly Declan. Kelly's paper reads less like a personal narrative and more like a brochure for the organization where she volunteered. At first, Professor Ramirez is impressed with the amount of detail that Kelly retained from volunteering, but after reading part of the paper, she becomes suspicious. To be safe, Professor Ramirez decides to copy a passage from Kelly's paper into her internet search engine to see if it matches any other published sources. It does; in fact, it is a direct match for an online brochure of a similar organization in a neighboring state. Professor Ramirez tests a few more sections from Kelly's paper and finds that 90% of it was plagiarized from this one source on the internet.

Plagiarism is taken very seriously at the college. Students accused of plagiarism are reported to the student review board, and if the board confirms that a student's work is not their own, the student is dismissed from the college. Students who have been dismissed for plagiarism are able to reapply to the college after waiting one semester, and if they are readmitted, they are placed on academic probation for a year.

Despite the college's policy, Professor Ramirez is conflicted about how to deal with this situation. She knows that Kelly had a very difficult semester. Her mother is ill with cancer, and during the semester, Kelly drove twice a week to her hometown two hours away to take her mother to doctor's appointments and chemotherapy. Knowing this, Professor Ramirez accommodated Kelly's schedule during the semester so that she did not have to drop the course. This is also Kelly's last semester before graduation, and she will be the first person in her family to graduate from college. Kelly also has a job lined up after graduation, for which Professor Ramirez wrote her a letter of recommendation, and if she does not graduate, she will most likely lose the job. Losing the job will be certain if Kelly is ejected from the college.

Professor Ramirez decides not to report the incident of plagiarism to the review board right away. She chooses instead to approach Kelly one-on-one and will proceed based on what Kelly has to say. During their meeting, it is apparent to Professor Ramirez that Kelly did complete the required service hours but was overwhelmed when it came to writing the paper. Kelly had let the assignment go until the very end, and then when she had to write it, she could only come up with one page rather than the three pages required. She added the plagiarized information to make the paper reach the required length. Kelly is genuinely remorseful and admits she is terrified of the consequences.

In the end, Professor Ramirez gave Kelly a zero for the assignment, but she still passed the class with a grade of a B. She did not feel that having Kelly kicked out of school would benefit the college or Kelly. Despite going against college policy, Professor Ramirez believes her behavior is consistent with her personal values of acknowledging that people make mistakes and deserve second chances. She personally felt that this behavior was out of character for Kelly and, had Kelly not been under tremendous personal and academic stress, she wouldn't have acted in this way.

Questions

1. Even though Professor Ramirez deviated from the college's policy regarding plagiarism, do you feel that she acted ethically?

2. If you were a student in this class and learned Professor Ramirez made an exception for this student, would you think she acted ethically? Explain.

3. In Table 11.1, the Six Pillars of Character are detailed. Which of these six pillars did Professor Ramirez display in consideration for her student, and how?

4. Professor Ramirez's actions ultimately brought into question whether or not the ends justify the means. Do you feel that her leniency in this case made her a stronger or more ethical leader? Explain.

Application

11.2 Case Study—In Good Company

For most companies in today's business world, profits (also referred to as "the bottom line") are the standard measurement of success. But the past decade has seen a dramatic rise in a different model: socially minded companies, which are for-profit companies formed with strong missions not just to make money but to be a force for good within their own operations, in their communities, and globally. Believing their missions are as important as, if not more important than, their bottom lines has led companies to develop and adopt a more comprehensive approach for defining corporate success. And a handful of states, like Vermont, are supporting and fostering this new way of doing business.

This new approach of measuring corporate success by more than just a myopic view of profits was spearheaded in 1994 with the development of an accounting framework known as the Triple Bottom Line (TBL or 3BL). In addition to considering financial profitability, the TBL includes measures of a company's commitment to corporate social responsibility through its social (people) and environmental (planet) impacts.

In addition to a new accounting system, a new corporate entity known as a Benefit Corporation, commonly referred to as a B Corporation or B Corp, was created for these new socially minded enterprises. The B Corporation is a legal structure for a business, like a limited liability company or a corporation. B Corporations are legally empowered to pursue positive stakeholder impact alongside profit. The B Corp structure requires companies' board of directors to consider other public benefits in addition to profit and also prevents shareholders from using stock value declines as a reason for seeking management dismissal or to pursue lawsuits against the corporation. Transparency is also built into the structure, requiring B Corps to publish annual benefit reports of their social and environmental performance using a comprehensive, credible, independent, and transparent third-party standard (B Lab, 2023). Key drivers behind the emergence of B Corporations are the increasing efforts of more conventional profit-driven companies to be seen as "green" and "good" as well as to "redefine the way people perceive success in the business world" (Kim et al., 2016, para. 11).

To see how B Corp entities are affecting the corporate and community landscape, consider the state of Vermont. In 2010, believing that companies focused on being a force for good increased the livability of their communities and are essential to a healthy state economy, Vermont became the second U.S. state to enact Benefit Corporation legislation. By 2019, Vermont boasted the highest number of B Corps per capita with more than 30 scattered throughout the state (ThinkVermont, 2019).

Vermont-based companies have a long history of ethically and socially aware business endeavors, beginning with beloved ice cream giant Ben & Jerry's. When the founders created the company in 1978 in an old gas station in Burlington, they made it clear they "didn't want to make a profit by taking advantage of someone" (Fee, 2018, para. 6). They committed to ensuring their ice cream business gave back to the community with a written mission statement declaring the Ben & Jerry's intent to balance the company's social and economic missions. The company made good on that promise, donating 7.5% of its pretax profits to charity. It also sourced its ingredients from other small local businesses. Over the years, the social and environmental missions of Ben & Jerry's have continued to expand both internally and externally, encompassing workers' rights, anti-racism, refugee asylum, global marriage equality and LGBTQ+ rights, and air quality and clean air, as well as climate issues (Ben & Jerry's, n.d.).

In addition, Vermont's Green Mountain Power was the first U.S. energy utility to achieve B Corp certification (Kelly, 2021). With the objective of supplying clean, efficient power and helping consumers to reduce their power bills, Green Mountain Power supplies electricity to almost 80% of the state, delivering energy that is 90% carbon free and more than 60% renewable (Fee, 2018). Through creative initiatives such as supplying customers with a Tesla Powerwall (a battery that acts like a generator and is charged off the grid with GMP's 90% carbon-free power or by a home's solar array), Green Mountain Power is working toward shifting Vermonters' energy dependence from the traditional power grid to more sustainable energy sources of solar power, higher-efficiency heat pumps, and geothermal systems. Green Mountain Power has consistently been ranked by *Fast Company* (Carlson, 2022) as one of the Most Innovative Companies in energy.

Today, Vermont is home to a thriving community of B Corps in a range of sizes and industries. Its investment in the flourishing B Corp community seems to be paying off; the state was ranked first on the 2017 Opportunity Index, which evaluates four aspects of a community's "well-being": economy, education, health, and community (Opportunity Nation & Child Trends, n.d.).

Questions

1. Discuss how the Triple Bottom Line and B Corporation concepts relate to each of the Six Pillars of Character that influence ethical leadership:
   a. Trustworthiness
   b. Respect
   c. Responsibility
   d. Fairness
   e. Caring
   f. Citizenship

2. Ethical leaders as discussed in the chapter use "moral means to achieve their goals." Discuss how this definition would apply to companies desiring to be B Corporations.

3. Transparency in B Corporations is a key element to their status and certification. How does this transparency relate to the chapter's discussion on honesty and the balance required to appropriately disclose information?

4. The chapter outlines three leadership values used to distinguish ethical leaders: ethical, modal, and end.
    a. Describe how each of these values might be reflected in a B Corporation.
    b. Describe how each of these values is reflected in Vermont's encouragement of B Corporations in the state.

5. The text defines ethical leadership as "the influence of a moral person who moves others to do the right thing in the right way for the right reasons." Do you think, after reading Case Study 11.2, that this definition applies only to "persons," or can it be expanded to entities such as companies, states, and other government entities? Why or why not?

6. Research a Vermont B Corporation. You may use one discussed in the case or search the directory provided at www.bcorporation.net/en-us/find-a-b-corp/ (filter on Vermont). Discuss the company's operations and mission with respect to the following elements of ethical leadership:

   a. How does the company and its leadership reflect the Six Pillars of Character?

   b. How does the company use moral means to achieve its goals?

   c. How are the goals of the company used to influence others, including the company's own employees?

   d. How are the concepts of transparency and honesty reflected in the operations and mission of this company?

   e. Power in the chapter is defined as "the capacity to influence or affect others." From the five bases of power listed in the chapter, select and discuss those that apply to this company.

      • Referent power—based on the follower's identification and liking for the leader

      • Expert power—based on the follower's perceptions of the leader's competence

      • Legitimate power—associated with having status or formal job authority

      • Reward power—derived from the capacity to provide benefits to others

      • Coercive power—derived from being able to penalize or punish others

   f. For each of the "values of a leader" listed as follows, describe how it applies to the company that you selected.

      • Ethical values

      • Modal values

      • End values

11.3 Sample Items From the Ethical Leadership Style Questionnaire

Purpose

1. To develop an understanding of your ethical leadership style

2. To understand how your preferred ethical leadership style relates to other ethical leadership styles

Directions

1. Please read the following 10 hypothetical situations in which a leader is confronted with an ethical dilemma.

2. Place yourself in the role of the leader or manager in the situation.

3. For each situation, indicate with an "X" your *most preferred response*. Your most preferred response is the response that best describes why you would do what you would do in that particular situation. Choose only one response. There are no right or wrong answers.

Response alternatives explained:

- *I would do what is right*: This option means you follow a set of moral rules and do what is expected of you when facing an ethical dilemma. You focus on fulfilling your moral obligations and doing your duty.
- *I would do what benefits the most people*: This option means you try to do what is best for the most people overall when facing an ethical dilemma. You focus on what will result in happiness for the largest number of individuals.
- *I would do what a good person would do*: This option means that you pull from who you are (your character) when facing an ethical dilemma. You act out of integrity, and you are faithful to your own principles.
- *I would do what shows that I care about my close relationships*: This option means that you give attention to your relationships when facing an ethical dilemma. You may give special consideration to those with whom you share a personal bond or commitment.
- *I would do what benefits me the most*: This option means that you do what is best for accomplishing your personal goals and objectives when facing an ethical dilemma. You are not afraid to assert your own interests when resolving problems.
- *I would do what is fair*: This option means that you focus on treating others fairly when facing an ethical dilemma. You try to make sure the benefits and burdens of decisions are shared equitably between everyone concerned.

Situations

1. You are the leader of a manufacturing team and learn that your employees are falsifying product quality results to sell more products. If you report the matter, most of them will lose their jobs, you may lose yours, and your company will take a significant hit to its reputation. What would you do in this situation?
   A. I would do what is right.
   B. I would do what benefits the most people.
   C. I would do what a good person would do.
   D. I would do what shows that I care about my relationships.
   E. I would do what benefits me the most.
   F. I would do what is fair.

2. You have an employee who has been having performance problems, which is making it hard for your group to meet its work quota. This person was recommended to you as a solid performer. You now believe the person's former manager had problems with the employee and just wanted to get rid of the person. If you give the underperforming employee a good recommendation, leaving out the performance problems, you will have an opportunity to pass the employee off to another group. What would you do in this situation?
   A. I would do what is right.
   B. I would do what benefits the most people.
   C. I would do what a good person would do.
   D. I would do what shows that I care about my relationships.
   E. I would do what benefits me the most.
   F. I would do what is fair.

3. Your team is hard-pressed to complete a critical project. You hear about a job opening that would be much better for one of your key employees' career. If this individual leaves the team, it would put the project in danger. What would you do in this situation?
   A. I would do what is right.
   B. I would do what benefits the most people.
   C. I would do what a good person would do.
   D. I would do what shows that I care about my relationships.
   E. I would do what benefits me the most.
   F. I would do what is fair.

4. An employee of yours has a child with a serious illness and is having trouble fulfilling obligations at work. You learn from your administrative assistant that this employee claimed 40 hours on a timesheet for a week when the employee actually only worked 30 hours. What would you do in this situation?

    A. I would do what is right.
    B. I would do what benefits the most people.
    C. I would do what a good person would do.
    D. I would do what shows that I care about my relationships.
    E. I would do what benefits me the most.
    F. I would do what is fair.

5. You are a manager, and some of your employees can finish their quotas in much less than the allotted time to do so. If upper management becomes aware of this, they will want you to increase the quotas. Some of your employees are unable to meet their current quotas. What would you do in this situation?
    A. I would do what is right.
    B. I would do what benefits the most people.
    C. I would do what a good person would do.
    D. I would do what shows that I care about my relationships.
    E. I would do what benefits me the most.
    F. I would do what is fair.

6. You are an organization's chief financial officer, and you are aware that the chief executive officer and other members of the senior leadership team want to provide exaggerated financial information to keep the company's stock price high. The entire senior management team holds significant stock positions. What would you do in this situation?
    A. I would do what is right.
    B. I would do what benefits the most people.
    C. I would do what a good person would do.
    D. I would do what shows that I care about my relationships.
    E. I would do what benefits me the most.
    F. I would do what is fair.

7. Two new employees have joined your accounting team right out of school. They are regularly found surfing the internet or texting on their phones. Your accounting work regularly requires overtime at the end of the month to get the financial reports completed. These employees refuse to do any overtime, which shifts work to other team members. The other team members are getting resentful and upset. What would you do in this situation?
    A. I would do what is right.
    B. I would do what benefits the most people.
    C. I would do what a good person would do.
    D. I would do what shows that I care about my relationships.
    E. I would do what benefits me the most.
    F. I would do what is fair.

8. You are the director of a neighborhood food cooperative. A member—a single parent with four children—is caught shoplifting $30 in groceries from the co-op. You suspect this person has been stealing for years. You consider pressing charges. What would you do in this situation?

   A. I would do what is right.
   B. I would do what benefits the most people.
   C. I would do what a good person would do.
   D. I would do what shows that I care about my relationships.
   E. I would do what benefits me the most.
   F. I would do what is fair.

9. You have been accused of discriminating against a particular gender in your hiring practices. A new position opens up, and you could hire a candidate of the gender you've been accused of discriminating against over a candidate of another gender, even though the latter candidate has slightly better qualifications. Hiring the former candidate would let you address this accusation and improve your reputation in the company. What would you do in this situation?

   A. I would do what is right.
   B. I would do what benefits the most people.
   C. I would do what a good person would do.
   D. I would do what shows that I care about my relationships.
   E. I would do what benefits me the most.
   F. I would do what is fair.

10. You are a professor. One of your best students buys an essay online and turns it in for a grade. Later in the term, the student begins to feel guilty and confesses to you that the paper was purchased. It is the norm at the university to fail a student guilty of plagiarism. You must decide if you will flunk the student. What would you do in this situation?

    A. I would do what is right.
    B. I would do what benefits the most people.
    C. I would do what a good person would do.
    D. I would do what shows that I care about my relationships.
    E. I would do what benefits me the most.
    F. I would do what is fair.

Scoring

To score the questionnaire, sum the number of times you selected each of the items A, B, C, D, E, and F. The sum of A responses represents your preference for *Duty Ethics*, the sum of B responses represents your preference for *Utilitarian Ethics*, the sum of C responses represents your preference for *Virtue Ethics*, the sum of D responses represents your preference for *Caring Ethics*, the sum of E responses represents your preference for *Egoism Ethics*, and the sum of F responses represents your preference for *Justice Ethics*. Place these sums in the Total Scores section that follows.

Total Scores

    A. Duty Ethics: _____
    B. Utilitarian Ethics: _____
    C. Virtue Ethics: _____
    D. Caring Ethics: _____
    E. Egoism Ethics: _____
    F. Justice Ethics: _____

Scoring Interpretation

The scores you received on this questionnaire provide information about your ethical leadership style; they represent your preferred way of addressing ethical dilemmas. Given a situation with an ethical dilemma, this questionnaire points to what ethical perspective is behind the choices you would make to resolve the dilemma. As you look at your total scores, your highest score represents your primary or dominant ethical leadership style, your second-highest score is the next most important, and so on. If you scored 0 for a category, it means that you put lower priority on that particular ethical approach to guide your decision making when facing ethical dilemmas.

- *If you scored higher on Duty Ethics*, it means you follow a set of moral rules and do what is expected of you when facing an ethical dilemma. You focus on fulfilling your moral obligations and doing your duty.
- *If you scored higher on Utilitarian Ethics*, it means that you try to do what is best for the most people overall when facing an ethical dilemma. You focus on what will result in happiness for the largest number of individuals.
- *If you scored higher on Virtue Ethics*, it means that you pull from who you are (your character) when facing an ethical dilemma. You act out of integrity, and you are faithful to your own principles.
- *If you scored higher on Caring Ethics*, it means that you give attention to your relationships when facing an ethical dilemma. You may give special consideration to those with whom you share a personal bond or commitment.
- *If you scored higher on Egoism Ethics*, it means that you do what is best for accomplishing your personal goals and objectives when facing an ethical dilemma. You are not afraid to assert your own interests when resolving problems.
- *If you scored higher on Justice Ethics*, it means that you focus on treating others fairly when facing an ethical dilemma. You try to make sure the benefits and burdens of decisions are shared equitably between everyone concerned.

By comparing your scores regarding each of these ethical perspectives, you can get a sense of what is important to you when addressing an ethical concern. Obviously, if you scored low on any of these categories, it suggests that you give less priority to that ethical perspective. All of the ethical perspectives have merit, so there is no "best" perspective to maintain.

This questionnaire is intended as a self-assessment exercise. Although each ethical approach is presented as a discrete category, it is possible that one category may overlap with another category. It is also possible that you may have an ethical leadership style that is not fully captured in this questionnaire. Since this questionnaire is an abridged version of an expanded questionnaire, you may wish to take the entire questionnaire to gain a more accurate reflection of your ethical approach. It can be taken at www.leaderdecisionmaking survey.com.

Application

11.4 Observational Exercise—Ethical Leadership

Purpose

1. To become aware of the dimensions of ethical leadership
2. To assess how actual leaders exhibit ethical leadership

Directions

1. For this exercise, you must observe a public presentation of a leader in your community. This can be a religious leader, a college president, a mayor, a city commissioner, the head of a social service agency, or some other community leader.
2. Record what you observe about the leader's ethics in the categories that follow. Try to be thorough in your descriptions of the leader's presentation.

Leader's name: _____

Leader's title: _____

Occasion: _____

1. The *character* of the leader: What was the leader like? What kind of person was the leader? What were the leader's strengths and weaknesses?

2. The *actions* of the leader: How does this leader go about accomplishing *goals*? Where does the leader stand on (1) showing respect, (2) serving others, and (3) showing justice?

3. The *goals* of the leader: What were the leader's main goals? Were the leader's goals clear to you and others in the audience? How would you assess the value and worth of those goals?

4. The *honesty* of the leader: What did you observe about this leader's honesty? Was the leader open and forthright? How authentic did you find this leader to be?

5. The *power* of the leader: Based on French and Raven's (1959) types of power, what kind of power did this leader exhibit? What did you observe about how this leader would use their power with others?

6. The *values* of the leader: Based on the presentation, what do you think this leader values? What is important to this leader? What values did this leader promote in their presentation?

Questions

1. What is your overall assessment of this leader's ethics?

2. What specific examples in the leader's presentation were particularly revealing of the leader's ethics?

3. Which factors of ethical leadership (character, actions, goals, honesty, power, and values) were most apparent in the leader's presentation? Discuss.

4. On a scale from 1 (*highly unethical*) to 10 (*highly ethical*), how would you describe this leader's ethical leadership? Defend your answer.

Application

11.5 Reflection and Action Worksheet—Ethical Leadership

Reflection

1. This chapter suggests that leadership has a *moral dimension* and that leaders have a responsibility to use their authority for the common good. Do you agree? Discuss.

2. When you consider the *character of a leader* and *what a leader does* (the leader's actions), which of these two factors is more important with regard to ethical leadership? Can a person with bad character be an ethical leader? Discuss your answers.

3. In this chapter, the circumstances at Abu Ghraib prison are used as an example of unethical leadership. Do you agree with this assessment? How do you view what happened at Abu Ghraib? What factors explain the leadership ethics in this situation?

4. This chapter includes a story about Richard Lee, the father who coached his son's Little League baseball team. What was your reaction to the story? Do you think Richard was an ethical leader? How would you have responded in this situation?

Action

1. Based on your responses to the Ethical Leadership Style Questionnaire, what are your core values? Do you think other people know your core values? Are you comfortable talking about these values with others? In your planning for the future (e.g., next five years), how will your values influence what you do? Discuss.

2. *Character* is a fundamental aspect of ethical leadership. What are your character strengths and weaknesses? List three specific actions you could take to strengthen your character.

3. In the Observational Exercise (11.4), you observed and analyzed the ethical leadership of a specific leader. If you were to apply the same analysis to your own leadership, how would you describe yourself? What factors best explain the ethics of your own leadership? If you were to try to become a more ethical leader, what specific changes should you make in your leadership? Discuss.

12

EXPLORING DESTRUCTIVE LEADERSHIP

INTRODUCTION

As stated in Chapter 1, this book is about *what it takes to be a leader*—the concepts underlying *constructive* leadership. But what happens when the leadership is *destructive*?

History is riddled with examples of individuals whose leadership has resulted in bad, even evil, outcomes. In the 20th century alone, the world has seen the likes of leaders from Adolf Hitler in Germany, whose Nazi regime was responsible for the deaths of an estimated 19 million people, to Syrian president Bashar al-Assad, whose attempt to control his country and put down rebellion has left more than 380,000 people dead and displaced 11 million others (BBC, 2020). But bad leadership is not just in the governmental realm. There are many instances of destructive leadership in business, nonprofit, religious, and social worlds, from corruption (such as Elizabeth Holmes of Theranos) and cover-ups (such as the Catholic Church and the sexual abuse of children by priests) to using a trusted medical position to sexually assault female college athletes (such as Dr. Larry Nassar at Michigan State University).

All of these examples have led people to wonder: *Why?* How are destructive leaders able to get and maintain power and commit such atrocities and wrongdoings? And why are people their followers?

Although hundreds of books have been written on good leadership, until relatively recently there have been very few on bad leadership. However, because of the many visible failures in leadership in the past decade, writing and research designed to explain the nature of destructive leadership have become more prevalent. In the general public and in the academic community, there is a growing demand to understand what destructive leadership is, why it happens, and what to do about it (Einarsen et al., 2007; Kellerman, 2004; Krasikova et al., 2013; Lipman-Blumen, 2005; Padilla, 2013; Schyns & Schilling, 2013; Tepper, 2007; Tepper et al., 2017; Waldman et al., 2018).

Destructive leadership has been called a variety of names, including "the dark side of leadership," "toxic leadership," "bad leadership," "pseudo-transformational leadership," "abusive leadership," and "unethical leadership." Common to all of these is the idea that leadership is not always good and helpful; sometimes it is bad and harmful. In this final chapter, we will discuss the opposite of caring and productive leadership—*destructive leadership*—focusing on how and why it occurs, its characteristics, and how to deal with it. To begin, we will define destructive leadership and what it entails. Next, we will introduce a framework called the Toxic Triangle and explain how the components within the triangle foster the existence of destructive leadership. We will break out and take a more in-depth look at each of the components within the triangle, beginning with how both the leader's personality and their behaviors contribute to destructive leadership. Then we will explore what makes followers susceptible to destructive leaders and how certain environments are conducive to enabling destructive leadership. Finally, we will discuss practical ways to confront and nullify destructive leadership.

DESTRUCTIVE LEADERSHIP EXPLAINED

At one time or another, most of us have experienced a leader (e.g., teacher, manager, coach, or employer) who seemed mean, unfair, manipulative, or very controlling. This person's leadership often created a whole range of negative emotions in followers, from fear and insecurity to anger and resentment. Individuals who lead in this way can best be described as destructive leaders. In this section, we will identify the characteristics of destructive leadership and define specifically what it means.

In the past 10 years, leadership scholars have focused considerable attention on identifying exactly what is involved in destructive leadership (Krasikova et al., 2013; Padilla et al., 2007). While there is not consensus about the definition of destructive leadership, scholars have identified certain characteristics that underlie the process and clarify its meaning.

First, destructive leadership involves the *excessive use of power, control, or influence*. Destructive leaders are authoritarian and oppressive; they exercise almost complete control over others and attempt to make others obedient to their wishes. As Hitler did in Germany during the 1930s and 1940s, a destructive leader will use coercion and force to influence others to accomplish their own objectives. A dogmatic, "my way or the highway" supervisor or boss is illustrative of this aspect of destructive leadership.

Similarly, the president of a company who makes the promotion of an employee contingent on providing the leader with sexual favors demonstrates inappropriate and excessive control. Using power indiscriminately, destructive leaders force followers to do what the leader wants. As extreme as it sounds, destructive leadership is a form of despotic control in which the leader is arbitrary and unrestrained in their use of power (Padilla et al., 2007).

Second, destructive leadership has a *selfish quality*—it focuses only on the leader's goals and objectives rather than on the common goals of both leaders and followers, or the goals of the organization (Padilla et al., 2007). In essence, a destructive leader does not listen to followers and their interests, demanding that they fall in step with the leader's desires. For example, the owner of a construction company might think that every one of his employees should do community service to enhance the image of his company in the community. As a result, he requires salaried employees to "volunteer" 10 hours of their off-work time each month at a local faith-based charity that builds homes for low-income families where he is also a board member. In this case, the leader's requirement makes the employees resentful, in part because the required work for his charity cuts into their family and leisure time and also because many of them are already volunteering for their own causes. The employees find what the leader is asking them to do unfair and counterproductive. When a leader selfishly fixates on only their own goals, it hinders others from feeling autonomous; it also prevents followers from being empowered, which in the end has a negative impact on the climate of the organization.

Third, destructive leadership involves *harmful behaviors* that adversely affect followers and the organization. Using harmful methods of influence, destructive leaders force followers to behave in ways that can have detrimental outcomes. To illustrate, consider how, for decades, leaders at many levels within the Catholic Church covered up sexual abuse by priests, often moving the offenders from one diocese to another without revealing their abusive behaviors. As a result, the offenders were able to continue abusing victims, causing incalculable harm to thousands of victims. Additionally, the Catholic Church has suffered enormous damage to its reputation, lost members' trust, and faced significant financial losses due to settlements paid to victims. Destructive leaders end up violating the organization's legitimate interests by sabotaging the organization's goals as well as the well-being and satisfaction of the followers (Einarsen et al., 2007; Krasikova et al., 2013).

In contrast to how we define leadership in Chapter 1 as the "process whereby an individual influences a group of individuals to achieve a common goal," we define destructive leadership quite differently. **Destructive leadership** is *the process whereby an individual exercises excessive control and coercion to force a group of individuals to accomplish the leader's own goals without regard to the impact on others or the organization.* Destructive leadership is about how leaders use power to force people, often against their will, to do things that the leader alone wants done. It is destructive because it abuses followers and damages the organization.

Toxic Triangle

Although it is common to think about destructive leadership as a "leader" problem, it is about more than the leader (Padilla, 2013). Destructive leadership does not exist within a vacuum; it takes root as a result of a complex set of interactions between the leader, the followers, and the context. To explain what fosters destructive leadership, Padilla et al. (2007) created a model called the Toxic Triangle that outlines the key components that make destructive leadership possible (see Figure 12.1).

Destructive Leaders

The primary component of the Toxic Triangle is *destructive leaders*, as shown in Figure 12.1. Understanding this component is at the core of understanding destructive leadership as a whole. Who are destructive leaders? How can they be characterized? Do they have unique personalities and engage in certain identifiable behaviors? Padilla et al. (2007) have proposed some answers to these questions.

First, destructive leaders typically demonstrate *charisma*, which is a special quality, or charm, that appeals to others and enhances the leader's ability to gain people's devotion (see Chapter 2). While charisma can be a positive trait, it is used by destructive leaders in harmful ways. Incorporated with charisma are leaders' strong rhetorical skills, vision, and energy, which destructive leaders use to win others over and to exploit followers for their own ends. To illustrate, consider the infamous example of cult leader Jim Jones, a charismatic minister who moved his congregation (the Peoples Temple) from San Francisco to Jonestown, Guyana. He was accused of

FIGURE 12.1   ■   Toxic Leadership Triangle

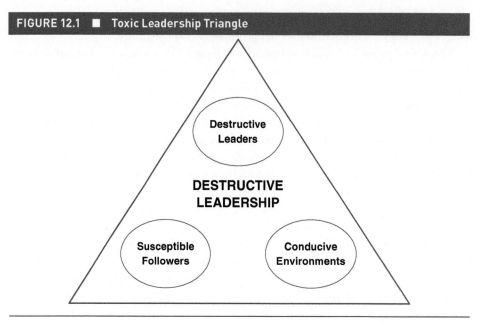

Source: Adapted from "The Toxic Triangle: Destructive leaders, susceptible followers, and conducive environments," by A. Padilla, R. Hogan, and R. B. Kaiser, 2007, *The Leadership Quarterly, 18*(3), 176–194.

abusing churchgoers and wanted to avoid U.S. government intervention into his church's affairs. Obsessed with power (see Chapter 11), Jones set up a commune where he manipulated and controlled his followers, eventually forcing them to commit mass suicide by drinking cyanide-laced Kool-Aid, resulting in the deaths of 913 people, 304 of whom were children. Jones was unmistakably a charismatic leader. But he used his leadership to abject ends.

Second, destructive leaders have an intense *need for power* (Padilla et al., 2007) and use this power primarily for personal gain and self-aggrandizement rather than for the common good. Serving others or the organization is not the focus of the destructive leader; rather, this leader coercively imposes their will on others, often devaluing followers to promote their own ends. For example, consider how Sheriff Joe Arpaio exercised his power over a period of 24 years in Maricopa County, Arizona. Promoting himself as "America's Toughest Sheriff," he ruled with an iron hand. He used the power of his office to go after undocumented immigrants who crossed the U.S. border, including conducting "immigration roundups." His behavior prompted a U.S. federal court to issue an injunction that barred him from conducting roundups, which he was later found to have ignored. While in office, Arpaio was accused of abuse of power, misuse of funds, failure to investigate sex crimes, unlawful enforcement of immigration laws, unconstitutional jail conditions, and racial profiling, among other things. Arpaio never wavered from promoting and executing his own outspoken viewpoints, but, destructively, he abused the power of his office, pursuing his own goals at the expense of advancing the common good.

Third, destructive leadership is associated with **narcissism**. In Greek mythology, Narcissus was a very handsome young hunter who, upon seeing his reflection in a pool of water, fell in love with his image and himself. Similarly, narcissistic leaders are enamored with themselves and their own leadership. They have a grandiose sense of self and like to receive constant attention from others. Because they are so preoccupied with their own approach to things, narcissistic leaders do not welcome the input of others. Narcissistic leaders act like they are special and freely pursue their own goals even when these goals may be unreasonable. Narcissism is destructive because it makes the leader insular, limiting their ability or willingness to receive feedback from others. These leaders lack empathy for others and are dismissive of the needs and concerns of others.

To illustrate, consider the owner of a high-end men's store in an upscale community who is very narcissistic. The design of the store and merchandise all reflect the owner's personality, and the owner loves his store and everything he has done to make it special. When sales are up, he attributes the success to his leadership and vision; when sales are down, it is other people's fault. When staff make helpful suggestions to improve operations, he listens and then does what he wants to do. The owner is totally focused on himself and has no time for others or their concerns. He has no empathy for employees who have to miss work because of a health problem (e.g., migraine headache) or family concern (e.g., sick child). When his sister, a single parent without health insurance, developed a chronic illness that required special medications, the owner never considered how he could help defray his sister's medical costs or help out with her children. Needless to say, the narcissistic and uncaring nature of his leadership made him a very difficult person to work for. Employees often felt discounted because he did not seriously consider their input and created a negative work environment. Not surprisingly, the store's employee turnover was very high.

In addition to charisma, need for power, and narcissism, Padilla et al. (2007) suggest it is not uncommon for destructive leaders to have had *negative or traumatic childhood experiences* that contribute to treating followers indifferently and exploiting them for their own purposes. Because of their troubled childhoods, destructive leaders can demonstrate an ideology of hate in which they turn their loathing of self toward others—treating others as despised enemies. Because of their own disturbed pasts, destructive leaders believe their abusive and hateful behavior toward others is legitimate. While it is impossible to directly associate childhood experiences with adult behavior, being aware of these issues can help explain some of the "why" behind destructive leadership.

Susceptible Followers

A second component of the Toxic Triangle is *susceptible followers* (see Figure 12.1). As we suggested earlier, destructive leadership does not occur in a vacuum; it occurs in situations where followers are susceptible to influence. For example, when followers are passive or submissive, their inaction can contribute to unfettered leadership and unintentionally support destructive leaders. Leaders and followers are interrelated in the leadership process. How followers act is strongly associated with how leaders lead.

According to Padilla et al. (2007), the types of followers who are susceptible to destructive leadership can be divided into two groups: *conformers* and *colluders*. As implied by the name, **conformers** comply with destructive leaders, in an effort to minimize the consequences of not going along. They conform because they lack a clearly defined self-concept and fear what will happen if they do not follow. Underlying their desire to conform could be unmet basic needs, negative self-evaluations, and immaturity. A good example of this involves members of a high school Tier 1 AAA Hockey team. They are on the team in hopes of getting exposure to recruiters for college or minor league hockey teams. Because the coach decides which team members will play in the games, the players put up with the coach's insults and public berating, as well as the coach's attempts to pit them against one another to create conflict, which many times turns physical. While the players' parents know of the coach's behavior, they, too, remain silent in order not to jeopardize their sons' chances of playing.

In contrast, **colluders** comply in the hopes of getting something out of it for themselves. They support the leader's agenda because it is advantageous to their own agenda. Underlying their desire to collude could be ambitiousness, selfishness, and the chance to support and be supported by a leader with similar beliefs and values. A good example of colluders involves elected officials such as legislators who vote along party lines on bills, even if they don't agree with the proposals or the proposals are not in the best interest of their constituents. Because the financial support and endorsement of their political parties is critical to these lawmakers, they vote for issues and bills they may not believe in to maintain the support of their party.

In addition to identifying susceptible followers as conformers and colluders, another explanation for why some followers are vulnerable to destructive leaders is set forth by Jean Lipman-Blumen in *The Allure of Toxic Leaders* (2005). In this book, she identifies a series of psychological factors on the part of followers that contribute to emergence of harmful leadership and explains why followers are sometimes compliant even with highly destructive leaders.

The list of factors described by Lipman-Blumen in Table 12.1 is helpful in understanding "why" our basic human needs make us susceptible to bad leadership.

1. *Our need for reassuring authority figures.* As far back as psychoanalyst Sigmund Freud's research in the early 1900s, much has been written about how people deal with authority. When we are very young, we depend on our parents to guide and protect us, but as we mature, we learn to be our own compass/authority/person and make our decisions without being dependent on others. However, as adults, some followers still have a high need for authority figures. They want their leaders to be big and strong like their parents used to be. They want to feel assured that they will be taken care of and protected. This need can open the door for destructive leaders to take advantage of followers and use them to meet their own ends. When followers' needs for a reassuring authority figure are strong, it makes them vulnerable to the dictates of abusive and destructive leaders. For example, in 2009, 50 participants in a self-help retreat in Arizona entered a sauna-like ceremony in a sweat lodge that was meant to provide spiritual cleansing. Even though some of the participants were in obvious distress and pleaded for help, James Arthur Ray, a prominent figure in the self-help industry at the time and leader of the retreat, instead pushed them further, encouraging them to tough out the sweltering conditions as part of a rebirthing process that would transform their lives. The participants trusted Ray, and as a result, 3 people died and 18 were hospitalized from overexposure to heat.

TABLE 12.1 ■ Psychological Factors and Susceptible Followers
1. Our need for reassuring authority figures
2. Our need for security and certainty
3. Our need to feel chosen or special
4. Our need for membership in the human community
5. Our fear of ostracism, isolation, and social death
6. Our fear of powerlessness to challenge a bad leader

Source: Based on *The Allure of Toxic Leaders* by J. Lipman-Blumen, 2005, p. 29; permission conveyed through Copyright Clearance Center, Inc. Republished with permission of Oxford University Press.

2. *Our need for security and certainty.* Psychologists who study people's belief systems have found that people have a need for consistency—to keep their beliefs and attitudes balanced. Our drive for predictability means we struggle in situations where things are disrupted and we do not feel "in charge" of ourselves or the events around us. It is in contexts like these that followers are susceptible to the lure of unethical leaders who have power. For example, imagine a person with a brain tumor who has received a serious diagnosis that has low survival statistics. In such a situation, most people trust their doctor and the advice of professionals at their local cancer center. But there are some people who feel so uncertain and insecure that they abandon traditional medicine and visit uncertified cancer centers outside the country that promise quick cures. All they want is someone to give them the security and certainty they believe is lacking in their situation. In difficult, trying times, it is human nature to look to "know-it-all" leaders for direction and support.

3. *Our need to feel chosen or special.* To explain people's need to feel chosen, Lipman-Blumen (2005) points to the religious leaders of the world, such as Moses and John Calvin, who emphasized to their followers that they were the "chosen ones"—they were special and had been singled out by a higher authority. Being a part of "the chosen" means one has truth on one's side while "others" do not. Being a part of the chosen and feeling that one is "right" gives a sense of security to followers but does so at the expense of appreciating the humanity of "the other." As an example, white supremacists' ideology is based on a belief that white people are superior to all other racial groups and should have control over people of other, "lesser" racial groups. Followers of white supremacy may feel chosen and special but at the high cost of treating others humanely. Toxic leaders know how to capitalize on people's needs to feel special, and they use those needs to their own ends.

4. *Our need for membership in the human community.* Psychologist William Schutz (1966) argued that one of the strongest interpersonal needs of people is to know whether

they belong to the group. Are we "in" or "out"? Are we included with others and acknowledged as a member of the community or not?

When a group or an organization is functioning positively, group membership is healthy for its members—they feel accepted, comfortable, valued, and inspirited. But people's need to be a member of the group can be exploited by destructive leaders. These leaders take advantage of individuals who are highly dependent on the group for their own personal meaning and purpose. Highly dependent followers may be willing to give up their individuality, beliefs, and integrity just to make sure they can retain their social belonging (Lipman-Blumen, 2005). Consider the disturbing hazing incidents at fraternities on college campuses that have resulted in the injuries and deaths of new members (pledges) who are willing to endure dangerous rituals because of their high need to belong to the group. Followers can become vulnerable to bad leadership when they are unable to moderate their own personal needs for belonging.

5. *Our fear of ostracism, isolation, and social death.* When an individual becomes a part of and *acquires* full membership to a group, the individual typically learns and begins to practice the norms of the group. Surrounded by the group, followers become comfortable with the group's values, mission, and beliefs. In addition, followers begin to like being a group member and doing what group members do, finding the inclusion and community of the group comforting.

   But being a part of the group also has a downside. This inclusion and community makes it difficult for an individual to break out of the group or dissent if the group's mission or values run counter to the individual's. Pressure to conform to the group makes it challenging for an individual to disagree with the group or try to get the group to change. When followers act against group norms or bring attention to the negative aspects of what the group is doing (e.g., act as whistle-blowers), they run a high risk of becoming ostracized and isolated from the group. For example, imagine you and some of your friends are all taking the same college history class and have decided to team up as a group to do the class's final project: a research paper and presentation on a significant historical event. The leader of your group, who is one of your closest friends, has found that you can buy a paper on your topic from an online service and wants everyone in the group to chip in the money to do it. You believe this is unethical. Do you tell the course instructor and risk being ostracized from your friends? Or do you "keep quiet," chip in to buy the paper, and maintain your relationships with your friends? The anxieties people feel regarding possibly being ostracized from the group make them susceptible to destructive leadership.

6. *Our fear of powerlessness to challenge a bad leader.* Finally, followers may unintentionally enable destructive leaders because they feel helpless to change them. Once a part of a group, followers often feel pressure to conform to the norms of the group. They find that it is not easy to challenge the leader or go against the leader's plans for the group. For example, in political parties, people often feel pressure to support the party's platform even when they feel diametrically opposed to it. Specifically, when a leader acts inappropriately or treats others in harmful ways, it is hard for followers

to muster the courage to address the leader's behavior. Groups provide security for followers, and the threat of losing this security can make it scary and uncomfortable to challenge authority figures. To speak truth to power is a brave act, and followers often feel impotent to express themselves in the face of authority. Although being an accepted follower in a group carries with it many benefits, it does not always promote personal agency. After all, who would support you if you challenged the leader? For example, imagine what it would be like to be a gay employee in an organization whose leadership is openly prejudiced against LGBTQ+ rights. Would you be likely to express disapproval of the leadership and its policies?

To summarize, destructive leadership does not arise only because of bad leaders; it emerges from the interaction between bad leaders and susceptible followers. Followers affect leaders, and leaders affect followers, simultaneously. Destructive leadership occurs in relation to susceptible followers. Destructive leaders evolve and can thrive when followers feel the need to conform or collude, and when they feel compelled to attempt to satisfy their needs for safety, uniqueness, and inclusion in a community.

Conducive Environments

As shown in Figure 12.1, the third component in the Toxic Triangle is **conducive environments**, which are unique situations or contexts that promote the development of destructive leadership. Knowing what comprises conducive environments is useful to understanding the basis for and complexities of destructive leadership. According to Padilla et al. (2007), conducive environments commonly include four factors: instability, perceived threat, certain cultural values, and the absence of checks and balances and institutionalization.

1. *Instability.* In times of crisis and confusion, followers seek direction and clarity; they want leaders to stabilize matters, often in the quickest way possible. Instability in the environment makes it convenient for calculating leaders to assert more power than they should and make decisions that are not within the bounds of the established organizational structure. When rules and systemic structures are not clearly established, opportunistic leaders can exploit the system to their own ends. Acting unilaterally, they can make radical changes. It is natural for all of us to want to find certainty in uncertain times, but we need to be vigilant about who we let lead and how they lead in these situations. Unstable contexts provide ripe opportunities for leaders to grab power and create rules that serve the leaders and their own purposes rather than the common good.

   A classic historical example of an unstable situation resulting in ineffective leadership is apparent in the events surrounding the assassination attempt on U.S. president Ronald Reagan on March 30, 1981. The president was shot while leaving the Washington Hilton after giving a luncheon speech for representatives of the American Federation of Labor and Congress of Industrial Organizations. He was immediately rushed to George Washington University Hospital where he was taken to surgery. Because his condition was unknown, there was great anxiety in the country and around the world. In the White House, there was chaos because there was no established protocol in place for this type of calamity. It did not help matters that Vice President George H. W. Bush was out of town giving a speech in Texas.

Behind the scenes at the White House, efforts by staff to stabilize matters were ineffective. In this disordered and tumultuous context, Secretary of State Alexander Haig decided on his own to address the press. He was out of breath and appeared very anxious, and when asked by the media who was making decisions for the government, Haig made a now famous statement: "As of now, I am in control here, in the White House." Furthermore, he made the mistake of erroneously claiming that after the vice president, he, the secretary of state, was third in the line of succession to the presidency rather than the Speaker of the House. Haig's attempt to lead was seen by many as overreaching his role and taking power that was not legitimately his to take. In the end, instead of providing calm, Haig's leadership resulted in greater uncertainty and anxiety.

2.   *Perceived threat.* Another situational factor that can create an environment that increases the likelihood of destructive leadership is perceived threat. People naturally want to be protected from threats that can occur on many levels, including physically, socially, or financially. Threats do not need to be real; they only need to be perceived as real. When individuals think they are going to be damaged or harmed by something, it is common for them to seek and accept assertive leadership. In addition, in situations where threat exists, many followers like others to take charge and show leadership. For example, immediately after the Boston Marathon bombing and before the perpetrators were found, people throughout Boston were willing to obey the police and "shelter in place" until the police found the suspects. Essentially, the people in Boston stayed inside their buildings and homes until they were told it was safe to go outside. Wanting to be protected from outside threats is closely related to Lipman-Blumen's (2005) concept of security, discussed earlier in this chapter. When we are fearful of being injured or hurt in some way, it is human to want to be taken care of by a strong leader. Feeling threatened, individuals are willing to give up their own agency to receive strong direction from others or to concede control to them.

For example, consider the movement across the United States by various groups and legislators to ban certain books in school libraries, classrooms, and entire districts, based on the books' content. A vast majority of the books targeted for removal in 2022 feature LGBTQ+ characters and identities and/or characters of color, and/or cover race and racism in American history, and/or provide sex education (Friedman & Farid-Johnson, 2022). The advocacy groups pushing the bans create a perceived threat by labeling these books as "obscene" and as having inappropriate content for children. These groups use language such as "parents' rights" and the "freedom to express religious or conservative views" to create the fear in others that these rights will be taken from them by allowing access to these books.

3. *Cultural values.* Broadly speaking, certain general values in society can increase the likelihood of destructive leadership. Based on the categories set forth by Hofstede (1980) in his classic work on cultural dimensions, Luthans et al. (1998) and Padilla et al. (2007) suggest that societies that demonstrate avoidance of uncertainty, collectivism, and high power distance are conducive environments for destructive leadership. First, societies characterized by high avoidance of uncertainty (e.g., Japan) rely on established social norms, rituals, and procedures to avoid uncertainty. Rules, structures, and laws make things more predictable. In situations that make followers feel uncertain, such as poverty or civil conflict, strong dictatorial leaders often provide hope to followers by making things more predictable. However, it is also within uncertain contexts that destructive leaders can easily capitalize on followers' needs by formulating rules, structures, and laws that give people what they are longing for—certainty.

    Second, societies characterized by collectivism (e.g., North Korea) identify with and emphasize broader societal interests rather than individual goals and accomplishments. They often have a strong leader and place a premium on collective efforts. Collectivist values engender people to prefer a leader who can lead the masses and unite them around a shared goal. Even where there is much diversity, collectivism serves as a way to support a strong leader who might be capable of bringing people together in a united front. Collectivist values make followers susceptible to rallying around and accepting a leader who promotes and promises an overarching unified cause that may or may not be in the best interests of the people. Having a common cause is valuable but not when it diminishes individuality and input from others.

    Finally, some cultures emphasize values characterized as high power distance (e.g., Saudi Arabia), which means that people accept the fact that power can be distributed unequally. High power distance is concerned with the way societies are stratified, thus creating levels between people based on power, authority, and material possessions. In cultures such as these, people see power and authority as facts of life, and disparities in education levels and wealth distribution are readily accepted. This context is conducive for destructive leaders because people are accustomed to the unequal power that is inherent in oppressive and totalitarian leadership.

4. *Absence of checks and balances and institutionalization.* The principle of **checks and balances** refers to the way power and influence are shared in an organizational system. It means that each part of the system is invested with power that counterbalances the influence of the other parts of the system. This principle ensures that power is not concentrated in the hands of a few individuals or groups. When checks and balances are not in place within a given organization, it opens up the opportunity for people to abuse power, advancing their own agenda at the expense of other groups within the system or the common agenda of the organization. For example, at the federal level in the United States, three branches of government (i.e., executive, judicial, and legislative) are designed to be checks and balances on each other, but if these checks

and balances are absent, one of the branches can take actions (e.g., the executive branch could issue a series of executive orders) that are in conflict with or usurp the power of the other branches. In practical terms, checks and balances are the safeguard that deters destructive leaders from seizing power unfairly and unjustly.

Similar to the checks and balances described, **institutionalization** is a process concerned with making rules and regulations in an organization. Strong institutions can be thought of as organizations in which there are clearly established rules and procedures and also accepted methods for changing or replacing them. Like checks and balances, institutionalization is a way for individuals and groups to explain how influence and power is shared within the organization. For example, Public School A could be described as a strong institution because it has a clear governance system with transparent rules and procedures about administrators' duties, as well as the rights and responsibilities of parents and students. In contrast, Public School B might be described as being institutionally weak because its governance rules and procedures are essentially undeveloped, unclearly written, and unenforceable. In new, small, and rapidly growing organizations, clear rules can be missing, which makes the context conducive for leaders who may act destructively toward followers (Thoroughgood et al., 2018). When institutionalization is strong, the opportunity for destructive leadership is lessened.

CONFRONTING DESTRUCTIVE LEADERSHIP IN PRACTICE

In contrast to the previous chapters that end with a discussion of how to "practice" leadership, this chapter ends with an examination of how *not to* "practice" leadership. It is concerned with how to restrain toxic leaders and how to change leadership from destructive to constructive. Consistent with the ideas presented in the Toxic Triangle (see Figure 12.1), we will discuss how to confront destructive leadership from three perspectives: the leader, the followers, and the context. Taken collectively, these perspectives provide a strong basis for developing strategies to combat destructive leadership.

Leaders

Most of us would agree that it is easy to recognize destructive leaders, but at the same time, it can be very difficult to get rid of them. The task is made more difficult because destructive leaders often possess charisma, which makes them persuasive. They have acquired power, which they like to exhibit and do so for their own ends. They are also narcissistic, which drastically reduces their ability to be empathic. Underlying all of this is their psychological need to resolve childhood traumas by treating others abusively. Destructive leaders are hard to deal with, and trying to change them or remove them from positions of leadership is extremely challenging and often impossible. To underscore these difficulties, imagine the challenges of dealing with someone like a religious cult leader such as Jim Jones in Guyana, or a dictator such as Adolf Hitler in Germany, or an entrenched corporate CEO like movie producer Harvey Weinstein (see Case Study 12.2—"Breaking the Silence"). In each of these cases, the toxicity of the leaders was apparent, but sufficient avenues for combating them were absent.

So what can organizations do about destructive leaders? One approach is to develop effective selection and development procedures that identify potentially destructive leaders (Padilla et al., 2007). In a business context, companies' human resource departments, which are charged with overseeing the recruiting, interviewing, and hiring of new employees, could make it their central mission to dissuade management from hiring or promoting individuals who exhibit the qualities of destructive leaders. Many companies require that potential employees take a battery of psychological tests to identify their strengths and weaknesses and whether they are a good match for the job and the organization's culture. These tests can make it easier to notice attributes of an applicant that might not be readily apparent in a general interview. For example, these tests can include assessments of an applicant's willingness to listen, empathic ability, need for control, and narcissism, to name a few. Candidates' scores on qualities such as these can provide an informed approach to eliminating certain people who present as having the potential to be problematic and destructive if they are given a leadership position within the organization. In addition, though harder to measure, candidates could be assessed in regard to their ethical and moral standards. Scoring low on ethical quality would be a clear indicator that a candidate could be destructive in their leadership, and therefore this individual could be removed from a pool of applicants (see more about ethical leadership in Chapter 11, "Addressing Ethics in Leadership").

In general, there is no panacea for dealing with destructive leaders. They will always exist and invariably have an insidious impact on the people and organizations they serve. In situations where communication or legal channels are available for individuals to express their concerns, it is incumbent on people to speak out, confront the leader, and demand change. In organizations where procedures exist to challenge or remove the leader, people should never fail to gather support and insist on change. This can often be a long and arduous process. But because destructive leaders are toxic and abuse power, individuals should not hesitate from challenging them and deposing them from office.

Followers

Reflecting on the Leadership Snapshot about Elizabeth Holmes and Theranos in this chapter, an important question worth addressing is "Why didn't the followers stop the destructive leadership of CEO Elizabeth Holmes?" By all accounts, she was a highly toxic leader. She focused exclusively on her own goals and destroyed those who got in her way or opposed her. But the company thrived for nearly 10 years under this despotic influence. How could this happen, and what can be done to prevent a situation like this from happening again?

One route available to followers is to disrupt destructive leadership by speaking out—to be whistle-blowers. For example, when certain employees at Theranos "blew the whistle" about company wrongdoing, they brought the company down by talking to journalists and getting the word out about abuse and illicit activities at Theranos. However, as illustrated in the Theranos case, whistle-blowers can pay a steep price for speaking up (Johnson, 2012). There are protections within the law for whistle-blowers, but whistle-blowing still demands courage and fortitude on the part of followers.

Padilla et al. (2007) suggest that followers can better respond to destructive leaders when the cultures they work within reinforce collaboration, employee initiative and involvement, and empowerment. This is true because destructive leaders use power unilaterally and an organizational culture that nurtures participatory involvement can provide a balance that can offset authoritarian power. Furthermore, organizations can build a culture that promotes staff development, particularly programs that focus on advancing the leadership potential of followers. Staff development helps address the problem of destructive leadership because it trains and builds individuals to be better leaders. It is also effective because destructive leaders often neglect staff development, because it is seen as threatening to their authoritarian leadership.

Finally, as discussed earlier in this chapter, there are psychological factors (see Table 12.1) that make followers susceptible to bad leaders. There are several ways for followers to address these factors and resist destructive leaders:

- *Convince themselves that they are OK, strong, and capable of confronting life's obstacles.* All individuals have it within themselves to be their own compass and act on the world from within their own agency.

- *Learn to handle ambiguity and live with uncertainty and accept these as natural and necessary.* We all encounter obstacles in life, and it is incumbent on each of us to look deeply within ourselves to find the strength and security to deal with the problem. Strong influence and support from the outside can give us this security, but we also can engage the strength within ourselves to handle the change and difficulties that confront us.

- *Do not become compliant with a destructive leader to satisfy our needs to feel special and chosen.* Being accepted by a destructive leader is no gift; this acceptance is inauthentic and self-defeating. Destructive leaders demand allegiance and unremitting devotion to their own self-serving goals. The cost of such commitment is too high and undeserved.

- *Do not lose our sense of who we are as people.* It is completely legitimate and healthy for followers to want to be a part of and accepted as a member of a group, but being accepted does not require giving away one's uniqueness to the intentions and norms of the destructive leader.

- *When necessary, followers need to muster all the strength available to them to act out against group norms when leaders are leading destructively.* Although there is a high risk of being isolated from the group, when the situation is abusive, followers have to step up and become whistle-blowers to stop the carnage and wrongdoing that the destructive leader has created.

- *Speak truth to power.* Followers need to reach within themselves and find the strength to express themselves in confronting and combating the leader. Groups are important to each of us, but pressure to conform should never get in the way of standing up for good when a leader is destructive. Everyone has the agency within to stand up and say no to bad leadership.

Context

The final area where destructive leadership can be addressed is within the context—the norms, rules, and procedures of the organization. One contextual approach that is particularly effective is to create a strong system of checks and balances among the different organizational units. Strong checks and balances are conducive to limiting or preventing destructive leadership because they require that the leader shares power with followers and accepts being monitored by followers regarding their use of power in any given area. Consider the example of a university political science department that has a strong system of checks and balances, which the faculty members carefully lay out in a procedural manual they call "the governance document." The 100-page document spells out very clearly the roles and responsibilities of faculty, particularly as these relate to the chairperson of the department. In regard to decision making within the department, the manual states that faculty members are allowed to declare their preferences and provide feedback to the chair regarding the scheduling of classes, their workload and committee work, and tenure and promotion decisions. The governance document is also explicit about the rules for merit pay, promotion, and workload. While the chairperson makes the decisions regarding how the department will operate, individual faculty members are encouraged to make their preferences known regarding how they want to be treated and what is fair. What is so important about the governance document is that it makes official the ways faculty can influence the chairperson and the ways the chairperson can influence the faculty. In short, the department addresses the problem of potential destructive leaders by having a system of governance that discourages it from ever emerging.

Another contextual approach that can act as a deterrent to destructive leadership is to maintain strong oversight of an organization through the use of independent boards of directors that are empowered to have access to and input into how the organization is run. For public companies in the United States, the U.S. Congress has enacted law to require greater board involvement and transparency. In response to the corporate scandals at Enron and WorldCom in the early 2000s, the Sarbanes-Oxley Act was authorized to protect investors by setting requirements for all U.S. public company boards, making these boards accountable for the accuracy and reliability of corporate disclosures. This has forced boards to more closely monitor corporate activity and made them and top managers more accountable for their actions (Perryman et al., 2010). In effect, it forces companies to be more transparent, reducing the likelihood of leaders abusing their power.

In addition, when boards of directors are not recruited and chosen by the CEO and are independent from CEO control, they can more effectively oversee the leadership within the organization. To be able to monitor top executives, it is important that boards of directors be involved in board member and executive selection, performance reviews, succession processes, policy-level oversight, and the power to sanction executives (Padilla et al., 2007). In effect, having a strong board of directors is another way to lessen the power and potentially abusive autonomy of top management.

Going back to the Theranos example, the board of directors that oversaw the company was handpicked by Elizabeth Holmes and made up of dignitaries, not scientists. As a result, the board members believed what Holmes told them about the science and technology behind Theranos's product, rather than developing an understanding of it on their own.

Finally, to control for abuse, organizations can attempt to monitor themselves by establishing norms and values that create a strong ethical climate within the organization, which helps establish ethical behavior (Perryman et al., 2010). When organizations encourage values of honesty, fairness, serving others, respect, and community, it becomes less probable that a leader will have the incentive or opportunity to act abusively or destructive toward followers.

LEADERSHIP SNAPSHOT

Elizabeth Holmes, Founder and Former CEO, Theranos

On the surface, Elizabeth Holmes was young and gifted with a single-minded passion to revolutionize the way diseases are diagnosed. At 19, she dropped out of Stanford University with a plan to drastically alter medical blood testing. The idea behind the company she named Theranos was transformative: using a few drops of blood from a single finger prick to look for everything from diabetes to cancer. This method would replace the numerous painful venous blood draws currently needed. And best yet, patients could do it from their own homes for a fraction of the cost.

It was an idea that intrigued high-powered individuals. Holmes, described as charismatic and mature with a deep, baritone voice that mesmerized listeners, was able to put together a distinguished board of advisers and investors including Rupert Murdoch, two former U.S. secretaries of state (Henry Kissinger and George Shultz), Oracle founder Larry Ellison, former U.S. senators Sam Nunn and Bill Frist, and former U.S.

Photo by Max Morse for TechCrunch - TechCrunch Disrupt San Francisco 2014, CC BY 2.0, https://commons.wik imedia.org/w/index.php?curid=45609 023

secretaries of defense William Perry and James Mattis. Even with its unproven technology, Theranos, and Holmes, managed to bring in $1 billion in funding from investors. At one point, the company was valued at $9 billion.

Elizabeth Holmes was born into a legacy of greatness. Her father was a descendant of the founder of the Fleischmann Yeast Company, and her great-great-grandfather established Cincinnati General Hospital and the University of Cincinnati's medical school. But by the time Elizabeth's father was born, the family fortune had been squandered by his grandfather and father. Chris Holmes, however, made sure his daughter knew of not only the great success of her forebears, but also the flaws of the later generations, emphasizing to her the negative impact that occurs from "people deciding not to do something purposeful" (Carreyrou, 2018, p. 10). It was what drew Elizabeth Holmes to study biotechnology—the promise of leaving her mark on the world by doing something that furthered the greater good, not just to become rich. In her sophomore year of college, Holmes wrote a patent application for an arm patch that would diagnose medical conditions. After sharing it with and receiving an encouraging response from a Stanford professor and a PhD student, she filed paperwork to start Theranos, leveraging her family's connections to raise money to fund it.

For 10 years, Theranos operated as if it were going to change the world, attracting top-notch engineers, chemists, and scientists to work there. Many of these essential employees worked in isolation from one another. Holmes, who was described as "driven and relentless," compartmentalized the firm's departments, quashing cross-departmental communication, so that only she had the full picture of the technology's development. She kept some of her most important employees on a "need-to-know" basis, demanding absolute loyalty from them and turning on them suddenly if she felt their fidelity was waning. She would also freeze people out when she was displeased with them, refusing to look at or talk to them, and fired people as easily as she hired them. Employee turnover at the company was exceedingly high.

Despite the corporate turmoil, Holmes's star was rising. She was interviewed by national news programs, and her face graced numerous magazine covers. *Inc.* magazine dubbed her "The Next Steve Jobs." Theranos continued to attract high-level investors and board members. As one employee said, Holmes had "this intense way of looking at you while she spoke that made you believe in her and want to follow her" (Carreyrou, 2018, p. 68).

As the company grew, Holmes expanded its senior staff, hiring Ramesh "Sunny" Balwani as executive vice-chairman. What Balwani's duties were wasn't clear, but from the get-go he inserted himself into every aspect of the company, "acting haughty and demeaning toward employees, barking orders, and dressing people down" (Carreyrou, 2018, p. 69). It wasn't widely known by employees at the time, but Holmes and Balwani were romantically involved and living together.

Theranos struggled in its efforts to develop the dreamed-of, and promised, blood-testing technology, but that didn't stop Holmes from developing partnerships with major companies, including drug retail giant Walgreens. Holmes told lies and half-truths and embellished details about the efficacy of Theranos's testing technology in order to convince partners to come on board. Walgreens signed on to have Theranos operate blood-testing centers in its pharmacies, opening 40 sites. Meanwhile, Theranos skirted rules and regulations to avoid oversight by the Food and Drug Administration of its procedures. The company did do blood testing using its device, called the Edison, but the results produced were often inaccurate, putting customers in danger.

During all this, Holmes traveled in private jets and had her own personal security detail, drivers, personal assistants, and a personal publicist who was on retainer for $25,000 a month. Theranos's company headquarters in Palo Alto, California, cost $1 million a month to rent and was furnished lavishly, including a $100,000 conference table (Bilton, 2019).

One of the company's greatest expenses, however, was legal fees. Theranos had as many as nine law firms on retainer, and the resulting legal fees were reported to have cost the company millions of dollars each month (Bilton, 2019). It was that team of high-powered lawyers that kept Theranos's dirty secrets from becoming public. There were plenty of people internally who tried to blow the whistle, but the company would retaliate with an intimidating barrage of lawsuits. Most employees who resigned or were fired were forced to sign binding confidentiality and nondisclosure agreements, barring them from discussing not only the company's technology, but its work culture as well.

One of those who did sound the alarm, Tyler Shultz, grandson of one of Holmes's biggest backers, George Shultz, paid a high price: Not only did he quit his job, but he and his grandfather, who doggedly defended Holmes and the company's promise, became estranged. Holmes attended George's 95th birthday party; Tyler did not.

Theranos's complicated structure of smoke and mirrors began collapsing in 2015 when *The Wall Street Journal*, owned by Theranos board member Rupert Murdoch's News Corporation, ran a story questioning the veracity of Theranos's lab results and the legitimacy of its core product, the Edison. The story revealed that the technology didn't work and that Theranos relied on third-party devices to administer its blood analysis tests. The fallout was enormous. The Securities and Exchange Commission (SEC), the Department of Justice, and the Federal Bureau of Investigation all began investigating Theranos. The company was sued by investors. Walgreens, its largest partner, terminated the relationship. *Forbes*, which once estimated Holmes's wealth at $4.5 billion, wrote it down to zero (Bilton, 2019).

The company, and Holmes, held on for two more years, with Holmes acting like nothing was wrong. Meanwhile, her employees were subpoenaed by the SEC and other government agencies. The company moved from its lavish headquarters to its laboratory facility in Newark, California, where employees, who were used to an in-house chef and all the latest conveniences, sat four to a table in a big open space. In December 2017, Holmes managed to secure a $100 million loan from an investment company, but months later, Holmes was charged with 11 criminal counts, including wire fraud and conspiracy. Theranos ceased operations in September 2018, and the investment company ended up getting all 90 of Theranos's patents. The other investors who had contributed $900 million to Theranos walked away with nothing. The employees of the doomed company lost more than just wages; many have had a difficult time securing new jobs with Theranos on their résumé (Bilton, 2019). It wasn't until 2022 that Holmes was finally tried on the criminal counts. She was convicted in November 2022 of four counts of defrauding investors and sentenced to 11 years and 3 months in prison, which she began serving in May 2023.

SUMMARY

This chapter is about destructive leadership, which is often thought of as "the dark side of leadership." In it, we describe the characteristics and underpinnings of destructive leadership using a model called the Toxic Triangle. This model differentiates three components of destructive leadership: destructive leaders, susceptible followers, and conducive environments. After analyzing what it is and why it occurs, we discuss practical ways to confront and nullify destructive leadership.

Destructive leadership involves the use of excessive control by leaders to force followers to achieve the leader's own goals without regard to the impact on others and the organization. Characteristically, destructive leaders demonstrate charisma, which they use to gain people's devotion and exploit followers for their own ends. Destructive leaders have intense needs for power, which they use for self-aggrandizement rather than for the common good. In addition, it is common for destructive leaders to be narcissistic, lacking empathy for others and dismissing others' concerns. They focus exclusively on their own goals even when these goals are unreasonable. Some have argued that leaders' negative or traumatic childhood experiences may be the origin or cause of their destructive leadership.

Destructive leadership does not occur in a vacuum; it occurs in situations where followers are susceptible. Some followers, called conformers, comply with destructive leaders to minimize the consequences of not going along. Others are colluders and comply because supporting the destructive leaders helps the followers achieve their own agendas. Psychological factors that help explain why followers become susceptible to destructive leadership include their needs for a reassuring authority figure, for security, to feel special, and to be a part of the human community; a fear of being ostracized; and feelings of powerlessness. Destructive leaders are able to capitalize on these needs to their own ends.

Some environments are especially conducive to destructive leadership. In unstable and crisis situations, followers want direction, and this need provides ripe opportunities for leaders to grab power and make decisions that are not for the common good. When situations are threatening, followers want to be taken care of and are more willing to give up their own agency to receive strong direction from a leader. Culturally, it is easier for destructive leaders to emerge when people have a high need to avoid uncertainty, when they emphasize collectivist causes over individuality, and when they are prone to accept power from the leader. Furthermore, situations without established rules that provide checks and balances are conducive to destructive leadership because safeguards to deter leaders from seizing power and acting destructively are lacking.

Though not easily accomplished, there are ways to combat destructive leadership. First, followers need to convince themselves that they are capable of confronting and handling life crises. They need to learn to address the psychological need they have to be accepted and taken care of by others, especially a leader.

Effective selection and development procedures in choosing employees or organization members can help weed out individuals prone to be abusive. Tests can be given to identify an individual's unwillingness to listen, low empathic ability, need for control, and narcissism. Organizations can promote and reinforce collaboration, employee initiative and involvement, and empowerment in the workplace while treating whistle-blowers with respect and encouraging them to identify abusive leaders.

Organizations can also establish norms, rules, and procedures that inhibit destructive leadership. Checks and balances require that leaders share power and accept monitoring of their use of power. Similarly, boards of directors, when given independence and oversight, make leaders accountable and less able to be abusive. Finally, organizations can establish strong ethical climates that support the values that make destructive leadership untenable.

KEY TERMS

checks and balances

colluders

conducive environments

conformers

destructive leadership

institutionalization

narcissism

Application

12.1 Case Study—Dr. Chen Likes Power

In the academic world, the old adage "publish or perish" has unmistakable meaning. This is especially so for Sophia Lopez, who has been an assistant professor in the school of pharmacy for several years and is currently up for promotion to associate professor with tenure.

Professor Lopez's department is headed up by Dr. Lilly Chen, a recognized scholar in medical and pharmaceutical research. Dr. Chen is known to get perks (e.g., a high-figure "consulting fee," a leased Lexus, and paid trips to conferences) from the pharma companies who give the school grants for research, which she uses her junior faculty and graduate students to conduct.

Dr. Chen has been at the university for 20 years and is widely known for her flamboyant and confident style. Besides her administrative duties, she has a busy travel schedule giving international presentations on drug discovery. Dr. Chen is a favorite of the university's upper administration because of her international reputation but also because she brings large government grants to the university for her research with pharmaceutical companies. As a result of these lucrative grants, Dr. Chen is known to have influence and power over university administrators and generally gets whatever she wants, and the administration looks the other way about the perks she gets from the pharma companies.

Dr. Chen's leadership within the school of pharmacy does not receive the same accolades. Although she is tolerated, Dr. Chen is not well liked among the school's faculty. As director of the school, she has the responsibility and power to set the school's mission and supervise its day-to-day operations, but when she carries out this work, she does so without regard for others' input. Faculty seldom say anything positive about Dr. Chen's administrative ability, often describing her as a leader who is driven, self-serving, and cavalier. Junior faculty are cautious around her and describe her as mean-spirited and authoritarian.

It is within this work environment that Sophia Lopez finds herself. Sophia is a single mom with two children who came to the United States from Mexico six years ago, having completed her doctoral degree with honors. She has a work visa that allows her to stay in the country, but the visa is reviewed annually. Any misstep in her employment situation could mean immediate deportation. Professionally, Sophia has worked very hard. She teaches a full load of classes each semester and also conducts research. She spends considerable time outside of class mentoring students, listening to their personal problems, and giving them support. Sophia has resisted the pressure to take part in Dr. Chen's research projects because she doesn't have time and it is not her area of specialty. Sophia has had three articles accepted for publication recently in clinical journals but not in the top-tier research journals. Annual teaching evaluations indicate that she is an average instructor.

For her upcoming annual review, Sophia needs a letter of support from Dr. Chen stating that Sophia's teaching and research meet the standards necessary for promotion. Sophia met with Dr. Chen to discuss the letter and to obtain her support, and although she was fearful about her meeting with the administrator, Sophia did not anticipate how threatening and overwhelming the meeting would actually be.

Regarding teaching, Dr. Chen said she expected everyone to be superior in the classroom and expressed disappointment in Sophia's average teaching evaluations, suggesting she devote more time to class preparations and improving her classroom teaching style. Sophia tried to defend herself and point out that she has a large teaching load (five classes) and is teaching more night classes than any other faculty. Dr. Chen dismissed her comments and told her to "quit whining." She also accused Sophia of spending too much time working at home instead of at the office, wondering if she was really working when at home or "just taking care of her kids and cleaning house."

Regarding Sophia's research, Dr. Chen was very frank, stating that she wanted her pharmacy school to be ranked in the top 10 nationally and that Sophia was "doing nothing" to help that ranking. Furthermore, Dr. Chen berated Sophia for her low productivity and called her "the weakest faculty member in the school." She pointed out that Sophia had only published three articles, none of which were cutting-edge scholarship. Dr. Chen reminded Sophia that when she was hired, she was given a sizeable startup grant to get her research off the ground, but Sophia accomplished little with these funds and made frequent excuses about her lack of time to publish articles on her research. Dr. Chen then wryly noted that the pharma company research projects she oversees have more credibility and are in higher-tier journals but that Sophia "seems to feel she is above working on that kind of research."

Needless to say, Sophia was devastated by Dr. Chen's review of her work. Dr. Chen seemed mean, heartless, and intimidating. Sophia likes the school of pharmacy and her colleagues but does not know how to make Dr. Chen recognize her value to the school. Sophia is also worried about her children and even more so about keeping her green card if Dr. Chen decides to let her go.

Questions

1. Destructive leaders often have charisma, needs for power, narcissism, negative life themes, and ideologies of hate. In what way does Dr. Chen exhibit these traits?

2. Have you personally ever had a boss who acted like Dr. Chen? What was it like, and how did you respond?

3. Table 12.1 lists six psychological factors that make followers susceptible to destructive leaders. Which three of these factors best help to explain Sophia Lopez's response to Dr. Chen? Discuss.

4. The Toxic Triangle suggests that destructive leadership comprises three components: destructive leaders, susceptible followers, and conducive environments. What role does each of these components play in this case, and how do these components interact to cause destructive leadership?

5. To guard against destructive leadership, institutions need rules and procedures that promote fairness for people at all levels of the organization. What rules and procedures would you establish for the pharmacy school in this case? How would these decrease the opportunity for leaders like Dr. Chen to be destructive toward others?

12.2 Case Study—Breaking the Silence

Harvey Weinstein was powerful, well connected, and wealthy. In 2011, he was named one of *Time* magazine's 100 Most Influential People in the World. Well known in the film industry, his name might not have been instantly recognizable to the average person, but that changed in 2017.

On the outside, Weinstein was a highly acclaimed film producer generously mentoring talented performers and launching them into stratospheric careers. He was a respected Hollywood gatekeeper, and garnering his favor meant entrance to an exclusive, lucrative industry and access to rare opportunities for career success.

The story, however, was somewhat different from the inside. Highly acclaimed? Definitely. Powerful, wealthy, and well connected? Most certainly. Respected? Yes, but the word *feared* came up just as often. Generous mentor? Not so much.

An article in *The New York Times* on October 5, 2017, threw open the shutters and revealed Weinstein's dark side. "Harvey Weinstein Paid Off Sexual Harassment Accusers for Decades" was the culmination of an investigation by journalists Jodi Kantor and Megan Twohey that revealed substantial allegations of sexual misconduct by Weinstein. The article outlined eight known settlements to effectively silence actresses and other female employees who had made sexual harassment claims against the media mogul. It was just the tip of the iceberg.

Weinstein and his brother, Bob, founded the Miramax film production company in 1979, which was a very successful venture, producing award-winning, blockbuster films. In 1993, Disney Productions purchased Miramax, infusing it with cash but leaving the Weinsteins in charge. Miramax had at least one Oscar-nominated film every year from 1992 until 2003 (Eltagouri et al., 2018). In 2005, Harvey and his brother left the company after a dispute with Disney and formed The Weinstein Company (TWC), a privately held production company of which the brothers had significant control through their ownership of 42% of the company's stock. As a condition of employment, TWC employees were required to sign nondisclosure agreements, binding them to a "code of silence"—they could not criticize the company or its leaders in a way that could harm their "business reputation" or "any employee's personal reputation" (Kantor & Twohey, 2017).

Under the Weinsteins' control, the working environments at both Miramax and TWC were considered unstable by many employees, with Harvey Weinstein described as a capricious leader. While reputed to be "charming and generous," showering those in his favor with gifts, cash, and personal or career assistance, Weinstein apparently had a "volcanic personality . . . given to fits of rage and personal (verbal) lashings of male and female employees alike" (Kantor & Twohey, 2017). Noting that the Weinstein brothers had a reputation for being ruthless in business dealings, employee Stuart Burkin, who started at TWC in 1991, said "'Miramax ran on fear. They're intimidating, they shout a lot, they foam at the mouth'" (Eltagouri et al., 2018).

But for actors and actresses, a meeting with Harvey Weinstein could open a world of possibilities, from lucrative scripts and acting roles to media coverage and endorsements. However, the price could be high. The *New York Times* article detailed allegations of decades of sexual harassment, coercion, and payoffs by Weinstein to actresses and female company employees, including actresses Ashley Judd and Rose McGowan, who divulged their experiences in the story. Many of the article's accounts were eerily similar, though very few of the women interviewed had ever met one another: A business meeting was arranged with Harvey Weinstein at either his office or a hotel restaurant, and the woman was to be greeted by an assistant, usually female, and told the meeting location had been changed to Mr. Weinstein's hotel suite, where the assistant would escort the woman and then abruptly leave. After that, Weinstein would try a variety of means to coerce or intimidate the women into sexual activities, including "appearing nearly or fully naked in front of them, requiring them to be present while he bathed or repeatedly asking for a massage or initiating one himself" (Kantor & Twohey, 2017).

The article set off a firestorm. Weinstein was dismissed as the head of TWC, and four members of the company's all-male board of directors resigned. And the allegations kept pouring in. The number of women coming forward to reveal their personal stories of Weinstein's conduct toward them multiplied quickly. Less than a week after *The New York Times* published its exposé, the *New Yorker* magazine published the findings of a 10-month investigation of its own by Pulitzer Prize–winning journalist Ronan Farrow. Thirteen more women, including actresses Rosanna Arquette and Mira Sorvino, shared their stories with *The New Yorker*, including allegations of rape and assault. The article highlighted what had been intimated by the victims and others involved: that Weinstein's behavior was common knowledge within the company and the entertainment industry.

> Sixteen former and current executives and assistants at Weinstein's companies told me that they witnessed or had knowledge of unwanted sexual advances and touching at events associated with Weinstein's films and in the workplace. They and others described a pattern of professional meetings that were little more than thin pretexts for sexual advances on young actresses and models. All 16 said that the behavior was widely known within both Miramax and the Weinstein Company. Messages sent by Irwin Reiter, a senior company executive, to Emily Nestor, one of the women who alleged that she was harassed, described the "mistreatment of women" as a serial problem that The Weinstein Company had been struggling with in recent years. Other employees described what was, in essence, a culture of complicity at Weinstein's places of business, with numerous people throughout his companies fully aware of his behavior but either abetting it or looking the other way. Some employees said that they were enlisted in a subterfuge to make the victims feel safe. A female executive with the company described how Weinstein's assistants and others served as a "honeypot"—they would initially join a meeting along with a woman Weinstein was interested in, but then Weinstein would dismiss them, leaving him alone with the woman. (Farrow, 2017a)

It wasn't only TWC employees who were aware of the behavior. For years there had been subtle public clues in comments by members of the entertainment industry including by late-night talk-show and Oscar hosts. As the stories continued to break regarding Weinstein, industry insiders began to come forward, confirming that Weinstein's misconduct was well known. Acclaimed filmmaker Quentin Tarantino, who collaborated with Weinstein on some of his biggest box office hits, shared that he had long been aware of Weinstein's misconduct, revealing that "I knew enough to do more than I did" (BBC, 2019).

Retaliation and fear of reprisal played a significant role in the perpetuation and concealment of Weinstein's activities. Those who resisted his advances contend that their careers were stalled or damaged by the long reach of Weinstein's network. Often, derogatory stories regarding their personal lives would suddenly begin appearing in the media. Farrow (2017a) shared the following:

> Virtually all of the people I spoke with told me that they were frightened of retaliation. "If Harvey were to discover my identity, I'm worried that he could ruin my life," one former employee told me. Many said that they had seen Weinstein's associates confront and intimidate those who crossed him and feared that they would be similarly targeted. Four actresses, including Mira Sorvino and Rosanna Arquette, told me they suspected that, after they rejected Weinstein's advances or complained about them to company representatives, Weinstein had them removed from projects or dissuaded people from hiring them. Multiple sources said that Weinstein frequently bragged about planting items in media outlets about those who spoke against him; these sources feared similar retribution.

In November 2017, Farrow's article "Harvey Weinstein's Army of Spies" appeared in *The New Yorker*, detailing how Weinstein had hired high-powered private security agencies and investigative journalists to collect information on the women and other journalists trying to expose the allegations against him. The agencies' intimidating tactics included stalking, using false names, misrepresenting themselves as journalists, and recording conversations without permission. Weinstein channeled the hiring and payment of these agencies and journalists through a legal firm in order to conceal and protect their work under the auspices of client privilege. Weinstein, however, personally monitored the investigations. Included in the service agreements with the agencies were "success fees" such as a $300,000 bonus if the agency provided information that "directly contributes to the efforts to completely stop the article from being published at all in any shape or form" (Farrow, 2017b).

More than 100 women have come forward with stories of sexual assault and harassment by Weinstein, with at least 19 of them accusing the media mogul of rape. Many of these actors are renown in the film industry, including Kate Beckinsale, Daryl Hannah, Heather Graham, Angelina Jolie, Julianna Margulies, Gwyneth Paltrow, Lupita Nyong'o, Monica Potter, Sean Young, and Uma Thurman (Moniuszko & Kelly, 2017).

Exposure of Weinstein's behavior and the magnitude of the accusations against him has had far-reaching consequences and resulted in several lawsuits against Weinstein and his company. In March 2018, in an effort to protect itself from the possible financial devastation of the pending lawsuits, TWC filed for bankruptcy protection. Through this filing, the company released victims of and witnesses to Weinstein's alleged misconduct from their signed nondisclosure agreements. "Since October, it has been reported that Harvey Weinstein used non-disclosure agreements as a secret weapon to silence his accusers. Effective immediately, those 'agreements' end," the company said in a statement. "No one should be afraid to speak out or coerced to stay quiet" (Associated Press, 2018).

Weinstein was subsequently arrested and indicted on criminal charges of rape and sexual abuse. Many of the prominent associations he had affiliation with or had garnered honors from rescinded the awards and memberships, most notably the Academy of Motion Picture Arts and Sciences (the organization behind the Academy Awards).

But the impact of Weinstein's downfall was felt far beyond Hollywood. As the list of accusers grew, it helped to ignite an explosive international movement against sexual harassment through the #MeToo hashtag campaign, which encouraged others to share their personal stories via social media. Dubbed the "Weinstein Effect," it opened the floodgates, and a torrent of allegations across industries and the globe resulted in the dismissal of several prominent business and political figures. In April 2018, *The New York Times* and *The New Yorker* were awarded the Pulitzer Prize for Public Service "for their coverage of the sexual abuse of women in Hollywood and other industries around the world."

In 2020, Weinstein was convicted of rape and assault charges in New York and sentenced to 24 years in prison. In 2022, the 70-year-old was charged with rape and indecent assault in a 2013 case in Los Angeles and in February 2023 found guilty and sentenced to 16 additional years.

Questions

1. The book lists three characteristics of destructive power. Discuss how each of these does or does not apply to this case.

2. The chapter discusses a model known as the Toxic Triangle, which outlines three key components that work together to make toxic leadership possible.

   a. Destructive leaders: The text lists three characteristics of a destructive leader. Discuss how each one applies to Harvey Weinstein and provide examples.

   b. Susceptible followers: A key component in enabling destructive leadership to take hold, the Toxic Triangle model discusses two categories of followers: conformers and colluders.

      i. Based on the model's definition, whom would you classify as conformers in this case? Why?

      ii. Whom would you classify as colluders? Why?

      iii. Do you think a follower of a destructive leader can be both a conformer and a colluder? Explain.

   c. Conducive environments, or the context that promotes the development of destructive leadership and includes the following four factors: Discuss how each of these factors contributed to the toxic environments of Miramax and TWC under the leadership of Harvey Weinstein.

      i. Instability

      ii. Perceived threat

      iii. Certain cultural values

         a. High avoidance of uncertainty

         b. Collectivism

         c. High power distance

      iv. Absence of checks and balances and institutionalization

3. The chapter lists the following factors that make humans susceptible to bad leadership. How does each of these apply or not apply to the followers in the case?
   a. A need for reassuring authority figures
   b. Our need for security and certainty
   c. A need to feel chosen or special
   d. Our need for membership in the human community
   e. Fear of ostracism, isolation, and social death
   f. Fear of powerlessness to challenge a bad leader

4. The text discusses various ways in which destructive leadership can be confronted and avoided in practice by leaders, followers, and context. For decades, Harvey Weinstein's unscrupulous practices were known by many but were not stopped.
   a. How was Weinstein able to thwart challenges to his behavior?
   b. Within the structure of the organization he created, do you see ways in which this behavior could have been confronted and dealt with much sooner than it was?
   c. What do you think it took to finally expose these behaviors and bring about change?

12.3 Abusive Leadership Questionnaire*

Purpose

1. To gain an understanding of the dimensions of destructive leadership
2. To obtain an assessment of your own destructive leadership tendencies

Directions

1. Make five copies of this questionnaire. It should be completed by you and five people you know (e.g., roommates, coworkers, relatives, friends).
2. For each of the 15 statements, use the following key to indicate the frequency with which you think this individual engages in the leadership behavior listed. Do not forget to complete this exercise for yourself as the leader.

Key:

1. I cannot see them ever using this behavior with others.
2. They very seldom use this behavior with others.
3. They occasionally use this behavior with others.
4. They use this behavior moderately often with others.
5. They use this behavior very often with others.

When _____ is the leader/supervisor, followers would say the following about their leadership:

Score Statements

	Never	Seldom	Occasionally	Often	Very Often
1. Ridicules others	1	2	3	4	5
2. Tells others their thoughts and feelings are stupid	1	2	3	4	5
3. Gives others the silent treatment	1	2	3	4	5
4. Puts people down in front of others	1	2	3	4	5
5. Invades the privacy of others	1	2	3	4	5

	Never	Seldom	Occasionally	Often	Very Often
6. Reminds others of past mistakes and failures	1	2	3	4	5
7. Doesn't give others credit for work that required a lot of effort	1	2	3	4	5
8. Blames others to save their own embarrassment	1	2	3	4	5
9. Breaks promises they make	1	2	3	4	5
10. Expresses anger at others when they are mad for another reason	1	2	3	4	5
11. Makes negative comments about people to others	1	2	3	4	5
12. Is rude to others	1	2	3	4	5
13. Does not allow others to interact with their coworkers	1	2	3	4	5
14. Tells others they are incompetent	1	2	3	4	5
15. Lies to others	1	2	3	4	5

Source: Tepper, B. J. (2000). Consequences of abusive supervision. *Academy of Management Journal, 43*(2), 178–190

Scoring

1. Enter the responses for Raters 1, 2, 3, 4, and 5 in the appropriate columns on the following scoring sheet. An example of a completed chart is provided in Example 12.1 below.
2. For each of the 15 items, compute the average for the five raters and place that number in the "average rating" column.
3. Place your own scores in the "self-rating" column.

Abusive Leadership Questionnaire Chart

	Rater 1	Rater 2	Rater 3	Rater 4	Rater 5	Average rating	Self-rating
1. Ridicules others							
2. Tells others their thoughts and feelings are stupid							
3. Gives others the silent treatment							
4. Puts people down in front of others							
5. Invades the privacy of others							
6. Reminds others of past mistakes and failures							
7. Doesn't give others credit for work that required a lot of effort							
8. Blames others to save their own embarrassment							
9. Breaks promises they make							
10. Expresses anger at others when they are mad for another reason							

	Rater 1	Rater 2	Rater 3	Rater 4	Rater 5	Average rating	Self-rating
11. Makes negative comments about people to others							
12. Is rude to others							
13. Does not allow others to interact with their coworkers							
14. Tells others they are incompetent							
15. Lies to others							

Scoring Interpretation

The scores you received on this questionnaire provide information about how you see yourself and how others see you as a leader. Specifically, the purpose of the instrument is to assess your tendencies to show aspects of destructive leadership. The higher your average score is on a particular behavior, the more you have a tendency to engage in this potentially destructive behavior with others. The chart allows you to compare your perceptions of yourself as a leader with the perceptions of others, especially in regard to behaviors that have the potential to be destructive. While it can be confirming when others see you in the same way as you see yourself, it is also beneficial to explore the observations of others that differ from your self-rating. None of us wants to consider ourselves a destructive leader, but sometimes we are unaware how certain behaviors by us toward others have potentially damaging effects. This assessment can help you learn of and understand the areas in which you are consistently doing the "right things" as well as areas in which you may seek to improve.

Example 12.1 Abusive Leadership Questionnaire Ratings

	Rater 1	Rater 2	Rater 3	Rater 4	Rater 5	Average rating	Self-rating
1. Ridicules others	3	2	2	2	2	2.8	1
2. Tells others their thoughts and feelings are stupid	1	1	1	1	1	1	1

	Rater 1	Rater 2	Rater 3	Rater 4	Rater 5	Average rating	Self-rating
3. Gives others the silent treatment	2	3	3	3	3	2.8	1
4. Puts people down in front of others	1	2	2	3	2	2	2
5. Invades the privacy of others	1	2	1	1	1	1.2	2
6. Reminds others of past mistakes and failures	3	2	2	2	1	2	1
7. Doesn't give others credit for jobs requiring a lot of effort	3	3	4	3	2	3	3
8. Blames others to save they own embarrassment	2	2	2	1	3	2	4
9. Breaks promises they make	4	3	4	4	5	4	2
10. Expresses anger at others when they are mad for another reason	3	3	4	3	2	3	5
11. Makes negative comments about people to others	3	3	4	4	3	3.4	1
12. Is rude to others	1	1	1	1	1	1	1
13. Does not allow others to interact with their coworkers	2	2	2	2	2	2	2
14. Tells others they are incompetent	2	3	3	4	3	3	1
15. Lies to others	1	2	2	1	2	1.8	4

Summary and interpretation: The scorer's self-ratings are higher (i.e., worse) than the average ratings of others on 1, 3, 6, 9, 11, and 14. The scorer's self-ratings are lower (i.e., better) than the average ratings of others on 5, 8, 10, and 15. The scorer's self-ratings on 2, 4, 7, 12, and 13 are the same as the average ratings of others.

12.4 Observational Exercise—Destructive Leadership

Purpose

1. To learn to identify characteristics of destructive leaders
2. To develop an understanding of how followers and context contribute to destructive leadership

Directions

1. For this exercise, you will observe a functioning leader and assess that person's tendencies to be destructive in how they treat followers. This leader can be a supervisor, a manager, a coach, a teacher, a fraternity or sorority officer, or anyone who has a position that involves leadership. You will also observe and take notes on the followers and the situation.
2. On a sheet of paper, briefly describe as completely as possible (1) the way the leader treated followers, (2) the way followers responded to the leader, and (3) the implied communication norms and rules that seemed to be operating in the situation.

Questions

1. Using the Toxic Triangle illustrated in Figure 12.1, draw a sketch that briefly highlights the leader's characteristics, the followers' responses, and the nature of the situation.

2. Identify one characteristic about this leader that made you feel uncomfortable. Could that characteristic lead to destructive leadership if not corrected? Discuss.

3. From your vantage point, how would you describe the way followers responded to the leader? Did followers act overly dependent in any way toward the leader? Do you think these followers would be susceptible to the leader unfairly dominating them? Discuss.

4. If you were asked to be a consultant to this group or organization, describe three specific changes you would make to lessen the possibility that destructive leadership could thrive in this situation.

Application

12.5 Reflection and Action Worksheet—Destructive Leadership

Reflection

1. As described in this chapter, destructive leaders are charismatic, are narcissistic, like power, and often have had some type of traumatic childhood experience. Of these characteristics, are there one or two that you may possess that might make you vulnerable to being a destructive leader? Describe those and discuss.

2. This chapter emphasizes that followers play a role in the emergence of destructive leaders. As you reflect on your own psychological needs, describe how your behavior in groups could contribute to giving a leader the opportunity to be destructive toward followers.

3. Think for a moment about a situation where you were part of a group or an organization (work, club, volunteer project, etc.). What were the communication rules and procedures in this context? Was the amount of influence and power the leader had clearly spelled out? Did you and other group members feel free to challenge the leader's actions? How would you describe your leader–follower relationship? Do you think you are or were vulnerable to being unfairly treated by this leader? Discuss.

Action

1. Of the 15 behaviors (e.g., ridicules others, gives others the silent treatment) mentioned in the Abusive Leadership Questionnaire, select 4 you could address to improve your leadership. Explain.

2. The practice section of this chapter describes several ways to confront destructive leaders. None of them are easy. The next time you are in a context where a leader is acting destructively toward followers, what will you do to stop the abuse? Discuss.

3. Focusing on Lipman-Blumen's (2005) psychological factors of susceptible followers (Table 12.1), discuss specifically how you could become a stronger follower and less susceptible to destructive leadership.

GLOSSARY OF KEY TERMS

ability: a natural or acquired capacity to perform a particular activity

accommodation: an unassertive but cooperative conflict style that requires individuals to attend very closely to the needs of others and ignore their own needs

actions: the ways one goes about accomplishing goals

adaptive leadership: examines how leaders help people address problems, face challenges, and adapt to change

adjourning stage: last stage in group development when the goals of a group have been fulfilled or the allotted time has run out and the members begin considering the implications of ending the group

administrative skills: competencies a leader needs to run an organization in order to carry out the organization's purposes and goals

approach: a general way of thinking about a phenomenon, not necessarily based on empirical research

assimilation: the process whereby those from different cultures were expected to adapt to and, in many cases, adopt the customs of the majority group

authentic leadership: looks at the authenticity of leaders and their leadership

authoritarian leadership style: a style of leadership in which leaders perceive followers as needing direction and need to control followers and what they do

avoidance: a conflict style that is both unassertive and uncooperative, and characterized by individuals being passive and ignoring conflict situations rather than confronting them directly

belonging: a positive feeling one experiences as a result of feeling welcomed and accepted as part of a group

"Big Five" personality factors: broad categories of personality traits (openness, conscientiousness, extroversion, agreeableness, and neuroticism)

challenge: to stimulate people to commit themselves to change

change: a move toward something different; a shift away from the way things currently are

character: one's qualities, disposition, and core values

charisma: magnetic charm and appeal; a special personality characteristic that gives people the capacity to do extraordinary things

charismatic leadership: a special gift that some people possess, that gives them the capacity to have an extraordinary impact on followers

checks and balances: the way power and influence are shared in an organizational system so that when power is invested in one part of the system it is counterbalanced with power invested in other parts of the system

cohesiveness: a sense of "we-ness"; the cement that holds a group together, or the esprit de corps that exists within a group

collaboration: a conflict style that requires both assertiveness and cooperation and occurs when both parties agree to a positive settlement to the conflict and attend fully to the other's concerns while not sacrificing or suppressing their own

colluders: followers who comply with destructive leaders because the leader's agenda may benefit their own and they hope to get something out of it

competition: a conflict style of individuals who are highly assertive about pursuing their own goals but uncooperative in assisting others to reach their goals

compromise: a conflict style that involves both a degree of assertiveness and a degree of cooperativeness

conceptual skills: capabilities that involve working with concepts and ideas, the thinking or cognitive aspects of leadership

concern for people: refers to how a leader attends to the people in the organization who are trying to achieve its goals

concern for production: refers to how a leader is concerned with achieving organizational goals

conducive environments: unique environments that are fertile for and promotive of the development of destructive leadership

confidence: feeling positive about oneself and one's ability to succeed

conflict: a felt struggle between two or more interdependent individuals over perceived incompatible differences in beliefs, values, and goals, or over differences in desires for esteem, control, and connectedness

conflict style: a patterned response or behavior that people use when approaching conflict

conformers: followers who comply with destructive leaders to minimize the consequences for themselves of not going along with the leader's agenda

connective leadership: focuses on how leaders can work with followers in ways that affirm followers' distinct identity and embrace their diversity

consideration behavior: a relationship leadership behavior in which the leader creates camaraderie, respect, trust, and regard with followers

constructive climate: a positive atmosphere that makes people want to attend and participate in the group

constructive feedback: honest and direct communication about a group member's performance

content conflict: involves struggles between leaders and others who differ on issues such as policies and procedures

content dimension: involves the objective, observable aspects of communication

contingency theory: a leadership theory that focuses on the match between the leader's style and specific situational variables

dark side of leadership: the destructive side of leadership where a leader uses their influence or power for personal ends

democratic leadership style: a style of leadership in which leaders treat followers as fully capable of doing work on their own and work with followers, trying hard to treat everyone fairly, without putting themselves above followers

destructive leadership: the process whereby an individual exercises excessive control and coercion to force a group of individuals to accomplish the leader's own goals without regard to the impact on others or the organization

determination: being focused and attentive to tasks; showing initiative, persistence, and drive

differentiation: an interaction process that occurs in the early phase of conflict that helps participants define the nature of the conflict and clarify their positions with regard to each other

diversity: variety or difference

emotional intelligence: concerned with a person's ability to understand their own and others' emotions, and then to apply this understanding to life's tasks; the ability to perceive and express emotions, to use emotions to facilitate thinking, to understand and reason with emotions, and to manage emotions effectively within oneself and in relationships with others

employee orientation: a relationship leadership behavior in which the leader takes an interest in workers as human beings, values their uniqueness, and gives special attention to their personal needs

end values: the outcomes or goals a leader seeks to achieve

equity: refers to treating people with justice and fairness; includes being concerned with whether people have the opportunities and resources to succeed and thrive

ethical leadership: examines a leader's character, duties, decision making, and decision outcomes

ethical values: concerned with the character or virtuousness of the leader

ethnocentrism: the tendency for individuals to place their own group (ethnic, racial, or cultural) at the center of their observations of others and the world

face saving: communicative attempts to establish or maintain one's self-image or another's self-image in response to threat

forming stage: the orientation phase when individuals spend time assessing their purpose for joining the group, attempt to figure out whether they fit into the group, and discover what is appropriate and acceptable behavior within the group

fractionation: the technique of breaking down large conflicts into smaller, more manageable pieces

Gallup: a public opinion research organization that conducts political polling and research in other areas of the social sciences

gender-based studies: studies that view how one's gender affects and differentiates one's leadership

goals: the aims or outcomes an individual seeks to achieve

"Great Man" theories: early trait theories of leadership that focused on identifying the innate qualities and characteristics possessed by great social, political, and military leaders (see also *trait approach*)

group: a set of three or more individuals who are in some way interdependent and mutually influence one another in an effort to achieve a common goal

group-building and maintenance roles: roles that promote cohesiveness among members and enhance their ability to work together as a group

group task roles: members' roles that contribute to the group's ability to perform its task

honesty: telling the truth and representing reality as fully and completely as possible

inclusion: the process of incorporating differing individuals into a group or an organization

individual roles: used by group members to satisfy their own needs, desires, and agendas; generally nonfunctional and unhelpful to the group

initiating structure: task leadership in which the leader organizes work, defines role responsibilities, and schedules work activities

institutionalization: concerned with making rules and regulations in an organization and methods for altering them

integrity: adhering to a strong set of principles and taking responsibility for one's actions; being honest and trustworthy

intelligence: having good language skills, perceptual skills, and reasoning ability

interpersonal skills: people skills; those abilities that help a leader to work effectively with followers, peers, and higher-ups to accomplish the organization's goals

laissez-faire leadership style: a style of leadership, sometimes labeled nonleadership, in which leaders ignore workers and their work motivations and engage in minimal influence

leader–member exchange (LMX) theory: focuses on the quality of leader–follower relationships

leadership: a process whereby an individual influences a

group of individuals to achieve a common goal

leadership style: the behaviors of leaders, focusing on what leaders do and how they act

learned behaviors: actions or behaviors people acquire through experience; ingrained things they come to understand throughout their life

map: a laid-out path to follow to direct people toward their short- and long-term goals

melting pot: a metaphor for a blending of many into one, or a heterogeneous society becoming homogeneous

modal values: values that are concerned with the means or actions a leader takes

multiculturalism: the presence of, or support for the presence of, several distinct cultural or ethnic groups within a society

narcissism: to be excessively enamored with and preoccupied with one's self

norming stage: third stage in group development where group cohesion develops as members begin feeling connected to one another

norms: the rules of behavior that are established and shared by group members

out-group members: individuals in a group or an organization who do not identify themselves as part of the larger group, and who are disconnected and not fully engaged in working toward the goals of the group

path–goal theory: a leadership theory that examines how

leaders use employee motivation to enhance performance and satisfaction

performing stage: fourth stage of group development where members now perform the work they have set out to do

personal style: unique habits regarding work and play, which have been ingrained over many years and influence one's current style

philosophy of leadership: a unique set of beliefs and attitudes about the nature of people and the nature of work that have a significant impact on an individual's leadership style

picture: an ideal image of where a group or an organization should be going

pluralism: the recognition that people of different cultures do not need to sacrifice their own traditions and values to become a part of one society

positive psychology: the scientific study of what makes life most worth living

power: the capacity to influence or affect others

prejudice: a largely fixed attitude, belief, or emotion held by an individual about another individual or group that is based on faulty or unsubstantiated data

principled negotiation: an approach to conflict that decides issues on their merits rather than through competitive haggling or through excessive accommodation

privilege: an advantage held by a person or group that is based on age, race, ethnicity, gender, class, or some other cultural

dimension, which gives those who have it power over those who don't

problem-solving skills: one's cognitive ability to take corrective action in a problem situation in order to meet desired objectives

process groups: groups whose communication style focuses on group members, how they are related, and how they communicate with one another

production orientation: task leadership in which the leader stresses the production and technical aspects of the job

realized strengths: personal attributes that represent our strongest assets

relational approach: an approach to leadership, defined as a relationship, in which the leader affects and is affected by followers, and both leader and followers are affected in turn by the situation that surrounds them

relational conflict: refers to the differences we feel between ourselves and others concerning how we relate to each other

relationship (process) behaviors: behaviors used by leaders that help group members feel comfortable with themselves, with each other, and with the situation in which they find themselves

relationship dimension: refers to the participants' perceptions of their connection to one another

relationship-oriented leadership: leadership that is focused primarily on the well-being of

followers, how they relate to each other, and the atmosphere in which they work

servant leadership: emphasizes the "caring principle" with leaders as "servants" who focus on their followers' needs in order to help these followers become more autonomous, knowledgeable, and like servants themselves

situational approach: an approach to leadership research based on the premise that different situations demand different kinds of leadership

skill: a competency developed to accomplish a task effectively

sociability: capability of establishing pleasant social relationships; being sensitive to others' needs and concerned for their well-being

social identities: the parts of our self-concept that come from our group memberships

social perceptiveness: having insight into and awareness of what is important to others, how they are motivated, the problems they face, and how they react to change

spiritual leadership: considers how leaders use values, a sense of "calling," and membership to motivate followers

standards of excellence: the expressed and implied expectations for performance that exist within a group or an organization

status quo: the current situation; the way things are now

stereotype: a generalized belief that everyone in a group shares the same qualities or characteristics

storming stage: the second stage of group development, also called the "conflict phase" where members become less interested in inclusion issues, such as how they fit into the group, and more interested in control issues, such as how they influence the group

strategic planning: a conceptual skill, the cognitive ability to think and consider ideas to develop effective strategies for a group or an organization

strengths: attributes or qualities of an individual that account for successful performance; positive features of ourselves that make us effective and help us flourish

structure: a blueprint for the work of a particular group that gives form and meaning to the purposes of its activities

synergy: the group energy created from two or more people working together, which creates an outcome that is different from and better than the sum of the individual contributions

systemic discrimination: occurs when patterns of discriminatory behavior, policies, or practices become a part of an organization and continue to perpetuate disadvantage to those being discriminated against

task behaviors: behaviors used by leaders to get the job done

task groups: focus most of their efforts on substantive content issues such as identifying and meeting the goals of the group, the business or work that the group needs to accomplish, or the procedures the group will follow

task-oriented leadership: leadership that is focused predominantly on procedures, activities, and goal accomplishments

technical competence: having specialized knowledge about the work we do or ask others to do

themes of human talent: relatively stable, fixed characteristics—similar to personality traits—that are not easily changed

theory: includes a set of hypotheses, principles, or laws that explain a given phenomenon

Theory X: a general theory created by Douglas McGregor in which leaders assume that people dislike work, that they need to be directed and controlled, and that they want security—not responsibility

Theory Y: a general theory created by Douglas McGregor in which leaders assume that people like work, that they are self-motivated, and that they accept and seek responsibility

Theory Z: a leadership theory tangentially related to Theory X and Theory Y, developed by William Ouchi, that

emphasizes common cultural values, beliefs, and objectives among its members with a focus on communication, collaboration, and consensual decision making

trait: a distinguishing personal quality that is often inherited (e.g., intelligence, confidence, charisma, determination, sociability, or integrity)

trait approach: an approach to leadership research that focuses on identifying the innate qualities and characteristics possessed by individuals (see also *"Great Man" theories*)

transformational leadership theory: a theory that describes leadership as a process that changes people and organizations

unconscious bias: used to describe when we have attitudes toward people or associate stereotypes with them without our conscious knowledge that we are doing so

unrealized strengths: personal attributes that are less visible

values: the ideas, beliefs, and modes of action that people find worthwhile or desirable

vision: a mental model of an ideal future state

weaknesses: limiting attributes that often drain our energy and result in poor performance

REFERENCES

Chapter 1

Allyn, B. (2019, May 20). *Top reason for CEO departures among largest companies is now misconduct, study finds.* National Public Radio. https://tinyurl.com/2rk23u77

Antonakis, J., Cianciolo, A. T., & Sternberg, R. J. (Eds.). (2004). *The nature of leadership.* Sage.

Barnard, C. (1938). *The functions of the executive.* Harvard University Press.

Bass, B. M. (1985). *Leadership and performance beyond expectations.* Free Press.

Bass, B. M. (1990). *Bass and Stogdill's handbook of leadership: A survey of theory and research.* Free Press.

Charity: Water. (2023). *Meet the founder.* https://www.charitywater.org/about/scott-harrison-story

Clifford, C. (2018, March 22). *How Charity: Water's founder went from hard-partying NYC club promoter to helping 8 million people around the world.* CNBC. https://www.cnbc.com/2018/03/22/how-scott-harrison-founded-charity-water.html

Conger, J. (1990). The dark side of leadership. *Organizational Dynamics, 19*(2), 44–55.

Conger, J. A., & Riggio, R. E. (Eds.). (2007). *The practice of leadership: Developing the next generation of leaders.* Jossey-Bass.

Curtin, J. L. (2022). *700 definitions and ways to lead.* Archway.

Fields, J. (2018, September 24). *Charity: Water founder on hedonism, redemption, and service. Good Life Project.* https://www.goodlifeproject.com/podcast/scott-harrison-charity-water/

Graen, G. B., & Uhl-Bien, M. (1995). Relationship-based approach to leadership: Development and leader–member exchange (LMX) theory of leadership over 25 years: Applying a multi-level multi-domain perspective. *Leadership Quarterly, 6,* 219–247. http://dx.doi.org/10.1016/1048-9843(95)90036-5

Hersey, P., & Blanchard, K. H. (1969). Life-cycle theory of leadership. *Training and Development Journal, 23*(5), 26–34.

House, R. J., Hanges, P. J., Javidan, M., Dorfman, P. W., & Gupta, V. (2004). *Culture, leadership, and organizations: The GLOBE study of 62 societies.* Sage.

Komives, S. R., Lucas, N., & McMahon, T. R. (2013). *Exploring leadership: For college students who want to make a difference* (3rd ed.). Wiley.

Komives, S. R., Wagner, W., & Associates. (Eds.). (2016). *Leadership for a better world: Understanding the social change model of leadership* (2nd ed.). Jossey-Bass.

Lipman-Blumen, J. (2000). *Connective leadership: Managing in a changing world.* Oxford University Press.

Lipman-Blumen, J. (2005). *The allure of toxic leaders.* Oxford University Press.

Modaff, D. P., Butler, J. A., & DeWine, S. (2017). *Organizational communication: Foundations, challenge, and misunderstandings* (4th ed.). Pearson.

Northouse, P. (2019). *Leadership: Theory and practice* (8th ed.). Sage.

Obama, M. (2022). *The light we carry: Overcoming in uncertain times.* Crown.

Obama, M. (2018). *Becoming.* Crown.

Obama, M. (2017, January 6). *Remarks by the First Lady at the National School Counselor of the Year event.* White House Office of the First Lady. https://obamawhitehouse.archives.gov/the-press-office/2017/01/06/remarks-first-lady-national-school-counselor-year-event

Reddin, W. J. (1967, April). The 3-D management style theory. *Training and Development Journal,* 8–17.

Rost, J. C. (1991). *Leadership for the twenty-first century.* Praeger.

Urban Farming Guys. (2023). *About.* http://theurbanfarmingguys.com/about

Vecchio, R. P. (1987). Situational leadership theory: An examination of a prescriptive theory. *Journal of Applied Psychology, 72*(3), 444–451.

White House Historical Association. (2018). *Michelle Obama.* https://www.whitehousehistory.org/bios/michelle-obama

Chapter 2

Addison, P. (2005). *Churchill: The unexpected hero.* Oxford University Press.

Antonakis, J., Cianciolo, A. T., & Sternberg, R. J. (Eds.). (2004). *The nature of leadership.* Sage.

Asmal, K., Chidester, D., & Wilmot, J. (2003). *Nelson Mandela: In his own words.* Little, Brown.

Bass, B. M. (1990). *Bass and Stogdill's handbook of leadership: A survey of theory and research.* Free Press.

Bruni, F. (2002). *Ambling into history: The unlikely odyssey of George W. Bush.* HarperCollins.

Clinton, C. (2004). *Harriet Tubman: The road to freedom.* Little, Brown.

Clinton, W. J. (2004). *My life.* Knopf.

Clinton, W. J. (2003). Foreword. In K. Asmal, D. Chidester, & J. Wilmot (Eds.), *Nelson Mandela: In his own words* (pp. xv–xvi). Little, Brown.

Conger, J. A. (1999). Charismatic and transformational leadership in organizations: An insider's perspective on these developing streams of research. *Leadership Quarterly, 10*(2), 145–170.

Coombs, D. S., & Cassilo, D. (2017). Athletes and/or activists: LeBron James and Black Lives Matter. *Journal of Sport and Social Issues, 41*(5), 425–444.

Curtis, N. (2016). *Better than new: Lessons I've learned from saving old homes (and how they saved me).* Artisan.

The Editors of Life Magazine. (2008). *The American journey of Barack Obama.* Little, Brown.

ESPN. (2019, March 10). *LeBron James: Stats.* http://www.espn.com/nba/player/stats/_/id/1966/lebron-james

Evans, K. D. (2017, April 18). *LeBron James Family Foundation and Akron Public Schools establish the I PROMISE School.* https://theundefeated.com/features/lebron-james-family-foundation-akron-public-schools-i-promise-school/

Gonzalez-Balado, J. L. (1997). *Mother Teresa: Her life, her work, her message.* Liguori.

Green, M. A. (2017, October 17). LeBron James is the greatest living athlete (and here's why). *GQ.* https://www.gq.com/story/lebron-james-greatest-living-athlete

Harris, J., & Watson, E (Eds.). (2007). *The Oprah phenomenon.* The University Press of Kentucky.

Hayward, S. F. (1997). *Churchill on leadership: Executive success in the face of adversity.* Prima.

House, R. J. (1976). A 1976 theory of charismatic leadership. In J. G. Hunt & L. L. Larson (Eds.), *Leadership: The cutting edge* (pp. 189–207). Southern Illinois University Press.

House, R. J., Hanges, P. J., Javidan, M., Dorfman, P. W., & Gupta, V. (2004). *Leadership, culture, and organizations: The GLOBE study of 62 societies.* Sage.

Illouz, E. (2003). *Oprah Winfrey and the glamour of misery.* Columbia University Press.

Judge, T. A., Bono, J. E., Ilies, R., & Gerhardt, M. W. (2002). Personality and leadership: A qualitative and quantitative review. *Journal of Applied Psychology, 87*(4), 765–780.

LeBron James Family Foundation. (2018, June 26). *The kids from Akron.* Facebook. https://www.facebook.com/LeBronJamesFamilyFoundation/

Keegan, J. (2002). *Winston Churchill.* Viking.

Kirkpatrick, S. A., & Locke, E. A. (1991). Leadership: Do traits matter? *The Executive, 5*(2), 48–60.

Life Books. (2008). *The American journey of Barack Obama.* Little, Brown.

Lyman, E. J. (2016). Mother Teresa declared a saint by Pope Francis. *USA Today.* http://www.usatoday.com

McDonald, K. B. (2007). *Embracing sisterhood: Class, identity, and contemporary Black women.* Rowman & Littlefield.

Meacham, J. (2008, August 22). What Barack Obama learned from his father. *Newsweek.* https://www.newsweek.com/

National Institute of Allergy and Infectious Diseases.

(2023, January 5). *Anthony S. Fauci, M.D., former NIAID director.* https://www.niaid.nih.gov/about/director

Nelson, M. (n.d.). *Barack Obama: Life before the presidency.* Miller Center, University of Virginia. https://www.millercenter.org/president/obama/life-before-the-presidency

Osterman, M. J. K., & Martin, J. A. (2018, May 30). The timing and adequacy of prenatal care in the United States, 2016. *National Vital Statistics Reports, 67*(3). https://www.cdc.gov/nchs/data/nvsr/nvsr67/nvsr67_03.pdf

Ott, T. (2020, May 12). *Anthony Fauci biography.* https://www.biography.com/scientist/anthony-fauci

Remnick, D. (2010). *The bridge: The life and times of Barack Obama.* Knopf.

Riley, R. L. (n.d.). *Bill Clinton: Life before the presidency.* Miller Center, University of Virginia. https://millercenter.org/president/clinton/life-before-the-presidency

Sandys, C., & Littman, J. (2003). *We shall not fail: The inspiring leadership of Winston Churchill.* Penguin.

Sebba, A. (1997). *Mother Teresa: Beyond the image.* Doubleday.

Segal, E. (2022, December 5). What Dr. Anthony Fauci teaches us about leadership in a crisis. *Forbes.* https://www.forbes.com/sites/edwardsegal/2022/12/05/what-dr-anthony-fauci-teaches-us-about-leadership-in-a-crisis/?sh=3650d51b9a1c

Shamir, B., House, R. J., & Arthur, M. B. (1993). The motivational effects of charismatic leadership: A self-concept based theory. *Organization Science, 4*(4), 577–594.

Solomon, J. (2000, June 18). Bush, Harvard Business School and the makings of a president. *The New York Times.* https://www.nytimes.com/

Spink, K. (1997). *Mother Teresa: A complete authorized bibliography.* HarperCollins.

Stogdill, R. M. (1974). *Handbook of leadership: A survey of theory and research.* Free Press.

Vardey, L. (1995). Introduction. In L. Vardey (Ed.), *Mother Teresa: A simple path* (pp. xv–xxxviii). Ballantine.

Wills, G. (1994). *Certain trumpets: The call of leaders.* Simon & Schuster.

Chapter 3

Barber, L. (2002, January 6). Ridley Scott: "Talking to actors was tricky—I had no idea where they were coming from." *The Guardian.* https://www.theguardian.com/film/2002/jan/06/features.awardsandprizes

Cumming, E. (2019, May 25). *Alien:* How Ridley Scott's masterpiece has stayed relevant for 40 years. *Independent.* https://www.independent.co.uk/arts-entertainment/films/features/alien-40-anniversary-ridley-scott-sigourney-weaver-ellen-ripley-a8801066.html

Harms, P. D., Wood, D., Landay, K., Lester, P. B., & Vogelsang Lester, G. (2018). Autocratic leaders and authoritarian followers revisited: A review and agenda for the future. *The Leadership Quarterly, 29,* 105–122.

House, R. (1996). Path-goal theory of leadership: Lessons, legacy, and a reformulated theory. *The Leadership Quarterly, 7,* 323–352.

IMDb. (2023). *Ridley Scott: Trivia.* https://m.imdb.com/name/nm0000631/trivia/

Keegan, R. (2022, January 13). What Ridley Scott has learned: "We don't know s***." *The Hollywood Reporter.* https://www.hollywoodreporter.com/feature/ridley-scott-interview-the-last-duel-house-of-gucci-1235073041/

Lewin, K., Lippitt, R., & White, R. K. (1939). Patterns of aggressive behavior in experimentally created "social climates." *Journal of Social Psychology, 10,* 271–299.

March for Our Lives. (2018, June 4). *March for Our Lives to launch nationwide voter registration tour.* PR Newswire. https://www.prnewswire.com/news-releases/march-for-our-lives-to-launch-nationwide-voter-registration-tour-300658989.html

March for Our Lives. (2019). *Mission & story.* https://marchforourlives.com/mission-story

March for Our Lives Houston. (2020). *National mission statement.* https://www.mfolhouston.org/mission-statement

McGregor, D. (1960). *The human side of enterprise.* McGraw-Hill.

Ouchi, W. G. (1981). *Theory Z: How American business can meet the Japanese challenge*. Addison-Wesley.

Schulman, M. (2017, September 14). The battle for *Blade Runner*. *Vanity Fair*. https://www.vanityfair.com/hollywood/2017/09/the-battle-for-blade-runner-harrison-ford-ridley-scott

Turan, K. (2010). Man of vision. *DGA Quarterly*. https://www.dga.org/Craft/DGAQ/All-Articles/1003-Fall-2010/Interview-Ridley-Scott.aspx

White, R., & Lippitt, R. (1968). Leader behavior and member reaction in three "social climates." In D. Cartwright & A. Zander (Eds.), *Group dynamics* (pp. 318–335). Harper & Row.

Chapter 4

Blake, R. R., & McCanse, A. A. (1991). *Leadership dilemmas: Grid solutions*. Gulf.

Blake, R. R., & Mouton, J. S. (1964). *The managerial grid*. Gulf.

Bowers, D. G., & Seashore, S. E. (1966). Predicting organizational effectiveness with a four-factor theory of leadership. *Administrative Science Quarterly*, *11*(2), 238–263.

Eagly, A., & Karau, S. J. (2002). *Sex differences in social behavior: A social-role interpretation*. Erlbaum.

Fessler, L. (2018, February 6). MacArthur genius Ai-jen Poo makes the economic case for listening. *Quartz at Work*. https://qz.com/work/1185580/national-domestic-workers-alliance-director-ai-jen-poo-makes-the-economic-case-for-listening

Kahn, R. L. (1956). The prediction of productivity. *Journal of Social Issues*, *12*(2), 41–49.

MacArthur Foundation. (2014, September 17). *Ai-jen Poo*. https://www.macfound.org/fellows/class-of-2014/ai-jen-poo#searchresults

Misumi, J. (1985). *The behavioral science of leadership: An interdisciplinary Japanese research program*. University of Michigan Press.

National Domestic Workers Alliance. (2021). *Domestic worker leadership programs*. https://www.domesticworkers.org/programs-and-campaigns/organizing-domestic-workers-and-developing-leaders/developing-leaders/

Poo, A. (with Conard, A.). (2015). *The age of dignity: Preparing for the elder boom in a changing America*. New Press.

Rohrlich, J. B. (1980). *Work and love: The crucial balance*. Summit Books.

Sherwood, A. L., & DePaolo, C. A. (2005). Task and relationship-oriented trust in leaders. *Journal of Leadership & Organizational Studies*, *12*(2), 65–81.

Stogdill, R. M. (1974). *Handbook of leadership: A survey of theory and research*. Free Press.

Zheng, W., Surgevil, O., & Kark, R. (2018). Dancing on the razor's edge: How top-level women leaders manage the paradoxical tensions between agency and communion. *Sex Roles*, *79*(11–12), 633–650.

Chapter 5

Bass, B. M. (1990). *Bass & Stogdill's handbook of leadership: Theory, research, and managerial applications* (3rd ed.). Free Press.

Blake, R. R., & McCanse, A. A. (1991). *Leadership dilemmas: Grid solutions*. Gulf.

Boal, K. B., & Hooijberg, R. (2000). Strategic leadership research: Moving on. *Leadership Quarterly*, *11*(4), 515–549.

Bradberry, T., Greaves, J., & Lencioni, P. (2009). *Emotional intelligence 2.0*. TalentSmart.

Brady, T. (2020, December 14). *How the "Notorious RBG" used persuasion to advance equality*. University of Chicago Harris School of Public Policy. https://harris.uchicago.edu/news-events/news/how-notorious-rbg-used-persuasion-advance-equality

Caruso, D. R., & Wolfe, C. J. (2004). Emotional intelligence and leadership development. In D. V. Day, S. J. Zaccaro, & S. M. Halpin (Eds.), *Leader development for transforming organizations: Growing leaders for tomorrow* (pp. 237–266). Erlbaum.

Centro de Textiles Tradicionales del Cusco. (2020). *About us*. http://www.textilescusco.org/about-us

Dibble, J. L., & Levine, T. R. (2010). Breaking good and bad news: Direction of the MUM effect and senders' cognitive representations of news valence. *Communication Research*, *37*(5), 703–722. https://doi.org/10.1177/0093650209356440

Goleman, D. (1995). *Emotional intelligence*. Bantam Books.

Gresko, J. (2020, September 20). *A rapper, an elevator and an elephant: Stories Ginsburg told*. Associated Press. https://apnews.com/article/us-supreme-court-the-notorious-big-ruth-bader-ginsburg-ap-top-news-notorious-big-2e653eead7305defa29afee753725f28

Gutgold, N. (2020, September 24). Your view: Impressions from my talk with Ruth Bader Ginsburg: A giant intellect with a warm heart. *The Morning Call*. https://www.mcall.com/2020/09/24/your-view-impressions-from-my-talk-with-ruth-bader-ginsburg-a-giant-intellect-with-a-warm-heart

Hallum, C. (2018, September 15). The Centro de Textiles Tradicionales del Cusco fights poverty. *Borgen Magazine*. https://www.borgenmagazine.com/centro-de-textiles-tradicionales-del-cusco/

Katz, R. L. (1955). Skills of an effective administrator. *Harvard Business Review, 33*(1), 33–42.

Lord, R. G., & Hall, R. J. (2005). Identity, deep structure and the development of leadership skill. *Leadership Quarterly, 16*(4), 591–615.

Mann, F. C. (1965). Toward an understanding of the leadership role in formal organization. In R. Dubin, G. C. Homans, F. C. Mann, & D. C. Miller (Eds.), *Leadership and productivity* (pp. 68–103).

Mayer, J. D., & Salovey, P. (1995). Emotional intelligence and the construction and regulation of feelings. *Applied and Preventive Psychology, 4*(3), 197–208.

Mayer, J. D., Salovey, P., & Caruso, D. R. (2000). Models of emotional intelligence. In R. J. Sternberg (Ed.), *Handbook of intelligence* (pp. 396–420). Cambridge University Press.

Mumford, M. D., Zaccaro, S. J., Connelly, M. S., & Marks, M. A. (2000). Leadership skills: Conclusions and future directions. *Leadership Quarterly, 11*(1), 155–170.

Mumford, T. V., Campion, M. A., & Morgeson, F. P. (2007). The leadership skills strataplex: Leadership skill requirements across organizational levels. *Leadership Quarterly, 18*(2), 154–166.

Salovey, P., & Mayer, J. D. (1990). Emotional intelligence. *Imagination, Cognition, and Personality, 9*(3), 185–211.

Van Buskirk, E., & Van Buskirk, D. (2012a). Chinchero, Peru: A message from Nilda. *Descendants of the Incas*. http://www.incas.org/chinchero-peru-a-message-from-nilda

Van Buskirk, E., & Van Buskirk, D. (2012b). El Centro de Textiles Tradicionales de Cusco. *Descendants of the Incas*. https://www.incas.org/center-for-traditional-textiles-of-cusco.html/

Walsh, C. (2015, May 29). Honoring Ruth Bader Ginsburg. *The Harvard Gazette*. https://news.harvard.edu/gazette/story/2015/05/honoring-ruth-bader-ginsburg

WorldStrides. (2016, April). *Meet Smithsonian expert Nilda Callañaupa Alvarez*. https://worldstrides.com/blog/2016/04/meet-smithsonian-expert-nilda-callanaupa-alvarez/

Yammarino, F. J. (2000). Leadership skills: Introduction and overview. *Leadership Quarterly, 11*(1), 5–9.

Zaccaro, S. J., Gilbert, J., Thor, K. K., & Mumford, M. D. (1991). Leadership and social intelligence: Linking social perceptiveness and behavioral flexibility to leader effectiveness. *Leadership Quarterly, 2*(4), 317–331.

Chapter 6

Anderson, E. C. (2004). *StrengthsQuest: Curriculum outline and learning activities*. Gallup.

Blagg, D., & Young, S. (2001, February 1). What makes a good leader. *Harvard Business School Alumni Stories*. https://www.alumni.hbs.edu/stories/Pages/story-bulletin.aspx?num=3059

Brown, B. (2017). *Braving the wilderness: The quest for true belonging and the courage to stand alone*. Random House.

Brown, B. (2023a). *Official bio*. https://brenebrown.com/media-kit/

Brown, B. (2023b). *Research*. https://brenebrown.com/the-research/

Buckingham, M., & Clifton, D. (2001). *Now, discover your strengths*. Free Press.

Cameron, K. S. (2012). *Positive leadership: Strategies for extraordinary performance* (2nd ed.). Berrett-Koehler.

Cameron, K. S., Dutton, J. E., & Quinn, R. E. (2003). Foundations of positive organizational scholarship. In K. S.

Cameron, J. E. Dutton, & R. E. Quinn (Eds.), *Positive organizational scholarship* (pp. 3–14). Berrett-Koehler.

Clifton, D. O., & Harter, J. K. (2003). Investing in strengths. In K. S. Cameron, J. E. Dutton, & R. E. Quinn (Eds.), *Positive organizational scholarship* (pp. 111–121). Berrett-Koehler.

DSN Staff. (2018, May 3). DSN announces the 2018 Global 100! *Direct Selling News*. https://www.directsellingnews.com/dsn-announces-the-2018-global-100/

Dutton, J. E., & Ragins, B. R. (2007). *Exploring positive relationships at work*. Erlbaum.

Fowler, R. D., Seligman, M. E. P., & Kocher, G. P. (1999). The APA 1998 annual report. *American Psychologist, 54*(8), 537–568.

Fredrickson, B. L. (2001). The role of positive emotions in positive psychology: The broaden-and-build theory of positive emotions. *American Psychologist, 56*, 218–226.

Gardner, H. (1997). *Extraordinary minds: Portraits of exceptional individuals and an examination of our extraordinariness*. Basic Books.

Gist, M. E., & Mitchell, T. R. (1992). Self-efficacy: A theoretical analysis of its determinants and malleability. *Academy of Management Review, 17*, 183–211.

Linley, A. (2008). *Average to A+: Realising strengths in yourself and others*. CAPP Press.

Linley, A., & Dovey, H. (2012). *Technical manual and statistical properties for Realise2*. CAPP Press.

Lockman, J. A., Petrone, C. G., Luzynski, C., Petrone, A. B., Holmes, M. H., & Dagen, A. S. (2023). Effectiveness of a strengths-based leadership coaching program for women. *Journal of Leadership Education, 22*(1). https://journalofleadershiped.org/jole_articles/effectiveness-of-a-strengths-based-leadership-coaching-program-for-women/

Luscombe, B. (2018, November 1). America's reigning expert on feelings, Brené Brown now takes on leadership. *Time*. https://time.com/5441422/expert-feelings-brene-brown-leadership/

MacKie, D. (2016). *Strength-based leadership coaching in organizations: An evidence-based guide to positive leadership development*. Kogan Page.

Mary, Kay. (n.d.). *About Mary Kay: Our founder*. https://www.marykay.com/en-us/about-mary-kay/our-founder

Peterson, C. (2006). *A primer in positive psychology*. Oxford University Press.

Peterson, C. (2009). Foreword. In S. J. Lopez & C. R. Snyder (Eds.), *Oxford handbook of positive psychology* (p. xxiii). Oxford University Press.

Peterson, C., & Park, N. (2009). Classifying and measuring strengths of character. In S. J. Lopez & C. R. Snyder (Eds.), *Oxford handbook of positive psychology* (pp. 25–34). Oxford University Press.

Peterson, C., & Seligman, M. E. P. (2003). Positive organizational studies: Lessons from positive psychology. In K. S. Cameron, J. E. Dutton, & R. E. Quinn (Eds.), *Positive organizational scholarship* (pp. 14–28). Berrett-Koehler.

Peterson, C., & Seligman, M. E. P. (2004). *Character strengths and virtues: A handbook and classification*. Oxford University Press; American Psychological Association.

Quinn, R. E., Dutton, J., & Spreitzer, G. (2003). *Reflected Best Self Exercise: Assignment and instructions to participants* (Product number 001B). University of Michigan Regents, Positive Organizational Scholarship Research Group.

Rath, T. (2007). *StrengthsFinder 2.0*. Gallup Press.

Rath, T., & Conchie, B. (2008). *Strengths based leadership: Great leaders, teams, and why people follow*. Gallup Press.

Roberts, L. M., Spreitzer, G., Dutton, J., Quinn, R., Heaphy, E., & Barker, B. (2005, January). How to play to your strengths. *Harvard Business Review*, pp. 75–80.

Seligman, M. E. P. (2002). *Authentic happiness: Using the new positive psychology to realize your potential for lasting fulfillment*. Free Press.

Seligman, M. E. P., & Csikszentmihalyi, M. (2000). Positive psychology. *American Psychologist, 55*(1), 5–14.

van Woerkom, M., Meyers, M. C., & Bakker, A. B. (2022). Considering strengths use in organizations as a multilevel construct. *Human Resource Management Review, 32*(3). https://doi.org/10.1016/j.hrmr.2020.100767

Chapter 7

Bass, B. M., & Avolio, B. J. (1994). *Improving organizational effectiveness through transformational leadership*. Sage.

Conger, J. A., & Kanungo, R. N. (1987). Toward a behavioral theory of charismatic leadership in organizational settings. *Academy of Management Review, 12*(4), 637–647.

Conger, J. A., & Kanungo, R. N. (1998). *Charismatic leadership in organizations*. Sage.

Covey, S. R. (1991). *Principle-centered leadership*. Simon & Schuster.

Festinger, L. (1957). *A theory of cognitive dissonance*. Stanford University Press.

Gleissner, M. (2017). *Everyday impact: Kakenya Ntaiya*. Image Impact International. https://imageimpact.org/everyday-impact-kakenya-ntaiya/

Green Bronx Machine. (2023). *About us*. https://greenbronxmachine.org/about-us/

Harvard T.H. Chan School of Public Health. (2018, March 8). *Voices in leadership: Kakenya Ntaiya, founder and president of the Kakenya Center for Excellence* [Video and transcript]. https://www.hsph.harvard.edu/voices/events/kakenya-ntaiya-founder-and-president-of-the-kakenya-center-for-excellence/

House, R. J. (1977). A 1976 theory of charismatic leadership. In J. G. Hunt & L. L. Larson (Eds.), *Leadership: The cutting edge* (pp. 189–207). Southern Illinois University Press.

Kakenya's Dream. (n.d.). https://www.kakenyasdream.org

King, M. L. (1963). *"I have a dream. . . ."* [Speech at the March on Washington]. National Archives at New York City. https://www.archives.gov/files/press/exhibits/dream-speech.pdf

Kouzes, J. M., & Posner, B. Z. (2003). *The leadership challenge* (3rd ed.). Jossey-Bass.

Mathias, R. (2022, June). A radical sea change. *Women*. https://www.jpost.com/pdf/Women%20Magazine%202022.pdf

Nanus, B. (1992). *Visionary leadership: Creating a compelling sense of direction for your organization*. Jossey-Bass.

National Geographic. (2023). Kakenya Ntaiya: Advocate for women and girls. https://www.nationalgeographic.org/find-explorers/kakenya-ntaiya

Ntaiya, K. (2012, October). Kakenya Ntaiya: A girl who demanded school [Video and transcript]. *TEDxMidAtlantic*. https://www.ted.com/talks/kakenya_ntaiya_a_girl_who_demanded_school/transcript

Ntaiya, K. (2018, November). Empower a girl, transform a community [Video and transcript]. *TEDWomen 2018*. https://www.ted.com/talks/kakenya_ntaiya_empower_a_girl_transform_a_community/transcript

Paz-Frankel, E. (2017, March 8). Inna Braverman: The young woman with big plans to harness the world's oceans for clean energy. *NoCamels Israeli Innovation News*. https://nocamels.com/2017/03/eco-wave-power-inna-braverman/

Queen of the waves: Inna Braverman. (2020, April 1). Business Sweden. https://www.business-sweden.com/insights/articles/queen-of-the-waves-inna-braverman

Sashkin, M. (1988). The visionary leader. In J. A. Conger & R. N. Kanungo (Eds.), *Charismatic leadership: The elusive factor in organizational effectiveness* (pp. 122–160). Jossey-Bass.

Sashkin, M. (2004). Transformational leadership approaches: A review and synthesis. In J. Antonaki, A. T. Cianciolo, & R. J. Sternberg (Eds.), *The nature of leadership* (pp. 171–196). Sage.

Senge, P. (1990). *The fifth discipline: The art and practice of the learning organization*. Doubleday/Currency.

Shamir, B., House, R. J., & Arthur, M. B. (1993). The motivational effects of charismatic leadership: A self-concept based theory. *Organization Science, 4*(4), 577–594.

Terry Fox Foundation. (2023). https://www.terryfox.org/

United Nations Climate Change. (2019, September 26). *Winners of the 2019 UN Global Climate Action Awards announced*. https://unfccc.int/news/winners-of-the-2019-un-global-climate-action-awards-announced#new_tab

Zaccaro, S. J., & Banks, D. J. (2001). Leadership, vision, and organizational effectiveness. In S. J. Zaccaro & R. J. Klimoski (Eds.), *The nature of organizational leadership: Understanding the performance imperatives confronting today's leaders* (pp. 181–218). Jossey-Bass.

Chapter 8

Bales, R. F., & Strodtbeck, R. L. (1951). Phases in group problem-solving. *Journal of Abnormal and Social Psychology*, *46*, 485–495.

Benne, K. D., & Sheats, P. (1948). Functional roles of group members. *Journal of Social Issues*, *4*(2), 41–49.

Bennis, W. G., & Shepard, H. A. (1956). A theory of group development. *Human Relations*, *9*, 415–437.

Cartwright, D., & Zander, A. (Eds.). (1968). *Group dynamics: Research and theory* (3rd ed.). Harper & Row.

Casad, B. J., & Bryant, W. J. (2016, January 20). Addressing stereotype threat is critical to diversity and inclusion in organizational psychology. *Frontiers in Psychology*, *7*(8). https://www.doi.org/10.3389/fpsyg.2016.00008

Corey, M. S., Corey, G., & Corey, C. (2017). *Groups: Process and practice* (10th ed.). Cengage.

Dansereau, F., Graen, G. G., & Haga, W. (1975). A vertical dyad linkage approach to leadership in formal organizations. *Organizational Behavior and Human Performance*, *13*(1), 46–78.

Dayal, A., O'Connor, D. M., Qadri, U., & Arora, V. M. (2017). Comparison of male vs female resident milestone evaluations by faculty during emergency medicine residency training. *JAMA Internal Medicine*, *177*(5), 651–657.

Duhigg, C. (2016, February 15). What Google learned from its quest to build the perfect team. *The New York Times Magazine*. https://www.nytimes.com/2016/02/28/magazine/what-google-learned-from-its-quest-to-build-the-perfect-team.html

Fisher, B. A. (1974). *Small group decision making: Communication and the group process*. McGraw-Hill.

Harris, T. E., & Sherblom, J. C. (2018). *Small group and team communication* (5th ed.). Waveland Press.

Hawthorne, M. A. (2015). Cultivating and sustaining generative teams. *Stanford Social Innovation Review*, 1–5. https://doi.org/10.48558/dpsf-5645

Homeboy Industries. (2019). *Our founder Father Greg*. https://homeboyindustries.org/our-story/father-greg/

Graen, G. B., & Uhl-Bien, M. (1995). Relationship-based approach to leadership: Development of leader–member exchange (LMX) theory of leadership over 25 years: Applying a multi-level, multi-domain perspective. *Leadership Quarterly*, *6*(2), 219–247.

Kouzes, J. M., & Posner, B. Z. (2023). *The leadership challenge* (7th ed.). Jossey-Bass.

LaFasto, F. M., & Larson, C. (2001). *When teams work best: 6,000 team members and leaders tell what it takes to succeed*. Sage.

Larson, C., & LaFasto, F. M. (1989). *Teamwork: What must go right/what can go wrong*. Sage.

Levi, D., & Askay, D. A. (2021). *Group dynamics for teams*. Sage.

Loomis, M. E. (1979). *Group process for nurses*. Mosby.

Malik, M., Wan, D., Ahmad, M. I., Naseem, M. A., & Rehman, R. U. (2015). The role of LMX in employees' job motivation, satisfaction, empowerment, stress and turnover: Cross country analysis. *Journal of Applied Business Research*, *31*, 1897–2000. https://doi.org/10.19030/jabr.v31i5.9413

Metzger, J. (2009). *What would Jane do? City-building women and a tale of two Chicagos*. Lake Claremont Press.

Miller, J. (2023, May 16). Why some companies are saying "diversity and belonging" instead of "diversity and inclusion." *The New York Times*. https://www.nytimes.com/2023/05/13/business/diversity-equity-inclusion-belonging.html

Napier, R. W., & Gershenfeld, M. K. (2004). *Groups: Theory and experience* (7th ed.). Houghton Mifflin.

Northouse, P. G. (2022). *Leadership: Theory and practice* (9th ed.). Sage.

Reichers, A. E., & Schneider, B. (1990). *Organizational climate and culture*. Jossey-Bass.

re:Work. (n.d.). *Tool: Foster psychological safety*. https://rework.withgoogle.com/guides/understanding-team-effectiveness/steps/foster-psychological-safety/

Reyes, D. L., Dinh, J., & Salas, E. (2019). What makes a good team leader? *The Journal of Character & Leadership Development*, *6*(1), 88–101.

Rozovsky, J. (2015, November 17). *Five keys to a successful Google team*. re:Work. https://rework.withgoogle.com/blog/f

ive-keys-to-a-successful-goo gle-team/

Schein, E. H. (2017). *Organizational culture and leadership* (5th ed.). Wiley.

Schutz, W. C. (1958). *FIRO: A three-dimensional theory of interpersonal behavior.* Holt, Rinehart & Winston.

Schutz, W. C. (1966). *The interpersonal underworld.* Science and Behavior Books.

Shaw, M. (1981). *Group dynamics: The psychology of small group behavior* (3rd ed.). McGraw-Hill.

Snyder, K. (2014, August 26). The abrasiveness trap: High-achieving men and women are described differently in reviews. *Fortune.* https://fortu ne.com/2014/08/26/performa nce-review-gender-bias/

Tamiru, N. (2023, June). *Team dynamics: Five keys to building effective teams.* Think with Google. https://www.thinkwi thgoogle.com/intl/en-gb/con sumer-insights/consumer-tr ends/five-dynamics-effectiv e-team/

Tuckman, B. W. (1965). Developmental sequences in small groups. *Psychological Bulletin,* *63*(6), 384–399.

Tuckman, B. W., & Jensen, M. A. C. (1977). Stages of small-group development revisited. *Group & Organization Studies,* *2*(4), 419–427.

UC Riverside Staff Assembly. (2019, June 10). *Matt Sakaguchi: What Google learned about team building—May 23, 2019* [Video]. YouTube. https://www. youtube.com/watch?v=N6h7B PzYjyA&t=12s

Vroom, V. H. (1964). *Work and motivation.* Wiley.

Williams, J. C., Multhaup, M., Li, S., & Korn, R. (2018). *You can't change what you can't see: Interrupting racial and gender bias in the legal profession.* American Bar Association and Minority Corporate Counsel Association. http://www.abajo urnal.com/files/Bias_interrup ters_report-compressed.pdf

Yalom, I. D. (1995). *The theory and practice of group psychotherapy* (4th ed.). Basic Books.

Chapter 9

Americans for the Arts. (n.d.). Cultural equity. Definitions. h ttps://www.americansforthe arts.org/about-americans-fo r-the-arts/cultural-equity/de finitions

Billboard staff. (n.d.). *Unmasking ADHD at work: How employees, managers and executives can increase productivity, reduce burnout.* Billboard.com. https://www.billboard.com/pr o/adhd-at-work-stockx-impro ving-productivity-reducing-b urnout/

Blaine, B. E. (2013). *Understanding the psychology of diversity* (2nd ed.). Sage.

Booysen, L. (2014). The development of inclusive leadership practice and processes. In B. M. Ferdman & B. R. Deane (Eds.), *Diversity at work: The practice of inclusion* (pp. 296–329). Wiley.

Brewer, M. B. (1991). The social self: On being the same and different at the same time. *Personality and Social Psychology Bulletin, 17*(5), 475–482.

Byyny, R. L. (2017). Cognitive bias: Recognizing and managing our unconscious biases. *The Pharos, 80*(1), 2–6.

Carnes, M., Devine, P., Isaac, C., Manwell, L., Ford, C., Byars-Winston, A., Fine, E., & Sheridan, J. (2012). Promoting institutional change through bias literacy. *Journal of Diversity in Higher Education, 5*(2), 63–77.

Devine, P. G. (1989). Stereotypes and prejudice: Their automatic and controlled components. *Journal of Personality and Social Psychology, 56*(1), 5–18.

Dishman, L. (2015, May 18). Millennials have a different definition of diversity and inclusion. *Fast Company.* http: //www.fastcompany.com/304 6358/the-new-rules-of-work /millennials-have-a-differen t-definition-of-diversity-and-i nclusion

Ferdman, B. M. (1992). The dynamics of ethnic diversity in organizations: Toward integrative models. In K. Kelly (Ed.), *Issues, theory, and research in industrial/organizational psychology* (pp. 339–384). Elsevier Science.

Ferdman, B. M. (2014). The practice of inclusion in diverse organizations. In B. M. Ferdman & B. R. Deane (Eds.), *Diversity at work: The practice of inclusion* (pp. 3–54). Wiley.

Ferdman, B. M., Barrera, V., Allen, A., & Vuong, V. (2009, August). Inclusive behaviors and the experience of inclusion. In B. G. Chung (Chair), *Inclusion in organizations: Measures, HR practices, and climate* [Symposium]. Academy of Management 69th Annual Meeting, Chicago, IL.

Ferdman, B. M., & Deane, B. R (Eds.). (2014). *Diversity at work: The practice of inclusion*. Wiley.

Goldman, Sachs Group. (2023). Q&A with Damien Hooper-Campbell, chief diversity officer at Zoom. *Alumni News*. https://www.gsalumninetwork.com/s/1366/18/interior.aspx?sid=1366&gid=1&pgid=252&cid=4123&ecid=4123&crid=0&calpgid=402&calcid=1281

Gudykunst, W. B., & Kim, Y. Y. (1997). *Communicating with strangers: An approach to intercultural communication* (3rd ed.). McGraw-Hill.

Harrison, D. A., & Sin, H. (2006). What is diversity and how should it be measured? In A. M. Konrad, P. Prasad, & J. K. Pringle (Eds.), *Handbook of workplace diversity* (pp. 191–216). Sage.

Harvey, C. P. (2015). Understanding workplace diversity: Where have we been and where are we going? In C. P. Harvey & M. J. Allard (Eds.), *Understanding and managing diversity: Readings, cases, and exercises* (pp. 1–7). Pearson.

Harvey, C. P., & Allard, M. J. (2015). *Understanding and managing diversity: Readings, cases, and exercises*. Pearson.

Healey, J. P., & Stepnick, A. (2017). *Diversity and society: Race, ethnicity, and gender* (5th ed.). Sage.

Herring, C., & Henderson, L. (2015). *Diversity in organizations: A critical examination*. Routledge.

Hirshberg, J. J., & Ferdman, B. M. (2011, August).

Leader-member exchange, cooperative group norms, and workplace inclusion in workgroups. In M. Shuffler, S. Burke, & D. Diaz-Granados (Chairs) (Eds.), *Leading across cultures: Emerging research trends from multiple levels* [Symposium]. Academy of Management 71st Annual Meeting, San Antonio, TX.

Hofhuis, J., van der Rijt, P. G. A., & Vluf, M. (2016). Diversity climate enhances work outcomes through trust and openness in workgroup communication. *SpringerPlus, 5*, 714.

Hunt, V., Layton, D., & Prince, S. (2015, January). *Diversity matters*. McKinsey & Company. https://www.mckinsey.com/business-functions/organization/our-insights/why-diversity-matters

Johnson, D. W., & Johnson, F. P. (2009). *Joining together: Group theory and skills* (10th ed.). Allyn & Bacon.

Komives, S. R., Wagner, W., & Associates (Eds.). (2016). *Leadership for a better world: Understanding the social change model of leadership* (2nd ed.). Jossey-Bass.

Loden, M. (1996). *Implementing diversity*. McGraw-Hill.

Miller, J. (2023, May 16). Why some companies are saying "diversity and belonging" instead of "diversity and inclusion." *The New York Times*. https://www.nytimes.com/2023/05/13/business/diversity-equity-inclusion-belonging.html

Mor Barak, M. E. (2014). *Managing diversity: Toward a globally inclusive workplace* (3rd ed.). Sage.

Myers, V. A. (2012). *Moving diversity forward: How to go from well-meaning to well-doing*. American Bar Association.

Oliver, M. B. (1999). Caucasian viewers' memory of Black and white criminal suspects in the news. *Journal of Communication, 49*(3), 46–60.

Ospina, S., & Foldy, E. G. (2010). Building bridges from the margins: The work of leadership in social change organizations. *The Leadership Quarterly, 21*(2), 292–307.

Pew Research Center. (2018, November 13). *Early benchmarks show "post-Millennials" on track to be most diverse, best-educated generation yet*. https://www.pewsocialtrends.org/2018/11/15/early-benchmarks-show-post-millennials-on-track-to-be-most-diverse-best-educated-generation-yet/psdt-11-15-18_postmillennials-00-00/

Ponterotto, J. G., & Pedersen, P. B. (1993). *Preventing prejudice: A guide for counselors and educators*. Sage.

Porter, R. E., & Samovar, L. A. (1997). An introduction to intercultural communication. In L. A. Samovar & R. E. Porter (Eds.), *Intercultural communication: A reader* (8th ed., pp. 5–26). Wadsworth.

Project Implicit. (n.d.). Blindspot's *Implicit Association Test*. https://implicit.harvard.edu/implicit/user/agg/blindspot/indexrk.htm

The Review. (n.d.). eBay's first chief diversity officer on humanizing diversity and inclusion. First Round Capital. https://review.firstround.com

/ebays-first-chief-diversity-officer-on-humanizing-diversity-and-inclusion

Rivera, L. A. (2015). *Pedigree: How elite students get elite jobs*. Princeton University Press.

Schutz, W. C. (1958). *FIRO: A three dimensional theory of interpersonal behavior*. Holt, Rinehart & Winston.

Sears, B., Mallory, C., Flores, A. R., & Conron, K. J. (2021). *LGBT people's experiences of workplace discrimination and harassment*. The Williams Institute at University of California, Los Angeles School of Law.

Shore, L. M., Randel, A. E., Chung, B. G., Dean, M. A., Holcombe Ehrhard, K., & Singh, G. (2011). Inclusion and diversity in work groups: A review and model for future research. *Journal of Management, 37*(4), 1262–1289.

Southern Poverty Law Center. (2022). *Whose heritage? Public symbols of the Confederacy* (3rd ed.). https://www.splcenter.org/sites/default/files/whose-heritage-report-third-edition.pdf

Special Populations and CTE Illinois Leadership Project. (2016). *Cultural diversity self-assessment*. http://illinoiscte.org/index.php/resources/cultural- competency-module

Streitmatter, J. (1994). *Toward gender equity in the classroom: Everyday teachers' beliefs and practices*. State University of New York Press.

Tajfel, H., & Turner, J. C. (1986). An integrative theory of intergroup conflict. In S. Worchel & W. Austin (Eds.), *Psychology of intergroup relations* (pp. 2–24). Nelson-Hall.

Thomas, D. A., & Ely, R. J. (1996, September–October). Making differences matter: A new paradigm for managing diversity. *Harvard Business Review*. https://hbr.org/1996/09/making-differences-matter-a-new-paradigm-for-managing-diversity

Time Staff. (2017, May 23). Read: New Orleans mayor on removing Confederate monuments. *Time*. https://time.com/4790674/mitch-landrieu-new-orleans-confederate-monuments-speech

Wilkie, D. (n.d.). How DE&I evolved in the C-suite. *SHRM Executive Network*. https://www.shrm.org/executive/resources/articles/pages/evolving-executive-dei-diversity-c-suite.aspx

Winfrey, O. (2018, August). Oprah talks to former New Orleans mayor Mitch Landrieu. *O, The Oprah Magazine*. http://www.oprah.com/inspiration/oprah-talks-to-former-new-orleans-mayor-mitch-landrieu_1

World Economic Forum. (2022, July 13). *Global gender gap report 2022*. https://www.weforum.org/reports/global-gender-gap-report-2022/in-full/2-4-gender-gaps-in-leadership-by-industry-and-cohort/

Chapter 10

Bachal, H. (2020, January 27). *Humaira: The game changer* [Video]. YouTube. https://www.youtube.com/watch?v=rugwMb_lO7k&ab_channel=HumairaBachal

Blake, R. R., & Mouton, L. S. (1964). *The managerial grid*. Gulf.

Brown, C. T., & Keller, P. W. (1979). *Monologue to dialogue: An exploration of interpersonal communication*. Prentice Hall.

Dream Foundation Trust. (n.d.). *What we do: Awareness & advocacy program*. https://dreamfoundationtrust.wixsite.com/home/awareness-advocacy-program

Dream Foundation Trust. (2023). *What we do: Dream Model Street School*. https://dreamfoundationtrust.wixsite.com/home/dream-model-street-school

Faruqi, A. (Producer), & Obaid-Chinoy, S. (Director). (2013). *Humaira: The dream-catcher* [Motion picture]. SOC Films.

Fisher, R. (1971). Fractionating conflict. In C. G. Smith (Ed.), *Conflict resolution: Contributions of the behavioral sciences* (pp. 157–159). University of Notre Dame Press.

Fisher, R., & Ury, W. (1981). *Getting to yes: Negotiating agreement without giving in*. Penguin Books.

Fisher, R., Ury, W., & Patton, B. (1991). *Getting to yes: Negotiating agreement without giving in* (2nd ed.). Penguin Books.

Folger, J. P., Poole, M. S., & Stutman, R. K. (1993). *Working through conflict: Strategies for relationships, groups, and organizations* (2nd ed.). Scott, Foresman.

Goffman, E. (1967). *Interaction ritual: Essays on face-to-face behavior*. Anchor Books.

Hocker, J. L., & Wilmot, W. W. (1995). *Interpersonal conflict* (4th ed.). W. C. Brown.

Kilmann, R. H., & Thomas, K. W. (1975). Interpersonal conflict-handling behavior as reflections of Jungian personality dimensions. *Psychological Reports*, *37*(3), 971–980.

Kilmann, R. H., & Thomas, K. W. (1977). Developing a forced-choice measure of conflict handling behavior: The "mode" instrument. *Educational and Psychology Measurement*, *37*(2), 309–325.

Knutson, T., Lashbrook, V., & Heemer, A. (1976). *The dimensions of small group conflict: A factor analytic study* [Paper presentation]. Annual meeting of the International Communication Association.

Lulofs, R. S. (1994). *Conflict: From theory to action*. Gorsuch Scarisbrick.

Maslow, A. (1970). *Motivation and personality* (2nd ed.). Harper & Row.

Putnam, L. L. (2010). Communication as changing the negotiation game. *Journal of Applied Communication Research*, *38*(4), 325–335.

Schmidt, W., & Tannenbaum, R. (1960). Management of differences. *Harvard Business Review*, *38*(6), 107–115.

Schutz, W. C. (1966). *The interpersonal underworld*. Science and Behavior Books.

Temple-Raston, D. (2013, January 3). After fighting to go to school, a Pakistani woman builds her own. *Weekend Edition Sunday* [Radio news program]. http://www.npr.org/2013/01/06/168565152/after-fig hting-to-go-to-school-a-pak istani-woman-builds-her-own

Terry, R. W. (1993). *Authentic leadership: Courage in action*. Jossey-Bass.

Watzlawick, P., Beavin, J., & Jackson, D. D. (1967). *Pragmatics of human communication*. Norton.

Wilmot, W. W., & Hocker, J. (2011). *Interpersonal conflict* (8th ed.). McGraw-Hill.

Chapter 11

Balch, O. (2023, April 11). *Ryan Gellert: "At Patagonia we have to be greener than green—and make a profit."* Reuters. https://www.reuters.com/business/sustainable-business/ryan-g ellert-patagonia-we-have-be-greener-than-green-make-pr ofit-2023-04-11/

Beauchamp, T. L., & Bowie, N. E. (1988). *Ethical theory and business* (3rd ed.). Prentice Hall.

Ben & Jerry's. (n.d.). *2017 social and environmental assessment report*. https://www.benjerry.c om/about-us/sear-reports/20 17-sear-report

B Lab. (2023). *Benefit Corporation vs. B Corp*. https://usca.bc orporation.net/benefit-corpor ation-vs-b-corp/

Bowie, N. E. (1991). Challenging the egoistic paradigm. *Business Ethics Quarterly*, *1*(1), 1–21.

Carlson, K. (2022, March 8). *Fast Company names GMP one of the top five most innovative companies in North America*. Green Mountain Power. https://greenmountainpower. com/news/fast-company-nam es-gmp-one-of-the-top-five-most-innovative-companies/

Chouinard, Y. (2023). *Earth is now our only shareholder*. Patagonia. https://www.patagonia.com/ownership

Ciulla, J. B. (2003). *The ethics of leadership*. Wadsworth/Thomson Learning.

Dean, G. (2022, September 22). Patagonia's founder just gave the company away—the latest unusual step in a history of corporate innovations, from being an early adopter of paid parental leave to donating $145 million to the environment. *Business Insider*. https://www.businessinsider.com/pa tagonia-yvon-chouinard-envir onment-staff-benefits-sustai nability-childcare-organic-do nate-2022-9

Ding, J. (2022, September 16). Business: Patagonia founder is giving away riches to save Earth; Yvon Chouinard and his company have long been leaders in corporate activism. *Los Angeles Times*, p. A8.

Environmental Protection Agency. (2022, December 3). *Textiles: Material-specific data. Facts and figures about materials, waste and recycling*. https://www.epa.gov/facts-and-fi gures-about-materials-wast e-and-recycling/textiles-ma terial-specific-data#Textiles Overview

Fee, G. (2018, August 30). Vermont businesses do well by doing good. *Stratton Magazine*. https://www.strattonmagazin e.com/good-works/do-well-d o-good/

French, J. R., Jr., & Raven, B. (1959). The bases of social power. In D. Cartwright (Ed.), *Studies in social power* (pp. 150–167). Institute for Social Research.

Human Rights Watch. (2019, December 16). *North Korea: Abusive rule 10 years after Kim Jong Il*. https://www.hrw.org/news/2021/12/16/north-korea-abusive-rule-10-years-after-kim-jong-il

Johnson, C. R. (2005). *Meeting the ethical challenges of leadership* (2nd ed.). Sage.

Josephson Institute. (2008). *The six pillars of character*. Josephson Institute.

Kanungo, R. N. (2001). Ethical values of transactional and transformational leaders. *Canadian Journal of Administrative Sciences, 18*(4), 257–265.

Kanungo, R. N., & Mendonca, M. (1996). *Ethical dimensions of leadership*. Sage.

Kelly, K. (2021, December 14). *GMP certified as a B Corp for third time, using energy as a force for good*. Green Mountain Power. https://greenmountainpower.com/news/gmp-certified-as-b-corp-for-third-time-using-energy-as-a-force-for-good/

Kim, S., Karlesky, M. J., Myers, C. G., & Schifeling, T. (2016, June 17). Why companies are becoming B Corporations. *Harvard Business Review*. https://hbr.org/2016/06/why-companies-are-becoming-b-corporations

McKinsey & Company. (2023, April 20). *Patagonia shows how turning a profit doesn't have to cost the Earth*. https://www.mckinsey.com/industries/agricul ture/our-insights/patagonia-shows-how-turning-a-profit-doesnt-have-to-cost-the-earth

Northeastern Global News. (2022, September 20). *The founder of Patagonia gave away his company to fight climate change. Is that really as good as it sounds?* https://news.northeastern.edu/2022/09/20/patagonias-founder/

1% for the Planet. (2023). *Membership overview*. https://membersupport.onepercentfortheplanet.org/membership overview

Opportunity Nation & Child Trends. (n.d.). *The 2017 Opportunity Index*. http://opportunityindex.org/wp-content/uploads/2017/12/2017-Opportunity-Index-Full-Analysis-Report.pdf

Patagonia. (2023). *Don't buy this jacket, Black Friday and the New York Times*. https://www.patagonia.com/stories/dont-buy-this-jacket-black-friday-and-the-new-york-times/story-18615.html

Pitta, D. A., Fung, H.-G., & Isberg, S. (1999). Ethical issues across cultures: Managing the differing perspectives of China and the USA. *Journal of Consumer Marketing, 16*(3), 240–256.

Resick, C. J., Hanges, P. J., Dickson, M. W., & Mitchelson, J. A. (2006). A cross-cultural examination of the endorsement of ethical leadership. *Journal of Business Ethics, 63*(4), 345–359.

Sonsev, V. (2019, November 27). Patagonia's focus on its brand purpose is great for business. *Forbes*. https://www.forbes.com/sites/veronikasonsev/2019/11/27/patagonias-f ocus-on-its-brand-purpose-is-great-for-business/?sh=1df15bd954cb

Suzuki, T. (2022, September 8). North Korea has spent $1.6 billion on nuke program over 50 years. *The Asahi Shimbun*. https://www.asahi.com/ajw/articles/14729561

ThinkVermont. (2019, November 5). *Vermont certified B corps: Using business as a force for good*. Vermont Department of Economic Development. https://thinkvermont.com/neighbors/vermont-certified-b-corps-using-business-as-a-force-for-good/

Velasquez, M. G. (1992). *Business ethics: Concepts and cases* (3rd ed.). Prentice Hall.

Chapter 12

Associated Press. (2018, March 20). Weinstein Co. files for bankruptcy protection. *Billboard*. https://www.billboard.com/articles/news/8254437/weinstein-co-files-for-bankruptcy-protection

BBC. (2019, May 24). *Harvey Weinstein timeline: How the scandal unfolded*. https://www.bbc.com/news/entertainment-arts-41594672

BBC. (2020, August 31). *Syrian president Bashar al-Assad: Facing down rebellion*. https://www.bbc.com/news/10338256

Bilton, N. (2019, February 20). "She never looks back": Inside Elizabeth Holmes's chilling final months at Theranos. *Vanity Fair*. https://www.vanityfair.com/news/2019/02/inside-elizabeth-holmess-final-months-at-theranos

Carreyrou, J. (2018). *Bad blood: Secrets and lies in a Silicon Valley startup*. Knopf.

Einarsen, S., Aasland, M. S., & Skogstad, A. (2007). Destructive leadership behaviour: A definition and conceptual model. *Leadership Quarterly*, *18*(3), 207–216.

Eltagouri, M., Rosenberg, E., & Hui, M. (2018, May 25). Rise and ignominious fall of Harvey Weinstein, in four acts. *The Washington Post*. https://www.washingtonpost.com/news/arts-and-entertainment/wp/2018/05/24/the-rise-and-ignominious-fall-of-harvey-weinstein-in-four-acts/

Farrow, R. (2017a, October 10). From aggressive overtures to sexual assault: Harvey Weinstein's accusers tell their stories. *The New Yorker*. https://www.newyorker.com/news/news-desk/from-aggressive-overtures-to-sexual-assault-harvey-weinsteins-accusers-tell-their-stories

Farrow, R. (2017b, November 6). Harvey Weinstein's army of spies. *The New Yorker*. https://www.newyorker.com/news/news-desk/harvey-weinsteins-army-of-spies

Friedman, J., & Farid-Johnson, N. (2022, September 19). *Banned in the USA: The growing movement to censor books in schools*. PEN America. https://pen.org/report/banned-usa-growing-movement-to-censor-books-in-schools/

Hofstede, G. (1980). *Culture's consequences: International differences in work-related values*. Sage.

Johnson, C. E. (2012). *Organizational ethics: A practical approach* (2nd ed.). Sage.

Kantor, J., & Twohey, M. (2017, October 5). Harvey Weinstein paid off sexual harassment accusers for decades. *The New York Times*. https://www.nytimes.com/2017/10/05/us/harvey-weinstein-harassment-allegations.html

Kellerman, B. (2004). *Bad leadership: What it is, how it happens, why it matters*. Harvard Business School Press.

Krasikova, D. V., Green, S. G., & LeBreton, J. M. (2013). Destructive leadership: A theoretical review, integration, and future research agenda. *Journal of Management*, *39*(5), 1308–1328.

Lipman-Blumen, J. (2005). *The allure of toxic leaders*. Oxford University Press.

Luthans, F., Peterson, S. J., & Ibrayeva, E. (1998). The potential for the "dark side" of leadership in post-communist countries. *Journal of World Business*, *33*(2), 185–201.

Moniuszko, S. M., & Kelly, C. (2017, October 27). Harvey Weinstein scandal: A complete list of the 87 accusers. *USA Today*. https://www.usatoday.com/story/life/people/2017/10/27/weinstein-scandal-complete-list-accusers/804663001/

Padilla, A. (2013). *Leadership: Leaders, followers, environments*. Wiley.

Padilla, A., Hogan, R., & Kaiser, R. B. (2007). The Toxic Triangle: Destructive leaders, susceptible followers, and conducive environments. *Leadership Quarterly*, *18*(3), 176–194.

Perryman, A. A., Sikora, D., & Ferris, G. R. (2010). One bad apple: The role of destructive executives in organizations. In L. L. Neider & C. A. Schriesheim (Eds.), *The "dark" side of management* (pp. 27–28). Information Age.

Schutz, W. C. (1966). *The interpersonal underworld*. Science and Behavior Books.

Schyns, B., & Schilling, J. (2013). How bad are the effects of bad leaders? A meta-analysis of destructive leadership and its outcomes. *Leadership Quarterly*, *24*, 138–158.

Tepper, B. J. (2000). Consequences of abusive supervision. *Academy of Management Journal*, *43*(2), 178–190.

Tepper, B. J. (2007). Abusive supervision in work organizations: Review, synthesis, and research agenda. *Journal of Management*, *33*, 261–289.

Tepper, B. J., Simon, L., & Man Park, H. (2017). Abusive supervision. *Annual Review Organizational of Psychology and Organizational Behavior*, *4*, 123–152.

Thoroughgood, C. N., Sawyer, K. B., Padilla, A., & Lunsford, L. (2018). Destructive leadership: A critique of leader-centric perspectives and toward a more holistic definition. *Journal Business Ethics*, *151*(3), 627–649.

Waldman, D. A., Wang, D., Hannah, S. T., Owens, B. P., & Balthazard, P. A. (2018). Psychological and neurological predictors of abusive supervision. *Personnel Psychology*, *71*, 399–421.

INDEX